**DATE DUE**

# Distinguished Asian American Political and Governmental Leaders

# Distinguished Asian American Political and Governmental Leaders

Don T. Nakanishi and Ellen D. Wu

*Distinguished Asian Americans Series*
An Oryx Book

GREENWOOD PRESS
Westport, Connecticut • London

Library of Congress Cataloging-in-Publication Data

Nakanishi, Don T.
  Distinguished Asian American political and governmental leaders / Don T. Nakanishi
  and Ellen D. Wu.
      p.   cm.—(Distinguished Asian Americans series)
    Includes index.
    ISBN 1–57356–325–0 (alk. paper)
    1. Asian Americans—Biography.   2. Statesmen—United States—Biography.   3. Politicians—United States—Biography.   I. Wu, Ellen D.   II. Title.   III. Series.
  E184.O6.N35   2002
  920'.009295073—dc21    2002016957

British Library Cataloguing in Publication Data is available.

Copyright © 2002 by Greenwood Publishing Group, Inc.

All rights reserved. No portion of this book may be
reproduced, by any process or technique, without the
express written consent of the publisher.

Library of Congress Catalog Card Number: 2002016957
ISBN: 1–57356–325–0

First published in 2002

Greenwood Press, 88 Post Road West, Westport, CT 06881
An imprint of Greenwood Publishing Group, Inc.
www.greenwood.com

Printed in the United States of America

The paper used in this book complies with the
Permanent Paper Standard issued by the National
Information Standards Organization (Z39.48–1984).

10 9 8 7 6 5 4 3 2 1

Every reasonable effort has been made to trace the owners of copyright materials in this book,
but in some instances this has proven impossible. The author and publisher will be glad to
receive information leading to more complete acknowledgments in subsequent printings of the
book, and in the meantime extend their apologies for any omissions.

Cover images are used by permission.

# Contents

*Introduction: From Exclusion and Disenfranchisement to Political Leadership—Asian Pacific American Elected Officials and Activists* vii

## Profiles

Aiso, John Fujio 3
Akaka, Daniel K. 5
Arakaki, James Y. 8
Ariyoshi, George R. 9
Barve, Kumar 12
Bloch, Julia Chang 13
Boggs, Grace Lee 16
Buchholdt, Thelma 20
Cayetano, Benjamin 24
Chan, Wilma 27
Chao, Elaine L. 29
Chau, Nguyen Minh 31
Chaudhary, Satveer 32
Chow, Ruby 33
Choy, Herbert Young Cho 36
Chu, Judy 38
Esteves, Jose S. 41
Eu, March Fong 42
Faleomavaega, Eni F. H. 45
Fong, Hiram L. 47
Fong, Matthew K. 48
Furutani, Warren 51
Gin, Mike 54
Guingona, Michael P. 56
Hayakawa, Samuel Ichiye 59
Hayashi, Dennis W. 61
Hirono, Mazie 64
Honda, Mike 65

Inouye, Daniel K. 69
Ito, Lance A. 72
Joe, Harry J. 75
Kealoha, James Kimo 77
Kim, Jay C. 78
King, Jean Sadako 81
Kochiyama, Yuri 83
Koh, Harold Hongju 86
Kwoh, Stewart 88
Kwok, Daphne 90
Lam, Tony 92
Lau, Cheryl Ann 96
Lau, Gordon 97
Lee, Bill Lann 99
Lee, Cheryl 102
Lee, Harry 104
Lim, Joaquin 106
Lim, John 107
Liu, Carol 108
Locke, Gary 109
Luke, Wing 112
Mansho, Rene 116
Matsui, Robert 117
Matsunaga, "Spark" Masayuki 120
Matsunaka, Stanley T. 122
Minami, Dale 123
Mineta, Norman Y. 125
Mink, Patsy T. 129
Miyagishima, Kenneth Daniel 131
Mollway, Susan Oki 132
Morita, Hermina M. 134
Nakano, George 136
Narasaki, Karen 138

Natividad, Irene 140
Oh, Angela Eunjin 144
Ong, Wing F. 146
Park, Michael 150
Quan, Gordon 152
Saiki, Patricia 154
Sangiolo, Amy Mah 156
Santos, Sharon Tomiko 157
Saund, Dalip Singh 159
Shin, Paull Hobom 161
Sibonga, Dolores 163
Singh, Shamina 165
Siv, Sichan Aun 167
Tahir-Kheli, Shirin R. 171
Tanaka, Paul K. 172
Teng, Mabel 174
Tokuda, Kip 176
Underwood, Robert 178
Uong, Chanrithy 180
Valderrama, David M. 183
Veloria, Velma Rosette 185
Vera Cruz, Philip Villamin 188
Waihee, John David, III 191

Wong, Barry 193
Wong, Delbert E. 194
Wong, Martha J. 196
Woo, Michael 198
Woo, S.B. (Shien-Biau) 200
Wu, David 202
Xiong, Joe Bee 205
Yaki, Michael 208
Yamane, Brian Y. 209
Yee, Leland 210
Yih, Mae 211
Yoneda, Karl Goso 212

*Appendix 1: Distinguished Asian American Political and Governmental Leaders by Birth Date* **215**

*Appendix 2: Distinguished Asian American Political and Governmental Leaders by Position* **217**

*Selected Bibliography* **219**

*Index* **221**

# Introduction: From Exclusion and Disenfranchisement to Political Leadership—Asian Pacific American Elected Officials and Activists

Significant demographic and political changes have marked the Asian Pacific American experience during the post–World War II era, especially since the mid-1960s. Large-scale immigration from Asia, for example, which began with the enactment of the Immigration Act of 1965, has had a dramatic impact on many states and regions across the United States, as well as on the Asian Pacific American population. From a largely native-born group of 1.5 million in 1970, there has been unprecedented growth and diversification among Asian Pacific Americans, who reached 12 million in 2000, with the majority now being foreign-born. Recent projections estimate that Asian Pacific Americans will continue to increase to nearly 20 million by 2020 (Ong and Hee 1993; Youngberg 2001). Politically, on the other hand, there has been a continuous increase in the political participation and representation of Asian Pacific Americans in both electoral and non-electoral politics (Nakanishi 1998), which has its origins in the Asian American movement and the civil rights movement of the 1960s (Louie and Omatsu 2001). Currently, there are more than 2,200 elected and major appointed officials in 33 different states and at the federal levels (Nakanishi and Lai 2001). Indeed, the Asian Pacific American population has shown that it has the organizational and leadership skills, financial resources, interethnic networks, and a growing sense of political efficacy to assert its policy positions, effectively confront broader societal issues that are damaging to their group interests, and contribute to the nation's democratic processes (Erie and Brackman 1993; Horton 1995; Saito 1998).

The heightened political participation of the Asian Pacific American population during the past several decades is particularly noteworthy when it is considered in the context of the historical legacy of disenfranchisement of Asian Pacific Americans in relation to the American electoral system. Early Chinese and Japanese immigrants, for example, were not allowed to vote and were excluded from fully participating in major aspects of American life because of a plethora of discriminatory laws and policies ranging from the Chinese Exclusion Act of 1882 to *Ozawa v. United States* (1922), which forbade Asian immigrants from becoming naturalized citizens (Daniels 1968; Saxton 1971; Chuman 1976; Ichioka 1977). These legal barriers prevented early Asian immigrants from being involved in electoral politics of any form—be it the type of ward politics practiced by European immigrants in the cities of the Atlantic or Midwest states or simply being able to vote for their preferences in a local or presidential election. This, of course, substantially delayed the development of electoral participation and representation by Asian Pacific Americans in Hawaii, California, and elsewhere until the second and subsequent generations who lived during the post–World War II period—over a hundred years after their initial period of immigration. And although the national news media have oftentimes touted them as America's "model minority"—a label that Asian Pacific leaders and scholars have disputed because of its simplistic implication that other minority groups can overcome racial and other discriminatory barriers by following the example of Asian Pacific Americans—this reputed success has disguised their historic lack of access and influence in the nation's most significant political and social decision-making arenas and institutions (Suzuki 1977; Chun 1980). Asian Pacific American civil rights groups have continued to remain vigilant in seeking the elimination of so-called "political structural barriers" like unfair redistricting plans and the lack of Asian language bilingual ballots, which many leaders believe have prevented Asian Pacific Americans from fully exercising their voting rights (Bai 1991; Kwoh and Hui 1993; Ong and Nakanishi 1996).

At the same time, Asian Pacific Americans, like other American racial minorities who have been historically disenfranchised from the American electoral system, have engaged in an array of nonelectoral political activities to advance or protect their group interests. Asian Pacific Americans were active participants in labor-organizing efforts in the Far West, Hawaii, New York, and in the Rocky Mountain states, and indeed were at the forefront of creating labor unions for agricultural workers in California and Hawaii (De Witt 1980; Kwong 1981; DeVera 1981; Yoneda 1983; Scharlin and Villanueva 1992). Like other racial minorities, Asian Pacific Americans also have a long history of seeking social justice and equal treatment by continuously engaging in legal challenges against discriminatory laws and practices in education, employment, housing, land ownership, immigration, and other significant public policy issue areas. Many of the legal cases involving Asian Pacific Americans like *Korematsu v. United States* (1943), *Lau v. Nichols* (1974), or *Equal Employment Opportunity Commission v. University of Pennsylvania* (1989) have become landmark civil rights decisions (Wang 1976; Carmody 1989; Irons 1983).

## About This Book

*Distinguished Asian American Political and Governmental Leaders* is the first-ever compilation of biographies of Asian Pacific American elected officials, major political appointees, judges, and activists. It provides information on the life histories and political accomplishments of 96 Asian Pacific Americans, who have participated in political, judicial and civil rights arenas of this nation from 1950 to the present. Most were trailblazers, being the first Asian Pacific American or the first of a particular Asian Pacific ethnic community, for example, Vietnamese Americans, to be elected or appointed to a leadership position. The late Dalip Singh Saund, for example, became the first Asian Pacific American and the first Indo-American ever elected to the U.S. House of Representatives when voters in Imperial and Riverside counties in Southern California elected him in 1957. Elaine Chao was the first Asian Pacific American and Chinese American woman appointed to a presidential cabinet post when George W. Bush nominated her to be the U.S. Secretary of Labor in 2001. And the late John Aiso became the first Japanese American, as well as Asian Pacific American, judge in California when he was appointed in 1953.

In selecting the leaders for this book, we tried to be as comprehensive as possible and to provide the reader with a glimpse of the diversity of electoral and nonelectoral forms of political participation and representation that

*Introduction*

Asian Pacific Americans have pursued (Nakanishi 1998). We have included biographies on each Asian Pacific American who has served or is serving as a state governor (Ariyoshi, Cayetano, Locke, Waihee); other statewide elected office (Eu, Fong, Hirono, Kealoha, King, Lau, Woo); the U.S. Senate (Akaka, Fong, Hayakawa, Inouye, Matsunaga); the U.S. House of Representatives (Faleomavaega, Kim, Matsui, Mineta, Mink, Saiki, Saund, Wu); and as a presidential cabinet member (Chao, Mineta). We also have provided a cross-section of 45 Asian Pacific American elected officials at the municipal and state levels for 12 states from Alaska to Massachusetts and from Minnesota to Texas. Among them are the first Cambodian, Hmong, and Vietnamese American elected officials, as well as some of the longest-serving Asian Pacific Americans, such as Harry Lee, who has been continuously re-elected as Sheriff of Jefferson Parish, Louisiana, since 1979. At the same time, we have included Asian Pacific Americans who have played major leadership roles in nonelectoral political pursuits, such as Yuri Kochiyama, Philip Vera Cruz, and Angela Oh, who have made significant contributions in the areas of human rights, union organizing, and race relations.

# Profiles

# John Fujio Aiso

**Born:** 14 December 1909, Burbank, California.

**Died:** 29 December 1987, Los Angeles, California.

**Education:** B.S., Brown University, 1931; J.D. Harvard University, 1934.

**Positions Held:** Head Instructor, United States Military Intelligence Service Language School (MISLS), 1941–1945; Commissioner, Los Angeles Superior Court; Judge, Los Angeles Superior Court; Judge, Appellate Department; Judge, Division Five of the California Court of Appeal for the Second Appellate District.

**Awards, Honors:** World War II Legion of Merit, honorary master's degree from Brown University, 1950; Government of Japan's Third Class Order of the Rising Sun Medal, 1984.

**Summary:** John Fujio Aiso was the head instructor of the United States Military Intelligence Service Language School (MISLS) during World War II and the first Nisei judge on the American mainland.

## Early Years and Education

John Fujio Aiso was born on 14 December 1909 in Burbank, California to Japanese immigrants. At an early age, Aiso demonstrated a penchant for political leadership, capturing the student body presidency by 600 votes at LeConte Junior High School in Hollywood, California. His early victory, however, was bittersweet. Protests from parents, the local press, and an anti-Asian student petition forced LeConte's administration to halt all student government activities until Aiso graduated.

Racial discrimination and tensions followed Aiso to Hollywood High School, where he was rejected from the Junior ROTC and dissuaded by the principal from trying out for a position on the cheerleading squad. He joined Hollywood's debate team, however, and became its captain and top speaker, leading the organization to a Southern California High Schools championship in 1926. Academically, Aiso also excelled, becoming the first Japanese American elected to the prestigious Ephebian Society, a high school honorary, and selected by Hollywood's faculty as class valedictorian.

Aiso first stepped into the national spotlight during a contentious brush with the American Legion's U.S. Constitution oratorical contest in 1925. Placing first in the preliminary competition, Aiso won the right to represent Hollywood in the regionals. The principal, however, informed Aiso that he needed to choose either valedictory honors or his spot in the speech contest. Amidst the highly public controversy, covered by the vernacular press and the *Los Angeles Times*, Aiso forfeited the latter, instead coaching second-place finisher Herbert Wenig to a victory at the state level. Wenig not only won the regional contest, for which he received $500, a trip to Europe, and a place at the Washington, D.C. finals, but he also won the national competition.

Graduating from Hollywood High School at the age of 16, Aiso spent his next year at Sijo Gakuen in Tokyo before returning stateside to enroll at Brown University in the fall of 1927. As an undergraduate, Aiso continued his trail of activity and success with a varsity award on the cross country team and a position on the interfraternity governing body, representing Delta Upsilon fraternity. Notably, Aiso, as captain of Brown's debate team, led his organization to an Eastern Intercollegiate Championship during the 1928–1929 academic year. He excelled at his studies; majoring in economics, he graduated cum laude and as valedictorian in 1931. Aiso wasted no time advancing to the next stage of his career, matriculating at the Harvard University Law School that fall. Three years later, J.D. in hand, Aiso moved east, where he successfully applied for the New York Bar and secured a clerkship with Patterson, Eagle, Greenough, and Day on Wall Street. Aiso's appetite for education was insatiable, however, and he spent 1936–1937 learning Japanese law at Chuo University in Japan.

## Career Highlights

Military conflicts shaped the next decade of Aiso's life. Beginning in 1937, the young lawyer spent three years as an employee of a subsidiary of the British-American Tobacco Company in the increasingly turbulent territory of Manchukuo, China, then a puppet state of the Japanese imperialist regime. Upon contracting hepatitis, Aiso returned home to the United States in 1940, where he was drafted shortly thereafter. In April of 1941, he reported for active duty. Aiso's first task as a private second class was truck repair, despite his obvious lack of knowledge, experience, and skill. Fortunately, his next assignment—service to the Japanese-language school run by the intelligence section of the Fourth Army—coincided much more closely with his qualifications. Initially placed in the program as a student, Aiso's facility with Japanese quickly propelled him to the position of assistant instructor and, finally, head instructor of the Military Intelligence Service Language School (MISLS), located first in San Francisco and later near Minneapolis. The school soon expanded from the 60 students enrolled on its opening day in November 1941 to over 6,000, including 4,500 Nisei, by the end of the war. Under Aiso's direction, the MISLS offered courses in Japanese history, geography, and reading in addition to basic language instruction. Graduates of MISLS performed intelligence work in the Pacific theater, where they interpreted and deciphered messages circulated by the Japanese military. "He saved many lives by being able to know what the Japanese army was doing," noted his surviving brother, Daniel (Morrison and O'Donnell 1987, 4). After nearly four years with MISLS, Aiso ventured back overseas in October 1945 to accept a legal position with the Civil Information Service in occupied Japan under General MacArthur. He left active duty in 1947 as a lieutenant colonel, the highest rank achieved by Japanese American servicemen and women in World War II.

Back home in the postwar period, Aiso resumed his legal career, first as a private attorney before being named a commissioner of the Los Angeles Superior Court in September 1952. The following year, he made history as the first mainland Nisei judge upon appointment to the Los Angeles Judicial District Municipal Court. Thereafter, he continued to serve in a number of distinguished positions, including the Los Angeles Superior Court (1953), the Appellate Department (1967), and Division Five of the California Court of Appeal for the Second Appellate District (1968), and served briefly as justice pro tem of the California Supreme Court. Upon retiring from the bench in 1972, Aiso served as special counsel to the law firm O'Melveny and Myers until undergoing a minor stroke in 1984.

The honors Aiso earned for his years of distinguished achievement included the Legion of Merit, which he received in 1965 for his military service, an honorary masters degree from Brown University, a scholarship fund named in his honor by the Japanese American Bar Association and the Japanese government's Third Class Order of the Rising Sun medal, conferred to only one other Nisei, for his service in occupied Japan from 1946 to 1948. The Monterey, California, Library of Defense Language Institute, formerly known as the MISLS, is named for Aiso, as is a street in downtown Los Angeles near the Japanese American National Museum in Little Tokyo. Tragically, Aiso's life ended prematurely on 29 December 1987 from head injuries sustained from an attack by an unknown assailant at an Arco gasoline service station in Los Angeles. Aiso is survived by his wife, the former Sumi Akiyama, his daughter, Ruth, and his son, John Jr.

### Sources

"Aisō, John." In *The Asian American Encyclopedia*, vol. 1, ed. Franklin Ng. New York: Marshall Cavendish, 1995, pp. 11–12.

"Aiso, John Fujio." In *Japanese American History: An A to Z Reference from 1868 to Present*, ed. Brian Niiya. New York: Facts on File, 1993.

Fugita, Steve. "John Fugue Aiso." In *Distinguished Asian Americans*, ed. Hyung-Chan Kim. Westport, CT: Greenwood Press, 1999, pp. 15–17.

*Japanese American Veterans Association Web site:* www.javadc.org [Accessed 10 July 2001].

McIlwain, James T. "Brown and the Yankee Samurai." facgov.brown.edu/facgov/facbulletin/March99Issue/mcIlwain.html [Accessed 10 July 2001].

Morrision, Patt and Santiago O'Donnell. "John Aiso, Prominent Nisei and Jurist, Dies After Mugger's Attack," *Los Angeles Times*, 31 December 1987, Metro part 2, page 4.

## Daniel K. Akaka

Sen. Daniel Akaka, D-Hawaii, speaks in 1999 during talks between Native Hawaiians and officials from the Interior and Justice departments. The talks were called for in a 1993 joint congressional resolution apologizing for Americans' role in the 1893 overthrow of Hawaii Queen Lili'uokalani. (Ronen Zilberman, AP/Wide World Photos)

**Born:** 11 September 1924, Honolulu, Hawaii.

**Education:** B.Ed. University of Hawaii, 1952; M.Ed. University of Hawaii, 1966.

**Positions Held:** Hawaii State Representative, U.S. House of Representatives, 1976–1990; Hawaii State Senator, U.S. Senate, 1990–present.

**Awards, Honors:** Named by A. *Magazine* as one of the 25 Most Influential Asian Americans, 1997.

**Summary:** Daniel K. Akaka is the nation's first U.S. senator of native Hawaiian descent.

## Early Years

Daniel Kahikina Akaka, the nation's first U.S. senator of native Hawaiian and Chinese ancestry, was born on 11 September 1924 in Honolulu, Hawaii. The youngest of eight children, Akaka's childhood and youth was marked by a devout religious faith. The family, members of the Congregationalist (Kawaiahao) church, participated in two devotions every day. His parents also espoused a strong sense of community—Akaka described them as a pair who "believed in feeding and helping others," always inviting their guests to 'Hele Mai E Ai' ('Come in and eat')" (Mavrides 1995, 1). The Akaka spirit of giving would become a common theme throughout the senator's career. As he once stated, "I feel I'm here on earth to give service. That has been the basis of my decisions" (Associated Press 1998).

Akaka's road to Congress began with a strong education. His family hailed from a modest background—the ten of them lived together in a small, two-bedroom house; his father, who had not progressed in school beyond the third grade, supported them by laboring for a sugar-processing pot manufacturer. As a child, Akaka aspired to work at Pearl Harbor, but his parents pushed him to concentrate on his studies so that he would have options beyond the state's sugar and coffee plantations. He then successfully completed high school at the Kamehameha School for Boys in 1942.

## Education

Before attending college, Akaka first worked as a welder for the Hawaiian Electric Company. In 1945, he joined the army as a welder mechanic for the Army Corps of Engineers in Saipan and Tinian. After the war, he graduated from the University of Hawaii with a bachelor of education degree in 1952. He also earned professional certificates in secondary education in 1953 and school administration in 1961 and a master's degree in education in 1966.

## Career Highlights

As an educator, Akaka performed a number of roles. He taught in rural, urban, and military schools before serving as a vice-principal and then principal until 1968. It was through education that Akaka first stepped into government. Beginning in 1953, he was a Hawaii Department of Education program specialist for 18 years. In 1963, he participated in the National Convention of the Department of Elementary School Principals in Hawaii as a delegate. A gracious host, Akaka presented leis, macadamia nuts, and even a rendition of "Blue Hawaii" to the 6,000 attendees. The increasingly well-known Akaka then started his term as Hawaii's chief program planner for the Department of Education in 1969. Two years later, he was named the state's director of economic opportunity.

Akaka first tried electoral politics in 1974 as the chosen running mate for Hawaii gubernatorial hopeful George R. Ariyoshi. He lost in the primaries but was named Ariyoshi's special assistant for human resources and the director of Hawaii's Progressive Neighborhood Program in 1975–1976.

On the nation's bicentennial, Akaka tried again for public office. This time, he aimed for—and won—Hawaii's second Congressional District seat in the U.S. House of Representatives with 80 percent of the vote. On his seven consecutive terms in the House, Akaka built a favorable "Hawaiian style" rapport with his colleagues. As a member of the House Appropriations Committee, he voiced his support for Hawaiian concerns such as tourism, sugar production, environmental protection, the pineapple industry, and native Hawaiian advocacy programs.

After moving to the Senate in 1990 to finish the remainder of the late Senator "Spark" Matsunaga's term, Akaka continued to push for his beloved home state. "I want the Senate to hear the people's voices. The agenda I have here [in the House of Representatives], I'll carry with me there," he said upon his appointment (Associated Press 1998). Indeed, one of his first challenges was successfully defending Hawaiian sugar growers in the face of lowered federal subsidies. Akaka also helped to persuade the government to open a Federal Emergency Management Agency field office in Hawaii to assist local authorities with natural disasters. He triumphantly rallied for a formal congressional apology in 1993 for the American overthrow of the Hawaiian monarchy a century earlier. In addition, he facilitated the formation of the Kahoolawe Island Conveyance Commission to oversee the goings-on of the area, once a U.S. military practice site, after its return to the Hawaiian people.

In Congress, Akaka has been involved in a diverse array of issues. He has served on the Energy and Natural Resources, Governmental Affairs, Indian Affairs, and Veterans' Affairs committees. He has membership in the Senate Democratic Policy Committee and co-chairs the Federal Government Service Caucus. Akaka opposed the confirmation of conservative Supreme Court Justice Clarence Thomas as well as President Reagan's proposal to initiate production of the MX missile. A committed liberal, Akaka is pro-choice and anti–capital punishment. On environmental questions, however, he has wavered between both sides, though usually an advocate for renewable energy research and development, tropical agriculture and aqua culture research, and marine protection. In 1995, he supported Alaskan oil drilling forces over the opening of the state's Arctic National Wildlife Refuge despite initially co-sponsoring a bill to protect the Yukon State's northern coastal plain. Under fire from environmentalists, he defended his choice by emphasizing the dependence of the Hawaiian economy on domestic oil supplies.

Notably, Akaka has also been a firm voice for Asian Pacific Islander interests, serving as secretary for the Congressional Asian Pacific Caucus and speaking at various API community functions. He has articulated the importance of voting to API political power. "Statistics show that the Asian Pacific population in America numbers 8.8 million, yet only little over one million Asian Americans are registered. We need to do a better job of turning out our people to vote.... Asian Pacific Americans need to work together as a community. We should focus on issues of commonality," he stated in 1996 (A. *Magazine* 1996, 28).

A. *Magazine* named Akaka one of 1997's 25 Most Influential Asian Americans in recognition of his actions during the Clinton administration's campaign finance controversy. Akaka, a member of the Senate committee responsible for investigating the White House's fund-raising practices, publicly denounced news media such as the *New York Times* and *National Review* as well as certain government officials for "giving inappropriate and misguided attention," such as racist stereotyping, assumptions, and harassment, to Asians and Asian American donors without distinguishing between the groups. The senator was subject to a number of malevolent phone calls and death threats as a result of his 20 March 1997 speech. A. *Magazine* writer Charles Park observed, "As reported hate crimes against Asian Americans continue to rise, and Congress moves to bar legal residents from making political donations, Asian Americans and other immigrants need conspicuous, competent leadership; Akaka ... stepped into fill the gap. Hopefully, other Asian Americans will take [this] cue to become more, not less, active in politics" (Park 1997, 60). He has been married to Mary Mildred Chong since 1948, and they are the parents of five children: Millannie, Daniel K., Jr., Gerard, Alan, and Nicholas.

## Sources

The United States Senate Web site: www.senate.gov [Accessed 20 April 1999].

"Daniel K. Akaka." *Congressional Yellow Book*. Leadership Directories, Inc., 1997.

"Daniel Kahikina Akaka." *AP Candidate Bios*. The Associated Press Political Service, 1998.

"The Magnificent 7." *A. Magazine* November 1996, p. 28.

Mavrides, Melanie J. "Daniel K. Akaka." In *Notable Asian Americans*, ed. Helen Zia and Susan B. Gall. Detroit: Gale Research Inc., 1995, pp. 1–2.

Park, Charles. "Senators Daniel Akaka, Daniel Inouye." In "The A. List 1997." *A. Magazine* December 1997/January 1998, p. 60.

# James Y. Arakaki

James Arakaki. (Courtesy of James Arakaki)

**Born:** 26 December 1940, Olaa, Hawaii.

**Education:** B.A., University of Hawaii–Manoa.

**Positions Held:** Member, Hawaii County Council, 1990–present.

**Awards, Honors:** Arakaki states, "Being a student of 'human engineering,' I do not seek personal awards and honors. I would rather give others the accolade[s] and honor that they deserve."

**Summary:** James Y. Arakaki is a member of the Hawaii County Council.

## Early Years and Higher Education

James Y. Arakaki was born on 26 December 1940, in an old plantation dispensary in Olaa, Hawaii, on the Big Island of Hawaii to Anmei and Yoshiko Arakaki. His mother chose the moniker "James," while his grandparents named him "Yasuichi," joining "Yasu," their family name, with "ichi," to symbolize his birth as a first-born son to a first-born son.

Recalls Arakaki, "One month before I was born, my father died while fishing off the coast of Hilo. His death made my mother a widow after only one year of marriage. After a year of living with her in-laws, my mother decided to move to Honolulu to start her new life. I was a very fortunate child being raised by grandparents, aunts, and uncles."

Arakaki was reared in local plantation camps. While the lifestyle made for "great kid-time days," he remembers, it "held no future." Thus, following his high school graduation, he "escaped" by joining the army, where he spent three years travelling across the United States before deciding not to make the military his career. He then enrolled at the University of Hawaii in Hilo, pumping gas and washing cars to pay his tuition, before transferring to the school's Manoa campus, where he earned his bachelor's degree in business economics.

## Career Highlights

With degree in hand, Arakaki entered the banking and finance field for ten years before becoming a Dale Carnegie instructor and sales careerist. While working in Honolulu, he met and married his wife Grace. The Arakakis have three children: Anne, an interior designer, Joan, a pharmacist, and Grant, a recent college graduate.

After many years in Honolulu, Arakaki moved back to the Big Island, and in 1978 started Dodo Mortuary Life Plan, Inc., where he is president. In 1990, Arakaki won a seat on the County Council of Hawaii and presently serves as its chairperson. James Arakaki has been very active in many community organizations such as the Japanese Chamber of Commerce, Hawaii Island Japanese Community Association, Hui Okinawa, Hilo Downtown Improvement Association, Ahualani Kumiai, Hawaii Allied Memorial Council, and the Kanoelehua Industrial Association. He has also served on the State of Hawaii Contractors Licensing Board.

## Source

County of Hawaii: County Council. http://www.hawaii-county.com/council/district03.htm. [Accessed 18 October 2001].

George R. Ariyoshi. (© Bettman/CORBIS)

# George R. Ariyoshi

**Born:** 12 March 1926, Honolulu, Hawaii.

**Education:** B.A., Michigan State University, 1949; J.D., University of Michigan, 1952.

**Positions Held:** Hawaii Territorial House of Representatives 1954–1958; Hawaii Territorial Senate, 1958–1959; Hawaii State Senate, 1959–1970; Hawaii Lieutenant Governor, 1970–1973; Hawaii State Governor, 1973–1986.

**Awards, Honors:** Distinguished Alumni Award, the University of Hawaii, 1975; Distinguished Alumni Award, Michigan State University, 1975; the Emperor's Silver Cup Award from the Japanese government, 1986; and honorary law degrees from the University of the Philippines at Quezon City, 1975, the University of Guam at Agana, 1975; and Michigan State University, 1977; and honorary doctorates in humanities from the University of Visayas, Philippines, 1977, Sokka University (Japan), 1984, and the University of Hawaii, 1986.

**Summary:** George R. Ariyoshi was the first governor of Asian descent in the United States. He served as Hawaii's top official from 1973 to 1986.

## Early Years

George Riyochi Ariyoshi was born to Japanese immigrants on 12 March 1926 in Honolulu. Like many other Issei in Hawaii, his mother, the former Mitsue Yoshikawa, hailed from Kumamoto, Japan; his father, Ryozo Ariyoshi, was a sumo wrestler in his homeland before emigrating to work as both a stevedore and a dry cleaning shop operator.

## Education

Young Ariyoshi was ambitious, declaring his goal to become a lawyer early in life. Encouraged by his parents, he treaded a focused path—after serving as class president in high school, he joined the army as an interpreter with the Military Intelligence Service in Japan at the end of World War II. Upon completion of his overseas assignment, he returned home for college. Although he had taken some courses at the University of Hawaii from 1944 to 1945, he ultimately earned his B.A. in political science and history from Michigan State University in 1949. Three years later, he graduated from the University of Michigan Law School.

## Career Highlights

Fresh out of the classroom, Ariyoshi realized his dream and established a solo practice in Honolulu. After working for a year, he plunged into political life by bidding for a seat in the territorial House of Representatives in 1954. Success continued to follow his ambitions, and he won the election. Four years later, he joined the territorial Senate; when Hawaii was finally admitted to the Union in 1959, he became one of the state's first senators.

In the Senate, Ariyoshi was named to several leadership positions, despite his quiet demeanor and general restraint as a speaker. He became chair of the heavyweight Ways and Means Committee, in 1964, the Senate Majority leader in 1965, and the majority floor leader in 1969.

The next year, Ariyoshi reemerged in local politics when the Democratic Party leader, gubernatorial hopeful John A. Burns, who had originally urged Ariyoshi to run for the territorial House in 1954, handpicked him as his running mate. The Burns/Ariyoshi ticket garnered 55 percent of the vote to win. Together, the pair pushed for economic growth, both domestically in areas such as tourism, as well as transnationally, urging for connections between Hawaiians and Asian Pacific countries.

When Governor Burns fell ill to cancer in 1973, Ariyoshi became the state's acting governor. In 1974, he decided to vie for the state's top position, and in November of that year, he became the nation's first Japanese American governor, defeating Honolulu Mayor Frank Fasi in the primaries and Republican Randolph Crossley in the general election.

Once in office, Ariyoshi espoused less aggressive views than he had held as Lieutenant Governor, choosing to concentrate on "preferred growth"—that is, fostering tourism while limiting new immigration—to combat the negative effects of simultaneous global recession, over development at the expense of the environment, and a swelling population. His measures toward these goals included a diverse 40-member Growth Management Task Force in 1977, traffic control in Oahu, and decreasing the numbers of goods imported into the islands.

In 1978, Ariyoshi faced Fasi again in the heated gubernatorial race. Ariyoshi, who highlighted his work in "bringing the people of the community together," and his "preferred growth" strategy, barely survived the renomination contest with Fasi and the general election against Republican state senator John Leopold (Associated Press 1986). The same year, the Hawaii Legislature passed a law limiting governors to two terms in office. Since it was not retroactively enforced, Ariyoshi was able to run for re-election in 1982. In his third attempt, he once again came head to head with Fasi, now an Independent, along with Republican businessman and state senator D.G. "Andy" Anderson, after defeating his own Lieutenant Governor, Jean Sadako King, in the Democratic primary. Criticizing her opponent, Sadako King claimed that he had not given her anything to do during his administration. Nevertheless, Ariyoshi won and went on to capture 45 percent of the votes in the general election with Fasi trailing in second place with 29 percent.

Outside of Hawaiian politics and national government, Ariyoshi has maintained an active life. Aside from his law practice, he worked for a number of firms and was partner of Cole, Gilburn, Goldhaber, and Ariyoshi Management, Inc. Ariyoshi served as chairman, president, and director of the Western Governors Association, the Hawaiian Insurance and Guaranty, Ltd., First Hawaiian Bank, Honolulu Gas Co. Ltd., the Pacific Basin Development Council, and the Hawaii Bar Association, among others. Within his ethnic community, he was an honorary co-chair of the Japanese American National Museum in Los Angeles and a member of the Japanese Cultural Center, Hawaii board of governors.

Ariyoshi has received a number of awards for his accomplishments, including the Distinguished Alumni Awards from the University of Hawaii and Michigan State University, the Emperor's Silver Cup Award in 1986, and honorary law degrees from the University of the Philippines at Quezon City, the University of Guam at Agana, the University of Visayas, and the University of Hawaii. He has been married to Jean Miya Hayashi since 1955, and they have three children, Lynne Miye, Todd Ryozo, and Donn Ryoji.

## Sources

"George Ryoichi Ariyoshi." *AP Candidate Bios*. The Associated Press Political Service, 1986.

"George Ryoichi Ariyoshi." *The Complete Marquis Who's Who Biographies*. Reed Elsevier, Inc., 1995.

Henry, Jim, "George R. Ariyoshi."" In *Notable Asian Americans*, ed. Helen Zia and Susan B. Gall. Detroit: Gale Research Inc., 1995, pp. 8–9.

# B

## Kumar Barve

**Born:** 8 September 1958, Schenectady, New York.

**Education:** B.S., Georgetown University, 1980.

**Positions Held:** Delegate, Maryland House of Delegates, 1990–present.

**Awards, Honors:** Legislator of the Year Award from the Montgomery County Medical Society in 1995, 1996, 2000; Named to the "honor roll" of legislators in 1996 by the Maryland Association of Nonprofit Organizations.

**Summary:** Kumar Barve is the first person of Asian Indian origin to be elected as a state legislator in U.S. history.

### Early Years and Education

Kumar Barve was born on 8 September 1958 in Schenectady, New York to Prabhakar and Neera Barve. After attending Paint Branch High School, he went on to Georgetown University, where he earned a bachelor of science degree in accounting in 1980.

### Career Highlights

Barve, a Democrat, was first elected to Maryland's House of Delegates in 1990 to represent approximately 110,000 residents of central Montgomery County. He served on the House Committee on Economic Matters, which oversees health care reform, business regulation, insurance, consumer protection, and state economic development strategy. Additionally, Barve was appointed chairman of the Science & Technology Subcommittee, and elected chairman of the Montgomery County Delegation. In this capacity he is the legislative leader of the largest county in the state of Maryland.

In 1993, Barve was a cosponsor and the primary architect of Maryland's landmark reform of health insurance. He also pushed for the 1995 law that allows HMO patients to use physicians outside of their HMO network. Recently, Barve was the prime architect of the landmark "e-commerce" Uniform Computer Information Transactions Act (UCITA). With its passage, Maryland became the first state in the nation to place this consumer and business protection statute in effect.

In recognition of his efforts, Barve received the Legislator of the Year Award from the Montgomery County Medical Society in 1995,

1996, and 2000, making him an unprecedented three-time recipient. He was also named to the "honor roll" of legislators in 1996 by the Maryland Association of Nonprofit Organizations.

In addition to his official duties, Barve, a self-described "really busy guy," works as chief financial officer for an environmental company in Rockville, Maryland.

### Source

Kumar Barve, personal communication to Ellen D. Wu, 2 October 2000.

# Julia Chang Bloch

Julia Chang Bloch. (Courtesy Julia Chang Bloch)

**Born:** 2 March 1942, Chefoo, China.

**Education:** B.A., University of California, Berkeley, 1964; M.A., Harvard University, 1967.

**Positions Held:** United States ambassador to the Kingdom of Nepal, 1989–1993; President, U.S.-Japan Foundation, 1996–present.

**Awards, Honors:** National Institute for Women of Color's Outstanding Women of Color Award, 1982; Organization of Chinese American Women Woman of the Year Award, 1987; National Association of Professional Asian Pacific Women Award, 1989; Asian American Leadership Award, 1989; Honorary Fulbright Fellowship, 1996.

**Summary:** A Chinese American, Julia Chang Bloch served as the nation's first ambassador of Asian ancestry. She was the United States ambassador to the Kingdom of Nepal from 1989 to 1993 and currently serves as the president of the U.S.-Japan Foundation.

### Early Years

The nation's first Asian American ambassador, Julia Chang Bloch, was born on 2 March 1942 in Chefoo, China, to Eva Yeh and Fu-Yun Chang. Chang Bloch, whose father had worked as the first Chinese director of the British-ruled customs service in Shanghai, spent her childhood surrounded by the intense political turmoil of the era. As a result, she fled the mainland at the age of nine with her family. This exodus would later shape her political stance as an American diplomat in Nepal. "Look, I am a refugee from Communism," she stated in 1991. "How do I feel? I made my choice with my feet.... We voted with our feet. How much more emphatic can you be than when you completely uproot yourself? My father was a very important man in China, and we left everything except the clothes on our back" (Fineman 1991, 1).

The Changs journeyed first by train to Canton, where they caught a junk to Hong Kong. From the British colony, they boarded an ocean liner bound for the United States. Chang Bloch caught her initial glimpse of her adopted country from the ship. "I still remember going on the President Wilson Lines, and I was so enthralled by the drinking fountain. I mean, the water just came out, and you could drink it.... My first impression of America was that water fountain," she reminisced (Fineman 1991, 1).

## Education

Within weeks, the family landed in San Francisco, where Chang Bloch would spend her formative years adjusting to a new culture and society. She did well, becoming a naturalized citizen in 1962 and graduating from the University of California, Berkeley in 1964 with a bachelor of arts degree in communications and public policy. She then took a position overseas with a two-year commitment to the Peace Corps teaching English in Chinese middle schools in Sabah, Malaysia. She wasted no time upon returning home and earned a masters degree in government and East Asia regional studies at Harvard University in 1967.

## Career Highlights

After obtaining her degree, Chang Bloch returned to the Peace Corps as a training officer for the East Asia and Pacific Region. As a trainer, her numerous responsibilities included the development and coordination of volunteer orientation programs, particularly concerning cross-cultural issues, overseeing official relations between the organization and host countries, and assisting in the screening of Peace Corps candidates' applications. In 1968, Chang Bloch transferred to the position of evaluation officer where she orchestrated and implemented tools for the assessment of the Peace Corps' work in Asia and Central America.

Chang Bloch's entry into Washington, D.C. circles occurred in 1971 when she accepted a position on the minority staff of the U.S. Senate Select Committee on Nutrition and Human Needs. "I decided I wanted to work for government, because, in China, government service is considered very respectable," she said. "It's a Confucian tradition that you want to serve your country" (Fineman 1991, 1). As a staff member for then-Senator Charles Percy (R-IL) from 1971 to 1976 and as the committee's chief minority counsel from 1976 to 1977, Chang Bloch again shouldered a myriad of responsibilities, among which were the preparation of legislative proposals, speeches, and reports—and overseeing the committee's funds.

In 1977, Chang Bloch once again changed hats when she was appointed the deputy director for the U.S. International Communication Agency's Office of African Affairs. She put her classroom and practical training to use, devoting time to American relations with sub-Saharan Africa as deputy director from 1977 to 1980 for the OAA, which had a $20 million budget and over 500 staff members. Chang Bloch also served as a liaison between the National Security Council, the State Department, and the Agency for International Development.

Before undertaking her next project, Chang Bloch invested one semester in research at Harvard's Kennedy School of Government. With her fellowship to its Institute of Politics, she investigated the connection between American diplomacy and domestic developments. At the close of her study, Chang Bloch continued her government work as a special assistant within the Agency of International Development (AID), where she examined humanitarian programs for Somalian refugees and facilitated communications between AID and the State Department. In 1981, she was named AID's assistant administrator for the Food for Peace and Voluntary Assistance Bureau, becoming the nation's first Asian American presidential appointee confirmed by the Senate. As the party responsible for coordinating the most wide-reaching hunger assistance program on earth, she managed over $2 billion of aid for 80 countries.

The most dire crisis during her term occurred in late 1983 through 1985 with the famine in Africa, during which the Agency of International Development delivered 3 million tons of food to approximately 40 million men, women, and children affected by the disaster. Of AID's actions, Chang Bloch recalled, "It was very controversial during the famine because we fought for the policy of the hungry child. But no scandal. No scandal. I used to dread that I'd wake up in the morning and find a story on the front page about thousands of tons of food rotting on the docks [in Ethiopia]. It was tough but rewarding" (Fineman 1991, 1).

In addition to the African emergency, Chang Bloch divided AID's resources among the World Food Program, various United Nations conferences, the Americans Schools and Hospitals Abroad Program, and a number of other federal and private agencies.

After six years with the Food for Peace and Voluntary Assistance Bureau, Chang Bloch stepped into familiar territory as the assistant administrator for AID's largest subdivision, the Asia and Near East Bureau. Again, the capable Chang Bloch juggled a substantial budget—$3.8 billion—and supervised a sizable staff of over 2,000 to coordinate relief programs for at least 26 nations. As before, she bridged the efforts of AID with other organizations, such as the World Bank and the International Monetary Fund.

In 1988, Chang Bloch returned to her alma mater, Harvard, to serve as an associate in the U.S.-Japan relations program at the university's Center for International Affairs. Similar to her previous fellowship, she researched American foreign policy, but specifically with Japan. Her query culminated in the publication of her findings in the Council on Foreign Relations' Yen for Development.

Chang Bloch made history in 1989 as the first U.S. ambassador of Asian ancestry, appointed by President George Bush as the American envoy to Nepal. " . . . You know, it was shocking, the first Asian American ambassador. It goes without saying that somebody realized there has never been an Asian American ambassador," she remarked (Fineman 1991, 1). Chang Bloch assumed her position as the Nepalese people were beginning to engage in a nationwide revolution for democratic reform. The monarchy, headed by King Birendra, responded to the movement negatively, often through violence.

As one of only 18 foreign ambassadors in Katmandu at the time, Chang Bloch was highly visible during the revolt. Her activism, which leaned toward the moderate Nepali Congress Party as opposed to left wing radicals, drew criticism from Communists. While Chang Bloch, a Republican, articulated her distaste for Communism, a remnant from her youth as a refugee from the Peoples' Republic of China, she explained that "Our policies [in support of democratization] are clear. I've been in the business for over 20 years. I've been in the government, and I never allow my personal feelings to get in the way of policy. I know the drill" (Fineman 1991, 1). Along those lines, she established Nepal's Democratic Program Initiative.

One of Chang Bloch's greatest challenges during her ambassadorship was completely unrelated to politics. While in Nepal, she saw her husband, attorney Stuart Marshall Bloch, whom she married on 21 December 1968, only four times a year. With good humor, she stated, "He says he's checking the Guinness Book of Records for the longest commute. It takes two days to get here. Well, we're used to it. But yeah, it's hard, and that's why I never thought of getting an ambassadorship," although she conceded that the post was indeed her "most fun job" ever (Fineman 1991, 1).

When asked in 1991 whether she would pursue another political position, Chang Bloch replied, "I'm too private a person, if you believe it, to join American politics. . . . My head tells me that I should move into the private sector" (Fineman 1991, 1). True to her word, she bid farewell to public policy in 1993, accepting a newly-created group executive vice presidency for corporate communications and governmental affairs at the Bank of America in San Francisco. Her primary task was to administer Bank of America's governmental, media, internal, and external communications programs. In 1996, she left the corporation for her first love, international affairs, assuming the presidency of the U.S.-Japan Foundation.

Chang Bloch has received countless accolades for her achievements, including the National Institute for Women of Color's Outstanding Women of Color title in 1982, an Organization of Chinese American Women Woman of the Year award in 1987, an Asian

American leadership award in 1989, the National Association of Professional Asian Pacific American Women Award in 1989, and an honorary Fulbright fellowship in 1996. Outside of her official capacities, she has been involved in various pursuits, such as ceramics, art collecting, and gourmet cooking, even co-authoring *Chinese Home Cooking* in 1986.

Chang Bloch acknowledges her seminal role in the advancement of women and Asian Pacific Islanders in American society. "I've learned that women and minorities need role models," she commented. The founding chair of the Organization of Chinese American Women and its Woman of the Year in 1987, Chang Bloch reflected, "I know every time I'm given a job, it's not just Julia Chang Bloch. It is a woman, and an Asian, also being tested. And I have always felt that I carry this triple burden, that if I don't do well, I am going to make [sic] more difficult for other Asians and other women" (Fineman 1991, 1).

## Sources

Fineman, Mark. "Speaking Her Mind; Diplomacy: The First and Only Asian-American Ambassador Shakes Up Nepal With Her Tough-Talking Style. 'I Would Really Have To Be A Nerd To Be Low Profile,' She Says." *Los Angeles Times*. 3 June 1991, p. E1.

Henry, Jim, "Julia Chang Bloch." In *Notable Asian Americans*, ed. Helen Zia and Susan B. Gall. Detroit, MI: Gale Research, Inc., 1995, pp. 19–20.

"Julia Chang Bloch." *The Complete Marquis Who's Who Biographies*. Reed Elsevier, Inc., 1997.

"Julia Chang Bloch Named Bank of America Group Executive Vice President." *Business Wire*, 2 June 1993.

# Grace Lee Boggs

**Born:** 27 June 1915, Providence, Rhode Island.

**Education:** B.A., Barnard College, 1935; Ph.D., Bryn Mawr College, 1940.

**Positions Held:** Member of numerous leftist political groups, including Johnson-Forest Tendency, Organization for Black Power, the National Organization for an American Revolution, the Inner City Organizing Committee, Michigan Freedom Now Party, and Detroit's Asian Political Alliance.

**Summary:** A Chinese American, Grace Lee Boggs has been involved in numerous leftist political organizations and campaigns since the 1940s. A longtime Detroit resident, she has worked most closely with the city's African American community.

### Early Years

Grace Lee Boggs was born on 27 June 1915 in Providence, Rhode Island above her father's downtown restaurant on Westminster Street. Although children were a rarity in the largely immigrant Chinese American community in that era, the waiters would say "Leave her on the hillside to die. She's only a girl," whenever Boggs would cry. As she recalled in her 1998 autobiography, *Living for Change*, "Later they told me this as a kind of joke. But for me, even as a child, it was no laughing matter. Early on, it gave me an inkling that all is not right with this world." It was this same innate sense of justice and willingness to question convention that provided the impetus for many, if not most, of her life decisions.

Before embarking on her career as a political activist, however, Boggs' experiences were not unlike those of other second generation Chinese Americans in the early 20th century. Her father, Ching Dong Goon, a.k.a. Chin Lee, and her mother, Ny Yih Lan, were both immigrants from the Southern Chinese region of Toishan in Guangdong province. They moved to the East Coast in about 1911 to pursue employment opportunities, which were extremely scarce for Chinese in the West at the time. By 1913, Chin Lee had opened a restaurant in Lawrence, Massachusetts, and within a short period of time was operating other branches in Boston, Providence, and

Buffalo. Then, in 1924, Boggs, her parents, and six siblings relocated to New York City where her father established the famed Chin Lee restaurant at 1604 Broadway. Boggs then spent the remainder of her childhood in the Queens Jackson Heights neighborhood.

## Education

The young Boggs displayed a flair for academics. Having skipped several years in school, she completed the eighth grade at twelve years of age before advancing to Elmhurst's Newton High School. In her senior year, she received a $100 annual Regents university scholarship, with which she enrolled at New York City's Barnard College. At that time, however, her future plans were unclear. "When I became a Barnard freshman in 1931, I was sixteen years old and very immature. When people asked me what I planned to do with a college education, I had no answer. The only thing I was clear about was that I was not going to become a teacher," she stated.

The turbulent politics and social circumstances of the 1930s eventually steered Boggs toward a philosophy major. In response to the decade's domestic and international crises, Boggs turned not to activism (the only action she participated in during her time at Barnard was a Briand Peace Pact campus demonstration) but to "asking . . . questions about the meaning of life and engaging in endless discussions" with friends. Unsatisfied, she filled her course schedule with philosophy classes. "When people asked me why I had become so interested in philosophy or what I was going to do with a major in philosophy, I was unable to explain. I could not even tell them what philosophy was about. All I knew was that I was feeling the need to think for myself," she recalled. "What other people had discovered, what other people thought was no longer enough for me."

After completing the requirements and graduating from Barnard in 1935, Boggs, like many other college-educated Asian Americans of the period, had no success in securing meaningful employment. Through happenstance, however, she learned of the availability of a Chinese graduate scholarship at Bryn Mawr College in Pennsylvania. She applied and was awarded full funding for her studies. At Bryn Mawr, Boggs relished her opportunity to study with Professor Paul Weiss, whom she described as one "who philosophized as if his life depended on it." Through Weiss, Boggs was exposed to the works of German thinkers Immanuel Kant and G.W.F. Hegel, the ideas of whom would profoundly influence her personal approach to life and humanity.

George Mead, one of the four founders of American pragmatism, was a third philosopher whose writings Boggs was first introduced to at Bryn Mawr. "In retrospect, it seems clear that what attracted me to Mead was that he gave me what I needed in that period—a body of ideas that challenged and empowered me to move from a life of contemplation to a life of action," she later stated. After finishing her dissertation, "George Herbert Mead: The Philosopher of the Social Individual," in 1940, Boggs left the East Coast for Chicago with little more than a few dollars, books, and clothes.

## Career Highlights

In Chicago, Grace Lee Boggs became involved with a number of neo-Trotskyist political groups and movements, including the South Side Tenants organization and the Workers Party. It was through the latter that she met CLR James, a black West Indian intellectual Marxist. Boggs joined his Trotskyist circle of colleagues known as the Johnson-Forest Tendency, which was first a branch of the Workers' Party, later a subgroup of the Socialist Workers' Party, and eventually an independent entity. She then moved back to New York in the late 1940s to work closely with James.

As a member of the Johnson-Forest Tendency and activist in international liberation movements, Boggs assisted in organizing within the party as well as among New York's laborers and participated in the development of the group's theories, philosophies, and publications. Among the Tendency's radical political views was the support of an independent black struggle and a critique of human relations with capitalist societies. The Johnson-Forest Tendency also established the Third Layer School where youth were instructors while intellectuals and older party members were students.

Before her split with James in 1962, Boggs came in contact with a number of political notables including Dr. Kwame Nkrumah, an anti-colonial activist who later became the first president of Ghana and the founder of the Organization of African Unity. Nkrumah proposed to Boggs not long after meeting her in 1945; Boggs refused because she "couldn't imagine [her]self being politically active in a country where [she] was totally ignorant of the history, geography, and culture." Years later, Nkrumah remarked to Grace Boggs' husband, Jimmy, "I hope you don't mind me saying this, but if Grace had married me, together we would have changed all Africa."

Instead, Boggs chose to wed Jimmy Boggs, an Alabama-born African American employed in Detroit's auto industry. The two first met in the fall of 1952 during a Third Layer School social in New York. Following Boggs' move to Detroit in 1953, the pair worked on *Correspondence*, the Johnson-Forest Tendency newsletter. After dinner one evening in June, Jimmy asked Boggs to marry him, initiating what would be a 40-year-long relationship. "I don't know why Jimmy asked me to marry him. Maybe he was testing me. If he was surprised by my affirmative response, there was no indication. We never discussed it. It all happened so naturally that there was nothing to discuss. Jimmy radiated a personal and political energy that I found very attractive. He was also more rooted and more secure in his identity as a human being than any man I had ever met," she explained.

Following A. Phillip Randolph's call to African Americans to March on Washington in 1941, Boggs decided to devote her energies to the black community. "From the March on Washington movement I learned that a movement begins when large numbers of people, having reached a point where they feel they can't take the way things are any longer, find hope for improving their daily lives in an action that they can take together," she stated. "I also discovered the power that the black community has within itself to change this country when it begins to move." Together with her husband, she quickly became immersed in the heart of Detroit's African American struggles to the extent that the FBI coined a new term, "Afro-Chinese," to describe her in their files.

Grace Lee Boggs' amazing body of work has included the creation of the Independent Negro Committee to Ban the Bomb and Racism and memberships in the Organization for Black Power, the National Organization for an American Revolution, and the Inner City Organizing Committee. She has also been involved in protesting discrimination both locally and nationally, organizing a Grassroots Leadership Conference, lecturing on revolutionary theory and practice, coordinating the all-black Michigan Freedom Now Party, and participating in a number of other campaigns. She has authored or co-authored a myriad of political works and contributed literature to various publications, including *Manifest for a Black Revolutionary Party*, co-written with Jimmy Boggs, and *Revolution and Evolution in the Twentieth Century*.

Boggs' activism was not limited to the African American community, however. Although admitting that "growing up [she] had been ambivalent about being Chinese, occasionally taking pride in [her] ancestry but more often ignoring it because [she] disliked the way that Caucasians reacted to [her] Chineseness," she became one of the six founders of Detroit's Asian Political Alliance in 1970 during the Asian American Movement. Among APA's activities were Chinese and Japanese history classes, screenings of political films, workshops for young U.S.-born Asians "to help discover and create their identities," and anti–Vietnam War/American aggression demonstrations.

In "Asian-Americans and the U.S. Movement," a pamphlet published by APA from a speech she delivered at the Asian American Reality Conference in December 1970, Boggs commented, "After the blacks, we Asians may be the ones who have the most to contribute to the struggle. . . . I believe we have something very important to contribute in the form of a historical perspective and in the concept of the human contradictions that have to be recognized and resolved and which we can see being tackled in Asia." Boggs herself visited China for the first time in the fall of 1984. Of her visit, she concluded, "The most important thing I learned during my two months in China was that I am more American than Chinese."

During the 1980s and early 1990s, Boggs continued with her dedicated political activism, showing no signs of age. Her activities included the urban-oriented Detroiters for Dignity and Save Our Sons and Daughters, which has supported community gardening, peace education, anti-violence programs, and Detroit Summer, "an Intergenerational Multicultural Youth Program/Movement to rebuild, redefine, respirit Detroit from the Ground Up" through such exercises as community gardens, public mural painting, community dinners, and leadership workshops. Her involvement focused on developing local, self-reliant communities.

Even after losing her husband to cancer in 1993, Boggs maintained a full schedule. She attended an environmental justice symposium in Washington, D.C. in February 1994, meeting with other Asian Pacific American delegates to discuss community-related concerns. Upon returning to Detroit, she helped to plan the city's first Environmental Justice Gathering and later the founding of the Detroiters Working for Environmental Justice, "whose goal is to build a grassroots movement to challenge the threats to our daily lives where we live, work, and play and to rebuild Detroit safer, healthier, and more self-reliant."

She also conducted an environmental justice workshop at the AARP Empowering Minority Elders Conference in Buffalo, New York in 1995, began serving as a stakeholder and member of the Youth Involvement/Citizen Activism team in Healthy Detroit, part of the Healthy Cities Movement established by the World Health Organization in 1984, and became involved in the New Detroit Race Relations Committee and City of Detroit Youth Commission in 1995.

That year, which she described as "exciting . . . because I was creating my own identity as an activist in Detroit movement and at the same time making new discoveries about my identity as an Asian American," Boggs attended her 60th year reunion at Barnard College. The high percentage of Asian Pacific American students at her alma mater astounded and affected her immensely. "When you have been a member of a minority so small as to be almost invisible, it is almost intoxicating to wake up one day and discover that your ethnic group is developing such a critical mass that what it does matters," she reflected. "Immediately upon my return to Detroit I sat down at my computer, typed in the title of the first chapter, and began writing the first draft of [my] autobiography."

As an octogenarian, Boggs again recognizes another turning point in her life. In the conclusion of *Living for Change*, she is philosophical at the prospects of the new millennium: "I rejoice at the changing of the guard and at the fact that the new generation, which is beginning to discover its mission, is more open than the generation that led the movements of the 1960s. . . . I am glad that I am still around not only as a participant but as a griot to pass on the story of how we got to this place—because, to paraphrase Kierkegaard, if the future is to be lived, the past must be understood."

## Sources

Boggs, Grace Lee. "Asian-Americans and the U.S. Movement." Pamphlet. Detroit: Asian Political Alliance, 1970.

———. *Living for Change: An Autobiography*. Minneapolis: University of Minnesota Press, 1998.

# Thelma Buchholdt

Thelma Buchholdt. (Courtesy of Thelma Buchholdt)

**Full Name at Birth:** Thelma Jean Garcia.

**Born:** Claveria, Cagayan Province, Philippines.

**Education:** B.A., Mount St. Mary's College, 1956; J.D., District of Columbia School of Law, 1991.

**Positions Held:** Member, Alaska State Legislature, House of Representatives, 1974–1982; Director, Office of Equal Employment Opportunity, State of Alaska.

**Awards, Honors:** "Filipinos of the Year Award," Philippine News, 1976; 1993–1994 Fil-Am Image Award.

**Summary:** Thelma Buchholdt is the first Filipino-American woman elected to a state legislature in the United States.

## Early Years and Education

Thelma Buchholdt was born to Eugenio and Diony de Leon Garcia in Claveria, Cagayan Province, Philippines. The oldest of three sisters, Rhoda, Jeannette, and Nancy, and two brothers, Eloy and Melvyn, Buchholdt notes that she came from a "politically active family. My mother was active in local and regional politics in the Philippines. My career was influenced by her example" (Brelsford 1983, 47).

The young Buchholdt showed early signs of promise, being promoted twice during her years at Claveria Elementary School—from second to third grade and from fourth to fifth grade. She then matriculated at three secondary institutions for one year each: the Claveria Institute in her hometown, Holy Ghost Academy in Laoag, Ilocos Norte, and the Academy of St. Joseph, also in Claveria, from which she graduated. Immigrating to the United States in 1951, Buchholdt decided to pursue her university education at Los Angeles's Mount St. Mary's College.

## Career Highlights

After earning her zoology degree in 1956, she spent eight years in Schenectady, New York, where she taught elementary school. She then relocated to Anchorage, Alaska in 1965, where she worked as an independent planning consultant on issues relevant to community organization, education, health, social services, and local government.

In 1974, Buchholdt launched her premier campaign for a seat in Alaska's state legislature to represent District 9. With her successful bid, she became the first female Filipino American to hold a seat in any state legislature outside of Hawaii and the first Filipino American State legislator. During her freshman term, she served on the Legislative Council's Subcommittee on Telecommunications and Subcommittee on Health Planning and vice chaired the Finance Committee.

Two years later, Buchholdt ran for reelection and emerged victorious. Noted San Francisco's *Philippine News* in January 1977, "The greatest credit must go to those who plunged into the political area as candidates and in the face of overwhelming political odds pulled out impressive victories." Citing Buchholdt as one outstanding example, the

*Philippine News* continued, "[she] stands out in light of the fact that, unlike her Hawaii or California counterparts, she had no effective mass ethnic base to count upon in her bid for reelection. She won the election the first time around on the basis of her platform and promises; she won reelection because she performed and delivered . . . [despite] a vicious racist campaign launched by one of her Anglo opponents in a predominantly Anglo district" (Quintana 1977, 3).

During her second term, Buchholdt vice chaired the Rules Committee while serving as a member of the Finance and Health, Education, and Social Services Committee and the Legislative Council. In 1978, she was reelected to a third term, during which she chaired the Health, Education, and Social Services Committee while participating on the Judiciary Committee and Committee for the Services to the Elderly. In 1980, she was again reelected to an impressive fourth term, during which she chaired the House Special Committee on Coal and joined the Finance, Rules, and Transportation Committees during the first session. Buchholdt then went on to serve on the Judiciary Committee and House Committee on Loans, and the Committee on Transportation and Natural Resources during the second session.

As a member of Alaska's state government, Buchholdt devoted her attention to a range of issues concerning education, human resources, and development, including advocacy for senior citizens, disabled children, victims of domestic violence, community schools, and a state health insurance plan. In the *Legislative Highlights* newsletter written for her residents of Spenard, her district, during her third term, Buchholdt also noted that "constituent casework is by far the most significant and challenging aspect of my legislative duties aside from my vote on legislation on the House floor" (Buchholdt n.d.).

At the start of her fourth term, Buchholdt emphasized the need to "maintain Alaskan solidarity. This decade [the 1980s] will present us with political challenges only our strong Alaskan solidarity can enable us to meet successfully." She also added, "I think we will succeed in maintaining political good will among and toward Alaskans through our sense of solidarity as one people. We can work together as urban and rural communities, cooperating with industry, the state and the federal government in the development of our state" (Buchholdt 1980, B4).

From Buchholdt's point of view, however, this solidarity did not preclude the support of women and ethnic and racial minorities. "As a minority woman in the legislature, I have had to deal with sexism and racism at every turn," she stressed. "I had to seize responsibility and do what I could. I fought to serve on the powerful Finance Committee and on other major committees" (Brelsford 1983, 47). One example of her efforts to direct attention toward underrepresented groups was her role in setting aside state funds in 1981 for the publication of *Profiles in Change: Names, Notes, and Quotes for Alaskan Women*, researched and written by Ginna Brelsford under the auspices of the Women's Political Leadership Project sponsored by the Alaska Commission on the Status of Women. In a message addressed to the readers, Buchholdt opined, "I have tried to be very realistic about public service. One must be committed to the public good to serve in the legislature. There are few other reasons for pursuing such a path. I do, however, believe that young women today have many opportunities and can make just about anything out of their lives." She continued, "We certainly need more women in the legislature and politics and I have fought for this. If you are truly committed to public service I encourage you to get involved at a young age. Choose a mentor or two, learn from them, join local organizations, develop your skills and your ability to serve will emerge" (Brelsford 1983, 47).

Additionally, Buchholdt has long been a prominent force among the local and national Filipino and Asian Pacific American communities. From 1973 to1975, she was the first woman president of the Filipino Community of Anchorage, Alaska, Inc. She played the lead role in obtaining initial planning funds for Anchorage's Asian Alaskan Cultural Center from the state legislature in 1980. Three years later, she convened a seven-member pilot volunteer Board of Directors, including herself, to plan for the design of the center and file its Articles of Incorporation with the state of Alaska. The center, which opened its doors in 1988, lists its main objectives as "the promotion of mutual respect and understanding of the Asian and American cultures, programs and projects of the Asian community in Anchorage, and business/trade and cultural exchanges between Alaska and the Asian/Pacific Rim countries" (Asian Alaskan Cultural Center 1999).

Buchholdt, who is of Ibanag-Ilocano background, has also presided over the Alaska chapter of the Filipino American National Historical Society (FANHS) from 1994 to the present. Currently, she serves as the National Vice President of FANHS, of which she is also a trustee. After persuading Alaska House speaker Ramona Barnes to appropriate funds for the research and documentation of the early history of Filipino contact and growth in Alaska in 1993, Buchholdt authored *Filipinos in Alaska: 1788-1958*, published by the Asian Alaskan Cultural Center in 1996. Assessing the history of this community, she explained, "Filipinos found Alaska a better place to live and work, and to raise their families. Filipinos recognized that their hard work and diligence were better appreciated in Alaska, and they stayed. They became part of Alaska and Alaska became their home" (Avery 1987, 8).

In 1982, Buchholdt was nominated for a fifth term in Alaska's House of Representatives but lost in the general election, due in part to the reapportioning of her precinct, thus forcing her to run in a new district where she was not well-known. Despite her defeat, Buchholdt has remained a significant presence in Alaskan and national politics. She continues to serve as one of Alaska's State Advisors to the U.S. Commission on Civil Rights, a position that she has held since 1972. From 1987 to 1988, she was the only Asian American and Filipino American woman elected as President of the National Order of Women Legislators. In the midst of these responsibilities, she also enrolled at the District of Columbia School of Law (now the Dave Clarke School of Law, University of the District of Columbia), earning her juris doctorate in 1991.

In 1995, Buchholdt was named the head of Alaska's Office of Equal Employment Opportunity. Regarding her appointment, Alaska's Governor Tony Knowles stated, "Thelma has worked tirelessly for decades with a diverse collection of groups and people in Alaska. I have asked her to join my team as an advocate for the state's non-discrimination and affirmative action programs, and to make job opportunities accessible to all Alaskans" ("The Governor's Report," 1995). On her new position, Buchholdt commented, "I know first hand how remote government appears to many people. I have spent my life working to bridge that gap" ("The Governor's Report, 1995).

Aside from her professional, political, and civic commitments, Buchholdt notes proudly that she has been a wife to Jon Buchholdt since 1957. The Buchholdts have four grown children: Titiana, an attorney, Chris, a business entrepreneur, Hans, a computer programmer and cartographer, and Dylan, an attorney.

While Buchholdt plans to retire soon from government work, she continues to hold a number of long-term, substantive goals at the dawn of the new millennium. These are "to remain politically active, to continue to nurture and shape my Filipino cultural heritage, and to continue practicing law, representing minority clients on a pro bono basis when necessary."

## Sources

"Answers to Frequently Asked Questions About the AACC." Pamphlet. Asian Alaskan Cultural Center, 1999.

Avery, Steve, "Author Documents Filipinos' Influence on Alaska History." *Kodiak Daily Mirror*. 7 January 1987.

Brelsford, Ginna. *Profiles in Courage: Names, Notes, and Quotes for Alaskan Women.* Anchorage: Alaska Commission on the Status of Women, 1983.

Buchholdt, Thelma. *Filipinos in Alaska: 1788–1958.* Anchorage: Asian Alaskan Cultural Center, 1996.

———. "Legislative Highlights." No date.

———. "Responsibilities Concern Buchholdt." *Anchorage Times.* 6 January 1980, p. B4.

"The Governor's Report." Juneau, AK: Office of the Governor, October 1995.

Quintana, Leandro D. " 'Filipinos of the Year' Selected." *Philippine News*, 1–7 January 1977, pp. 1, 3.

# C

## Benjamin Cayetano

Benjamin Cayetano. (Photo by George Kodama)

**Born:** 14 November 1939, Honolulu, Hawaii.

**Education:** A.A., Los Angeles Harbor College, 1966; B.A., University of California, Los Angeles, 1968; J.D., Loyola University, 1971.

**Positions Held:** Member, Hawaii State Legislature, 1974–1986; Hawaii State Lieutenant Governor, 1986-1994; Hawaii State Governor, 1994–present.

**Awards, Honors:** Asia-Pacific Academic Consortium for Public Health's Excellence in Leadership Award, 1991, UCLA Medal, 1995, UCLA's Edward A. Dickson Alumnus of the Year Award, 1998, Namesake for UCLA Asian American Studies Center's "Benjamin Cayetano Professor in Public Policy and American Politics" endowed academic chair.

**Summary:** Benjamin Cayetano, governor of Hawaii, is the highest ranking Filipino-American elected public official to date.

### Early Years

Benjamin Jerome Cayetano's childhood typified in many ways that of an "at-risk youth." The son of Filipino immigrants Bonifacio Marcos and Eleanor Infante, Cayetano, born 14 November 1939, lived in

Kalihi, an industrial, low-income area of Honolulu. Living in his father's custody after his parents divorced when he was six, Cayetano and his brother had an unorthodox upbringing, tagging along with Bonifacio on weekends to the restaurants where he worked as a waiter. The Cayetano siblings spent many nights "on the kitchen floor" or "on the beach," as Cayetano later remembered, in the company of older Hawaiian beach boys (Gupta 1995, 26).

Cayetano's primary and secondary school years were checkered by juvenile delinquency and stifled ambitions, despite early signs of academic promise. His mother, for example, discouraged him from pursuing law school after he became inspired to do so by an eighth grade class report he wrote on Clarence Darrow, the Scopes trial defense attorney. Behaviors such as smoking and fighting constantly plagued him and led to time in jail on one occasion. "I think I was trying to fit the stereotype of the Kalihi kid—to be rough and not afraid to use your dukes," he stated (Silva 1996, 33).

Cayetano performed poorly in school—"I was too interested in cars and other things and I was on the verge of flunking out," he recalled—but graduated nevertheless from Honolulu's Farrington High School in 1958 (Silva 1996, 33). He married his sweetheart, Lorraine Gueco, and soon thereafter, they began raising their children, Brandon, Janeen, and Samantha.

Accepting his responsibilities, a matured Cayetano worked steadily to support his family as a junkyard laborer, an electrician's apprentice, and a truck driver. However, he encountered trouble once again during a skirmish in a drive-in restaurant, resulting in another jail sentence. The threats faced by Cayetano behind bars cemented his resolve to avoid similar circumstances in the future, and upon his release, he began to work on state highway crews. Although interested in becoming a draftsman, he was unable to secure a position due in large part to discrimination. "In those days, I never met a Caucasian who wasn't a boss," he said (Silva 1996, 33). He also recounted an instance when a Japanese American employer bypassed his job application for that of a co-ethnic. It then occurred to Cayetano that he needed more education to increase his options, and he decided to move in 1963 to attend Los Angeles Harbor College in Wilmington, California. He vowed not to return to Hawaii until he was "something" (Gupta 1995, 27).

## Education

On the mainland, both Cayetano and his wife, Lorraine, endured seven years of hard work in order to obtain his degrees while maintaining their home life. Cayetano attended classes in the daytime and worked part time in the afternoons, while Gueco waitressed in the evenings at the Los Angeles International Airport. Eventually, he earned his A.A. in 1966, his B.A. as a political science major and an American history minor in 1968 from the University of California, Los Angeles, and his J.D. from Los Angeles' Loyola University in 1971.

## Career Highlights

Having achieved his goal to become "something" (in fact, according to Cayetano, he is the only lawyer among the 900 people in his high school graduating class), Cayetano moved back to Hawaii in 1971 to begin his law career. While working for a firm, he was appointed to the Hawaii Housing Authority by then-governor John A. Burns. This was to be the first of his many positions in the islands' political scene. He then ran successfully for Honolulu's Pearl City district's seat in the state House of Representatives in 1974, defeating a Japanese American candidate in the majority Japanese American district, followed by two terms in the state Senate that ended in 1986.

In the House, he was chair of the Energy and Transportation Committee, and while in the Senate, he headed the Ways and Means, Economic Development, and Public Utilities and Transportation Committees. A well-known figure, the *Honolulu Star-Bulletin* dubbed Cayetano one of the "ten most effective legislators" for four consecutive years.

Cayetano continued to practice law as a bar examiner in the Hawaii Supreme Court, was a member of various state judicial panels, an advisor to the University of Hawaii Law Review, and a partner in the firm Schutter, Cayetano, Playdon. As Hawaii's Lieutenant Governor from 1986 to 1994, he supported Japanese investments in Hawaii and equal opportunity for minorities. He was also particularly interested in economic diversification through educational reform to make Hawaii "someplace other than a tourist destination" with a population of "room maids and bell boys" (Gupta 1995, 28). One of his projects was the state-sponsored After-School Plus (A+) program, the first of its kind in the country, which provides after-school activities for 27,000 "latchkey" children of working parents.

Commonly perceived as independent, even arrogant, and on the fringes of the Democratic Party, Cayetano nevertheless became Hawaii's governor—the nation's first Filipino-American to hold the position—in 1994, albeit with less than 36 percent of the vote split among himself, Frank Fasi, and Patricia Saiki. As governor, one of Cayetano's initial achievements of which he was "most proud" was the brokering of a land exchange between the state and the Campbell Estate, resulting in the addition of 1,000 acres for public use. "This exchange will be of long-term benefit to Hawaii," stated Cayetano in a 1996 interview with *Filipinas* magazine (Silva 1996, 33). He listed affordable housing, reduced traffic congestion, and possible construction of a new University of Hawaii campus as a result.

The most pressing issue of Cayetano's first term, however, was the economy. Facing one of the greatest financial crises in the state's history, Cayetano dealt with a fiscal shortfall of $750 million, resulting in the downsizing of the state's jobs, education, health, and social service projects. Bankruptcies reached record highs and unemployment rates rose above national averages as military opportunities were eliminated in the wake of the end of the Cold War, and the weakening of the sugar industry, while tourism, one of Hawaii's bedrock industries, dropped as a result of Asia's widespread financial troubles.

Hawaii's economic slump proved to be Cayetano's most significant hurdle in his campaign for reelection as well. His approval ratings among the frustrated electorate declined, hitting unprecedented lows in April 1998. Cayetano, however, managed to overcome voter dissatisfaction, claiming impending improvements and promising measures in support of business without sacrificing the concerns of the working class. He barely beat his competition, Maui mayor Republican Linda Lingle, coming away only 5,253 votes, or 1.3 percent, ahead.

Aside from money management, education continues to remain at the top of his gubernatorial agenda. In his state of the state address in January 1999, he declared, "Contrary to the cries of our critics, Hawaii's public schools are not the worst in the nation. We are not the best either—and I take no comfort in the fact that our schools are average. Like you—I want our schools to be the best that they can be. Therefore, while my administration will continue to support the funding requirements for public education over the next four years, we will look to developing ways to measure and improve students and performance" (www.hawaii.gov 1999). Among his policy proposals for his second term are autonomy for the University of Hawaii, greater access to technical education, a system of performance measures, and locally-controlled "Schools for the New Century."

Outside of Hawaii, Cayetano is perhaps best known for his stance on gay marriage. During his first term as governor, his administration came under the glare of the national spotlight for its role in the public debate. Cayetano supported state recognition of legal rights for all domestic partners regardless of sex.

Cayetano's performance in the face of such challenging issues has earned him accolades such as the Asia-Pacific Academic Consortium for Public Health's Excellence in Leadership Award in 1991, the UCLA Medal in 1995, and UCLA's Edward A. Dickson Alumnus of the Year Award in 1998. Additionally, during the 1998-1999 school year, the UCLA Asian American Studies Center announced a campaign to create the endowed "Benjamin Cayetano Professor in Public Policy and American Politics" academic chair.

As the nation's first governor of Filipino ancestry, Cayetano has emphasized his role as "the governor of all the people of Hawaii" (Silva 1996, 33). However, he has also acknowledged his ethnic roots, staying active in the Filipino-American community and visiting Philippine President Fidel Ramos in 1995. During that trip, he also stopped in his father's hometown, Urdaneta, Pangasinan, where he was greeted with excitement and fanfare. Of his accomplishments, Cayetano simply explained, "In helping everyone, the disadvantaged in particular, you also help your own group get equal opportunity. The bigger task is how to govern.... I make a contribution by breaking stereotypes. If I work hard, remain honest, and compassionate, and act as a good leader, I open all doors for all kinds of people" (Silva 1996, 33).

## Sources

"Benjamin Cayetano." *AP Candidate Bios*. The Associated Press Political Service, 1998.

Gupta, Himanee. "Benjamin Cayetano." In *Notable Asian Americans*, ed. Helen Zia and Susan B. Gall. Detroit: Gale Research Inc., 1995, pp. 26–28.

*Hawaii State Web site:* www.hawaii.gov [Accessed 20 April 1999].

Lavilla, Stacy. "Wu, Cayetano Savor Tight Victories." *Asian Week*. 18 November 1998, p. 9.

*Selections from Crosscurrents, the Newsmagazine of UCLA's Asian American Studies Center*, ed. Glenn Omatsu. Fall/Winter 1998 and Spring/Summer 1999.

Shinn, John. L., III. "Cayetano Sworn in as Hawaii Gov." *Filipino Reporter*. 15 December 1994, p.1.

Silva, John L. "Straight Outta Kalihi." *Filipinas Magazine*. 31 May 1996, p. 33.

# Wilma Chan

**Born:** Boston, Massachusetts.

**Education:** B.A., Wellesley College, M.A., Stanford University.

**Positions Held:** Oakland Board of Education, 1990–1993, President, 1991–1993; President, Alameda County, California Board of Supervisors.

**Awards, Honors:** Citations from the California Hospital Council, the National Asian Women's Health Center, Native American Health Center, Rotary International, and the East Bay Asian Youth Center.

**Summary:** Wilma Chan is a representative in the California State Assembly. She is one of the first Asian American women to hold such a position and the first Asian American to serve as president of the Alameda County, California Board of Supervisors.

## Early Years and Education

A Chinese American, Wilma Chan was born and raised in Boston, Massachusetts. She earned her bachelor of arts degree from Wellesley College and her masters' degree in education policy analysis and administration from Stanford University.

## Career Highlights

Chan has maintained a highly active and involved profile as a west coast "transplant." In 1990, she was elected to Oakland's Board of Education, serving as its president from June 1991 to January 1993. She also expressed her interest in education as program coordinator for Effective Parenting Information for Children, a nationally recognized school-based prevention program.

In 1994, Chan successfully secured a bid for a seat on the Alameda County Board of Supervisors. As a supervisor, she represented District 3, which includes the Chinatown, China Hill, San Antonio, Downtown, East Lake, and Fruitvale areas of Oakland, the cities of San Leandro and Alameda and the unincorporated community of Hillcrest Knolls. Four years later, she won her reelection to the board unopposed.

As a member and president of the Alameda County Board of Supervisors, Chan compiled a distinguished record of accomplishments, particularly on behalf of children and youth. She worked to expand the number of school-based health clinics, led lobbying efforts to restore benefits to legal immigrants, organized the first children's collaborative in Alameda and San Leandro, initiated a pilot welfare-to-work project in Oakland's San Antonio neighborhood, and developed the strategic plan for the future of health care services in Alameda County. She also chaired the board's Health Committee and was a member of the Budget and Personnel, Administration, and Legislative Committees. In addition, Chan served on the San Francisco Bay Conservation and Development Commission and the Alameda County Retirement Board and headed the Children and Families First Commission.

The first Asian Pacific American to assume the presidency of the Alameda County Board of Supervisors, Chan made history again as one of the first Asian Pacific American women to occupy a seat in California's state assembly with her electoral victory in 2000. When she announced her intention to run in June 1999, she emphasized the significance of Chinese American representation in the state legislature. "We need to elect more Chinese Americans on a state level," said Chan. "There are many Chinese American politicians on the local level—that's a very positive trend we've seen in the last 10 years, but we need Chinese Americans in the California Legislature." She added, "We have [Gov.] Gary Locke in Washington State and [U.S. Rep.] David Wu in Oregon, but there are no Chinese Americans in the California Assembly. There are a lot of issues that need to be voiced" (Ni 1999).

Public education and health care continue to be major priorities on Chan's agenda. "These are complicated issues; I know them well," said Chan, who is married to a public school administrator and is the mother of two. She raised the possibility of government-backed incentives for college students to pursue careers in education, since "We have to attract good teachers." She also hopes to devote attention to tuberculosis and geriatrics during her tenure in the state assembly. For example, she observed that "The population of elderly will double within 25 years in Alameda County. We'll need to provide services or nursing homes. The population is aging, there are not enough services, and we can deliver the existing services better." Overall, Chan seems confident about the responsibilities of her high-profile position. "I'm the best person for the seat," she declared. "I know the district and how to solve real problems. It's important to know the issues from the ground up and not just have ideas" (Ni 1999).

For her contributions, Chan has been recognized by a number of local and national organizations, including the California Hospital Council, the National Asian Women's Health Center, Native American Health Center, Rotary International, and the East Bay Asian Youth Center.

**Source**

Ni, Perla, "Wilma Chan Announces Assembly Bid: Chinese Americans Need a Presence, Says Alameda County Chief Supervisor." *Asian Week*. 17–23 June 1999.

# Elaine L. Chao

Elaine L. Chao. (Courtesy of the Office of the Secretary of Labor)

**Born:** 1953, Taiwan.

**Education:** B.A., Mount Holyoke College, 1975; MBA, Harvard University, 1979.

**Positions Held:** Chairwoman, Federal Maritime Commission, 1988–1989; Deputy Secretary, Department of Transportation, 1989–1991; Director, Peace Corps, 1991–1992; President and CEO, United Way of America, 1992–1996; Secretary of Labor, 2001–present.

**Summary:** Elaine Chao is the first Asian Pacific American woman to hold a post in a presidential cabinet as George W. Bush's Secretary of Labor.

## Early Years and Education

Elaine L. Chao was born in Taiwan in 1953 to James and Ruth Chao. At the age of eight, she emigrated from Taipei by ship with her mother and two younger sisters to the United States to join her father, who had been studying for three years at St. John's University in Queens, New York. "It was a wonderful trip for a small child of eight," recalled Chao of the month-long sea passage. "My first port of call was Los Angeles. That's where I laid my first foot on America. There's a wonderful photo, a black-and-white, grainy picture of my mother, with a very tentative look on her face, holding the hand of her oldest child. That's me" (Baum 1992, E1).

Growing up in an immigrant family in Jamaica, Queens, Chao's childhood experiences clearly shaped her future outlook. Her father, for example, extolled the conservative values of meritocracy, education, and hard work, teaching her and her sisters home-repair skills while completing his studies and establishing his own shipping and trading business, Foremost Maritime Corporation. Eventually, his successes enabled the family to move from Queens to Long Island, eventually settling in wealthy Westchester County, New York.

Chao knew no English when she first moved from Taiwan, learning her new tongue by "copying everything into my notebook" (Lardner and Swoboda 2001, A23). She adjusted well, leaving home after school to attend Mount Holyoke College in Massachusetts, where she earned her bachelor's degree in 1975 followed by an MBA from Harvard University in 1979, programs which she supplemented with coursework at the Massachusetts Institute of Technology, Dartmouth College, and Columbia University.

## Career Highlights

With degrees in hand, Chao became an international banker at New York's Citicorp, where she worked from 1979 to 1983. Selected as a White House Fellow that year, she worked on the Domestic Policy Council, specializing in transportation and trade issues. She then relocated to San Francisco to accept a vice president of syndications position at Bank America's Capital Markets Group. In 1986, recruited by Transportation Secretary Elizabeth Dole, she returned to the nation's capital to serve as a Deputy Administrator of the

Federal Maritime Administration. After two years, she was named head of the commission. In 1989, she advanced to the position of Deputy Transportation Secretary, where, among her other duties, she assisted in coordinating merchant marine and air defense fleets during the Persian Gulf War.

Chao also campaigned for George Bush, Pete Wilson, and other California Republicans, becoming chair of Asian Americans for Bush/Quayle in 1988. Her conservative standing, such as her opposition of the 1991 Civil Rights Act, whose quotas Chao viewed as retarding the meritorious achievements of people of color, however, drew ire from other, more liberal-leaning Asian Pacific Americans.

Nevertheless, Chao's steady work and continuous hobnobbing with Washington's power players paid off; in 1991, President Bush appointed her to head the Peace Corps, an organization which, coincidentally, was established the same year that Chao emigrated to the United States. Chao defended her qualifications from critics, including one who declared, "The Peace Corps is being demeaned again by throwing someone in there to be window dressing" (Baum 1992, E1). "[My] memories of living in a developing nation are part of who I am today and give me a profound understanding of the challenges of economic development—an understanding which will make my tenure as Peace Corps director, I hope, a very special one," she stated (Baum 1992, E1).

The organization that Chao inherited was saddled with what one official described as "strain, confusion, and chaos," including debates over its rapid expansion into Eastern European countries, which some believed were considerably more privileged than the "traditional" target areas. However, in agreement with Bush, Chao firmly believed that the Peace Corps had a significant role to play in these emerging democracies. When the Peace Corps was established, she noted, "It was envisioned that one day the Soviet Union, the archenemy, would be free, democratic, and peaceful. We are seeing the fruition of a 30-year dream and the Peace Corps is involved in that" (Baum 1992, E1).

After a year as its director, Chao stepped down with the close of the Bush administration. She became president and CEO of the United Way, chosen from among 600 candidates. The organization was reeling from the financial fraud of her predecessor, William Aramony, and the resultant loss of millions of dollars in donation monies. One of her first decisions was to cut her salary from $390,000 to $195,000 in an effort to restore the public's faith in the United Way. In her four years as its head, Chao reformed the United Way, pronouncing it a "transformed organization" in 1996 (Weil 196, A22).

Following her tenure at the United Way, Chao served as a distinguished fellow at the Heritage Foundation. She also remained active on the boards of a number of companies and organizations, including Dole Food, Northwest Airlines, and the National Association of Security Dealers, Inc., the parent company of the NASDAQ Stock Market. She also devoted her efforts to the reelection of her husband, Republican Mitch McConnell, the senior senator from Kentucky.

In January 2001 Chao again made history as the first Asian Pacific American woman to be appointed to a cabinet secretary position as Secretary of Labor in the administration of George W. Bush. His first nominee, Linda Chavez, withdrew her nomination in the midst of a personal controversy. Regarding his selection, Bush said, "Her successful life gives eloquent testimony to the virtues of hard work and perseverance, and to the unending promise of this great country" (Gerstenzang 2001, A1). The President's statements echoed similar themes to Chao's own assessment of her accomplishments: "I am a woman. I am a minority. I am young. I get past this by just letting people get to know me" (Baum 1992, E1).

## Sources

Baum, Geraldine. "An Insider Moves Out, Up." *Los Angeles Times*. 19 January 1992, p. E1.

"Elaine Chao." *Chicago Sun-Times*. 12 January 2001, p. 22.
Gerstenzang, James. "The Presidential Transition; Bush Picks New Labor Nominee, Trade Chief." *Los Angeles Times*. 12 January 2001, p. A1.
Gupta, Himanee. "Elaine Chao." In *Notable Asian Americans*, ed. Helen Zia and Susan B. Gall. Detroit, MI: Gale Research Inc., 1995, pp. 39–40.
Jackson, Robert. "As President of United Way, Elaine Chao Reformed Agency." *Denver Rocky Mountain News*. 14 May 1996, p. 34A.
Lardner, George Jr., and Frank Swoboda. "Chao Knows Her Way Around Labor; Union Leaders Welcome a Solid Conservative." *Washington Post*. 12 January 2001, p. A23.
Weil, Martin. "United Way Chief Says She Intends to Resign." *Washington Post*. 19 May 1996, p. A22.

# Nguyen Minh Chau

Nguyen Minh Chau. (Courtesy of Nguyen Minh Chau, © Les Henig Photography)

**Born:** 18 January 1937, South Vietnam.

**Education:** B.A., Mount Holyoke College, 1960; M.A., University of Michigan, 1962; M.S., Columbia University, 1982.

**Positions Held:** Commissioner, Maryland Governor's Advisory Commission on Asian Pacific Americans; Member, City Council, Garrett Park, Maryland, 1995–present.

**Awards, Honors:** Distinguished Leadership Award, National Association for Community Leadership; Award, National Association of Asian Pacific American Women, Graduate and past board member, Leadership Washington and Leadership Maryland.

**Summary:** Nguyen Minh Chau is the first Vietnamese American woman elected to public office in the United States.

## Early Years and Education

Nguyen Minh Chau was born on 18 January 1937 in South Vietnam. She attended Saigon's Institution Saint Paul before moving to the United States in 1958 to pursue her bachelor of arts degree in sociology at Mount Holyoke College in South Hadley, Massachusetts. After graduating in 1960, she went back to Vietnam for a brief period before returning to the United States to settle permanently. Chau then enrolled at the University of Michigan in Ann Arbor, where she earned a master of arts in community adult education in 1962. Afterwards, she elected to spend a third year at Michigan taking 30 credit hours of courses in order to become a specialist in education. In 1982, she also completed the necessary coursework in business policy through the master's degree program for business executives at Columbia University's Graduate School of Business.

## Career Highlights

Beginning in 1971, Chau spent 28 years with Opportunity System, Inc., an African American company in Washington, D.C., as a project director and as an executive Vice

President. She identifies "being an Asian in an African American firm" as one of the greatest challenges of her career, because "issues tend[ed] to be viewed as 'Black and White.'" At the same time, she proudly notes that she "took the firm from its infancy as an 8(a) minority firm to the thriving company that it was when I left in 1999."

Chau also considers her gender to be one of the major difficulties she faces as an employee in a "male-oriented culture, at all levels of the corporate ladder," which "made it difficult for me to be fully part of the 'gang.'" Undeterred, however, she has been the president and owner of NiMiC Corporation, a professional consulting firm, in Garrett Park, Maryland, since 1982.

In 1995, Chau made history as the first Vietnamese American woman elected to public office in the United States with her appointment to the Garrett Park, Maryland, city council. "It is hard for me to pinpoint what precisely happened that caused me to pursue politics and government—but I always feel deeply that I have been fortunate to have many opportunities in my life, and municipal government enables me to have an advantageous edge in seeking to 'do the right thing' by the people that I have come into contact with," she explains. "Politics is a natural requisite for success in dealing with people—I strive to be mindful of people's needs, hopes, and fears in dealing with them, and I constantly strive to identify a narrow margin of agreement that pulls them together."

In addition to her duties as a city council member, Chau maintains an active civic and community profile. She is a member of the Communications Committee of the Maryland Municipal League, a commissioner on the Maryland Governor's Advisory Commission on Asian Pacific American Affairs, a participant in Leadership Montgomery, and chair of both the Montgomery United Way's Needs Assessment Committee and the Accountability and Assessment Committee of the Montgomery County Business Roundtable for Education. She has also been a board member of both the Maryland Humanities Council and the Governor's Commission on Celebration 2000. For her contributions, Chau has received a number of honors, including a Distinguished Leadership Award from the National Association for Community Leadership and a citation from the National Association of Asian Pacific American Women. As for her future goals, Chau simply states that she plans to "continue the volunteer community development effort that I have done to date."

## Sources

Personal communication to Ellen D. Wu, 25 February 2001.

## Satveer Chaudhary

Satveer Chaudhary. (Courtesy Office of the Honorable Satveer Chaudhary)

**Born:** 12 June 1969, Fridley, Minnesota.

**Education:** B.A., St. Olaf College, 1991; J.D., University of Minnesota Law School, 1995.

**Positions Held:** State Representative, Minnesota House of Representatives, 1996–2000; State Senator, Minnesota Senate, 2000–present.

**Awards, Honors:** Legislator of the Year, Minnesota Community College Student Association; Nominee, Freshman Legislator of the Year, *Politics in Minnesota* magazine; Listed in *Who's Who in American Politics* and *Outstanding Young Men of America* national directories.

**Summary:** Satveer Chaudhary is the first Asian Indian elected to the Minnesota state legislature and the fourth Asian Indian elected to a legislature in United States history.

### Early Years and Education

Satveer Chaudhary was born on 12 June 1969 in Fridley, Minnesota, to Raj and Surendra Chaudhary. He attended Columbia Heights High School before matriculating at St. Olaf College, where he received his bachelor of arts in 1991. The following year, he enrolled at the University of Minnesota Law School, graduating as a juris doctor in 1995.

### Career Highlights

Chaudhary launched his professional and political career with a number of notable positions. He worked for both the Hennepin County's Attorney Office in Minneapolis and Minnesota Attorney General Hubert H. Humphrey III. In addition, Chaudhary has served as a Foreign Policy Aide to U.S. Senator Edward M. Kennedy (D-Mass.) and State Affirmative Action Officer for the Minnesota Democratic Farmer-Labor Party. In 1996, he was elected to the first of his two terms as a member of the Minnesota House of Representatives before moving to the Minnesota Senate in 2000. As a state senator, Chaudhary is vice-chair of the Transportation and Education, Crime, and Finance Committees.

In addition to his legislative duties, Chaudhary is a member of the Crime Victim and Witness Advisory Council, A Blanket of Hope, and the Big Brothers Program. He also co-chairs the Anoka County, Minnesota Legislative Delegation and was a former board member of the Minnesota World Trade Center Board and the Oxford Union Debating Team.

Chaudhary is the first Asian Indian elected to the Minnesota state legislature and the fourth Asian Indian elected to a legislature in United States history. Significantly, he co-founded the Minnesota Asian-Indian Democratic Association and is a member of the honorary advisory council to the Asia-Pacific Endowment for Community Development. For his achievements, Chaudhary was recognized as Legislator of the Year by the Minnesota Community College Student Association and was nominated for Freshman Legislator of the Year by *Politics in Minnesota* magazine. He is also listed in *Who's Who in American Politics* and *Outstanding Young Men of America*, two prominent national political directories.

### Sources

Personal communication to Ellen D. Wu, 18 January 2001.

# Ruby Chow

**Full Name at Birth:** Mar Seung Gum.

**Born:** 1920, Seattle, Washington.

**Education:** Coursework completed at Garfield and Franklin High Schools, Seattle, Washington.

**Positions Held:** Member, King County Council, Washington State, 1973—1985.

**Awards, Honors:** Seattle Magazine Top Ten Women in the Northwest, 1965; Asian American Living Pioneer Award, 1997.

**Summary:** Chinese American Ruby Chow was the first Asian Pacific American woman elected to public office in the Pacific Northwest. She served as a member of the King County Council in Washington State from 1973 to 1985.

## Early Years and Education

Chinese American Ruby Chow was born in 1920 in Seattle, Washington's Chinatown to Jim Mar, who arrived in the United States in 1885, and his wife Wong See. "I remember living near Third Avenue and Washington Street when I was about four or five, and we lived on Jackson Street, Beacon Hill and near Providence Hospital," she reminisced in January 1979. "My father had come over here to work on the railroad and later he worked as a foreman of a salmon cannery for the Calverts, for the San Juan Fishing Company. I came from a family of ten, seven brothers and two sisters" (Estes 1979, 4). Raising a house full of children must have been challenging to the Mars, who were once approached by a Chinese woman who offered to purchase the 5-year-old Chow. Wong See angrily refused, stating that she would rather feed her children out of garbage cans.

The young Chow attended Seattle's Bailey Gatzert Elementary and Washington Junior High before moving on to Garfield and Franklin High Schools. In addition to taking classes, she worked as a waitress and sales girl at the National Dollar Stores to help her mother, who was widowed when Chow was about 12 years of age. "Those were just about the only jobs available in those days, and you were lucky to get them. Every penny helped," she explained (Estes 1979, 4). After her mother passed away when Chow was 17, she dropped out of Franklin High to waitress for $2 a day at a local Chinese restaurant. Even after her death, Wong See's tenacity throughout the difficult times has provided a source of strength for Chow. "My mother never complained.... She never nagged. When she had something to say, she said it, and that was it. In those days, we didn't have time to be depressed, to think about alcohol or drugs. We just had to get out there and work to survive," she said (Chen 1997, 8).

Chow married at age 19 and gave birth to two children soon thereafter. The marriage, however, dissolved following a move to New York City in the early 1940s. She stayed in the city and waited tables at local night clubs, an experience which turned out to be beneficial for her future King County, Washington constituents. In New York, she met her second husband, a Chinese opera performer named Ping Chow, whose company was stranded in the United States while touring during World War II. Lacking money and English competency, Ping Chow joined the American military. After he left the army, the two wed and moved to Seattle in 1943.

## Career Highlights

After five years of laboring for other establishments in the city's Chinatown, the Chows opened Ruby Chow's Restaurant—the first of its kind outside the enclave—in 1948. Their risk paid off. "It wasn't difficult getting the restaurant started," she recalled. "Both my husband and I were surprised. Most of my clientele from Chinatown followed us there, and first thing we knew, we were packed. We could only serve 65 people at once, but we were an overnight success. It was as if we were out on a football field and someone threw the ball. I picked it up and ran" (Estes 1979, 4).

For 30 years, the couple operated their popular eatery, expanding it when necessary to accommodate the many area politicians, bureaucrats, police officers, journalists, and other notables, including legendary martial artist Bruce Lee, who worked and resided there for almost four years, all of whom, along with common Seattle folk, flocked to Ruby's to sample Ping Chow's cooking.

The Chows also used their restaurant as a means of helping family members and friends in need, especially those who fled to the United States following the 1949 Communist victory in Mainland China. "If I had spent more time concentrating on making money, I think I would have been more financially successful. However, I think I have been much more successful in helping mankind. Money is important too, but I have always felt that I was put on earth to do something for people," she stated. "Both my husband and I feel this way. This is a good thing about us, the two of us. He enjoys this kind of work as much as I do" (Estes 1979, 4).

Beyond the restaurant, Chow has also been involved in Seattle's Chinese American community in a number of other ways. In response to what she believed was an ineffective approach to the community's problems by the male-dominated Chong Wah Benevolent Association, Chow rallied six other women to get themselves elected to the board. From 1975 to 1976, she was the first female president of the association. As noted by Chinese American writer Frank Chin in 1994, "The old stranded generation of the last Wah Kiew 'overseas Chinese' has never recovered from the shock of Ruby Chow, who, through her Chinese Community Service Organization, brought American-born, English speaking, non-Cantonese, northern Chinese outsiders, and women onto the Chong Wah board. To this day, the only Chong Wah in the world where women sit down with the men to make decisions about the Chinese community is Seattle" (Watson 1994, B1).

Among her other commitments have been the northwest regional directorship of the National Welfare Council for Chinese People, a charter membership, board membership and past presidency of the Seattle Chinese Community Service Organization. "Aunty Ruby" was also the founder and 18-year director of the prize-winning Seattle Chinese Community Girls' Drill Team. In addition, she assisted her fellow co-ethnic, Wing Luke, in his campaign for a seat on the Seattle city council.

Chow's involvement has also extended beyond city, state, and even national borders. She and her husband Ping have long been loyal supporters of the Nationalist Chinese Government in Taiwan, even journeying overseas to present the island's officials with a scroll from the Seattle Chinese community. In the late 1970s, when the issue of normalizing relations with the People's Republic of China was a pressing question for American diplomacy, she did not hesitate to voice her opinion on the matter. "It is my feeling that the Republic of China has been a friend and ally for many years and is a truly democratic country. They believe in the same things that we believe in here in the United States," she declared. "There are 22 million overseas Chinese, including 17 million in Taiwan, so that makes 50 million Chinese people working toward the same goals that we have here in the United States. And we sit here and sell them down the river" (Estes 1979, 5). Nearly twenty years later, she continued to maintain close ties with Taiwan as an appointee on its Overseas Chinese Affairs Commission.

Chow took her strong sense of community with her to elected office in her 50s. When asked by journalist Jane Estes why she waited until near-retirement age to immerse herself in Seattle's civic affairs, she replied, "I felt that I had accomplished quite a bit in my life. My five kids were grown up, and the community and friends felt that I could branch out and use what I had learned on a broader scale" (Estes 1979, 4). She ran successfully on the Democratic ticket for the fifth district seat on the King County Council in 1973 and spent the next twelve years as a vocal advocate of traditionally marginalized groups. In fact, she deliberately chose the fifth district because it was an area of "multiethnic people, low income, with many elderly and handicapped people. You name it, it's there" (Estes 1979, 5).

During her three terms on the King County Council, she championed a number of issues as both a member and chairwoman, including improving the Metro bus service and building more bus shelters in the face of cutbacks, since her constituents comprised the highest ridership of the system in the entire county. She also worked to expand affirmative action for women and minorities, providing aid for their businesses, securing funding for the construction of a new county jail, and supporting various other human service programs.

As the first Asian Pacific American woman elected to office in the Pacific Northwest and the first Asian Pacific American woman to chair a legislative body, Chow has earned her rightful place in the history books, along with approximately 50 awards and even two King County public parks as her namesakes. Her accomplishments have inspired her children, including Cheryl, her only daughter, who is a member of the Seattle City Council, and Mark, one of her four sons (the others being Brien, Edward, and Shelton), who is a Seattle District Court Judge. As Chin observed, her successes are admirable because "Ruby Chow's made it on guts, not manners or looks, bribery or blackmail. She was always the first" (Watson 1994, B1).

### Sources

Chen, Katy. "A Legend in Her Own Time: Ruby Chow." *Northwest Asian Weekly*. 15 21 March 1997, pp. 8, 14.

Coughlin, Dan. "Ruby Chow to Call it Quits After this Term." *Seattle Post-Intelligencer*. 27 November 1984, p. D1.

Estes, Jane. "Ruby Chow: The Council's Good Fortune." *Northwest*. 21 January 1979, pp. 4, 5.

Watson, Emmett. "A Rare Lady Served Suey, County Well." *Seattle Times*. 27 December 1994, p. B1.

# Herbert Young Cho Choy

**Born:** 6 January 1916, Makaweli, Hawaii.

**Education:** B.A., University of Hawaii, 1938; J.D., Harvard University, 1941.

**Positions Held:** Senior Judge, United States Court of Appeals, Ninth Circuit, 1971–1984; Senior Judge, United States Court of Appeals, Ninth Circuit, 1984–present.

Herbert Young Cho Choy. (Courtesy of Herbert Choy)

**Awards, Honors:** Decorated, Order of Civil Merit, Republic of Korea, 1973, Fellow, American Bar Foundation, 1994.

**Summary:** Judge Herbert Young Cho Choy is the first person of Korean ancestry in the United States to become a lawyer, the first person of Asian descent appointed to the federal bench, and the first and only person from Hawaii to date on the U.S. Court of Appeals, Ninth Circuit.

### Early Years

Herbert Young Cho Choy, not only the first Korean American attorney to practice law in the United States, but also the first Asian Pacific American appointed to a U.S. federal court, was born on 6 January 1916 in Makaweli, Kauai, Hawaii, to Doo Wook and Helen (Nahm) Choy, both of whom had immigrated to Hawaii from Korea as small children. When Choy was five, his father decided to move the family from Kauai to the capital of Honolulu, enabling him to negotiate for tailoring contracts with the military. Eventually, Doo Wook Choy, with his "Choy Tailor Mades," conquered the military uniform market on the islands. As a teenager, Choy contributed to the family economy as well, working ten hours a day in a pineapple processing plant for 12½ cents an hour. "I was mighty glad to do it," he recalled. "There were people waiting in line behind me" (McKillips 1972, E1).

As with many children, young Choy observed, and was inspired, to pursue law by the activities of adults around him. He was impressed by the ability of an attorney neighbor to provide his father with guidance concerning his business. While his parents felt that Choy's shy, quiet demeanor was perhaps more suited to the medical profession, they strongly encouraged him to do well in his studies no matter what subject. Choy, a pupil at Honolulu's Royal School, approached his schoolwork, particularly reading, with zeal. In his spare time, he worked at the public library and enjoyed the Boy Scouts, sports, and surfing.

## Education

After graduating from high school in 1934, he attended the University of Hawaii. During his college years, he received encouragement from Walter Short, the school's job placement director, who suggested that he participate in some extracurricular activities that would enable him to "learn how to stand up and talk and be understood" (Wong 1995, 64). Choy heeded his advice, becoming a member of the UH debate team and the theater guild and even taking singing lessons.

His dedication paid off with his acceptance to Harvard Law School, which he attended following his college graduation in 1938. After three competitive years, Choy earned his J.D. and returned to Hawaii, where he passed the bar and began work as a law clerk for the city and county of Honolulu. When World War II broke out in December 1941, he temporarily set aside his career to serve in the armed forces, both as a 1st Lieutenant in the Hawaii Territorial Guard and as a Lieutenant Colonel in the United States army. At the School of Military Government in Charlottesville, Virginia, he met his future wife, Dorothy Helen Shular, a school teacher, whom he married on 16 June 1945.

## Career Highlights

In 1946, he resumed his professional life as an associate of the multiethnic Hawaii law firm Fong and Miho, becoming a partner after just six short months. Choy stayed with the practice until 1957, when he assumed the position of Attorney General for the Territory of Hawaii for one year. He then returned to Fong, Miho, Choy, and Robinson, largely due to his colleagues' need of assistance to handle the backlog of cases, and remained on staff until 1971. During his years in the firm, he was also involved in a number of outside commitments, including the Chief Justice of Hawaii's advisory committee on the construction of judiciary buildings from 1970 to 1971, the compilation committee to compile Revised Laws of Hawaii from 1953 to 1957, and the committee to draft Hawaii rules of criminal procedure for the Supreme Court from 1958 to 1959.

In 1971, President Richard M. Nixon appointed him to the Ninth Circuit U.S. Court of Appeals in Honolulu. Of the landmark event, Choy simply stated, "It was a great honor to be the first Asian federal judge, but it does not make me feel special. I feel a great responsibility to make a good judicial record for the sake of future judges of Asian ancestry, my state, and my family" (Wong 1995, 64). He also thanked his parents "for the many hardships they faced as immigrant plantation children" and his wife Helen "for 26 years of our co-adventure in life." Choy added, "Perhaps, over all, I am grateful to this great nation" (Honolulu Advertiser 1971, A9).

Throughout his decades on the bench, including a senior judgeship since 1984, Choy has paid special attention to cases involving American Indian treaties, issues of land ownership, and fishing concerns, often favoring the arguments of Native Americans. He explained his liberal views as such, "I think it is because I am of a minority group. American Indians were the former owners of all the land in our country. When what little they have left is encroached upon by others, naturally I have a great deal of sympathy for them" (Wong 1995, 64).

Choy's judgeship has impacted his home life as well. While he and his wife Dorothy Helen do not have any children, they have "adopted" a number of his law clerks into their family, including 48 "children" and 20 "grandchildren," for whom they host a reunion every five years (Wong 1995, 64).

In his spare time, Choy enjoys tennis and sculling. A former surfing enthusiast, he was forced to give up the sport at age 53 due to injuries sustained in a surfing accident. "I might get tennis elbow but I won't drown," he noted with humor in 1972 (McKillips 1972, E1). He has also been involved in a number of community organizations over the years, including Big Brothers of Hawaii and the Hawaii Medical Service Association.

### Sources

Resume and biographical materials provided by Judge Herbert Choy.
"Herbert Choy," *The Complete Marquis Who's Who Biographies*. Reed Elsevier, Inc., 1998.
"Many Honor Judge Choy at Induction to Federal Seat." *Honolulu Advertiser*, 2 June 1971, p. A9.
Wong, Grace. "Herbert Choy." In *Notable Asian Americans*, ed. Helen Zia and Susan B. Gall. Detroit, MI: Gale Research Inc., 1995, pp. 63–65.

## Judy Chu

**Born:** 7 July 1953, Los Angeles, California.

**Education:** B.A., University of California, Los Angeles, 1974; M.A., California School of

Judy Chu. (Courtesy of Judy Chu)

Professional Psychology, 1977; Ph.D., California School of Professional Psychology, 1979.

**Positions Held:** Member, City Council, Monterey Park, California, 1988–2000; Mayor, Monterey Park, California, 1990–1991, 1994–1995, 1999; Member, California State Assembly, 2000–present.

**Awards, Honors:** Humanitarian Award for Research, Los Angeles Commission on Assaults Against Asian Women, 1985, Asian Pacific Family Center Achievement Award, 1989, UCLA Alumni Award for Excellence in Public Service, 1991, Asian Youth Center Lifetime Achievement Award, 1994, Image Award, Organization of Chinese Americans, Los Angeles, 1997, National Women's Political Caucus of California Special Award for Services to Youth and Education, 1998.

**Summary:** Judy Chu is one of the pioneers of Asian American women's politics. She has been a member of the Monterey Park, California, city council since 1988 and has thrice served as the municipality's mayor.

## Early Years

Judy Chu was born on 7 July 1953 in Los Angeles, California, to Judson Chu, a second generation Asian American, and his wife May, an immigrant from Canton, China. While she spent her childhood among African Americans in her South Central neighborhood, she was also active among the city's Chinese American community. "You know how it is with the Chinese families," she said. "They take you off to Chinatown to do activities with Chinese people," which for the young Chu included the Chinese Drum and Bugle Corps and Chinese school (interview with Ellen D. Wu, 24 July 1998).

However, it was not until after her graduation from Buchser High School in Santa Clara in 1970 that she experienced what she called a "cultural awakening" through a Study Tour of Taiwan sponsored by the island's government. "I'd grown up kind of rejecting my identity. Being an Asian American, I had always wanted to be American and didn't have a lot of role models growing up, so I didn't see any particular reason to be Asian," she remembered. "When I went, I was exposed to a lot of Asians at once, and I was just amazed by the variety of Asians." Chu noted that she "pretty much saw myself as an American before [the trip], and afterwards I saw myself as a Chinese American" (interview with Ellen D. Wu, 24 July 1998).

## Education

This heightened consciousness inspired her active involvement with Asian American concerns during her college years at the University of California at Los Angeles. After taking her first Asian American Studies class, she realized that she had been "ashamed of her cultural background" for so long because she was a "minority in this society" (personal communication with Ellen D. Wu, 15 August 1989). Outside of the classroom, she joined the Asian American Alliance, serving as editor of the group's newsletter, worked to increase the number of Asian American Studies classes available to students, demonstrated against the Vietnam war, and worked as a teaching assistant for a course on Asian American women. In addition, she volunteered for various Asian American women's groups and for Asian Joint Communications, a grassroots organization devoted to Asian American prisoners and drug addicts, later becoming a paid employee.

After earning her bachelor of arts degree in math in 1974, she went on to graduate from the California School of Professional Psychology in Los Angeles with a master's degree in clinical psychology in 1977, followed by a doctorate in 1979.

## Career Highlights

She ventured into academia as a part-time faculty member at UCLA's Asian American Studies Center, teaching classes on Asian American women and contemporary issues from 1980 to 1986. In 1984, she also co-wrote and co-edited a volume on Chinese Americans of Los Angeles entitled *Linking Our Lives*. From 1981 to 1986, she served as psychology professor at Los Angeles City College, followed by two years as a disabled students counselor at the same institution. Finally, in 1988, she accepted a position as a professor of psychology at East Los Angeles College, where she remains today.

Chu's work in higher education led her into her first foray in mainstream politics in 1985. Based on her professional credentials as well as her experience with community organizing, colleagues and friends encouraged her to run for the Garvey District School Board, which included parts of Monterey Park, Rosemead, and San Gabriel, California and whose electorate was 29 percent Asian Pacific American at the time. She won the election with the highest number of votes, becoming the first APA on the board.

Following her three year term on the Garvey board, Chu next ran for the city council of Monterey Park, campaigning on a growth-control platform. Again, she captured the highest number of votes in the election.

Notably, she earned 89 percent of the Chinese American votes and 75 percent of the Japanese American votes, along with the support of 35 percent of the Latino electorate and 30 percent of the white electorate.

In July 1991, Chu found herself caught in the midst of an intra-ethnic controversy regarding her position on bilingual 911/emergency dispatchers. A faction of the city's Chinese American community interpreted her actions to be against hiring bilingual personnel. She was accused of being "anti-Chinese" and "not Chinese enough" (Fong 1994, 236–237). Despite the situation, she managed to win her second bid for the Monterey Park city council, becoming the first Asian Pacific American reelected to the body. She ran successfully for a third term in 1997. During Chu's years on the council, she has also thrice served as mayor: 1990–1991, 1994–1945, and 1999–2000.

Throughout her tenure, Chu has remained optimistic about the city's intra- and inter-ethnic and racial diversity in spite of its occasional complications. "[It] presents a microcosm of the issue facing our nation as we enter the 21st century. With our innovative city staff, I know that we will rise to meet the challenges ahead" (Ku 1994, 11). Chu sought a seat in the California State Assembly in 1994 and in 1998 but lost both elections. She won in 2000.

As one of Monterey Park's leaders, Chu has actively contributed to her community, particularly in terms of coalition building between various ethnic groups. She founded a Conflict Resolution Training Program at a local high school as well as Harmony month, which received the grand prize for programs addressing diversity from the League of California Cities. She also facilitated the implementation of youth programs, a pilot child care service, and measures encouraging economic development, voter registration, and the reduction of gun violence.

Among Chu's myriad of past and present involvement within the local and national Asian Pacific American community are the Asian Youth Center in San Gabriel Valley, of which she was the founder, the Asian Pacific Islander Advisory Committee of the U.S. Census Bureau, the Asian Task Force of the United Way, the Chinese American Citizens Alliance, and the Organization of Chinese Americans. She is also active among women's groups such as the National Women's Political Caucus, the National Organization for Women, and the California Elected Women's Association for Education and Research.

Chu has received a plethora of honors for her outstanding service. These include "88 for 1988," the *Los Angeles Times'* selection of distinguished leaders in the Greater Los Angeles area, the Alumnae of the Year award from the California School of Professional Psychology in 1988, Public Official of the Year from the Alliance of Asian Pacific Labor in 1992 and 1995, the Outstanding Founder Award for National Philanthropy Day in Los Angeles in 1995, the Image Award from the Association of Chinese Americans of Greater Los Angeles in 1997, and a special award for Services to Youth and Education in 1998 from the National Women's Political Caucus of California.

Chu has been married to Michael Eng since 1978.

## Sources

Biographical materials provided by Judy Chu.

Chu, Judy. Interview with Ellen D. Wu. Monterey Park, California. 24 July 1998. Quoted by permission of Judy Chu.

Fong, Timothy P. "Monterey Park and Emerging Race Relations in California." In *Origins and Destinations: 41 Essays on Chinese America*. Los Angeles: Chinese Historical Society of Southern California and the UCLA Asian American Studies Center, 1994, pp. 227–241.

Hong, Howard. "Chu Announces Candidacy for Re-Election; Defends Stance on 911." *Asian Week*. 17 January 1992, p. 12.

Ku, Beulah. "Chu Sworn In as Mayor: Claims Civic Government Will Be Accessible." *Asian Week*. 6 May 1994, p. 11.

Lee, Bobbie and Gerard Lim. "Judy Chu Makes Bid for State Assembly: Monterey Park Councilwoman to Focus on California's Economy, Crime, and Education." *Asian Week*. 28 January 1994, p. 1.

# E

## Jose S. Esteves

Jose Esteves. (Courtesy of Jose Esteves)

**Born:** 3 October 1946, Philippines.

**Education:** B.S., University of the Philippines, 1969, 1971; MBA, University of the Philippines, 1975.

**Positions Held:** Vice Chair, Milpitas Planning Commission; Member, Milpitas, California City Council, 1998–present.

**Awards, Honors:** Milpitas Citizen of the Year; Outstanding Service in the Interest of a Better Milpitas.

**Summary:** Jose S. Esteves is a member of the Milpitas, California, City Council.

### Early Years and Education

Jose S. Esteves, the son of Pastor M. Esteves, Sr., and Filomena V. Esteves, studied at the University of the Philippines, earning two bachelor's degrees, one in Civil Engineering (1969) and one in Industrial Engineering (1971), followed by a Masters in Business Administration in 1975.

### Career Highlights

Jose Esteves has held a number of significant positions in both his professional and political career. He served on the Milpitas, California, Community Advisory Commission and the County of Santa Clara, California's Justice System Advisory Board and Roads Commission. He also worked as a department information systems specialist for the Superior

Court of California in Santa Clara County. Esteves was the top applicant among 30 prospects for a seat on the Milpitas Planning Commission. In 1998, he was elected to the Milpitas City Council with the highest number of votes, defeating an incumbent, a former mayor, and a 14-year member of the Unified School District. Esteves also maintains an active profile in his local community, volunteering with the Milpitas Chamber of Commerce, the Knights of Columbus, the Silicon Valley Lions Club, and Milpitas High School.

For his dedication, Esteves has received a number of honors, including Milpitas Citizen of the Year, Milpitas High Schools' Mentor of the Month, and a citation for Outstanding Service in the Interest of a Better Milpitas.

### Source

Correspondence with Jose Esteves.

## March Fong Eu

**Born:** 29 March 1929, Oakdale, California.

**Education:** B.S., University of California, Berkeley, 1943; M.Ed., Mills College, 1947, Ph.D., Stanford University, 1956; Postdoctoral work at Columbia University and California State College–Hayward.

**Positions Held:** California State Assembly, 1966–1974; California Secretary of State, 1975–1994; U.S. Ambassador to Micronesia, 1994–1998.

**Awards, Honors:** Named to *Ladies Home Journal*'s America's 100 Most Important Women list, 1988; Chinese Americans United for Self Empowerment (CAUSE)'s 1996 Citizen of the Year Award.

**Summary:** March Fong Eu was the first Asian American assemblywoman in California's state legislature as well as the first Asian American State official. She was California's secretary of state from 1975 to 1994.

### Early Years

Third generation Chinese American March Fong Eu, the youngest daughter of Yuen and Shiu Shee Kong, was born in the back room of a laundry on 29 March 1929 in Oakdale, California. Like many other Cantonese in the United States at the time, her parents found laundries to be one of their few alternatives for employment. Eu would later reflect that while her childhood was "not unhappy," her parents toiled "seven days a week, morning, noon, and night, washing and ironing clothes" in their Richmond, California operation (Washabaugh 1995, 75). For Eu herself, however, future prospects proved to be vastly different.

Former California Secretary of State March Fong Eu announces that she will run again for office in 2002 at a news conference at the Capitol in Sacramento, Calif., March 13, 2001. (Steve Yeater, AP/Wide World Photos)

## Education

Eu enrolled at Salinas Junior College for one year after high school before transferring to the University of California, Berkeley, from which she graduated in 1943. She then followed her bachelor of science degree with a master's degree in education from Oakland's Mills College in 1947, a doctorate in education from Stanford University in 1956, and postdoctoral work at Columbia University and California State College–Hayward.

## Career Highlights

She did not, however, make an immediate segue into government. Drawing upon her experience as a dental hygienist at the UC San Francisco Medical Center and the Oakland Public Schools, Eu first explored health education as the superintendent of dental health for the Alameda County school system and as a lecturer at Mills College. She was also president of the American Dental Hygiene Association in 1956–1957. The birth of her two children, Matthew Kipling Fong and Marchesa Suyin Fong did not slow her down, and in 1956, she was chosen for the first of three terms as a member of the Alameda County Board of Education.

Ten years later, Eu made history as the first Asian American assemblywoman in California's state legislature. During her eight years as the representative for Oakland and parts of Castro Valley, Eu was active on the committees of natural resources and conservation, commerce, and public utilities along with the select committee on medical malpractice; she was also the chair of the select committee on agriculture, foods, and nutrition. As a state representative, she received national attention for taking a sledgehammer to a toilet on television to protest pay restrooms for women, which she was later successful in helping to abolish.

Eu is best known, however, for her 19 years as California's Secretary of State. Capturing an unprecedented three million votes in the 1974 election, Democrat Eu pushed for a myriad of reforms during her two-decade reign. She noted among her proudest accomplishments her role in expanding means of voter outreach and accessibility to the polls, including "motor voter" registration, availability through the Department of Motor Vehicles, voter registration by mail, bilingual ballots, and electoral procedures to accommodate the disabled, hearing impaired, and the elderly.

As California's Secretary of State, Eu also directed her attention to victims' rights and crime, particularly after an unfortunate personal experience in 1986. That year, an assailant attacked her with an ax, robbing her in her Hancock Park home (he was later caught, convicted, and sentenced to 25 years in prison). While in office, she also established a modern storage facility for the state's archives and sponsored a traveling exhibit in 1979 to alert the public to the existence and availability of the archive's materials. Eu was also an advocate of women's concerns, as evident from her earlier involvement with the pay toilet issue, initiating efforts to better California's approach to child care and pregnancy rights, including the formation of Information and Guidance Centers for women. Additionally, Eu was instrumental in the founding of California's World Trade Commission.

Eu's focus on her position was interrupted only briefly in 1988, when she considered a run for the U.S. Senate. However, campaign rules dictated that her husband, wealthy Hong Kong businessman Henry Eu, whom she married in 1971, disclose his financial holdings, and his refusal to do so rendered her ineligible for the race. She then continued as Secretary of State until 1994, when she accepted President Clinton's nomination to be the ambassador to Micronesia, an archipelago near Indonesia and a former American trust territory. Before the Senate confirmation hearing in February that year, she stated, "When I initially talked to the president about being an ambassador, I wanted a country in Asia or the Pacific. For a long time I felt that Americans didn't know enough about Pacific countries. Of course we're now finding out about how important global trade and our relations are with the Asian countries" (Lin 1994, 1).

After her work in Micronesia, Eu returned home, devoting her energies to son Matt Fong's own bid for the U.S. Senate, appearing in TV ads and even selling her own Chinese calligraphy and brush paintings to raise money for his campaign. Notably, as *Asian Week* writer Samson Wong observed, in this case "blood [was] thicker than partisanship" (Wong 1998, 15)—Fong ran on the Republican ticket. Although Eu and Fong hold different political beliefs, they do share similar views that Asian Americans "are all first-class Americans," and feel that racism in the government could be effectively combated from within the ranks (Wong 1998, 15).

Many individuals and organizations have recognized Eu's contributions as a prominent political figure to U.S. society as a whole. Her distinctions include being named to *Ladies Home Journal*'s America's 100 Most Important Women list in 1988 and Chinese Americans United for Self Empowerment (CAUSE)'s 1996 Citizen of the Year Award. Eu, in fact, is quite cognizant of her pioneering efforts on behalf of all marginalized peoples in America. As she stated, "The real legacy that I am leaving is that I have been in public office for so long. In doing so, I think I have opened a lot of doors for women and minorities" (Lin 1994, 1).

## Sources

"Eu Resigns to Take Ambassadorship." *San Francisco Chronicle*. 11 February 1994, p. A21.

Gillam, Jerry. "March Fong Eu Quits as Secretary of State." *Los Angeles Times*. 11 February 1994, p. 3.

Lim, Gerard. "March Fong Eu Tapped by Clinton to be Micronesia's New Ambassador." *Asian Week*. 24 September 1993, p.1.

Lin, Sam Chu. "Eu Bids Farewell to Colleagues in California State Government." *Asian Week*. 7 January 1994, p. 1.

"March Fong Eu." *The Complete Marquis Who's Who Biographies*. Reed Elsevier, Inc. Updated 3 June 1997.

Washabaugh, Cindy. "March Fong Eu." In *Notable Asian Americans*, ed. Helen Zia and Susan B. Gall. Detroit, MI: Gale Research Inc., 1995, pp. 75–77.

Wong, Samson. "Political Potstickers: Oh Mom, Not That Story. . . . " *Asian Week*. 9 September 1998, p. 15.

# F

## Eni F. H. Faleomavaega

American Congressman Eni Faleomavaega from American Samoa takes the wheel aboard the SV *Rainbow Warrior* as it cruises toward the French atoll of Nururoa to protest the forthcoming French underground nuclear tests. (Steve Morgan, AP/Wide World Photos)

**Born:** 15 August 1943, Vailoatai Village, American Samoa.

**Education:** B.A., Brigham Young University, 1966; J.D., University of Houston, 1972; L.L.M., University of California, Berkeley, 1973.

**Positions Held:** Deputy Attorney General, American Samoa, 1981–1984; Lieutenant Governor, American Samoa, 1984–1989; Territorial Delegate from American Samoa, 1988–present.

**Awards, Honors:** Brigham Young University Alumni Service Award, 1979, Named Chieftain Faleomavaega, Leone Village, American Samoa.

**Summary:** Eni F.H. Faleomavaega is the sole member of Congress of Samoan ancestry.

### Early Years and Education

A native Samoan, Eni F. H. Faleomavaega was born on 15 August 1943 in Vailoatai Village in American Samoa to Eni and Taualai Hunkin. After attending Vailoatai and Laie Elementary Schools, he moved to Hawaii to enroll at Kahuku High School, graduating in 1962. He then journeyed to the Mainland where he studied at Brigham Young University in Provo, Utah, as a political science and history major. After earning his bachelor of arts degree in 1966, he joined the U.S. army and served in Vietnam. Following his honorable discharge in 1969, he returned to school, spending one year at Texas Southern University before transferring to the University of Houston Law School. He completed his juris doctor degree at Houston in 1972 and master of law from the University of California, Berkeley's Boalt Hall the following year.

## Career Highlights

After college, Faleomavaega was an administrative assistant to Paramount Chief A.U. Fuimaono, America Samoa's first elected representative to Washington, D.C., in 1973. He served Fuimaono for two years before working as a staff counsel to the U.S. House of Representatives Committee on Interior and Insular Affairs until 1981. Faleomavaega then returned home to the territory's deputy attorney general position for three years. In 1984, he was elected Lieutenant Governor of American Samoa.

During his term, he was named chair of the Governor's Task Force for Reorganization of the Administration and the Governor's Advisory Committee on Grants Programs. As a member of the national lieutenant governor's mission, he traveled to Egypt, Jordan, and Saudi Arabia in 1987; that year, he also went to Paris as part of the South Pacific Leaders Orientation Mission. Additionally, he was the keynote speaker and head of American Samoa's delegation to the 1986 Pacific Trade/ Omvestment Conference and led the territory's delegation to the 1987 South Pacific Conference in Noumea, New Caledonia.

Following his term as Lieutenant Governor, Faleomavaega, a Democrat, made a successful bid for the islands' seat in the U.S. House of Representatives in 1988. On Capitol Hill, Faleomavaega has been a member of the House Committees on Resources and International Relations, although he cannot participate in House votes as a territorial delegate. He is also involved in a number of caucuses, including the American Indian, Indian-American and India, Progressive, Congressional Gaming, and Congressional Coastal collectives. Faleomavaega is also part of the Filipino Veterans Congressional Task Force.

Aside from his legislative commitments, Faleomavaega remains active within his profession as a member of the U.S. Supreme Court Bar and the American Samoa Bar, and a speaker at the First Pacific Regional Law Conference of the Western Samoa Law Society. His activities are diverse, and include involvement with the National Conference of Lieutenant Governors, the National Association of Secretaries of State, and the National Indian Prayer Breakfast Group, and a charter membership in the Pago Pago chapter of the Lions Club.

Faleomavaega also continues to maintain a military connection as part of the U.S. Army Reserve and as a captain in the U.S. Army Judge Advocate General's Corps (JAG). From 1982 to 1990, he was a member of the 100th Battalion of the 442nd Infantry Reserve Unit of Fort DeRussy, Hawaii, and is president of the Samoa chapter of the Go For Broke Association.

For his accomplishments, Faleomavaega received Brigham Young University's Alumni Service Award in 1979 and was named the Matai Orator, or "Faleomavaega," of the Faiivae family in Leone, American Samoa.

In the context of the growing role of Asian Pacific Islanders and other minorities in the government, Faleomavaega has expressed concern that APIs do not have a political voice proportional to their financial contributions to the country's major parties. "There's not much result, in my opinion, in the ration of Asian Americans in political appointments," he said. " . . . The politicians only come in time for money, but then after that they forget the Pacific American community" (A. Magazine 1996, 28).

Still, he harbors an optimistic outlook, as stated in a 1998 Asian American Heritage Month celebration speech: "When I envision America, I don't see a melting pot designed to reduce and remove racial differences. The America I see is a brilliant rainbow—a rainbow of ethnicity and cultures, with each people proudly contributing in their own distinctive and unique way. That is what America is all about, and Asian Pacific Americans wish to find a just and equitable place in our society that will allow them—like all Americans—to grow, succeed, achieve, and contribute to the advancement of this great nation as we enter the next century, the 'Pacific Century' " (www.house.gov/faleomavaega, 1999). He is married to Hinanui Bambridge Cave of Papeete, Tahiti, and they have five children.

## Sources

Congressman Eni F. H. Faleomavaega Web site: www.house.gov/faleomavaega [Accessed 5/13/1999].
"Eni F. H. Faleomavaega." *The Complete Marquis Who's Who Biographies*. Reed Elsevier, Inc. Last updated 17 July 1997.
"The Magnificent 7." *A. Magazine*. 30 November 1996, p. 28.

# Hiram L. Fong

Hiram L. Fong. (© Bettmann/CORBIS)

**Born:** 15 October 1906, Honolulu, Hawaii.

**Education:** B.A., University of Hawaii, 1930; J.D., Harvard University, 1935.

**Positions Held:** Member, Hawaii Territorial House of Representatives, 1938–1952; Hawaii State Senator, U.S. Senate, 1959–1977.

**Awards, Honors:** Horatio Alger Award, 1970, Japanese American Citizens League Citation for Outstanding Service, 1970, University of Hawaii Distinguished Alumnus Award, 1991, Induction in the Junior Achievement Hawaii Business Hall of Fame, 1995, United Chinese Societies Model Chinese Father of the Year, 1996, Outstanding Citizen Achievement Award, Organization of Chinese Americans, 1996.

**Summary:** Hiram L. Fong is the nation's first U.S. senator of Asian ancestry.

## Early Years

Hiram Leong Fong, the nation's first Asian American senator, was born in Honolulu, Hawaii on 15 October 1906 to Cantonese immigrants, Lum Fong and Chai Ha Lum. The family resided in the low income area of Kalihi, where Fong spent his childhood. His father and mother supported their eleven children by working as a contract laborer on Hawaii's sugar plantations and as a maid, respectively. At an early age, he faithfully contributed to the household income by picking algorroba beans, shining shoes, selling newspapers and seafood, delivering poi, and caddying for local golfers. He was also an employee at the Pearl Harbor Navy Yard from 1924 to 1927.

## Education

Fong's precocious work ethic was fertile training ground for academic life. After graduating from Honolulu's McKinley High School, he attended the University of Hawaii for three years, where he was active as a member of the debate, volleyball, and rifle teams, adjutant of the ROTC, associate editor of the yearbook, and editor of the campus newspaper. In 1929, he was a contestant at the National Rifle Championships. In spite of his demanding extracurricular commitments, he earned a bachelor of arts degree with honors in 1930. He then went to Harvard Law School, paying his way as chief clerk of Suburban Water System and graduated in 1935.

## Career Highlights

With his J.D. in hand, Hiram L. Fong returned to his home state to open the firm of Fong, Miho, Choy, and Robinson. He also applied his legal education to the civic arena as a deputy attorney for three years for the city and county of Honolulu. In 1938, Fong won his bid for the territorial legislature. During his 14 years in territorial government, Fong was the speaker from 1938 to 1954 and was also a vocal advocate of Hawaiian statehood. From 1942 to 1944, he fought in the U.S. Army Corps as well. Then, in 1959, with the Aloha State's admission to the Union, Fong made history as both Hawaii's first senator and as the first Asian Pacific Islander elected to the U.S. Senate.

During his 18 years in Congress, Fong, a member of the post office and civil service, judiciary, and appropriations committees, pushed for the fledgling state's interests as well as those of less privileged groups. He argued successfully for $50 million in federal monies to build highways between military bases on the islands, persuading skeptics that Hawaii deserved its share of transportation funding even though it did not lie adjacent to other states. He also sought aid to support the University of Hawaii's East West Center and local voting procedures, particularly in regard to immigrants and native Hawaiians. Though a Republican, Fong also backed the liberal 1964 Civil Rights and the 1965 Immigration Acts and other components of President Lyndon B. Johnson's "Great Society" vision. Later, he assisted the Nixon White House in recruiting minority players into the administration.

Fong's distinguished career was not restricted to the Hill, however. He was a delegate to several international conventions, such as the 150th Anniversary of Argentine Independence in Buenos Aires and the 1974 World Interparliamentary Union in Tokyo. He was also the only Asian Pacific Islander to be twice-nominated for president by the Republicans. Possessing a knack for business, he has been a director and board member of several companies, including Finance Factors, Grand Pacific Life Insurance Company, Finance Investment Company, Market City, Ltd., and Ocean View Cemetery, Ltd. He is also the owner and operator of Senator Fong's Plantation and Gardens, 725 acres of landscape and wildlife open to tourists located at the base of the Ko'olau Mountains in Kaneohe, Hawaii.

A pioneer, Fong has received numerous honors, such as the 1970 Horatio Alger award, a Japanese American Citizens League citation for outstanding service, a University of Hawaii alumnus award, a place in the Junior Achievement Hawaii Business Hall of Fame, and the United Chinese Society's Model Chinese Father of the Year title in 1996. That year, the Organization of Chinese Americans also bestowed upon him its Outstanding Citizen Achievement Award. Senator Fong is married to Ellyn Lo of Honolulu, and they have four children: Hiram, Jr., Rodney L., Merie-Ellen Gushie, and Marvin Allen.

## Sources

Henry, Jim. "Hiram K. Fong." In *Notable Asian Americans*. ed. Helen Zia and Susan B. Gall. Detroit, MI: Gale Research Inc., 1995, pp. 79–80.

"Hiram Leong Fong." *The Complete Marquis Who's Who Biographies*. Reed Elsevier, Inc. Last updated 24 June 1997.

Ng, Assunta. "OCA Conference Draws 2,000." *Northwest Asian Weekly*. 19 July 1996, p. 1.

Senator Fong's Plantation and Gardens Web site: www.fonggarden.com [Accessed 13 May 1999].

# Matthew K. Fong

**Born:** 1953.

**Education:** B.S., United States Air Force Academy, 1975; MBA, Pepperdine University; J.D., Southwestern Law School.

**Positions Held:** California State Treasurer, 1994-1998.

**Awards, Honors:** Distinguished Alumnus Award, Pepperdine University, 1992.

**Summary:** Matthew K. Fong, son of former California Secretary of State, March Fong Eu, is the first Asian Pacific American to serve as California's State Treasurer.

## Early Years

Born in 1953, politics and government have been a consistent theme throughout Matthew Kipling Fong's life. At 12 years old, Fong canvassed door to door for his mother, March Fong Eu, a California state legislator and Secretary of State from 1975 to 1994. As a teen, he attended the 1968 Democratic National Convention in Chicago, meeting the rich, famous, and powerful, including Shirley MacLaine and Rosie Grier.

## Education

Following the lead of his father, Fong attended the United States Air Force Academy in Colorado Springs, Colorado, after graduating from high school. A recipient of the USAF Meritorious Service Mediator for outstanding management performance, he earned his bachelor of science degree in 1975 and then worked for a compulsory five years in the Air Force.

After completing his service, Fong returned to political circles as the campaign manager for his mother's third bid for California's Secretary of State position. He then joined her staff, collaborating on issues involving Asian countries, such as the California World Trade Commission. Later, when asked about his experiences as one of Eu's "employees," Fong jokingly replied, "The toughest part of working for my mother, probably typical of any son working for their family, is trying to get paid more than the minimum wage" (Lin 1994, 1).

Gradually, Fong's career plans solidified; he earned an MBA from Pepperdine University and a J.D. from Southwestern Law School in pursuit of his goal to become an international business lawyer. As a neophyte attorney, he accepted a job in business law with the Los Angeles-based international law firm of Sheppard, Mullin, Richter, and Hampton.

## Career Highlights

Amidst the demands of a budding legal career, Fong continued to be active in both civic and political circles. A USAF reserves officer, Fong counseled students interested in joining the military after high school; he was also a board member of the Los Angeles County Museum of Natural History. Meanwhile, he honed his politicking skills as the co-chairman of both the 1988 Bush/Quayle campaign in the Golden State, and Pete Wilson's bid for the U.S. Senate, and as an executive board member of California's Republican Party.

Fong had mulled for years over his political party allegiance—March Fong Eu, after all, was a formidable figure in the state's Democratic establishment—but finally crossed over to the GOP after his work with the USAF, his small business ties, and his conclusion that the Democrats no longer espoused a forceful defense policy. Regarding the family "split," Fong commented humorously, "Asian Americans need to be on both sides of the aisle. That's why I don't complain about my mother being a Democrat" (Chen et al. 1996, 56).

Fong's first attempt at elected office was in 1990 with his run for state controller. He lost the bid to a Democrat, Gray Davis, in the general election but was appointed by then-Governor Pete Wilson the following year to the powerful State Board of Equalization, the body that governs California's revenues from 13 separate tax programs, including state and property revenues. The five members of the board essentially regulate all legislation dealing with the state's taxes. While serving on the board, Fong, representing southern and central regions of Los Angeles County, called for a decrease in both manufacturing taxes and government intervention in business.

In 1993, Fong vied again for a state position, announcing his intention to run for state treasurer. He presented his platform as one of fiscal reform: "[If elected,] I'll use the power of the treasurer's office to help identify and eliminate wasteful government spending, push for tax policies that nurture economic growth, encourage new investment in California's economy, and work to keep the state's long-term debt financing under control" (*Los Angeles Times* 1993, B8). He successfully waged his campaign, winning by a half-million votes while spending only $2 million as compared to his opponent's $7 million in campaign expenditures.

As California's treasurer, Fong was leading the world's seventh largest economy, handling such monies as $160 billion in pension fund assets—California's Public Employees Retirement System is the nation's largest—and overseas investments. He also served as a member of Newt Gingrich's informal advisory group that met bimonthly for private dinners. Of the arrangement, Fong remarked, "Gingrich and I have gotten to know each other as we work on issues such as tax reform, cutting government waste, and immigration" (Wu 1996, 11). In 1996, for example, Fong's input helped to persuade the House Speaker to retain funding measures in an immigration reform bill hours before the vote in Congress. "For a party that stands for family values, how could we deny the right of an American citizen to be with their children or their parents?" he asked. "If I wasn't in the room, nobody would have spoken out to protect legal immigration. My issues are fiscal, economic, but I was able to use my position to have much wider influence" (Chen et al. 1996, 56).

Fong's visibility and presence placed him among Gingrich's list of possible running mates for the 1996 GOP presidential hopeful, Bob Dole. Although he realized that he was not in the "top tier" of candidates, Fong was "very flattered and very honored" in addition to being "very realistic." He also pointed to Gingrich's suggestion as a hopeful sign for minorities. "Until this time, if anyone asked if an Asian could be president, I would say no," he remarked. "This is the first in a long series of steps to get people used to the idea that Asian Americans can provide real leadership at local, state, and national levels" (Chen et al. 1996, 56).

Matthew Fong rose to the challenge in 1998 as the Republican candidate for California's Senate seat. Backed by party heavyweights, including Gingrich, Jack Kemp, Trent Lott, and Rudolph Giuliani, Fong ran a close race against the incumbent Barbara Boxer. An advocate of increased military spending, flat rate income tax, and a closer balance between environmental and economic policy, he also expressed his support for pro-choice during the first trimester of pregnancy, parental consent abortion laws, a boycott of Swiss banks (which at the time were under investigation for breaches of Holocaust victims' rights concerning their accounts), inquiries into the Indonesian government's violations against its ethnic Chinese citizens, the candidacy of openly gay philanthropist James Hormel for the ambassadorship to Luxembourg, and the importation of skilled overseas workers to fill job openings in Silicon Valley. In general, however, Fong maintained conservative views such as opposition to gun control and campaign finance reform.

Although Asian Americans of all political persuasions comprised a major segment of his supporters, Fong lost the November election. Accepting his defeat, he paused to reflect on his pioneering efforts. "Who would ever have thought that the great-grandson of Chinese laborers who came to America for a better opportunity would be standing here?" he asked. However, he also noted that ethnic and racial distinctions were never to be the most salient concerns of any campaign. "Here in this great country, it's not important to accentuate our differences that we're hyphenated Americans—African Americans, Latino Americans, Asian Americans—but that we're Americans" (Soo 1998, 16).

Fong continued, "We are not Republican or Democratic but tonight, after the election, we are Californians . . . and so as a Californian and one who is very proud, I stand to say, God bless Barbara Boxer, but tomorrow is another day." He then succinctly summed up his future plans: "We're coming back" (Soo 1998, 16).

## Sources

Booth, William. "Onetime Democrat Narrows Gap in Challenge to Sen. Boxer." *Washington Post.* 25 August 1998, p. A3.

Chen, Liliana, et al. "Power Brokers 1996: The 25 Most Influential Asian Americans." *A. Magazine.* December 1996/January 1997, p. 56.

Henry, Jim. "Matthew K. Fong." In *Notable Asian Americans,* ed. Helen Zia and Susan B. Gall. Detroit, MI: Gale Research Inc., 1995, pp. 80–82.

Janofsky, Michael. "California G.O.P. Senate Nominee Goes from Long Shot to Star." *The New York Times.* 14 August 1998, p. A12.

Lin, Sam Chu, "Eu Bids Farewell to Colleagues in California State Government." *Asian Week.* 7 January 1994, p. 1.

"Matt Fong to Run for State Treasurer in '94." *Los Angeles Times.* 11 August 1993, p. B8.

Soo, Julie D. "Boxer Bests Fong in Final Round." *Asian Week.* 11 November 1998, p. 16.

"A Unifying Strategy for Fong, Chin: The State's Top Republican Asian Americans Hope to be Stronger Together for November." *Asian Week.* 5 August 1998, p. 10.

Wu, Frank H. "Washington Journal: Fong for Vice President?" *Asian Week.* 11 July 1996, p. 11.

# Warren Furutani

**Born:** 10 October 1947, San Pedro, California.

**Education:** B.A., Antioch College.

**Positions Held:** Member, Los Angeles Board of Education, 1988–1996, President 1991–1992; Member, Los Angeles Community College Board of Trustees, July 1999–present.

**Awards, Honors:** Asian Pacific American Legal Center Community Service Award, Asian Pacific Woman's Network Woman Warriors Award for Education, Los Angeles Asian Pacific Heritage Month Committee Education Service Award, Asian American Architects and Engineers Lifetime Achievement Award.

**Summary:** Warren Furutani is a longtime Asian Pacific American community activist and the first APA to be elected to the Los Angeles Board of Education.

## Early Years

Fourth-generation Japanese American Warren Furutani was born in San Pedro, California, on 10 October 1947 to Charles "Chuck" Hiroshi Furutani and Mary Yamada, two native Californians who met at the Rohwer, Arkansas concentration camp during World War II before moving to New York, where they married. The couple then returned to the west, where they raised Furutani and his three brothers, Norman, Alan, and Stony.

Although Furutani spent his childhood in Southern California and attended Gardena High, he did not always live the "typical" Japanese American life of the post-war generation. "A major influence in my life was the fact that my dad was a Sansei of Nisei age," explained Furutani. "This meant that he was more Americanized and as a result we were always a little out of step with the JA community. My Dad was a jazz musician (drums), drove hot rods and motorcycles and chafed from the conformity of the JA community. He always preached to us not to be afraid of being different." But, admitted Furutani, "as sure as he wanted us to look at things from a different perspective, I wanted to be like everyone else." He managed to do so in many ways as an "above average student" who enjoyed guitar, the visual arts, and sports "[growing] up in the innocence of the 50s and early 60s" (personal communication to Ellen D. Wu, 11 July 2000).

## Education and Career Highlights

After high school graduation, however, Furutani was "thrust into the turmoil of the times." His friend, Julie Jefferson, a young African American woman, was a major influence on his thinking at the time. "After high school, Julie left for college in the South. She left a middle class Negro and came back an angry black militant," he recounted. "This impacted me as I tried to find out why she changed. As with other things, she brought me along on her political odyssey. Finally, while in South Park listening to Stokely Carmichael, a light bulb came on over my head. Stokely said, 'The most important thing for Black people to do is to define themselves, for themselves and by themselves.' I interchanged Asian and it said the same thing to me. We had to define ourselves and stop living up to the definitions others had for us. I'm still challenged by that" (personal communication to Ellen D. Wu, 11 July 2000).

Thus began Furutani's grassroots political odyssey. Exempt from the draft, he joined a special program at the College of San Mateo in Northern California where he became an activist and was one of the first Asian Pacific Americans arrested for political activities at school. "After San Mateo, the San Francisco and Berkeley 'strikes' kicked off and I officially became an 'outside agitator,' " he stated (personal communication to Ellen D. Wu, 11 July 2000). By his early 20's, Furutani had become, in the words of the editors of *Roots: An Asian American Reader*, a "well known community worker and speaker in the Asian community" (Tachiki et al. 1976, 335). A self-described "activist" and "public relations man" for the Los Angeles arm of the Asian American Movement, Furutani campaigned for Asian American Studies programs and equal opportunity programs at college campuses throughout California. In a 1971 interview with the *Amerasia Journal*, he stated, "In terms of [Asian American] Studies, I see it as a very essential thing. I see it as the beginning point, a point that's going to turn people on, something that is going to get people excited about the movement. I think that in many cases around the country Asian American Studies is being looked at as an ends and not as a means to an end" (*Amerasia* Staff 1971, 74).

In addition to university-related concerns, Furutani was heavily involved in anti–Vietnam War demonstrations, participating in numerous allies and marches, including many of the larger gatherings in the Los Angeles area during the period, and served as the National Community Involvement Coordinator for the Los Angeles chapter of the Japanese American Citizens League. "I proudly wore the mantle of 'outside agitator' for those years of my youth," he stated (personal communication to Ellen D. Wu, 11 July 2000).

One of Furutani's projects as outside agitator was the Manzanar Pilgrimage, a commemorative activity he conceptualized with Victor Shabada. "When we started talking about camp, the Nisei generation, my parents' generation, would say, 'That's best left not discussed. Let's just bury the hatchet,'" he recounted. "As we, the sansei, began to talk more about the camps, people told me it wasn't very important, but they started getting very upset. 'Why the hell are you bringing this up? Why do you want to talk about this shit for?' I would say, 'If it's not important, why are you so upset?'" (Mendez 1995, 1).

Since the late 1960s and early 1970s, Furutani has lectured and spoken at "almost every major university in the United States (except the South)" and in "communities around the country from the backs of pickup trucks and on countless street corners" about racism, imperialism, and other socio-political issues. Having "traded in" his "denim work shirt and army jacket for more traditional dress," Furutani has also worked "all kinds of different jobs" in the past three decades, including positions with the UCLA Asian American Studies Center, the Asian Community Fund, and the Asian Pacific Policy and Planning Council.

In April 1987, Furutani, who earned his B.A. from Antioch College's Los Angeles campus "much later in life" (personal communication to Ellen D. Wu, 11 July 2000), was elected to the Los Angeles Board of Education, becoming the first Asian Pacific American member in its history. Reelected in 1991, he served as its president for the 1991/1992 year. Furutani considers his most notable achievement during his tenure on the board to be democratizing the decision-making processes of the school board. "Until I got there it was a closed-door institution," he stated.

"Maybe because the busing wars had taken their toll, all the members closed their doors to the community. I opened them up by bringing accessibility back to the district. This opened the door to reform efforts like LEARN and much more school based management (personal communication to Ellen D. Wu, 11 July 2000).

"Being on the Board was the toughest job I've ever had," continued Furutani. "Still is. There were and still are many many problems to overcome. I was moderately successful at best, but I'm not done yet" (personal communication to Ellen D. Wu, 11 July 2000). Recently, his continuing interest in education is manifested in his participation on the elected Los Angeles Community College Board of Trustees. "I'm trying to re-engage the thousands of students who have dropped out of school or are not ready for any kind of post-secondary education. Interestingly enough, I am trying to re-institute a college readiness program like I attended at the College of San Mateo. I must have come full circle."

Furutani holds a number of other significant positions in both professional and civic capacities. Since 1998, he has been a consultant to the California State Assembly Speaker's Office of Member Service and sits on the advisory board for the Southern California Conservation Corporation and the Los Angeles Southwest Community College Foundation, of which he was president. Furutani also chairs the newly formed Board of Governors for Los Angeles' Little Tokyo Service Center.

In recognition for his contributions, Furutani has received the Asian Pacific American Legal Center Community Service Award, Asian Pacific Woman's Network Woman Warriors Award for Education, Los Angeles Asian Pacific Heritage Month Committee Education Service Award, and the Asian American Architects and Engineers Lifetime Achievement Award. Furutani is married to the former Lisa Abe, a Sansei born in Kyoto, Japan. The couple has two sons, Sei Malik, born in 1982 and named for Malcolm X, with whom he shares his birthday, and Joey Tadashi, born in 1985.

In reflecting about the movements of the 60s and 70s in relation to today's situation, Furutani seems hopeful for continuing progress in the Asian Pacific American community. "When I started my so-called career as an activist in the late 60s and early 70s, everybody was either a third-generation Japanese American or Korean American. Or Chinese and Filipino, American born. Now the American born is pretty hard to find in the overall numbers," he observed. "I have found that the new immigrant communities have really stimulated the political landscape. I really feel a new resurgence of activism, particularly among students today" (Mendez 1995, 1). His outlook is pragmatic, but optimistic: "Education is still a focal point. I'm excited about the API community. We have become a critical mass and we are coming of age politically. I want to help usher in this new era" (personal communication to Ellen D. Wu, 11 July 2000).

## Sources

Amerasia Staff, "An Interview with Warren Furutani." Amerasia. 1:1 March 1971, pp. 70–76.

Mendez, Carlos. "Fighting the Good Fight Tests Warren Furutani." Asian Week. 3 March 1995, p. 1.

Personal communication to Ellen D. Wu, 11 July 2000.

Tachiki Amy, et al. "An Interview with Warren Furutani." In Roots: An Asian American Reader. Los Angeles: UCLA Asian American Studies Center. 1976, pp. 335–340.

# G

## Mike Gin

Michael A. Gin. (Courtesy of Michael Gin)

**Born:** 6 February 1963, Inglewood, California.

**Education:** B.S., University of Southern California, 1984.

**Positions Held:** Councilman, City of Redondo Beach, California, 1995–present; Mayor Pro Tem, 1998–1999; Member, California Republican Party State Central Committee, 1998–present.

**Awards, Honors:** 1993 Redondo Beach's Young Man of the Year; 1999 CAUSE Citizen of the Year.

**Summary:** Mike Gin is Councilman for the City of Redondo Beach, California's District 3.

### Early Years and Education

Mike Gin was born on 6 February 1963 in Inglewood, California to William Min Gin, native of China's Guangdong Province, and Albertine Gin, originally from San Francisco. Gin attended Leuzinger High School, Lawndale, CA, where he served as student body president, and graduated in 1980 as class valedictorian. His early years made a lasting impression on the young Gin. "I believe that my community involvement (and eventual political aspirations) started when I was in high school," he explains. "When I became a sophomore in high school, I decided to join a service club called Key Club [a service organization sponsored by Kiwanis International for high school youth]. My original intentions for joining Key Club were for purely social reasons. The Club was considered one of the 'in' clubs at my school and, frankly, I wanted to be part of the 'in' crowd."

"Somehow, I managed to become a candidate for membership [despite strict community service requirements]. It was through these community activities that I began to understand and appreciate the importance of volunteerism and community service." Emphasizes Gin, "There are so many good things in our world that would not exist were it not for the hard work and dedication of community service volunteers. To this day, participating in community activities is an important part of who I am."

He next matriculated at the University of Sourthern California, Los Angeles where he earned his B.S. in computer science in 1984. His time spent as a member of the USC Student Senate's Academic Affairs Committee hinted at his later involvement in local politics.

## Career Highlights

Since college, Gin has maintained an active profile in both his professional and civic lives. From 1980 to 1991, he was a Senior Member of the Technical Staff, TRW, Inc. in Redondo Beach, where he worked on a variety of space- and defense-related software systems, including image processing and ground station software for NASA's Hubble Space Telescope. In addition, he served for two years on the company's Affirmative Action Advisory Committee. From 1991 to 1998, Gin was employed as a computer scientist for El Segundo, California's Infonet Services Corporation. There, he provided software development and computer systems support for a variety of Infonet's network reporting products. Since 1998, he has served as a Project Leader for Infonet's Production Support Team, where he is responsible for managing and directing activities associated with customer and technical support of Infonet's network reporting products.

On the political side, Gin has served in a number of capacities, including the Los Angeles and California State Republican Party Central Committees and the Redondo Beach Recreation and Parks and Planning Commissions. "During my tenures on the Preservation and Planning Commissions, I had the opportunity to work with many businesses and residents on a variety of issues," he notes. "I also learned many lessons about making decisions on numerous issues (some controversial) that were never clear-cut. Most of the time the decisions came down to carefully balancing disparate, but worthy community needs on both sides of the issue. I've come to believe that while it is important to possess underlying principles that guide you as a decision maker, it is important to listen and keep an open mind about all issues."

These lessons made an impact. "I enjoyed my service on the Preservation and Planning Commissions so much that my political aspirations and goals came into focus," he recalls. "I decided to run for the open seat in my City Council District in 1995." That year, Gin was elected outright in Redondo Beach's municipal primary election to represent District 3 on the City Council, capturing 62.5 percent of the votes cast in a four-candidate race. The goals he envisioned for Redondo Beach were to improve public safety, to enhance and maintain parks and other open spaces, and to enhance and improve the business climate in the city.

Gin followed his first victory with a second in 1999 when he ran unopposed for his second term. From 1998 to 1999, he was chosen by his colleagues to serve as Redondo Beach's Mayor Pro Tem. As a member of the city council, Gin was involved with the Board of Directors of the Independent Cities Association, the Redondo Beach Sister Cities Committee, the Los Angeles County Sanitation District, and the Independent Cities Risk Management Authority. He also chaired the Redondo Beach City Council/Redondo Beach School Board Subcommittee.

Outside of his office-related duties, Gin has worked with a number of community organizations, including the Redondo Beach Chamber of Commerce and the Redondo Beach

Jaycees. Additionally, he is a member of Chinese Americans United for Self-Empowerment (CAUSE)'s Board of Directors and chairs the Chinese Heart Council of the American Heart Association. In recognition of his accomplishments, he has received the 1993 Redondo Beach's Young Man of the Year Award, sponsored by the Redondo Beach Jaycees and Chamber of Commerce, and one of the CAUSE Citizen of the Year Accolades honoring all Los Angeles–area Chinese American municipal elected officials in 1999.

As a self-described newcomer to Asian Pacific American political life, Gin brings a fresh perspective to municipal government with an eye toward the future. "During my 2nd and last term on the City Council (I will be forced out by term limits in 2003), I'd like to continue to emphasize the goals listed above," he declares. "In addition, I'd like to help improve the technology in our city to create an environment where all city services can be accessed from a home computer. The concept of E-government will become more and more important over the next few years."

## Source

Personal communication to Ellen D. Wu, 5 October 2000.

# Michael P. Guingona

**Born:** 17 March 1962, San Francisco, California.

**Education:** B.A., University of California, Los Angeles, 1985; J.D., University of San Francisco School of Law, 1989.

**Positions Held:** Mayor/Council member, Daly City, CA City Council 1993–present.

**Summary:** Michael P. Guingona is the first Filipino American city council member and mayor of Daly City, California, where Filipino and Filipino Americans comprise over 25 percent of the population.

## Early Years and Education

Michael Patrick Guingona was born on 17 March 1962 in San Francisco, California, to Concepcion Limjap and Jose Guingona. Because his parents were separated at the time of his birth, his mother and stepfather, Eddie Lichauco, known to him as "Uncle Ed," raised him. Guingona noted that his brother, Dave, took the responsibility for "teaching me everything I know" (Almendrala 1983, 17). He attended the University of California, Los Angeles, where he majored in history and was a member of the Phi Alpha Theta History Honor Society and Beta Theta Pi fraternity. After earning his B.A. in 1985, he went on to study at the University of San Francisco School of Law, graduating in 1989. As a student at USF, he maintained an active life in addition to his classes, joining the Phi Alpha Delta Law Fraternity and International Law Society, serving as a Street Law instructor and

Michael Guingona. (Courtesy of Michael Guingona)

participating in the Community Legal Education Program.

## Career Highlights

From 1990 to 1999, Guingona worked as a deputy public defender in the Office of the Public Defender for the city and county of San Francisco, representing indigent defendants in all phases of criminal proceedings from arraignment through trial. In his nine years as a staff attorney, he tried over 35 cases in Municipal and Superior Court. Guingona left the Office of the Public Defender after nine years to start his own practice in San Francisco, emphasizing criminal defense. Guingona is a member of the Bar Association of San Francisco, the California Trial Lawyers Association, and the California Public Defenders Association. He also serves as a board member of the Filipino Bar Association of Northern California and chaired the Asian American Recovery Services of San Francisco from 1992 to 1994.

In 1996, Guingona accepted positions with two Bay Area institutions, the San Mateo County Transportation Authority and the San Mateo County Transit District. As the Vice-Chair and board member of the Transportation Authority, Guingona is responsible for expenditures in an extensive transportation program funded by a 20-year half-cent sales tax approved by San Mateo County voters in 1988. He oversees such projects as Caltrain improvements, street and highway concerns, and bicycle programs. As a board member for the Transit District, he provides public policy direction for programs and activities of the independent transportation district and its 1,300 employees, encompassing all of San Mateo County, with operations extending from Palo Alto through downtown San Francisco.

In addition to his legal and advisory capacities, Guingona has a third major realm of commitment, local politics. In this, he follows in the footsteps of several family members, including his great grandfather, Galiciano Apacible, former Governor of Batangas, Philippines, and his uncle, Teofisto Guingona, who has served as President Pro Tempore of the Philippine Senate and Executive Secretary of Philippine President Ramos. The youthful attorney made history first in 1993 as the first Filipino American member of the five-seat Daly City, California city council and again in 1995, when he became the youngest mayor in Daly City's history. Noted Alice Bulos, chairwoman of the Filipino-American Democratic Caucus in Northern California at the time, "It's a historic event for the empowerment of Filipinos" (Pimentel 21 June 1993, A13).

Because Guingona ran a close race against another minority, businessman Mario Panoringan, the contest generated considerable debate among the municipality's Filipino Americans, who made up 27 percent of the city's 92,000 residents at the time. Although the campaign resulted in somewhat of a community divide, Guingona expressed an interest in bridging the gaps and fulfilling the expectations of his constituents. "I would like to play a major role in the healing process," he stated. "I don't want to create an us versus them [situation]. I hope to be able to show them [Filipinos] that there's more of them in me than they believe," he stated soon after his victory (Pimentel 21 June 1993, A13).

As a city council member and mayor of Daly City, Guingona's duties have included determining policy direction on matters related to the day-to-day operations of the municipal government, such as the budget, capital improvement projects, public safety, parks, recreation and youth programs, and other quality of life issues. Additionally, he has represented the interests of the city's denizens, provided regional leadership through the San Mateo County Council of Cities and the San Mateo City County Association of Governments, and served as a member of the Daly City Redevelopment Agency and North San Mateo County Sanitation District Board of Directors.

In his spare time, Guingona, who is married to Teresa Ferrer Guingona and the father of Kai Michael Guingona, enjoys outrigger canoeing, softball, Philippine martial arts, swimming, and running. Having accomplished so much so early in his career, Guingona commented, "I'm a work in progress. I'm gonna make mistakes and I'm gonna learn from those mistakes" (Pimentel 16 July 1993, A1).

## Sources

Alemendrala, Laarni C. "What's Luck Got To Do With It?" *Filipinas*. August 1993, pp. 17, 46.

Pimentel, Benjamin. "Filipinos Finally Get Voice on Daly City's Council: Community has High Hopes for Guingona." *San Francisco Chronicle*. 21 June 1993, p. A13.

———. "The First Step: Filipinos Finding a Political Voice." *San Francisco Chronicle*. 16 July 1993, p. A1.

# H

## Samuel Ichiye Hayakawa

Samuel Ichiye Hayakawa. (© Bettmann/CORBIS)

**Born:** 18 July 1906, Vancouver, B.C., Canada.

**Died:** 27 February 1992, San Francisco, California.

**Education:** B.A., University of Manitoba, 1927; M.A., McGill University, 1928; Ph.D., University of Wisconsin, La Crosse, 1935.

**Positions Held:** California State Senator, U.S. Senate, 1976–1982; Special Adviser to Secretary of State for East Asian Affairs, 1983–1990.

**Awards, Honors:** President Emeritus, San Francisco State University, 1973; Honorary Chairman, U.S. English Foundation, 1983–1992.

**Summary:** Samuel Ichiye Hayakawa is one of only three U.S. senators of Japanese ancestry to date. A controversial figure, he opposed many liberal and leftist movements such as the Third World student strike at San Francisco State College in 1969 and the Japanese American Redress and Reparations movement of the 1980s.

### Early Years and Education

Samuel Ichiye (S.I.) Hayakawa was born on 18 July 1906 in Vancouver, British Columbia. His immigrant parents owned an import-export business but Hayakawa opted for a college education rather than inheriting the family company. He graduated from the University of Manitoba in 1927 and earned his M.A. in English from Montreal's McGill University the following year. Hayakawa then crossed the border to enroll in the University of Wisconsin at La Crosse's doctoral program in English and American literature, earning his degree in 1935 upon the completion of his dissertation on the works of Oliver Wendell Holmes. At U.W.–La Crosse, Hayakawa met his wife, Margedant Peters, whom he married in 1937. He also acquired his nickname, "Don," at the school from colleagues who thought his Canadian-English to be reminiscent of an Oxford University don.

## Career Highlights

An accomplished linguist, in 1941 Hayakawa authored *Language in Action*, a well-known semantics textbook based on the theories of Alfred Korzybski, the discipline's founder. Hayakawa, who believed the field to be "the study of what it is that goes haywire when people misunderstand each other—or themselves—and what to do about it," wrote *Language in Action* to warn his audiences of the perils of propaganda, using Adolf Hitler as an example (Freedberg 1992, A1). The volume drew both accolades—it was chosen as a Book of the Month Club selection—and fire—academics scorned the popular, rather than scholarly, writing style. The criticism did not deter him, however. *Language in Action* has been translated into nine other tongues, and Hayakawa produced more than six other books and assisted in compiling a number of English dictionaries and reference materials.

Meanwhile, Hayakawa stayed in higher education, teaching first at U.W.–La Crosse and later at the Illinois Institute of Technology. His decision to remain in the Midwest turned out to be a fortuitous one, as he managed to avoid incarceration in the Japanese American concentration camps during World War II. He continued to climb the academic ladder, taking a professorship at San Francisco State College (now San Francisco State University) in 1955, becoming the school's president three years later.

The hotbed of the San Francisco campus in the 1960s turned out to be the setting that vaulted Hayakawa to national prominence. "He had 15 minutes of glory, he put San Francisco State on the map, and he was to use that fame to get himself elected to the Senate," observed Eric Solomon, a member of the faculty, in retrospect (Freedberg 1992, A1). Handpicked by then-Governor Ronald Reagan, Samuel Ichiye Hayakawa represented the institution's intolerance of student movements. He enlisted the aid of police to wield control over the mass actions. During the 1968 Third World Student Strike calling for, among the demands, Asian American Studies, Hayakawa yanked the speaker cords from a soundtrack during a protest rally to "break up this reign of terror," in his words (Freedberg 1992, A1). Of his actions, which were nationally televised, Hayakawa exclaimed, "This has been the most exciting day of my life since my tenth birthday, when I rode a roller coaster for the first time!" (Umemoto 1989).

The following semester, Hayakawa designated a "select committee" of faculty members to negotiate with student strikers. More liberal than he, they orchestrated a compromise with the students which Hayakawa refused to sign. The resolution, which led to the establishment of the first School of Ethnic Studies in the nation, ended the longest and bloodiest student strike in U.S. History (Umemoto 1989).

As suggested by Solomon, Hayakawa used his visibility in combating the strikers to help him win one of California's seats in the U.S. Senate. While his first attempt in 1973 was thwarted on a technicality—he had changed political parties shortly before the race, violating election rules—he won his bid in 1976 at the age of 70, soundly beating Democrat incumbent John V. Tunney.

On the Hill, Hayakawa continued to draw attention from his peers and the public alike for his unusual and distinctive conduct. The 5'3" tam-o-shante–sporting senator did not attend his own inauguration—"My feet are cold" was his explanation—and he was too "bushed" to attend a black-tie dinner for rookie legislators his first term (Freedberg 1992, A1). He was named the Senate's least effective member by *Washingtonian Magazine* and was rated #93 out of the 100 senators for poor voting attendance. A narcoleptic, Hayakawa often napped during Senate sessions, prompting another nickname, "Sleepy Sam." His tendency to doze off on the Senate floor, coupled with his frequent colorful remarks—"When I first went to Washington, I thought, 'What is lil' ol' me doing with these 99 great people?' Now I ask myself, 'What am I doing with these 99 jerks?' "—made him the target of media personalities like Johnny Carson (Freedberg 1992, A1). He later criticized television and the press for tarnishing his image and costing him his reelection.

In his six years as California's junior senator, Hayakawa voted conservatively on a myriad of issues, backing the lowering of minimum wage and opposing bilingual education for immigrants, for example. Regarding the Panama Canal, he stated, "We stole it fair and square," although he later supported its return to Panamanian control (Freedberg 1992, A1).

Most disturbing to his co-ethnics was his flat-out denial of the federal government's wrongdoing toward Japanese Americans during World War II, arguing that the concentration camps had been "perfectly understandable" (Freedberg 1992, A1). In a speech delivered at the 1978 Japanese American Citizens League national conference, he opined, "Everybody lost out during the war, not just Japanese Americans," and the community's demand for redress was "ridiculous." In a separate incident, he stated, "[when] a small but vocal group demands a cash indemnity of $25,000 [per person] for those who went to relocation camps, my flesh crawls with shame and embarrassment" (Hatamiya 1993).

Aside from his term in the Senate, Hayakawa served as special advisor for East Asian and Pacific Affairs to Secretary of State George Schultz from 1983 to 1990. He also successfully led the 1986 crusade to designate English as California's official language. In his waning years, he continued to work on publications and collaborated with the University of California, Berkeley on an oral history project of his life. In his spare time, he enjoyed sports, particularly fencing, and participated for many years in the starting line-up of San Francisco's annual Reno's VIP-charity softball game.

Hayakawa died in 1992 at age 85 of a stroke and bronchitis complications, leaving behind his wife, Margedant, sons Alan and Mark, and daughter Wynne. Fellow California Representative Norman Mineta (now Secretary of Transportation) reflected, "Senator Hayakawa's service in Congress was pioneering for Americans of Japanese ancestry. He and I disagreed on many issues, but what we had in common was the belief that California and the United States are made stronger when Americans from all ethnic communities join together to participate without discrimination in government and in other public institutions" (Hong 1992, 1).

### Sources

Freedberg, Louis. "Ex-Senator Hayakawa Dies at 85; He Gained Fame in '60s as Fiery President of S.F. State." *San Francisco Chronicle*. 28 February 1992, p. A1.

Hatamiya, Leslie T. *Righting a Wrong: Japanese Americans and the Passage of the Civil Liberties Act of 1988*. Stanford: Stanford University Press, 1993.

Henry, Jim. "Samuel Ichiye Hayakawa." In *Notable Asian Americans*, ed. Helen Zia and Susan B. Gall. Detroit, MI: Gale Research Inc., 1995, pp. 106–107.

Hong, Lisa J. "Ex-Senator Hayakawa Didn't Run With Crowd." *Asian Week*. 6 March 1992, p. 1.

Umemoto, Karen. " 'On Strike!' San Francisco College Strike, 1968–1969: The Role of Asian American Students." *Amerasia*. 15:1 1989, pp. 3–41.

## Dennis W. Hayashi

**Born:** 31 May 1952, Los Angeles, California.

**Education:** B.A., Occidental College, 1974; J.D., University of California Hastings College of Law, 1978.

**Positions Held:** National Director Japanese American Citizens League, 1991–1993; Director of Office of Civil Rights, Department of Health and Human Services, 1993–1999; Director of Civil Rights Department, California

Department of Fair Employment and Housing.

**Awards, Honors:** Named one of *A. Magazine*'s 25 Most Influential Asian Americans in 1993.

**Summary:** Dennis Hayashi is a pioneer Asian Pacific American in civil rights advocacy, having served as the Department of Health and Human Services' Director of the Office of Civil Rights from 1993 to 1999.

## Early Years and Education

A native of Los Angeles, Dennis W. Hayashi was born on 31 May 1952 to Nisei parents George I. and Yukiko H. Hayashi. He attended Occidental College as a philosophy major, graduating cum laude in 1974 with a bachelor of arts degree. He studied at the University of California's Hastings College of Law in San Francisco, earning his juris doctorate in 1978.

## Career Highlights

While in school, Hayashi clerked for one year for U.S. District Court Judge Robert Takasugi of San Francisco. In 1979, he began his 12 years of service with the Bay Area's Asian Law Caucus, a nonprofit civil rights advocacy organization that focuses on Asian Pacific Islanders in America. Concentrating on employment and racial discrimination issues, Hayashi worked on a number of high-profile lawsuits, such as *Korematsu v. United States*. Fred Korematsu, a Japanese American, attempted to evade the government's evacuation and internment orders in May 1942 to stay with his Italian American girlfriend. He was caught, jailed, and later convicted when the Supreme Court ruled in 1944 that the exclusion of a "single racial group" as ordered by Congress and the president, was constitutional in the times of "pressing public necessity" (Hatamiya 1993).

The decision remained in the nation's law books until a legal team representing Korematsu and two other plaintiffs reopened it using a writ of error coram nobis, which is applied in instances of fundamental error or manifest injustice after the defendants have completed their sentences. U.S. District Court Judge Marilyn Patel ruled in favor of Korematsu in November 1983, vacating his convictions. Hayashi's work on Korematsu's case was part of the larger struggle for Japanese American redress and reparations in the 1970s and 1980s.

As an Asian Law Caucus attorney, Hayashi also represented a group of Vietnamese fishermen protesting racist treatment by the U.S. Coast Guard, San Francisco firefighters of color, and the family of Chinese American hate crime victim, Jim Loo, who was attacked and killed in a North Carolina pool hall in 1989 by two white men, Robert and Lloyd Piche, who mistook him for a Vietnamese.

In 1991, Hayashi became the director of the Japanese American Citizens League, the nation's oldest Asian Pacific Islander civil rights advocacy group, a fitting role for the son of former Japanese American concentration camp prisoners. For two years, he coordinated the organization's major projects, monitoring the seven regional offices while acting as JACL's spokesperson.

Hayashi became the Clinton cabinet's highest ranking Asian American on 5 May 1993, with his nomination to the directorship of the federal government's Office of Civil Rights in the Department of Health and Human Services. As director of the OCR, Hayashi oversees the ten regional branches of the agency and regulates the activities of beneficiaries of the Health and Human Services Department for proper conduct according to civil rights regulations.

Following his appointment on 27 June, he immediately voiced his support for immigrants' rights. "We need to educate our community about immigration. Asian Pacific Americans have not been active in the shaping of immigration policy," he told attendees at the Asian Pacific American Heritage Council Leadership

Conference in 1995 (Carroll 1995, 1). He expressed concern over the divisiveness of issues such as health care access among undocumented aliens and general misinformation about the subject, stating, "In Washington, in areas of public policy, perception and reality are often at odds" (Carroll 1995, 1).

Hayashi has noted that 37 million Americans do not benefit from basic health care coverage, while others encounter discriminatory, inferior treatment. "Every day, one out of four expectant mothers either sees no doctor at all for prenatal care, or waits to do so until just before delivery. Every day elderly people are forced to make terrible choices—choices between food or rent and necessary but expensive medication," he stated at a March 1994 reception hosted by the Asian and Pacific Islander American Health Forum. "Health security is more than financial insurance. It is also assurance of equal and unbiased quality" (Le 1994, 1).

Hayashi is also a firm proponent of affirmative action. In a July 1995 *Asian Week* piece, he argued, "Affirmative action has historically helped the APA community and remains an essential tool to address ongoing discrimination. . . . Our country's moral, legal, and practical interests are advanced by affirmative action.... [It] continues to embody and promote a commitment by America to achieve equality, fairness, and inclusiveness" (Hayashi 1995, 4).

In March 1999, Hayashi left the Department of Health and Human Services to accept a directorship in California's Department of Fair Employment and Housing. Among his duties in his newest position are to investigate and resolve discrimination complaints and promote and enforce anti–hate crime legislation.

Outside of the Asian Law Caucus, the Office of Civil Rights, and now California's Department of Fair Employment and Housing, Hayashi has been a major player in both the Asian Pacific Islander and legal communities. His impressive resume lists his work as the co-founder of the National Network Against Anti-Asian Violence, former membership on the Asian Pacific American Democratic Council, the California Council on Prevention of Hate Violence, the Civil Rights transition cluster for Clinton/Gore, and the boards of directors for the National Asian Pacific Association, San Francisco Coro Foundation, San Francisco Legal Assistance Foundation, and Child Care Law Center. He was also a former instructor at the New College of San Francisco's California Law School and an associate grievance director for the San Francisco local of the Hotel and Restaurant Employees International Union. Occidental College's Alumnus of the Year in 1994 and one of *A. Magazine*'s 25 Most Influential Asian Americans in 1993. Hayashi is also a prolific writer and has contributed to a number of publications, including the *Washington Post*, the *Los Angeles Times*, *Yale Law Review*, and *Asian American Policy Review*.

## Sources

Carroll, Pedro. "Conference Focuses on Benchmark APA Issues." *Asian Week*. 19 May 1995, p. 1.

"Dennis Hayashi." *The Complete Marquis Who's Who Biographies*. Reed Elsevier, Inc. Last updated 20 May 1997.

Espiritu, Yen Le. *Asian American Panethnicity: Bridging Institutions and Identities*. Philadelphia: Temple University, 1992.

Hatamiya, Leslie T. *Righting a Wrong: Japanese Americans and the Civil Liberties Act of 1988*. Stanford: Stanford University Press, 1993.

Hayashi, Dennis. "On Principle." *Asian Week*. 28 July 1995, p. 4.

Le, Anh. "Asian American Democratic Leaders Promise Health Care and Justice For All." *Asian Week*. 8 April 1994, p. 1.

Lee, Denny. "Dennis Hayashi." In "The A.100: 100 Most Influential Asian Americans of the Decade." *A. Magazine*. October/November 1999, p. 95.

"Power Brokers: The 25 Most Influential People in Asian America." *A. Magazine*. 31 October 1993, p. 25.

Wu, Douglas. "Dennis Hayashi." In *Notable Asian Americans*, ed. Helen Zia and Susan B. Gall. Detroit, MI: Gale Research Inc., 1995, pp. 107–108.

# Mazie Hirono

Mazie Hirono. (Courtesy of the State of Hawaii, Office of the Lieutenant Governor)

**Born:** 3 November 1947, Fukashima, Japan.

**Education:** B.A., University of Hawaii at Manoa; J.D., Georgetown University, 1978.

**Positions Held:** Hawaii House of Representatives, 1980–1994; Hawaii Lieutenant Governor, 1994–present.

**Summary:** Mazie Hirono is the first foreign-born Asian Pacific American woman to be elected to public office at the statewide level. She is the current Lieutenant Governor of Hawaii.

## Early Years and Education

Mazie Keiko Hirono was born in Fukashima, Japan on 3 November 1947. At age eight, she immigrated to Hawaii with her family and was naturalized two years later. Raised by her mother, Laura Chie Sato, she attended the state's public school and then enrolled at the University of Hawaii at Manoa. A Phi Beta Kappa inductee, Hirono earned her bachelor of arts degree in 1970 and her juris doctorate from Georgetown University in 1978.

## Career Highlights

Her first position as a fledgling lawyer was as Hawaii's deputy attorney general for the Anti-trust Division. She then served as a house counsel for INDEVCO in Honolulu from 1982 to 1983, followed by a year of solo practice in Honolulu and another four with the firm Shim, Tam, Kirimitsu, Kitamura and Chang.

As a working attorney, Hirono simultaneously launched her political career. A delegate to the state's Democratic Party Convention from 1972 to 1982, she next won a seat in Hawaii's House of Representatives in 1980, which she held for seven terms until 1994. As a state representative, Hirono actively supported a number of issues, such as women's rights, and introduced 120 successful bills into the House. From 1983 to 1984, when she was chair of the Committee on Housing, she backed Hawaii's Land Reform Act, which allowed working families to purchase the lots upon which their homes stood. She also advocated the buying rights of condominium residents. Later, as the five-year chair of the Consumer Protection and Commerce Committee, she delved into consumer concerns related to professional licensing, banking, and insurance.

In 1994, Hirono became the first immigrant Asian woman to hold a statewide elected office in the United States when she bid successfully for the Aloha State's lieutenant governorship as the running mate of Democrat Benjamin Cayetano. Interestingly, Hirono attributes the victory in part to Hawaii's significant Asian Pacific Islander population, adding that the diverse electorate has enabled her to address more universal, rather than strictly race or ethnic based, concerns with "cosmopolitan appeal." However, she also notes that the substantial API presence does impact the state government's agenda on issues such as immigration, rendering officials "more sensitive and supportive of immigrants" (Soo 1998, 12).

As Lieutenant Governor, Hirono's duties have been manifold, encompassing the realms of business, economy, and labor. Not surprisingly, fostering tourism, Hawaii's top industry, is high on her agenda as chair of the Governor's Advisory Council on Airlines Relations. Hirono has devoted her efforts to facilitate air travel to Hawaii through expanded service, fewer obstacles, such as visa waivers for Korean tourists, and improved safety, including more "user friendly" FAA regulations.

On the other hand, Hirono has worked to broaden Hawaii's economy to alleviate the state's dependence on visitor dollars. Among her areas of emphasis are aviation training, science and technology, and workforce development. She is an executive committee member of both Hawaii School-to-Work, a program which links Hawaii's students from 90 institutions to 200 businesses in order to improve job training, and America's Promise Hawaii, a volunteerism project.

Additionally, Hirono has chaired the Workers' Compensation Task Force, piloting legislative reforms leading to 37 percent rate reductions and the fewer eligibility restrictions to enable more state businesses to apply for insurance coverage. She also doubles as Hawaii's Secretary of State, co-chairs the Governor's Conference on Arts and Education, and is the only Hawaiian to sit on the executive committee of the Pacific Disaster Center, which investigates natural disasters and relief strategies. Furthermore, she has introduced anti–hate crime measures in the Hawaii Legislature and pushed for the creation of an independent Office of Elections to redirect the overseeing of Hawaii's voting procedures from her office to a Chief Election Officer.

Outside of government, Hirono has also maintained commitments to several civic organizations. She was on both the Nuuana YMCA and the Moiliili Community Center boards of directors. She has also coordinated or been honorary chair of various charity and cultural events, including the Race for the Cure and Hawaii Heart Walk.

In the wake of the Democratic National Committee's campaign finance scandal in the mid-1990s, Hirono was one of two APIs named to the party's 55-member executive committee, serving as deputy chair, as part of the Democrats' efforts to make amends with the Asian Pacific Islander community. She also led a task force responsible for identifying means through which the party could garner API support.

## Sources

ehawaii.gov: www.hawaii.gov/ltgov [Accessed 13 May 1999].

Eljera, Bert. "Apologies from DNC." *Asian Week.* 18 September 1997, p. 13.

"Mazie Keiko Hirono." *The Complete Marquis Who's Who Biographies.* Reed Elsevier, Inc., 1997. Last update 5 June 1997.

Soo, Julie D. "Island Politics: Race Seems Less of an Issue than on the Mainland—But Is It?" *Asian Week.* 21 October 1998, p. 12.

Wu, Frank H. "Washington Journal: Demos Make Refunds." *Asian Week.* 10 July 1997, p. 10.

# Mike Honda

**Born:** 27 June 1941, California.

**Education:** B.S., B.A., M.A., San Jose State University.

**Positions Held:** Member, San Jose Unified School Board, 1981–1990; Member, Santa Clara County Board of Supervisors, 1990–1996; Member, California State Assembly, 1996–2000; Member, U.S. House of Representatives (California, 15th District), 2001–present.

**Awards, Honors:** Asian-Pacific Policy and Planning Council 1997 Award; the Silicon Valley Asian Pacific American Democratic Club 1998 Norm Mineta Lifetime Achievement Award; Asian American Recovery Services, Inc., 1999 Dedicated Leader Award; Asian Law Alliance 2000 Community Impact Award; and the Asian Pacific Islander California Action Network 2000 Award; Bay Area Independent Elders Program Award; the Latino Peace Officers Association; Dr. Mar-

Mike Honda. (Courtesy of Mike Honda)

tin Luther King, Jr., Association of Santa Clara Valley 1997 Award; and the State Teachers Retirement Board 1998 Award.

**Summary:** Mike Honda was a member of the California State Assembly from 1996 to 2000 and currently represents California's 15th district in the United States House of Representatives.

## Early Years

A third-generation Japanese American, Mike Honda was born in California on 27 June 1941. As a young child, Honda was interned along with his family in one of the federal government's concentration camps during World War II, an experience that shaped his political outlook as an adult. "All my life I grew up in the midst of frustration," he recounted. "My parents raised us as a family, but their life was frustrating because of camp and being up-rooted. We know we were sent to camp without due process of law. So everything that violates due process, I want to be around to address it as an educator and as a policy maker" (Lin 1995, 7).

## Education

In 1953, the Honda household reestablished roots in San Jose, California, where Honda enrolled at San Jose State University. After a hiatus from course work in response to President John F. Kennedy's call to serve the nation—he worked for two years among isolated agrarian communities in El Salvador with the then-fledgling Peace Corps—Honda returned to school, earning a B.S. in biology, a B.A. in Spanish, and an M.A. in education.

## Career Highlights

As an educator, Honda held a series of positions, including teacher, Vice Principal, Principal, and Administrator, devoting special attention to the learning needs of the disadvantaged as well as academically gifted students. His professional career segued smoothly into a political career with his first elected position as a member of the San Jose Unified School Board, where he served from 1981 until 1990.

That year, he was elected to the Santa Clara County Board. As a Santa Clara Supervisor, Mike Honda worked to institute welfare reforms, facilitate the construction of the Lexington Overpass on Highway 17, advocated safety improvements along Highway 152, and supported environmental issues such as the Santa Clara County Open Space Authority and the protecting of hillsides from development. Limited to two terms on the board, Honda next set his sights on the state capital. "The opportunity is there for me to go to Sacramento where there's a lot of work to be done—work that will affect local government, local issues, human services, and education," he remarked near the end of his second term. "There's even more of an opportunity now, since the federal government is looking at shifting a lot of the responsibilities to the state level. With my background and experience in education, in community advocacy, and in government," he continued, "I think I've got the background and experience to seek out solutions and resolutions at the state level" (Lin 1995, 7). Apparently, voters agreed; in March 1996, Honda captured a seat in California's State Assembly, representing the South Bay's 23rd District, including San Jose and unincorporated areas of Santa Clara County—an area where APIs comprised over 25 percent of the electorate. He then followed with a second victory in 1998.

In the Assembly, Honda chaired the Public Safety Committee and is a member of the Education, Revenue and Taxation, and Public Employees, Retirement, and Social Security (PERSS) Committees. Not surprisingly, his legislative priority was education—calling vigorously for more stringent guidelines for determining California's teacher credentials—along with highway safety, domestic violence prevention, and economic development. Notably, he considered the passage of AB2804, which promotes teacher recruitment, retention, and retirement benefits, one of his most significant achievements in Sacramento.

With his election, Honda became only the second API member of his cohort in the State Assembly. "It's frustrating that we don't have more Asian Americans in the assembly, or any other office for that matter," he opined. "When you look at L.A., which probably has the highest concentration of Asian Americans, I don't think there's an elected official in the city. When you look at the county itself, there are maybe four—if that many—and most of them are in the Gardena area. The representation of Asians in elected office is dismal. It's not that we don't have the people or the talent. We need to have more people in policy-making positions because of what we can bring to the table as far as forging policies and laws that will govern all of us" (Lin 1995, 7).

One such issue that turned the public eye toward Honda himself was that of Japan's wartime atrocities in Asia during the period 1931–1945. In 1999, Honda sponsored a controversial resolution urging Japan to apologize with "clear and unambiguous" gestures for its actions against American veterans, former sex slaves, and other victims. "We're saying no to atrocities; we're saying yes to peace," he stated (Watanabe 1999, A3).

Dissenters, including Nikkei Assemblyman George Nakano (D-Torrance), feared that the passage of the legislation and its vocal support by an API legislator in particular would "perpetuate the myth that we are foreign" by blurring the lines between domestic and international issues, in the words of one activist, revive latent animosities, and spark an ill-timed backlash against Asian Pacific Americans in the wake of the Democratic campaign finance scandals. "I believe that I spent four years behind barbed wire because people could not distinguish between Americans like myself and the Japanese government because of the color of my skin," stated Nakano. "And I fear that this thinking still exists today" (Pimentel 1999, A17).

In response, Honda carefully amended his resolution to repudiate anti-Asian sentiments while simultaneously recognizing the efforts that Japan had already made toward apologies and reparations. Nevertheless, he stood his ground: "This is one way of closing a chapter for Japan in a way that allows them to move into the next century on a better footing with its neighbors," he argued. "An apology would go a long way in the healing of people and reparations would go a long way to helping survivors and victims" (Pimentel 1999, A17).

During the 2000 election year cycle, Honda entered the race to replace Republican Congressman Tom Campbell, who gave up his congressional seat run against the incumbent Senator Dianne Feinstein (D-California). In March 2000, Honda won an impressive victory in a five-way race for the Democratic nomination. Although outspent by former Carter administration defense official, Bill Peacock, who sunk nearly $1 million of his own money into the race, Honda won the highest percentage of the vote in the open primary. His campaign focused on issues such as health care, education, and the economy. He highlighted his work on patients' rights, increasing monies for teacher training and salaries, and tax credits to pay for interest on nearly $25 billion in bonds for public school revitalization, and limiting regulation on the Internet while improving its accessibility for all. Although the political journal Congressional Quarterly declared "no clear favorite" to succeed, Honda defeated his Republican opponent, state Assemblyman Jim Cunneen, by 12 percentage points. In Congress, Honda sits on the Budget and Transportation committees.

Outside of his official duties, Honda maintains an active profile among area API communities. For example, he chaired the California Asian Pacific American Experience–Silicon Valley Event, "Heading East Musical/Exhibit," in 1998. Among the organizations that have honored him for his services are: the Asian-Pacific Policy and Planning Council, the Silicon Valley Asian Pacific American Democratic Club, Asian American Recovery Services Inc., Asian Law Alliance, and the Asian Pacific Islander California Action Network. His commitments, however, have not been limited to the API community; other groups which have bestowed recognition on the Assemblyman include the Bay Area Independent Elders Program, the Non-Profit Association of Northern California, the Latino Peace Officers Association, Dr. Martin Luther King, Jr., Association of Santa Clara Valley, YMCA, and the State Teachers Retirement Board, among others.

Honda is married to Jeanne Honda, an elementary school teacher in San Jose. They are the parents of Mark and Michelle.

## Sources

Lin, Sam Chu. "Second in Sacramento: Santa Clara Supervisor Mike Honda Wants to Correct APA Underrepresentation in California State Legislature." *Asian Week*. 20 October 1995, p. 7.

Ma, Jason. "Easy Victory for Mike Honda." *Asian Week*. 15 March 2000, p. 13.

Pimentel, Benjamin. "Reactions Mixed to Assemblyman's Call for Japanese Apology; Some Asian Americans Believe Timing Is Off." *The San Francisco Chronicle*. 26 August 1999, p. A17.

Watanabe, Teresa. "Measure Urges Japan to Apologize for Atrocities." *Los Angeles Times*. 24 August 1999, p. A3.

Wong, Gerrye. "Political Lessons: Mike Honda Brings Experience as a Teacher to Assembly." *Asian Week*. 4 November 1998, p. 9.

Wong, William. "A Resolution Dividing Asian-Americans." *San Diego Union-Tribune*. 3 September 1999, pp. B8, B12.

# I

## Daniel K. Inouye

Daniel K. Inouye. (Courtesy of the Office of the Honorable Daniel K. Inouye)

**Born:** 7 September 1924, Honolulu, Hawaii.

**Education:** B.A., University of Hawaii, 1950; J.D., George Washington University, 1952.

**Positions Held:** Member, Hawaii Territorial House of Representatives, 1954–1959; Member, U.S. House of Representatives, 1959–1962; Hawaii State Senator, U.S. Senate, 1962–present.

**Awards, Honors:** For World War II service, the Bronze Star, Purple Heart with Cluster, Distinguished Service Cross, later updated to Medal of Honor (2000); named by A. *Magazine* as one of the 100 Most Influential Asian Americans of the Decade, 1999.

**Summary:** The nation's first senator of Japanese ancestry, Daniel K. Inouye is the highest ranking Asian Pacific American in Congress today.

### Early Years

Daniel Ken Inouye, born on 7 September 1924 in Honolulu, Hawaii, had a childhood fairly typical of most Nisei on the islands. The oldest of four children born to Hyataro Inouye, a file clerk, and his wife, Kame Imanaga Inouye, young Daniel was named for his mother's adopted father, a Methodist minister. Inouye attended Honolulu's public schools as well as Japanese language schools. In his spare time, he made pocket money by giving his friends haircuts and parking cars at the old Honolulu stadium. He also enjoyed a number of hobbies, including stamp collecting, tinkering with chemistry and crystal radio sets, and raising homing pigeons. After graduating from McKinley High School in 1942, he entered the University of Hawaii as a pre-medical student. As for all of his Japanese American contemporaries, the 7 December 1941 attack on Pearl Harbor marked a watershed period in Inouye's life. His ambition to become a doctor led the 17-year-old Inouye to his first brush with the war, where he "witnessed a lot of blood" while applying his first-aid training to treating civilian casualties from the conflict (www.senate.gov/~inouye.html 1999). The following March, Inouye enlisted in the Army and was assigned to the now famous, all-Japanese 442nd Regimental Combat Team. As one of the "Go For Broke" soldiers, Sergeant Inouye endured three difficult months of the Rome-Arno campaign with the U.S. Fifth Army, followed by an assignment in the French Vosges mountains, where he and his fellow Nisei soldiers rescued the "Lost Battalion" of Texas surrounded by German forces. Over the two weeks of bloody battle, Inouye was promoted to platoon leader, earning his bronze star and battlefield commission as a second lieutenant.

Inouye's greatest sacrifice in the war came in Italy toward the end of the conflict. While attacking enemy lines, Inouye, leading his platoon, caught a bullet in his abdomen. It exited his body but nearly hit his spine. Undaunted, he forged ahead, facing a machine gun alone. In defense of his men, he threw two hand grenades at the Axis forces. In retaliation, a German rifle grenade destroyed his right arm at close range. Still fighting, Inouye released his remaining grenade and fired shots from his weapon before being hit by a bullet in his leg. He spent 20 months in army hospitals recovering from his wounds. Inouye was again honored for his outstanding service to the army, receiving a Bronze Star, Purple Heart with Cluster, 12 other medals and citations, and being named a captain with a distinguished service cross, one of the military's highest distinctions.

## Education

Inouye's veteran status enabled him to re-enter school on the G.I. bill, and in 1950, he graduated from the University of Hawaii, not in the sciences, as was his pre-war plan, but in government and economics. Two years later, he received his J.D. from the George Washington University law school. As a law student, he was active in several capacities, foreshadowing his future in the U.S. Congress, including the professional law fraternity, Phi Delta Phi, the George Washington Law Review editorial board, and the Democratic National Committee.

## Career Highlights

After law school, Daniel Ken Inouye then returned to his home state to work in local government. After serving as a deputy public prosecutor for the city of Honolulu, he successfully ran for the territorial House of Representatives in 1954. He quickly assumed a House majority leadership position before moving to the territorial Senate in 1958. Inouye's work in the territorial government paid off in 1959 when he was elected to the U.S. Congress as the new state's first Representative on Capitol Hill. A popular and prominent figure, he made history capturing the largest number of votes for any candidate in a Hawaiian election as well as becoming the first Japanese American in the national legislature. The following year, he was re-elected to a full term.

Inouye's oath of office was particularly poignant, as one of his colleagues, Representative Leo O'Brian recalled in the early 1960s. "Tuesday last was the third anniversary of the admission of Hawaii. Today is the third anniversary of the most dramatic and moving scenes ever to occur in this House. On that day, a young man, just elected to Congress from the brand new state, walked into the well of the House and faced the late Speaker Sam Rayburn. The House was very still. It was about to witness the swearing in, not only of the first Congressman from Hawaii, but the first American of Japanese descent to serve in either House of Congress. 'Raise your right hand and repeat after me,' intoned Speaker Rayburn. The hush deepened as the young Congressman raised not his right hand but his left and he repeated the oath of office. There was no right hand, Mr. Speaker. It had been lost in combat by that young American soldier in World War II. Who can deny that, at that moment, a ton of prejudice slipped quietly to the floor of the House of Representatives" (www.senate.gov/~inouye.html 1999).

As Hawaii's Representative, Inouye sat on the Banking and Currency and Agriculture committees, where he voiced the concerns of the local sugar and pineapple industries. Then, after three years, he moved to the Senate, where he has remained ever since.

A loyal Democrat, Inouye was an advocate of the liberal programs of Presidents John Fitzgerald Kennedy and Lyndon B. Johnson in the 1960s, particularly those concerning civil rights, racial discrimination, and welfare. Initially, he also supported America's role in Southeast Asia but later changed his views, voting to end the conflict in Vietnam and advocating the War Powers Act of 1973, which called for a ceiling on the President's power to engage U.S. armed forces overseas without the backing of Congress.

Inouye has been in the national spotlight several times throughout his senatorial career. He delivered the keynote address at the 1968 Democratic National Convention. He was a member of the Senate Select Committee on Presidential Campaign Activities, which was responsible for investigating the Nixon administration's role in the Watergate scandal, and he chaired the Senate Select Committee on Secret Military Assistance to Iran and the Nicaragua Opposition in 1987. Again, Inouye investigated presidential use and abuse of authority as he scrutinized the Iran-Contra affair.

Well-respected among his colleagues, Inouye has served in several other significant positions during his time in the Senate, including the chair of the 1976 Senate Select Committee on Intelligence, member of the powerful Senate Appropriations Committee and chair of its Defense Appropriations subcommittee, and the Democratic Steering and Coordination Committee. Inouye has also focused continuously on issues of social justice as Hawaii's senator, defending abortion rights, public school desegregation, gun control, and consumer advocacy. It was he who proposed formation of the Commission on Wartime Relocation and Internment of Civilians, which held a series of hearings on the Japanese American concentration camp experience in nine cities nationwide in 1981 and released a 467-page report that was instrumental in the passage of the 1988 Civil Liberties Act, granting former Japanese American internees redress and reparations.

His senior status on the Senate Appropriations Committee and his background as a soldier in the 442nd Regimental Combat Team was also crucial to improving the appropriations process. In a persuasive letter to his colleagues, he stated, "I hope that when the time for the decision is upon us, you will join me in remembering those men from the internment camps who proudly and courageously demonstrated their 'last full measure of devotion' in the defense of their country. Although these men will not receive benefits from the provisions of this bill, I am certain that they will gratefully rest in peace"(Hatamiya 1993).

Aside from the Japanese American redress campaign, Inouye also served the API community as an executive committee member of the Congressional Asian Pacific Caucus. In 1997, he introduced bills in Congress to facilitate the naturalization of Philippine nationals who served in the United States military during World War II. A. *Magazine* recognized

Inouye for his outstanding contributions to the Asian Pacific American community by honoring him as one of the 100 Most Influential Asian Americans of the Decade in 1999.

The senator has also been a staunch advocate for Native American concerns, such as sovereignty, gaming, and taxation, acting as both chair and vice chair of the Senate Committee on Indian Affairs. In 1998, when asked by the Native American newspaper, *Lakota Times* why he was "one of the most Indian-friendly senators we have," despite having almost no Native Americans in his state, Inouye responded, "Because I'm an American. And I know a little about the history of the United States as it relates to Native Americans. And I've said this many times, those pages in our history book are dark, shameful. And the least I can do as an American is clean up those pages. It's a shameful chapter, a chapter we should—all of us—hang our heads in shame over" (*Lakota Times* 1998, A2).

Daniel Inouye has been married to Margaret Shinobu since 1949; they have one son, Daniel Ken Inouye, Jr.

## Sources

The United States Senate Web site: www.senate.gov/~inouye [Accessed 14 April 1999].
"Daniel K. Inouye." *AP Candidate Bios*. The Associated Press Political Service, 1998.
Hatamiya, Leslie T. *Righting a Wrong: Japanese Americans and the Passage of the Civil Liberties Act of 1988*. Stanford: Stanford University Press, 1993.
Henry, Jim. "Daniel K. Inouye." In *Notable Asian Americans*, ed. Helen Zia and Susan B. Gall. Detroit, MI: Gale Research Inc., 1995, pp. 126–127.
Lee, Denny. "The Establishment." In "The A. 100: 100 Most Influential Asian Americans of the Decade." *A. Magazine*. October/November 1999, p. 95.
Park, Charles. "Senators Daniel Akaka and Daniel Inouye." In "The A. List 1997." *A. Magazine*. December 1997/January 1998, p. 60.
"Sen. Dan Inouye: I am a Native American." *Indian Country Today (Lakota Times)*. 23 March 1998, p. A2.

# Lance A. Ito

Judge Lance Ito presides over a hearing in the O.J. Simpson double-murder trial in Los Angeles, January 20, 1995. (Mark J. Terrill, AP/Wide World Photos)

**Born:** 2 August 1950, Los Angeles, California.

**Education:** B.A., University of California, Los Angeles, 1972; J.D., University of California, Berkeley, 1975.

**Positions Held:** Municipal Court Judge of Los Angeles Judicial District of Los Angeles County, 1987–1989; Judge, Los Angeles County Superior Court; Assistant Presiding Judge, Los Angeles Superior Court.

**Awards, Honors:** Trial Judge of the Year, Los Angeles County Bar Association, 1992; Most Influential Asian American of the Year, *A. Magazine*, 1995.

**Summary:** Lance A. Ito of the Los Angeles Superior Court is the most recognized Asian Pacific American judge today. He is best known for presiding over the highly publicized O.J. Simpson trial in the mid-1990s.

## Early Years and Education

A third-generation Japanese American, Lance A. Ito was born in Los Angeles, California, on 2 August 1950. His Nisei parents, recently released from Heart Mountain concentration camp in Wyoming, were both school teachers. Ito attended Los Angeles public schools, graduating from John Marshall High School in 1968. He spent his undergraduate years as a Bruin at the University of California, Los Angeles, earning his B.A. in political science in 1972. He next moved north to attend law school at the University of California, Berkeley's Boalt Hall, graduating in 1975.

## Career Highlights

As a fledgling attorney, Ito first worked for the firm of Irsfield, Irsfield, and Younger for two years, after which he accepted a position as a prosecutor for the district attorney's office, where he remained for a decade, devoting his energies to issues related to street gangs and organized crime. In the mid-1980s, he served on the Los Angeles County Association of Deputy District Attorney's Board of Directors, held a vice-chairmanship of California's State Task Force on Youth Gang Violence, and a membership on the state's Task Force on Victim's Rights.

In December of 1997, California's Governor George Dukmejian took notice of Ito's accomplishments, selecting him as the first Municipal Court judge of the Los Angeles Judicial District of Los Angeles County. Two years later, Dukmejian re-appointed Ito to a judgeship in the Los Angeles County Superior Court. In 1990, the county's voters voiced their satisfaction with Ito's performance in the local election for the position. Likewise, his peers noted his achievements handling such cases as the 1991 securities fraud prosecution of Charles Keating of the Lincoln Savings and Loan Association, one of the many nationwide Savings and Loans scandals of the period. His colleagues named him trial judge of the year for the Los Angeles County Bar Association in 1992.

Ito's reputation led him to preside over one of the most highly-publicized court battles of the 20th century—the trial of former National Football League running back and Hall of Famer O.J. Simpson in which he was accused of murder. This case thrust Ito into the national spotlight. "At that point—when on four networks and across a dozen nations there was no other news—he was the focal point, the locus, of a hundred million frozen stares," noted *A. Magazine*, whose editors named him the most influential Asian American personality in 1995. "At that point he became the most famous Asian American on the planet; now, and perhaps in history" (Yang 1995/1996, 35). The trial propelled Ito into pop-culture icon status, inspiring the "Dancing Itos" on NBC's *Tonight Show*, references in hip-hop rap lyrics, and one of the top choices for Halloween costumes mid-decade. *People* magazine even dubbed Ito the #1 "unlikely heartthrob" in its 1995 "Celebrity Romance" issue.

At times, Lance Ito was also the target of racist remarks, including inappropriate comments delivered in a supposedly-Japanese accent by New York Senator Alfonse D'Amato. These experiences not only left a deep impression on Ito but also prompted him to address the problem by raising awareness within the Asian Pacific American community. "During the course of the Simpson case, I tried to ignore the media frenzy that was going on. But one thing I could not ignore was the racist parodies and caricatures," he told an audience of 400 at the Korean American Bar Association banquet in 1996. "I have to tell you that I found them to be deeply offensive. I found them to be deeply distracting. And I found them to be deeply disturbing. The astonishing thing was, some of the worst offenders came from areas of our country where there are major Asian populations" he said (Lin 1996, 10).

For Ito, the ordeals of the trial were instructive. "The amazing thing for me was that these people were not afraid to come after me. They seemed to think that Asian Americans are fair game. They seem to think that we won't fight back. They seem to think that we will suffer these indignities and these insults in silence" (Lin 1996, 10). He continued, "The lesson that I learned from this experience [is that] if they can come after me, they can come after each and everyone of us here tonight, our families, and our friends." Cautioned the judge, "No one is immune from the racist sickness that still infects our country" (Lin 1996, 10).

To combat the problem, Ito suggested that the Asian Pacific American community foster civic virtues among new immigrants and "seek to survive and prosper with the mainstream." Additionally, he noted, "We must also avoid conflict with our fellow minority groups" (Lin 1996, 10).

## Sources

"Briefs: Judge Ito Speaks on Internment." *Asian Week.* 2 July 1998, p. 8.

Henry, Jim. "Lance A. Ito." In *Notable Asian Americans,* ed. Helen Zia and Susan B. Gall. Detroit, MI: Gale Research Inc., 1995, pp. 132–134.

Lin, Sam Chu. "Ito Warns of Social Trends: 'No One Is Immune From Racist Sickness,' Judge Says." *Asian Week.* 8 March 1996, p. 10.

Van Gelder, Lawrence, "D'Amato Mocks Ito and Sets Off Furor." *The New York Times.* 6 April 1995, p. B1.

Yang, Jeff. "Lance Ito." In "Powerbrokers III: 1995's 25 Most Influential Asians in America." *A. Magazine.* December 1995/January 1996, p. 35.

# J

## Harry J. Joe

Harry J. Joe. (Courtesy of Jenkens & Gilchrist, PC)

**Born:** 8 December 1948, Dallas, Texas.

**Education:** B.A., University of North Texas, 1970; J.D., Washington University, 1975.

**Positions Held:** Member, City Council of Irving, Texas, 1989–1997; Mayor Pro Tem, 1991–1992, 1995–1997.

**Summary:** Harry J. Joe was a member of the Irving, Texas, city council from 1989 to 1997 and its mayor pro tem in 1991-1992 and 1995-1997.

### Early Years and Education

A Chinese American, Harry J. Joe was born on 8 December 1948 in Dallas, Texas, to Fay G. (Fong Ong) and Kay (Sau Kwan) Joe. He attended the University of North Texas, where he earned his bachelor of arts degree in 1970. He then went on to Washington University in St. Louis, graduating as a Doctor of Jurisprudence in 1975.

### Career Highlights

Joe notes that "observation of the civil rights movement in the 1960s encouraged me to pursue a career in law and in seeking public office." He embarked on this career in a number of ways. After joining the American Immigration Lawyer's Association, Joe became the chairperson of its Texas Chapter from 1980 to 1981, a member of its Board of Governors, and a National Officer from 1982 to 1989. He also served as an adjunct professor of law at Southern Methodist University's School of Law from 1982 to 1994, where he taught immigration law.

In 1987, Joe began a two-year term on the City of Irving, Texas's Planning and Zoning Commission. At the conclusion of his service, he successfully bid for a seat on the city council. "Running for and winning election to public office," he remarked, was one of his "proudest accomplishments." He spent eight years on the Irving City Council, including two turns as Mayor Pro Tem from 1991 to 1992 and 1995 to 1997. Additionally, Joe presided over Irving's Republican Club from 1997 to 1998. Currently, Joe is a member of Jenkens and Gilchrist Law Firm in Dallas, Texas.

## Source

Personal communication with Ellen D. Wu, 12 December 2000.

# K

## James Kimo Kealoha

**Born:** 29 April 1909, Pahoa, Hawaii.

**Died:** 24 August 1983, Honolulu, Hawaii.

**Education:** Hilo High School, Hilo, Hawaii, 1926.

**Positions Held:** Representative, Hawaii Territorial House of Representatives, 1934–1938; Senator, Hawaii Territorial Senate, 1938–1940; Member and Chair, Hawaii County Board of Supervisors, 1940–1946, 1948–1960; Lieutenant Governor, Hawaii, 1960–1964.

**Summary:** James K. Kealoha was the state of Hawaii's first lieutenant governor.

### Early Years and Education

A Chinese Hawaiian, James K. Kealoha, also known as Lee Yat Wo, was born on 29 April 1908 in Pahoa, located on the island of Hawaii, to Alice Makiuni Kealoha and Lee Chau, a Cantonese grocer who first emigrated to Hawaii to work on the local plantations. After graduating from Hilo High School in 1926, Kealoha clerked for Kwong See Wo, a Hilo-area grocery, raised papayas, and opened his own market, which remained operational until 1948. He married Muilan Young in 1929; and the couple raised two daughters, Leihulu Emma and Leiohu Lillie.

### Career Highlights

Kealoha first entered the political arena in 1934 at the age of 26, when he won a seat in Hawaii's Territorial House of Representatives. After two terms in the House, during which he served as speaker pro-tem, he next moved to the Territorial Senate, where he was named president pro-tem. Notably, in 1938, Kealoha transferred his loyalties from the Democratic to the Republican party.

Known as the "boy wonder" of Hawaiian politics due to his popularity with constituents, Kealoha continued to further his political career with his election to the Hawaii County Board of Supervisors in 1940, the first of his three terms. After one unsuccessful bid for Hawaii county chairman in 1946, he won six consecutive elections for the county chair.

The Republican party named Kealoha the running mate of gubernatorial candidate William F. Quinn in 1959. Upon defeating the Democratic team of John Burns and Mitsuyuki Kido, the pair assumed the top two positions in the new state.

Unfortunately, Kealoha's historic victory would be his last in formal politics. Following an unsatisfying term as lieutenant governor, during which he wielded little power and performed mostly symbolic duties, Kealoha ran unsuccessfully against Quinn in the 1962 Hawaii state Republican primary for the governor's seat. Four years later, he bid for Hawaii's seat in the United States Congress against Masayuki "Spark" Matsunaga; he followed the loss against the incumbent Matsunaga with a frustrated attempt for the mayorship of Hawaii County in 1968.

Aside from politics, Kealoha worked briefly as the executive officer for the Hawaii exhibit at the New York World's Fair and as a financial manager for a group of Hawaiian investors at the Montreal World Expo in the 1960s. Kealoha also returned to his horticultural roots, farming papayas in Hawaii and operating a farm in Salem, Oregon. He died on 24 August 1983 at Honolulu's St. Francis Hospital at the age of 75.

## Sources

"James K. Kealoha, No. 2 Official When Hawaii Became a State." *The New York Times*. 26 August 1983, p. B16.

Ng, Franklin. "James K. Kealoha." In *Distinguished Asian Americans: A Biographical Dictionary*, ed. Hyung-chan Kim. Westport, CT: Greenwood Press, 1999, pp. 153–155.

# Jay C. Kim

**Born:** 27 March 1939, Seoul, South Korea.

**Education:** B.S., University of Southern California, 1967; M.S., University of Southern California, 1969; M.A., California State University, Los Angeles, 1979.

**Positions Held:** Mayor, Diamond Bar, California, 1991–1992; Representative, 41st District, R-CA, U.S. Congress, 1992–1998.

**Awards, Honors:** 1985 Small Business Association's Small Businessman of the Year, Award for National Excellence, Contractor of the Year, Outstanding Achievement in Business and Community Development Award, Engineer of the Year Award, 1993 Ellis Island Medal of Honor Award.

**Summary:** Jay C. Kim is the nation's first Congress member of Korean ancestry. He represented California's 41st district in the House of Representatives from 1992 to 1998.

## Early Years

Jay C. Kim was born on 27 March 1939 in Seoul, South Korea. Kim's father, a restaurant manager, named him Chang Joon Kim, which means "Golden Splendid Law" in Korean, to celebrate the long-awaited birth of his only child. Kim's mother, Woon Kil Choi, lovingly pampered their sickly son, showering him with care and attention. "I handled him like precious gold or jade.... I gave him only the best food I could find," she recalled. "I decided that I would make sure Chang Joon received the finest education possible, even though I myself have never even entered a school gate." Kim relished his [treasured] status in the family and would even pray that he would not have any siblings "because he wanted to monopo-

Rep. Jay Kim, R-Calif. at his Capitol Hill office April 27, 1998. (Courtesy of Joe Marquette, Associated Press, AP)

lize our love," remembered his mother (Spiegel and Kang 1993, A1).

His happy boyhood days were soon darkened by the outbreak of the Korean War. Like many others at the time, Kim's father hid from the Communists inside the family home. His mother was forced to help maintain the operation of railroad tracks. In time, the Kims left Seoul on foot for the town of Taejon, 90 miles away, where they stayed for three years.

## Education

After attending two universities in Korea and serving briefly in the South Korean Army, Kim arrived in the United States on a student visa in 1961. First attending a California community college, he eventually transferred to the University of Southern California, where he earned a bachelor's degree in civil engineering in 1967 and a master's degree in environmental engineering in 1969. A decade later, Kim obtained a second graduate degree, a master's degree in public administration, from California State University, Los Angeles.

Notably, he had not pursued his father's dream for him—law school. A dutiful son nonetheless, he tried his best to fulfill his wishes. "I didn't tell my father I was studying engineering. I was afraid he might have a heart attack," he admitted. "I told him I was doing international law. And he was not that unhappy" (Lam 1996, 48).

In 1962, Kim married Jung Ok (June) Kim, his sweetheart from Seoul. The challenge of balancing family life with college and work as a dishwasher, busboy, and newspaper delivery person was substantial, and the Kims sent their first two children (a son and a daughter; they later had another son) to Korea to live with Choi in the meantime. Despite the hardships, Kim looks back fondly on his early years in the United States, a time he remembers as an era of "tremendous pride in America, of people loving each other, helping each other out" (Lam 1996, 48). He readily embraced his adopted home. As he settled into life in the states, he legally changed his name from Chang Joon to Jay and obtained permanent residency.

## Career Highlights

After graduating from USC, Kim worked as a city engineer for both Ontario and Compton, CA before venturing into entrepreneurship in 1976 with the founding of his company, Jaykim Engineers Inc., a Southern California–based engineering design firm. Established with $25,000 out of his own pocket and an additional $100,000 loan from the Small Business Association, Jaykim Engineers grew steadily with continued assistance from the Small Business Association for 14 years. In 1985, Kim was named SBA's small businessman of the year for his region.

However, the success of Jaykim Engineers was marred by accusations of incompetence, poor workmanship, and inflated labor and overhead costs from several of its clients as well as auditors. Jaykim Engineers also faced an unrelated dilemma in the early 1990s as one of five minority-owned firms chosen to demolish remnants of buildings damaged by the 1992 Los Angeles uprising. Kim later decided to sell the company to avoid conflicts of interest due in part to this assignment.

Like his business ventures, Kim's political career has seen both success and scandal. His involvement began in the 1970s as a cofounder of the Korean American Political Association, serving as its president in 1974. Kim's first office occurred in 1990, when he successfully ran for a seat on the Diamond Bar, CA city council less than a month after building his home within the city limits. His victory surprised locals, including one city employee who remarked, "Most people who run for office here have come up through the social organizations like the Kiwanis Club, or they've been active for a long time in community causes. . . . It seemed like Jay Kim just came from nowhere" (Spiegel and Kang 1993, A1).

Chris Stewart, one of Kim's campaign advisors, described him as "a very naive candidate," particularly concerning his handling of funds (Spiegel and Kang 1993, A1). State auditors charged that he neglected to report some of his investments, holdings, and campaign donations, including himself and Jaykim Engineers, Inc., and also that he had taken some questionable tax deductions on contributions to other candidates.

Kim approached the city government as a business, pushing the council to vote for privatization of certain services, resulting in the layoff of approximately 125 people from Diamond Bar's payroll. Jay Kim began his term as the mayor of Diamond Bar in 1991. The next year, when reapportionment resulted in the creation of a new 41st Congressional district covering parts of Los Angeles, Orange, and San Bernadino counties, local Republican Party leaders approached him to run for the House of Representatives seat. As a prominent civic leader, a successful entrepreneur, and a churchgoing man with solid "family values," Kim had the "ideal profile," as Dr. Forest Tennant, a San Gabriel Valley, California, Republican leader described, to appeal to the district's conservative, affluent voters (Spiegel and Kang 1993, A1).

Defeating five Republican hopefuls, Kim ran into other obstacles—a violation of a local campaign sign ordinance, a lawsuit from his former campaign manager citing Kim's failure to pay a bonus after the primaries, and an FBI investigation of Jaykim Engineers, Inc., during the general election due to suspected illegal corporation contributions. Despite his problems, however, Kim fought off Democratic candidate Bob Baker to become the first Korean American member of Congress.

As in Diamond Bar, Kim's outlook on Capitol Hill was "to make government run more like business" (Spiegel and Kang 1993, A1). An example of his hands-off ideology was his support of abortion rights, which he believed were not within the legislature's jurisdiction. A right-wing Republican, he also opposed deficit spending, "hostile tax laws," economic stimulus, and "motor voter" registration, while advocating government measures to boost U.S. businesses overseas and ethics in government.

His zeal for the position—Kim had perfect attendance and made daily speeches on the House floor—earned him the distinction of most outstanding and outspoken legislator among his party's freshmen. Additionally, he was awarded the Ellis Island Medal of Honor, which recognizes immigrants who have made outstanding contributions to the United States, in 1993.

Despite his public image as a humble immigrant—"If you're an immigrant in this country, you can lose everything except an accent. Henry Kissinger had an accent. I'm not elegant. I'm an engineer" (Spiegel and Kang 1993, A1)—Kim distanced himself from the Korean American community during his time in Congress, emphatically stating that he was not its advocate. "I'm not sure how I can help," he remarked (Ward 1992, B3). He supported anti-immigration legislation, and made his stance clear in remarks like "We can't build a wall from the Pacific Ocean to the Gulf of Mexico, but something must be done" (Ward 1992, B3). In fact, Kim pointedly distanced himself from the Asian Pacific American community throughout his years on Capitol Hill. "We're all American, period," he stated emphatically (Lam 1996, 66). He strongly articulated his disapproval of identifying as "American Asian, or Asian American. I think we've got to be more careful about hyphenating all the time" (Lam 1996, 66).

His dissociation drew criticism from other Asian Americans in Washington, such as Phil Tajitsu Nash, who observed that "Kim was reluctant to participate in Asian Pacific American activities or to hire Asian Pacific American staff. He seemed uncomfortable with his fellow Asian Pacific American legislators." Another remarked, "He was shown a hell of a lot of bipartisan comradeship by his other colleagues of APA background and other APA political activists. Yet, he personally attacked or bad-mouthed us" (Nash 1998).

Unfortunately, the contentiousness of the Congressman's career on Capitol Hill did not stop with the immigrant issue. Kim, re-elected in 1994 and 1996, again found himself mired in controversy as charges of campaign finance infractions, including upwards of $250,000 in illegal contributions, resurfaced. He had denied wrongdoing for several years but eventually pleaded guilty to misdemeanor charges and was sentenced in 1998, along with his wife June, to two months of electronically-monitored home detention, thousands of dollars in fines, and 200 hours of community service. His conduct has rendered the future of his political career tenuous. For example, in a March 1998 *Asian Week* article, Nash commented on the "total lack of support for him from any of his natural allies [Asian Pacific Americans] since his sentencing" (Nash 1998).

Still, regardless of his ambiguous standing in the Asian American community and his somewhat spotty career record, Kim represents for many the possibilities for the foreign-born in America. "When I ran, a lot of people told me I wasn't going to make it because I'm Asian. The election gives the message to the whole world that this is nonsense," he once noted (Ward 1992, B3). Regrettably, Kim realizes that his accomplishments are bittersweet. "I have tried hard to live honestly without violating laws. My disappointment is indescribable.... My dream was to use this opportunity to become a great congressman" (Spiegel and Kang 1993, A1).

### Sources

Hong, Terry. "Jay C. Kim." In *Notable Asian Americans*, ed. Helen Zia and Susan B. Gall. Detroit, MI: Gale Research Inc., 1995, pp. 155–156.
"Jay C. Kim." *AP Candidate Bios*. The Associated Press Political Service, 1996.
"Jay Kim." *Congressional Yellow Book*. Leadership Directories, Inc. 1997.
Lam, Karen. "The Man Outside: Karen Lam Talks to Jay Kim, Congressional Maverick." A. *Magazine*. August/September 1996, pp. 34–35, 48, 66.
Nash, Phil Tajitsu. "Jay Kim Couldn't Hide: Should He Run?" *Asian Week*. March 19–25, 1998.
Spiegel, Claire, and K. Connie Kang. "The Fast, Rocky Rise of Jay Kim: As the First Asian Immigrant Elected to the Congress, His Success Was a Cause of Celebration and Hope for Millions of Other Asian-Americans. Now, Federal Investigations Have Shaken His Career." *Los Angeles Times*. 27 October 1993, p. 1. Home Edition.
Ward, Mike. "Local Elections/41st Congressional District: Republican Kim Would Make History with Win." *Los Angeles Times*. 21 June 1992, Orange County Edition, p. 3.

# Jean Sadako King

**Born:** 6 December 1925, Honolulu, Hawaii.

**Education:** B.A., University of Hawaii, 1948; M.A., New York University, 1946; M.F.A., University of Hawaii, 1968.

**Positions Held:** Hawaii State Representative, 1972–1974, State Senator, 1974–1978; and Lieutenant Governor, 1978–1982.

**Summary:** Jean Sadako King is the first Asian Pacific American to be elected to public office at the statewide level. She served as Hawaii's Lieutenant Governor from 1978 to 1982.

### Early Years

Jean Sadako McKillop, was born on 6 December 1925 in Honolulu, Hawaii. Her father, William Donald McKillop, was a Canadian-Scot who had journeyed to the Big Island to work as Captain Cook's first postmaster and later became a bookkeeper at the Captain Cook Coffee Company. Chiyo Murakami, her mother, was the Nisei daughter of Japanese coffee growers in Kona. Describing her mother years later, King recalled, "Looking at her picture, I'd also say she was pretty independent minded with a very clear sense of what she thought was important, and right." One such conviction was to marry McKillop despite the rarity of interracial unions in the early 1920s. "My mother did a very courageous thing when she married my dad," said King (Saiki 1985, 119).

After the wedding, the young couple moved to a house in the area near Piikoi and Beretania Streets in Honolulu. It was in this home that King was born. The family moved to two other locations around the city, and as a result, King attended Likelike School, Aliiolani School, and English Standard School, during her early years. Encouraged to engage in creative activities by her third grade teacher, Mrs. Hurd, one of King's favorite pastimes as a child was writing stories, which she would read aloud to her classmates. She also cultivated her literary talents crafting tales in Japanese school, which she attended every day after regular school as well as Saturdays.

## Education

King spent her junior and senior high school years at Sacred Heart Academy, an institution known for its rigorous academic standards. "It was quite a sacrifice for my parents to send us to private schools ... but my mother was determined we have what she saw as the best education available," she explained (Saiki 1985, 121–122). King took full advantage of her opportunities, graduating as class valedictorian and editor of the school yearbook. "When I was growing up, I was never given the feeling there were things I couldn't do," she said (Chu 1989, 415). She also balanced her coursework with a full load of after-school activities, including Japanese dancing, tap, hula, and typing and shorthand lessons, as suggested by her pragmatic father. The skills paid off soon thereafter, when she landed a job as a billing clerk at Honolulu Iron Works during World War II. Due to her demonstrated speed and accuracy, she was soon promoted to a stenographer position.

Following her graduation, King enrolled at the University of Hawaii. On campus, she maintained an active schedule, working as a class assistant for a psychology lab, tutoring English for members of the swim team, serving as a class officer and co-features editor of the UH newspaper, *Ka Leo*, and voted a Ka Palalpala Cosmopolitan Beauty Queen and Rainbow Relay Queen. After earning her B.A. in 1948, she journeyed to the mainland to attend New York University for its history masters' program. Her MA thesis on the 1946 Hawaii sugar strike was drawn in part from her personal experience with grassroots politics on the islands. "The '46 sugar strike was the first time I went door to door," she said. "I was a university student and helped hand out union leaflets" (Saiki 1985, 122). Finally, over a decade later, she returned to school for her MFA degree from the University of Hawaii in 1968. For her second masters' thesis, she organized the production and presentation of the English premiere of a contemporary Japanese anti-war play by Miyamoto Ken.

## Career Highlights

Politics, however, remained a powerful draw for King. As with many of her Asian Pacific American peers, she decided to join the Democratic Party—despite her parents' Republican affiliation—for its relatively inclusive, multiethnic orientation. In 1972, she served as campaign manager for Japanese American standout Patsy Mink, after having previously served as a Senate staff member, and a researcher and speech writer for Hawaii's Speaker of the House. She also inaugurated a 10-year turn in public office, serving one term each as state representative (1972–1974), state senator (1974–1978), and lieutenant governor (1978–1982), becoming one of the two highest ranking Asian Pacific American women in a statewide elected position to date. Interestingly, King did not view her race or gender as any type of disadvantage in her political work. "In Hawaii, being an Asian woman is not an impediment since there are quite a number of us. . . . Ethnicity is just a means of identification, not discrimination," she explained (Chu 1989, 411). However, she ran unsuccessfully for governor in 1982 and retired from politics thereafter.

King, formerly married to James A. King from 1948 to 1972 and mother of a son and daughter, summarized her political philosophy as such: "There are things I care a lot about. What Hawaii is like, what it's going to be like five years from now, ten, twenty-five. Whether government is open, and responsive. Whether or not people, our people here, have choices. It's very very important for an individual to feel that she or he has a choice, a say about what their life is like, what direction it's going—whether it's their family life, their education, their job, their environment, their sense of security in old age" (Saiki 1985, 125).

Over the span of her career, King devoted her energies to a number of salient issues, including affordable housing, the admittance of the general public into official government meetings, and environmental preservation vis-à-vis urban development. Most significantly, she chaired the first Environmental Protection Committee in the state house and its sister organization in the Senate, overseeing the passage of the 1972 Environmental Protection Act and the 1975 Shoreline Protection Act.

### Sources

Chu, Judy. "Asian Pacific American Women in Mainstream Politics." In *Making Waves: An Anthology of Writings By and About Asian American Women.* New York: Beacon Press, 1989, pp. 405–421.

"King, Jean Sadako." In *The Asian American Encyclopedia*, Volume 3, ed. Franklin Ng. New York: Marshall Cavendish, 1995, pp. 829–830.

Saiki, Patsy Sumie. *Japanese Women in Hawaii: The First 100 Years.* Honolulu: Kisaku, Inc., 1985, pp. 116–134.

## Yuri Kochiyama

**Full Name at Birth:** Mary Nakahara.

**Born:** 1921, San Pedro, California.

**Education:** Compton Junior College, 1939–1941.

**Positions Held:** Member of numerous leftist political organizations, including Nisei-Sino Service Organization, the Hiroshima Maidens (atomic bomb survivors), Congress of Racial Equality (CORE), Asian Americans for Action, and Republic of New Afrika. Participant in political campaigns on issues concerning political prisoners including Mumia Abu-Jamal, Yu Kikumara, and David Wong, along with movements for black revolutionary nationalism, Third World liberation, Japanese American redress and reparations, jobs for workers of color, and ethnic studies on university campuses.

**Awards, Honors:** Japanese American Citizens League Civic Award; Named to A. *Magazine*'s 100 Most Influential Asian Americans of the Decade, 1999.

**Summary:** Internationally known human rights activist Yuri Kochiyama has been involved in numerous capacities in leftist political organizations dating back to the 1950s.

### Early Years

Internationally renowned human rights activist Yuri Kochiyama was born Mary Nakahara in San Pedro, California, in 1921, and lived an "ordinary" childhood and youth until the outbreak of World War II. Politics impacted her life at an early age when her father, Seichi Nakahara, was imprisoned by the FBI in 1941 on false charges of espionage for Japan. As a result of his traumatic detainment, his health suffered, and he died on 21 January 1942, just one day after he was permitted to return home from the federal penitentiary on Terminal Island. Friends and family who attended the funeral were subject to FBI surveillance.

The next year, the entire Nakahara family was among the 120,000 Japanese Americans incarcerated for the duration of World War II in government concentration camps. As for many of her co-ethnics, the experience marked a major watershed period in Kochiyama's life.

At this time, she began her life-long political activism by organizing a letter writing campaign to Nisei men in the armed forces. She also worked with other young internees to open a USO for Japanese American soldiers, who were not permitted at the time to join the regular USO. Kochiyama also met her future husband, Bill Kochiyama, a GI who was visiting the Jerome, Arkansas camp where she was imprisoned.

## Career Highlights

The Kochiyamas married after the war and moved to New York City, where they raised six children: Billy, Audee, Aichi, Eddie, Jimmy, and Tommy. During the 1950s and 1960s, the Kochiyamas became increasingly involved in a number of human rights organizations and issues, including the Nisei-Sino Service Organization, the Hiroshima Maidens (atomic bomb survivors), Congress of Racial Equality (CORE), and Asian Americans for Action. After settling in Harlem in 1963, the Kochiyamas joined the Harlem Parents Committee and enrolled in the Harlem Freedom School, along with their three eldest children, to learn African American history. Their home became a virtual community center throughout the years as countless guests passed through the Kochiyama family home to share their experiences and ideas on various political movements. One such visitor was Malcolm X. Kochiyama met him at a hearing for her son at a Brooklyn court on 16 October 1963. She relayed the encounter to *Giant Robot* magazine in 1998:

> I remember when he walked into the foyer of the court, all the young blacks ran down and they circled him and they were shaking his hand, but since I wasn't black, I didn't feel like I should go down there. There was that article a few months before in *Life* magazine where a white gal came into Harlem and saw Malcolm at the Shabazz restaurant and said, "What can I do for you Malcolm?" and he just said, "Nothing," and she went away crying. I thought, "Wow, that could be me making the same mistake. But as I saw all those blacks around him, I kept thinking, "Gee, doggone it," I wanted to meet him so much and I asked one of the court leaders, "Do you think there's any chance of meeting him?" and he said, "Why don't you try and see? All he can do is tell you to go away."
>
> So I went slowly down there until I was 15 feet away, watching them, and then all of a sudden, in one instant, he looked up almost looking like he was wondering, "What is this old Asian woman doing?" But I thought it was now or never, so I went right over there and said, "Malcolm, can I shake your hand?" "Of course," he said, "For what?" and I said, "Oh, I want to congratulate you." And he said, "What for?" I said, "Well, for what you're doing for your people." He asked, "What am I doing for my people?" and I had to think of a quick answer and said, "You're showing direction." And all of a sudden he just looked up and smiled and he came out of the circle onto the other side and shook my hand. (*Giant Robot* 1998)

She then added, however, that she differed with him on his opinions regarding the issue of integration. He then extended an invitation to her to visit him at his office to probe the matter further.

Although she never made it to his office, Yuri Kochiyama began attending the meetings of Malcolm X's Organization of Afro-American Unity and then later the Malcolm X Liberation School. The Kochiyamas invited Malcolm X to their home in 1964 to meet delegates of the Hiroshima-Nagasaki Peace Mission. That day, she recalled, "Everyone was so impressed by him" and his ideas linking racism with capitalism and international politics (*Giant Robot* 1998).

Malcolm X kept in contact with the Kochiyamas during his travels to Africa and Asia. Kochiyama was the one to cradle his head at the Audubon Ballroom in New York immediately following his assassination in

1965. His influence on Kochiyama's world perspective was so profound that even after his death, she continued to apply his ideology to her personal struggle for human rights. In 1969, Yuri joined the Republic of New Afrika (RNA), a Black Nationalist group. At that time, she also began to use her Japanese name, Yuri, in lieu of her Anglo name, "Mary," to symbolize her beliefs.

Kochiyama's involvement in human rights campaigns spanned the 1970s, 1980s, and 1990s. She worked on issues concerning political prisoners including Mumia Abu-Jamal, Yu Kikumara, and David Wong, black revolutionary nationalism, Third World liberation, Japanese American redress and reparations, jobs for workers of color, and ethnic studies on university campuses. She has actively participated in organizing annual Day of Remembrance events, the Malcolm X Commemoration Committee, and the W.E.B. Du Bois Foundation. She also lectured extensively at colleges across the country. She participated in a 1977 takeover of the Statue of Liberty by a Puerto Rican National Rights Group. "We had to do something that would get the media to put enough pressure to get the five [Puerto Rican nationals] out of prison," she recalled in *Giant Robot*. "I was the only Asian.... We held it for nine hours.... It was exciting" (*Giant Robot* 1998).

Despite suffering a stroke in the 1990s, she continued to labor selflessly for the causes close to her heart. In 1998, she spent one quarter at the University of California at Los Angeles Asian American Studies Center as a scholar-in-residence. During this time, she hosted several informal brown-bag lunches with students during which she posed the simple, but important question to the newest generation of activists, "What is the mission of your generation?" In a series of speeches delivered on college campuses in 1996, Kochiyama offered a possible answer to her own challenge. "This generation's mission just might be that of 'expanding one's horizon and decolonizing one's mind,' that the cross-over to making coalitions, working with and supporting others, can be better facilitated.... Because you are young and have dreams and want to do something meaningful, that in itself, makes you our future and our hope" (Kochiyama 1998).

Diane C. Fujino, Kochiyama's biographer, commented on the significance of Kochiyama's activism in Asian American and American politics and history in her article, "Revolution's from the Heart: The Making of an Asian American Woman Activist, Yuri Kochiyama":

> I see Yuri's greatest strengths as her ability to build bridges between communities and movements, and her deep love for people, grounded in revolutionary policies.... Some may interpret Yuri's actions as those of a humble, non confrontational, other-focused, behind-the-scenes worker perpetuating the stereotypic passive role of the Asian American woman. But as a revolutionary nationalist, Yuri hardly fits this characterization. Whether or not she considers herself to be one, Yuri is a leader. She defies stereotypes, takes radical stances on controversial issues, inspires hundreds of young people to join the movement, and bridges various liberation struggles throughout the world.

### Sources

"The A. 100: 100 Most Influential Asian Americans of the Decade." *A. Magazine*. October/November 1999, p. 84.

Fujino, Diane C. "Revolution's from the Heart: The Making of an Asian American Woman Activist, Yuri Kochiyama.'" In *Dragon Ladies: Asian American Feminists Breathe Fire*, ed. Sonia Shah. Boston: South End Press, 1997, pp. 169–181.

*Giant Robot* staff. "Yellow Power." *Giant Robot*. Spring 1998, pp. 61–81.

Kochiyama, Yuri. *Discover Your Mission: Selected Speeches and Writings*, ed. Russell Muranaka et al. Los Angeles: UCLA Asian American Studies Center, 1998.

# Harold Hongju Koh

Harold Koh, U.S. assistant secretary of state for democracy, human rights and labor, in 1999. (Burhan Ozbilici, AP/Wide World Photos)

**Born:** 1954.

**Education:** B.A., Harvard University, 1975; Honours B.A., Magdalen College, Oxford University, 1977; J.D., Harvard University, 1980.

**Positions Held:** Assistant Secretary of State for Democracy, Human Rights, and Labor, 1998-2000.

**Awards, Honors:** Richard E. Neustadt Award for best book on American presidency, American Political Science Association 1991; Guggenheim Fellowship, 1996; Asian American Bar Association of New York's Outstanding Lawyer of the Year Award, 1997; Named to A. Magazine's 100 Most Influential Asian Americans of the Decade, 1999.

**Summary:** Harold Hongju Koh, the Assistant Secretary of State for Democracy, Human Rights, and Labor, was one of the highest ranking Asian Pacific Americans in the Clinton Administration. He is also the first Korean American cabinet member in the United States.

## Early Years and Education

Harold Hongju Koh has experienced the repercussions of international relations from his earliest days. As a 6-year-old, the American-born Koh witnessed his father, a HLS-trained senior United Nations diplomat, renounce his Korean homeland for life as a political exile. The profound impression of his father's public refusal to serve the South Korean military regime never left the future diplomat. Noting the irony of the situation, he recently observed, "[Now,] I am assistant secretary for human rights, and South Korea is free and diplomatic" (*Harvard Law Bulletin* 2000).

Koh earned his B.A. from Harvard University in 1975, a second bachelor's degree from Oxford University's Magdalen College in 1977, and a J.D. from his alma mater, Harvard, in 1980.

## Career Highlights

After graduation, Harold Hongju Koh taught at a number of prestigious institutions around the world, including Magdalen and All Souls Colleges at Oxford, the Hague Academy of International Law, the University of Toronto, and the George Washington University Law Center. Koh also authored over 70 articles on international law, human rights, constitutional law, and international business and trade, along with several books on similar subjects.

Koh's accomplishments have earned him repeated recognition, including the 1991 Richard E. Neustadt Award from the American Political Science Association for the best book on the American Presidency and a 1996 Guggenheim Fellowship. Additionally, he has received an honorary doctor of laws from the

City University of New York Law School and the Asian American Bar Association's 1997 Outstanding Lawyer of the Year award. In 1997, *American Lawyer* magazine named him one of the nation's 45 top public sector attorneys under the age of 45.

Before accepting his position in Washington, Koh clerked for Judge Malcolm Richard Wilkey of the United States Court of Appeals for the DC Circuit Court and Justice Harry A. Blackmun of the United States Supreme Court. In addition to his work in private practice and at the Office of Legal Counsel at the U.S. Department of Justice, he also served as Yale University's Gerard C. and Bernice Latrobe Smith Professor of International Law and director of the school's Orville H. Schell, Jr. Center for International Human Rights. In the early 1990s, he represented human rights cases before the U.S. Supreme Court against the federal government regarding its policy of repatriating refugees from countries such as Haiti and Cuba.

Nominated Assistant Secretary of State for Democracy, Human Rights and Labor by President William Jefferson Clinton on 10 September 1998, Koh was confirmed by the Senate on 21 October 1998. As Secretary of State Madeline Albright's "right-hand aide," Koh espoused three basic principles in his approach to human rights work: advocating for human rights based on principle, not politics; speaking the truth about human rights conditions, abuses, and policies, and understanding universal human rights to be fully consistent with Asian values as he learned them and as they are practiced by Asian communities in the United States and abroad. "My job is to try to advance and increase human freedom through reporting, persuasion, criticism, and advocacy," he explained (*Harvard Law Bulletin* 2000).

Among Koh's goals as Assistant Secretary of State were focusing mainstream U.S. foreign policy on human and worker rights concerns and utilizing transnational legal processes and a variety of political strategies to facilitate the incorporation of human and worker rights approaches by other governments. He set high standards for himself. "At the end of each day, I try to think about who has been helped by what I have done. If I don't think I have done enough, I try to do more the next day," he avowed (*Harvard Law Bulletin* 2000).

Koh appreciated the challenges of his position, including its global mandate and the opportunities it affords to witness "the indomitability of the human spirit" (*Harvard Law Bulletin* 2000).

For Koh, named one of A. *Magazine's* 100 Most Influential Asian Americans of the Decade, the toughest obstacle of all as assistant secretary of state may have been balancing the demands of his home life in New Haven with his career in Washington. He is dedicated to participating in the daily family life of his wife, Mary Christy Fisher, and his children, Emily and William. "It's unbelievably restorative to come back from a war zone and hear your kids talk about Little League and ballet lessons," he says. "The quest for human rights, is, above all, a struggle to give people a normal life. I am fighting to give other people this kind of normalcy" (*Harvard Law Bulletin* 2000).

### Sources

The Embassy of the United States of America, Helsinki, Finland Web site: www.usembassy.fi/washfile/1998/09101998_407.htm [Accessed 4 January 2000].

Harvard Law Bulletin Web site: www.law.harvard.edu/alumni/bulletin/article1b.html [Accessed 4 January 2000].

Lee, Denny. "Harold Hongju Koh." In "The A.100: 100 Most Influential Asian Americans of the Decade." A. *Magazine*. October/November 1999, p. 92.

www.minorities-jb.com/asian/politics/archives/koh9.html [Accessed 4 January 2000].

U.S. Department of State Web site: www.state.gov/www/about_state/biography/koh.html [Accessed 4 January 2000].

# Stewart Kwoh

Stewart Kwoh. (Courtesy of Stewart Kwoh)

**Born:** 16 September 1948, Nanking, China.

**Education:** B.A., University of California at Los Angeles, 1970.; J.D., University of California at Los Angeles, 1974.

**Positions Held:** President, Southern California Chinese Lawyers' Association, 1988–1989; Commissioner, Future Courts of Commission, 1991–1993; Founding Board Member and Vice Chair, National Asian Pacific Legal Consortium, 1992–present; Executive Director, Asian Pacific American Legal Center of Southern California, 1983–present.

**Awards, Honors:** ACLU award, 1993; President's Award, Southern Christian Leadership Conference of Greater L.A. and Martin Luther King Legacy Association; Public Affairs Award, CORO, 1993; Mayor's Awardee, L.A. City Human Relations Commission, 1996; Civil Rights Award, Chinese American Civil Rights Organization, 1996; Honorary Doctor of Law Degree, Williams College, Massachusetts, 1996; Civil Rights Award, Japanese American Citizens League, 1997; Macarthur Foundation Fellowship, 1998.

**Summary:** Stewart Kwoh is the president and executive director of the Asian Pacific American Legal Center of Southern California, the nation's largest and most diverse legal assistance and civil rights organization targeting Asian Pacific Americans. In June 1998, Kwoh was named a Macarthur Foundation Fellow, becoming the first Asian Pacific American attorney and human rights activist to receive this highly prestigious honor, commonly known as a "genius grant."

## Early Years

Stewart Kwoh was born on 16 September 1948 in Nanking, China, to Chinese Americans Edwin and Beulah (Quo) Kwoh. Kwoh's overseas birth reflects the transnational history of his family; his father Edwin was sent by Kwoh's great-grandfather, the first Presbyterian minister in China, to America to study. After World War II, Edwin returned to his homeland with his American-born wife Beulah, in hopes of helping to rebuild the war-torn country. Two months after the birth of their son, the Kwohs traveled first to Shanghai and then back to the United States, where they settled in Los Angeles. Facing racism and discrimination in the area job market, the Ivy League–educated Edwin became a salesman, while Beulah, a graduate of both the University of California, Berkeley, and the University of Chicago, taught community college courses before going on to become a Hollywood actress.

The young Kwoh cultivated a socially and politically conscious outlook from an early age, due in large part to his religious upbringing and the civil rights movement. As a student in the city he met a number of other youth from varying backgrounds through his involvement in the Brotherhood USA Camp of the National Conference of Christians and Jews.

## Education

After graduating from Los Angeles' John Marshall High School, Kwoh attended the University of California, Los Angeles (UCLA), where he continued to develop his interest in social and political issues, serving as the president of the Asian American Student Alliance, supporting the establishment of the Asian American Studies Center, protesting against the Vietnam War, and tutoring immigrant children in Chinatown.

A pre-med major at UCLA, Kwoh earned his bachelor of arts degree in 1970. Before continuing on to law school, he spent a brief period in Hong Kong studying in Chinese. He then returned to his alma mater, from which he received his J.D. degree in 1974.

Fresh out of law school, Kwoh opened the Law Office of Fay and Kwoh from 1975 to 1978 and the Law Office of Kwoh and Ono from 1979 to 1982. The following year, he co-founded the Asian Pacific American Legal Center (APALC) of Southern California with a number of other attorneys and community leaders who envisioned providing the growing Asian Pacific American populace with multilingual, culturally sensitive legal services and education. "We decided the time had come for a publicly supported legal center," Kwoh explained. "We knew at the grass-roots level that we weren't the 'model minority'" (Yokoi 1993, 6).

As the executive director of the APALC since its inception, Kwoh has guided the organization to its premier position as the nation's largest and most diverse legal assistance and civil rights institution that specifically targets Asian Pacific Americans, offering guidance on such issues as citizenship, domestic violence, exploitative labor, and government benefits. "We see ourselves as service providers and advocates for the Asian Pacific American community and as bridge builders with the larger community of Los Angeles," stated Kwoh (Yokoi 1993, 6). Among these "bridge building" endeavors are the Multicultural Collaborative, a committee of 11 minority organizations dedicated to designing a comprehensive plan for human relations in Los Angeles which Kwoh helped to establish after the 1992 civil uprising. Kwoh has also facilitated the development of a joint dispute resolution program between the Martin Luther King Dispute Resolution Center and the Asian Pacific American Dispute Resolution Center which aims to resolve interethnic conflicts by teaming African American, Korean American, and other mediators. Another significant project supported by the APALC in tandem with the Southern Christian Leadership Conference and the Central American Resource Center is the Leadership Development in Interethnic Relations (LDIR) which has trained hundreds of participants in human relations skills.

In addition to the APALC, Kwoh maintains active involvement in a diverse array of professional and civic capacities. Among others, he has taught courses at the UCLA Law School on civil rights and "Asian Americans and the Law" and serves on the Council on Foreign Relations, the California Citizens Commission on Higher Education, the Asian Pacific Revolving Loan Fund, the Pat Brown Institute of Public Affairs, and the National Asian Pacific American Legal Consortium, the nation's first pan-Asian civil rights organization, of which he is a founding board member and vice chair.

For his many accomplishments, Stewart Kwoh, the husband of Patricia Lee Kwoh and father of Steven and Nathan Kwoh, has received numerous accolades, including an honorary doctorate in 1996 from Williams College in Massachusetts, civil rights awards from the Chinese American Civil Rights Organization and the Japanese American Citizens League, and a mayor's award from the Los Angeles City Human Rights Commission. In 1998, Kwoh was named a Macarthur Foundation Fellow, commonly known as a "genius grant," becoming the first Asian American attorney and human rights activist to receive this highly prestigious recognition.

Kwoh, described by colleagues and other notables as a "visionary," and "master bridge-builder," articulates his life and community vision as: "The greatest dream I have is for Asian Pacific Americans to be treated as an equal. In the meantime, we have to build up our institutions. We need to develop a whole system of values, justice and equality and to be able to harmonize it within the Asian Pacific American community, then with other groups" (Kang 1995, A1).

## Sources

Kang, K. Connie. "Building Bridges to Equality." *Los Angeles Times*. 7 January 1995, p. A1.

"Kwoh, Stewart." *Who's Who among Asian Americans 1994/95*. Detroit: Gale Research, 1994, p. 315.

Yokoi, Iris. "Asian Legal Center Celebrates 10 Years." *Los Angeles Times*. 10 October 1993, p. 6.

# Daphne Kwok

Daphne Kwok. (Photo by Hilary Schwab)

**Born:** 22 May 1962

**Education:** B.A., Wesleyan University, 1984; M.PA., Baruch City College, 1989.

**Positions Held:** Executive Director of Organization of Chinese Americans, Inc., since September 1990.

**Awards, Honors:** Presidential Classroom's 25th Anniversary Outstanding Alumni Award; Member, American Jewish Committee's 1997 National Women's Leadership Group delegation to Israel; Asian Americans for Equality Dream of Equality Award, 1998; Delegate, 1999 American Swiss Foundation's Young Leaders Conference in Vevey, Switzerland; Named one of *A. Magazine*'s 100 Most Influential Asian Americans of the Decade, 1999.

**Summary:** Daphne Kwok, one of the country's most visible Asian Pacific American activists, is the executive director of the Organization of Chinese Americans, Inc., a national, non-profit, civil rights organization.

## Early Years and Education

Daphne Kwok began her life's passion, Asian American advocacy, in her teen years when she founded the International Club at her high school. Her enthusiasm persisted at Wesleyan University in Middletown, Connecticut, where she presided over the campus's Asian Interest Group as an undergraduate. Following her graduation in 1984, when she earned her B.A. in East Asian studies and music, Kwok founded and chaired the Wesleyan Asian Alumni Council.

## Career Highlights

These accomplishments mark the beginning of Kwok's eventful career focusing on the concerns of Asian Pacific Americans. Among her many involvements are the Organization of Chinese American Women, the National Democratic Council of Asian and Pacific Americans, and the D.C. Mayor's Office for Asian and Pacific Islander Affairs. In 1985, she chaired the Northern Virginia Asian American Democratic Committee, which supported the successful Virginia Gubernatorial campaign of Gerald Baliles that year. In 1997, she engaged in a similar project, serving on the Northern Virginia Asian Pacific Americans for Don Beye for Governor Task Force.

Armed with her masters in public administration degree from Baruch College of New York—a diploma she earned as part of a one-year National Urban Fellowship in 1989—Kwok accepted the Executive Directorship of Organization of Chinese Americans, Inc., a national, nonprofit civil rights organization, in September 1990. Previously, she had been an OCA member since 1985 and president and board member of the OCA's Northern Virginia Chapter.

As OCA's head administrator, Daphne Kwok juggles several important responsibilities: overseeing the programs and services for 44 chapters and 35 college affiliates representing over 10,000 members, monitoring salient issues pertaining to not only Chinese Americans but the Asian Pacific American community at large. She also manages the headquarters staff, coordinates the OCA National Convention, and solicits funding for the organization. She served as project director for federal educational grant programs on employment discrimination, drunk driving, and AIDS. She is a major media representative for the community, having made numerous television and print media appearances.

In 1996, Kwok coordinated the National Asian Pacific American Voter Registration Campaign which involved 19 different national Asian Pacific American organizations. The successful movement registered over 70,000 voters and produced a celebrity-laden Public Service Announcement proclaiming the Get-Out-The-Vote message directed at students. The following year, Kwok was chosen as the interim chair of the National Council of Asian Pacific Americans, the first national network of Asian Pacific American social welfare organizations. Kwok was formally elected as chair of NCAPA in May 1999.

During the midst of anti-Asian sentiment in government affairs in the late 1990s, Kwok stood as a firm defender of Asian Pacific American rights. Among her other contributions, Kwok testified before the Congressional Asian Pacific Caucus on the impact of federal counter intelligence and security investigations on Asian Pacific Americans at the Department of Energy in 1999. She also expressed her views on behalf of the APA community before the U.S. Commission on Civil Rights regarding the implications of the treatment of Asian Pacific Americans as a result of the 1997 campaign finance controversy.

In her "spare time," Kwok continues to maintain active involvement with her alma mater, Wesleyan. She was chosen to serve a three-year term as an Alumni Elected Trustee of the university in 1991, the first Asian Pacific American to do so in the history of the school. She also headed Wesleyan's Asian/Asian American Study Group on Admissions and was vice chair of the board's student affairs committee. From 1994 to 1997, she chaired the Wesleyan Washington, D.C. Alumni Council, and in 1997, she became the agent for the class of 1984.

Kwok has received a myriad of accolades for her dedication to the civil rights of Asian Pacific Americans. Her honors include the Presidential Classroom's 25th Anniversary Outstanding Alumni Award, a place on the American Jewish Committee's 1997 National Women's Leadership Group delegation to Israel, the 1998 Asian Americans for Equality Dream of Equality Award, and a delegate position to the 1999 American Swiss Foundation's Young Leaders Conference in Vevey, Switzerland.

Named one of A. *Magazine*'s 100 Most Influential Asian Americans of the Decade, in 1999, Kwok explained the motivation behind her life's work: "My interest in empowering Asian Americans is what drives me" (Lee 1999, 83).

## Source

Lee, Denny. "Daphne Kwok." In "The A. 100: 100 Most Influential Asian Americans of the Decade." A. *Magazine*. October/November 1999, p. 83.

# L

## Tony Lam

Tony Lam. (Courtesy of Tony Lam)

**Born:** 4 October 1936, Hai Phong Port, North Vietnam.

**Education:** French Baccalaureate General Education Degree, Part I.

**Positions Held:** Member, Westminster City Council, Westminster, California, 1992–present.

**Summary:** Tony Lam is the first Vietnamese American elected to public office in the United States. He has served on the Westminster, California ("Little Saigon") city council since 1992.

### Early Years and Education

Tony Lam was born on 4 October 1936 in North Vietnam's Hai Phong Port. His father, Cat Lam, worked as a teacher and a French clothier, while his mother, Nghien Lam, was a landowner and proprietor of a bakery in the city of Thanh Hoa.

One of seven children, the young Lam became separated from his family in 1946 during the war between the French and the Vietminh. "I had a tough time the first few days," he remembered. "All I had was one [pair of] short[s] and one jacket; at night I slept on the earthen floor" (interview with Ellen D. Wu, 1999). He located a family friend with whom he stayed for a brief period before continuing on to search for his brothers. Along the way, he crossed paths with resistance forces who offered him a job as a cattle herder. Later, when they discovered Lam's vocal talents, they placed him in what he described as a "propaganda team . . . singing from village to village to motivate the populace." After a few months, his brothers found him, and he reunited with the rest of his family in Thanh Hoa (interview with Ellen D. Wu, 1999).

Lam's mother found it difficult to care for her children, however, so Lam and one of his brothers joined the Vietminh military academy soon thereafter. After a year, they ventured back to Hai Phong Port where his father was still living. There, Lam resumed his studies. "While I was in school, I was always one of the best students . . . in any class," he remembered proudly. As a student, Lam maintained an active schedule, working as a professional singer for a variety show to earn his tuition. He also sponsored and coached a soccer team. "[I] was very active then in a lot of ways, always tried to be independent. That's my character," he explained. Additionally, he invested time in learning English from a French record entitled *L'anglais sans pain* (interview with Ellen D. Wu, 1999). His dedication was rewarded after his family moved south following the battle of Dien Bien Phu in 1954. There, directors of a local orphanage asked Lam to serve as a translator for famed U.S. Navy doctor Tom Dooley.

When his father lost his job as a chief accountant with a French dredging company, Tony Lam dropped out of high school to join the French navy in 1955. Describing himself as "thin and tiny" at the time, Lam was 10 pounds below the weight requirement, however, and had to have a friend stand in for him (interview with Ellen D. Wu, 1999). Fortunately, the switch was successful, and Lam was sent first to boot camp before being assigned to a logistical support group while training to be a bookkeeper.

While in the military, Lam was sent to the United States to study American damage control procedures. To prepare, he took several English as a Second Language (ESL) courses. In the end, however, he declined the opportunity since it entailed an additional eight years of service. Nevertheless, he had gained and reinforced valuable linguistic tools that would later prove to be extremely useful.

## Career Highlights

Following his honorable discharge from the military in 1958, Lam secured a position with United States Agency for International Development (USAID) government contracts. As a storekeeper, interpreter, and assistant superintendent to the bridge department, he worked for one year with the American company Johnson, Drake, and Piper to build the Saigon Bien Hoa highway. In 1959, he accepted a job as an interpreter with the Chinese Technical Mission from Taiwan's Joint Commission on Rural Reconstruction (JCRR). Over the course of five years, he was promoted to assistant director of agriculture, traveling to many of Vietnam's provinces to help develop methods to improve agronomy, animal husbandry, fishing, and forestry techniques for farmers. One of his projects, for example, was conducting a survey on hog marketing in Hong Kong.

Next, he returned to USAID under the U.S. embassy as an area specialist and then an assistant director for rural affairs, overseeing all Vietnamese personnel. His tasks at USAID, similar to those with the Chinese Technical Mission's JCRR, also included the formulation of strategic hamlet programs to provide farmers and other villagers with clothing, food, health care, resettlement assistance, and other necessities.

In February 1965, Lam accepted a position with the Rand Corporation. As assistant analyst, he conducted a study for the U.S. Defense Department on motivational forces of the VietCong. Later that year, he was hired by an engineering firm specializing in deep harbor visibility studies as an office manager. From 1965 to 1969, Lam worked as an independent U.S. government contractor, providing construction and stevedoring services.

Government contracting proved to be quite lucrative for Tony Lam, and he was able to build a business with his brother, the Lam

Brothers Corporation, which exported seafood and operated a cold storage facility and fish meal and dehydrated rice companies. Working 18-hour days, Lam amassed a sizable income and was able to provide his family with more than modest surroundings including a 16-bedroom villa, servants, and luxury cars. They enjoyed the fruits of his success until political circumstances put an end to their comfortable lifestyle.

"When Vietnam fell, I fell with it," said Lam. "I lost practically everything" (interview with Ellen D. Wu, 1999). Almost overnight, he transformed from one of the country's wealthy elite to a war refugee. In April 1975, after assisting with mass evacuations at military air bases in Vietnam and the Philippines for 48 hours straight, he fled his homeland to Camp Asan in Agana, Guam.

Once in Guam, he was called to serve as a refugee camp manager by the Marine Corps Commanding Office. For three months, he exercised his leadership skills, assigning refugees to barracks and selecting Vietnamese women to work in the mess halls "so the rice was not half-cooked, not overcooked" (interview with Ellen D. Wu, 1999). He organized ESL classes, arranged for showings of Kung Fu films, beauty pageants, bike races, volleyball contests, and a Fourth of July celebration for entertainment, and set up a post office, camp radio station, and law and order group for Asan's 125,000 residents.

From Guam, Lam moved with his wife Hop, whom he had married in 1961, six children Cathy (Hang), Jackie (Huyen), Phillip (Duong), Robert (Hung), Carol (Hanh), and Napoleon (Hieu), mother-in-law, and two sisters-in-law to Camp Pendleton in El Toro, California. There, he again volunteered as a camp coordinator, assisting with the relocation of 30,000 refugees.

The Lams then spent a brief period in Sarasota, Florida, where they were sponsored, before undergoing secondary migration—typical of Southeast Asian refugees—back to the West Coast. Following a three-day, three-night cross-country bus trip, they moved in with Lam's brother's family and his parents in Huntington Beach, California. The quarters, however, were extremely cramped, so Lam rented a house for his family. Furnishings, however, took longer to acquire. "We slept on the floor. We ate on the floor. Our children studied on the floor," he remembered (interview with Ellen D. Wu, 1999).

Both Lam and his wife worked several jobs to support their large family. "My family, we never go to welfare," he stated. Lam pumped gas at a local service station for minimum wage and landed a second position with a company that manufactured navy practice bombs. His wife, Hop, started first with a mail order business and then added shifts at a medical supplier and a guitar factory. "The first day I picked [her] up, I couldn't recognize her because she [was] covered with dust [from sanding the instruments]," he recalled (interview with Ellen D. Wu, 1999).

In 1978, the Lams purchased their first home in the United States, located in the city of Westminster, California. They chose the area based on its proximity to Asian markets and restaurants in Chinatown and Camp Pendleton employment prospects, in addition to the favorable Orange County climate. In Westminster, Lam's civic involvement flourished. For years, he assisted recent Vietnamese arrivals, who had sought him for help, because he was once a camp manager and because, in his own words, "I never say no to anybody." As a resident of Westminster, he volunteered as a citizens advisor to local schools and attempted to rally his co-ethnics into a mutual assistance group. His new jobs as a deputy district manager with the Equitable Life Insurance Company and as a marketing agent for Air France also afforded him more free time, which he then spent organizing within the community. In 1979, he was elected to one year on the Community Development Council on Orange County's Board of Directors, and in 1981, he headed Westminster's Tet festival. In 1982, Lam gained his U.S. citizenship. The next year he co-founded the Vietnamese American Chamber of Commerce and then served as its third president in 1983.

One of Lam's long-running pet projects has been the designing, development, and promotion of the Little Saigon district in Westminster. "We wanted to create something here that will remind us of who we are," Lam told *Asian Week* in 1996 (Eljera 1996, 13). He lobbied state, county, and city officials with Van Tran, another Vietnamese American and a field representative for a state assemblyman, along with the then-mayor of Westminster, Chuck Smith, for the installment of "Little Saigon" signs along the adjacent 405/22 freeways. Against some opposition, the signs were approved in 1988. The process, however, made it clear to him that his community would need more influence to accomplish its goals. "I realized that it is important to be an elected official to have more weight to talk to others, to get anything done," he stated (interview with Ellen D. Wu, 1999).

As a result, he decided to run for a vacated seat on the Westminster City Council in 1992. One of six candidates, including Jimmy Tong Nguyen, another Vietnamese American, Lam narrowly defeated his closest opponent by a mere 138 votes. Notably, most of his support came from non-Vietnamese at the polls, since only 2,000 Vietnamese Americans out of Westminster's 80,000 total population at the time were registered to vote. With his victory, the self-described "Tax Fighter, Crime Fighter" became the first Vietnamese American to hold elected office in the nation.

In June 1994, Lam participated in a controversial recall election demanded by a local union. He successfully defended his position only to face a second re-election in November of that year. Again, he won, attributing his victories as an "unknown person" in part to his steady dedication. "I walked precinct[s] a lot," he said. "Some slammed the door in front of my face, but I came back again. I explained that I want to serve the city well with my experience, not because I'm a Vietnamese—I'm American, and I'm proud to be an American... voting me in, we can have a good diversity" (interview with Ellen D. Wu, 1999).

After winning his fourth election in 1998, Lam encountered opposition from factions within the Vietnamese community. When he chose not to take a public stand on the controversy surrounding a local merchant's display of pro-communist symbols, picketers boycotted Viendong, his Garden Grove, California restaurant which he opened in 1984. Consequently, he spent $52,000 in legal fees and $13,000 to hire security guards to keep the doors open. "I'm standing firm," he declared in the midst of the demonstrations (interview with Ellen D. Wu, 1999).

As for the future, Lam has no plans to run for mayor of Westminster, believing that he would "divide the community even more," nor does he aspire to bid for state office because of the difficulty of breaking in to California's established political networks. Regardless of the direction his career takes, Lam feels "very proud" of his pioneering efforts. He noted that he is frequently approached by young Vietnamese Americans, encounters that he takes seriously. "I feel that I'm a role model, that I want to help the youngsters as a stepping stone for the next generation. I want them to get into mainstream America and be proud of our heritage as well," he stated. "I want to prove that there's a lot of good citizens that contribute to the mainstream America instead of the negative things" (interview with Ellen D. Wu, 1999).

## Sources

Eljera, Bert. "Big Plans for Little Saigon: Third in a Series on Asian American Cultural Centers in Celebration of Asian American Heritage Month." *Asian Week*. 17 May 1996, p. 13.

Lam, Tony. Interview with Ellen D. Wu. 8 June 1999. Westminster, California.

Mydans, Seth. "A Vietnamese-American Becomes a Political First." *The New York Times*. 16 November 1992, p. A11.

Resume provided by Tony Lam.

# Cheryl Ann Lau

**Born:** 7 December 1944, Hilo, Hawaii.

**Education:** B.M., Indiana University; M.M., Smith College; Ph.D., University of Oregon, Eugene; J.D., University of San Francisco.

**Positions Held:** Nevada Secretary of State, 1991–1994; General Counsel, U.S. House of Representatives, Washington, 1995–1996.

**Awards, Honors:** Ballot News Election Official of the Year; Common Cause "Ethnics in Government" Award.

**Summary:** Cheryl Lau is the first Asian American elected official in the state of Nevada. She served as Nevada's Secretary of State from 1991 to 1994.

## Early Years and Education

Cheryl Ann Lau was born on 7 December 1944 in Hilo, Hawaii. As a young woman on the islands Lau showed promise in the performing arts and spent much of her time practicing the flute and piano as well as playing in a local band. Her interests, which ranged from classical to country, jazz, and even her own compositions, coupled with her talent, led her to the Indiana University School of Music, where she earned her bachelor's degree in flute and piano performance, followed by a masters degree in music education and administration from Smith College, and a Ph.D. in musicology from the University of Oregon, Eugene.

## Career Highlights

Her first step as a doctor of music was to relocate to Taiwan to teach at the College of Chinese Culture and Soochow University. "I wanted to learn a little more about my culture," explained Lau, who is of Chinese ancestry (*Asian Week* 1992, 6). After teaching in the Republic of China, Lau returned home to accept a tenure track position on the faculty of California State University, Sacramento's music department, specializing in musicology. In time, she became the director of the graduate division as well.

Mid-career, a tragic turn of events redirected Lau from her music professorship to the legal profession. "My first husband was murdered, so I wanted to learn more about the criminal justice system," she explained (Lee 1994, 3). She then left CSU to work as a researcher for Nevada's Department of Transportation and to enroll at the University of San Francisco law school. She passed the bar exam in 1986 and then accepted a deputy attorney general position under Nevada Attorney General Brian McKay to sharpen her legal skills and understanding of contract policies.

A transition from law to government was the next logical step for Lau, who has had a long-standing interest in politics. Despite minimal experience as a mailroom employee and a telephone bank campaign worker, Lau plunged into the 1990 race for Nevada's Secretary of State. The position had been vacated just shortly before when the former Secretary of State took over the outgoing Attorney General's seat. In an unusual victory, Lau soundly defeated her Democratic opponent by 30,000 or nearly 10 percent, of the votes.

Lau's small business background undoubtedly appealed to her Republican supporters. Her parents, Ralph Ky and Beatrice Lau, owned Hilo Dry Goods, a modest clothing and souvenir store in Hawaii, which they steadily rebuilt from bankruptcy. Working in the family's shop made her aware of both the concerns and accomplishments of the country's small business owners and their employees.

While in office, Lau tackled a number of issues dealing with business, including reforms in corporation laws to facilitate the license applications process. Changes in Nevada's elections protocol earned Lau recognition as the Common Cause Ethics in Government and *Ballot News* Election Official of the Year awardee. Additionally, as chair of Nevada's Women's Commission, she addressed domestic violence, the glass ceiling, and female role models. Other areas of interest included security legislation and Lake Tahoe preservation.

As Nevada's Secretary of State, Lau continued to be active within her party. In 1992, she became the vice chair of the Republican National Convention's platform committee. Again, Lau used her position to highlight the roles of business and economy in government.

At the close of her term in 1994, Lau ran for Governor of Nevada, but lost in the Republican primary to state assemblyman Jim Gibbons. The defeat did not halt her political career, however; the following year, Newt Gingrich named her general counsel to the U.S. House of Representatives. She also accepted the chair position of Asian Americans for Dole-Kemp.

Lau has been a voice for Asian American women in politics. "I think the world has changed so much that an Asian woman can be anything she wants to be," she remarked. "We have special characteristics, like patience and grace, which make us suited to leadership roles. I hope we see more Asian women in business and politics" (Lee 1994, 3). While she is optimistic, she is also realistic. She was one of a number of Asian Pacific Islander petitioners who approached the U.S. Civil Rights Commission about the anti-Asian bias in the federal investigation of the Clinton administration's fundraising practices. Lau seems to recognize the inevitable "spokesperson" labeling of all Asian Pacific Islanders in politics and government. "I have tried to travel to other states and speak to Asian groups, encouraging them to get involved," she said. "I feel a sense of responsibility in doing well—not bringing disgrace or doubt in our culture and traditions" (Lee 1994, 3).

## Sources

"Community Profile: Cheryl Lau, Nevada Secretary of State." *Asian Week*. 15 May 1992, p. 6.

Gupta, Himanee. "Cheryl Lau." In *Notable Asian Americans*, ed. Helen Zia and Susan B. Gall. Detroit, MI: Gale Research, Inc., 1995, pp. 177–178.

Lee, Bobbie. "Cheryl Lau Has Visions of a Bold, New Nevada." *Asian Week*. 2 September 1994, p. 3.

Mukherjee, Tiarra. "Political Clout: Why Asian Americans Don't Have It . . . What We Can Do to Get It." A. *Magazine*. 31 October 1992, p. 10.

Wong, Bill. "Yellow Pearls: Ethnic Bonding." *Asian Week*. 25 September 1997, p. 6.

Wu, Frank H. "Washington Journal: The John Huang Affair." *Asian Week*. 7 November 1996, p.11.

# Gordon Lau

**Born:** 22 August 1941, Honolulu, Hawaii.

**Died:** 19 April 1998, San Francisco, California.

**Education:** B.A., University of San Francisco; J.D., University of San Francisco.

**Positions Held:** Member, San Francisco Board of Supervisors, 1977–1979; Chair, San Francisco–Shanghai sister city committee, 1981–1988.

**Awards, Honors:** Gordon J. Lau Elementary School, San Francisco, named for Lau (posthumously), 1998.

**Summary:** Gordon Lau was the second Asian Pacific American to sit on the powerful Board of Supervisors of San Francisco with his appointment in 1977. Lau then became the first elected Asian Pacific American member of the board later that year.

## Early Years and Education

A Chinese American, Gordon Lau was born on 22 August 1941 in Honolulu, Hawaii to a warehouse man and clerk typist. At the age of 12, his family relocated to San Francisco to obtain higher quality medical care for his mother, Elizabeth. There, Lau spent the remainder of his formative years, graduating from Chinatown's St. Mary's Elementary School and St. Ignatius High School. He then earned his B.A. in history and J.D. from the University of San Francisco.

## Career Highlights

Armed with his law degree, Lau launched an active career in grassroots and electoral politics. In the 1960s, he joined the Young Turks, an Asian American community-oriented organization that worked within the Chinese Community. The group pushed for civil rights, health and employment issues, and tenants' and workers' concerns. The efforts of Lau and his activist cohorts, including Judge Lillian Sing, UC Berkeley professor L. Ling-chi Wang, and business leader Harold Yee, resulted in the formation of a number of local community service groups, such as Chinese for Affirmative Action, Asian Inc., and Self-Help for the Elderly. "We were young, and we were troublemakers," recalled Sing in 1998. "We were willing and had the courage to air our dirty laundry in public" (*Asian Week* 1998, 4).

Lau's contributions received attention from San Francisco Mayor George Mascone, who appointed him to the city's Board of Supervisors, San Francisco's equivalent to a city council, in 1977. The second Asian Pacific American to sit on the powerful board (George Chinn was appointed by Mayor Joseph Alioto in 1973), Lau then became the first elected Asian Pacific American member of the BOS later that year with his victory at the polls, paving the way for future city leaders such as Tom Hsieh, Leland Yee, Mabel Teng, and Michael Yaki. "He was a real trailblazer," said former supervisor Angela Alioto in 1998. "He set a path and made it wider for Asian Americans to become appointed and elected to the board" (Heredia 1998, A13).

As one of the Bay Area's top officials, Lau pushed for a number of key community issues, including the diversification of the San Francisco Police Department to include more women and people of color and provision of multilingual voting facilities for non–English speakers. He also backed rent control against the wishes of area landlords, some of whom were Chinese Americans. "It took a lot of courage for him to do that," noted Henry Der, former executive director of Chinese for Affirmative Action, in 1998. Despite the opposition, added Der, "He represented individuals grounded in addressing the needs of the people. He exemplified the small guy and people who had no access to the system" (Eljera 1998, 9).

Roland Quan, a member of Lau's campaign committee, also remarked in 1998 that the former supervisor "evolved from a young candidate to someone who could bring all sides together." Lau's down-to-earth personality, observed Quan, was evident from his openness about his personal past. "One of his favorite stories was about how he worked as a garbage collector in San Francisco when he was a young man," said Quan. "He used to tell us that he was the first Chinese American garbage collector [in the area]" (Eljera 1998, 9). In fact, Lau's dedication to community-based issues earned him a reputation as a meticulous researcher, rather than a politician, constantly preoccupied with soliciting votes from his constituency. "It's the way I am," he stated in an October 1979 interview with the *San Francisco Chronicle*. "But I guess it's a minus when you're campaigning" (Heredia 1998, A13).

Lau completed his two-year term in 1979, at which time he lost his reelection, but continued to remain heavily involved in civic affairs. Former San Francisco Mayor Dianne Feinstein named him the chairman of the San Francisco–Shanghai sister city committee, where he served from 1981 to 1988. Former San Francisco Mayor Frank Jordan observed that in this position, Lau provided him "the best liaison I had with the Asian community. He did more to open up positive lines of communication to that community than anyone else I know" (Heredia 1998, A13). Lau's other projects included fund-raising to rebuild his alma mater, St. Mary's, at the former site of the International Hotel in Chinatown at Jackson and Kearney, strategic support for Proposition H, a successful ballot measure to retrofit the Central Freeway.

Upon his untimely death from gall bladder complications at the age of 56 on 19 April 1998, local and state leaders reflected on his groundbreaking work. "He was significant [for the same reason] Jackie Robinson is significant. He was a first . . . when the Board of Supervisors used to be all white people and a few women," said state senator John Burton in 1998 (Heredia 1998, A13). Bay Area Rapid Transit (BART) Board President James Fang commented, "San Francisco has a special place with Shanghai and China because of his efforts" (Heredia 1998, A13). Kandace Bender, spokesperson for Mayor Willie Brown, issued the following statement: "Supervisor Lau was one of San Francisco's great pioneers, as a strong advocate of civil rights, as the city's first elected Asian American supervisor, as founding father of the Shanghai sister city relationship. He will be in our hearts and minds this week when we meet with Mayor Xi of Shanghai to plan San Francisco's next visit to Shanghai, a continuation of the heritage Mr. Lau began" (Heredia 1998, A13).

In November 1998, the San Francisco Board of Education unanimously voted to rename Commodore Stockton Elementary School the Gordon J. Lau Elementary. The Chinatown school, one of the city's largest, whose student body is approximately 50 percent Asian, was known as the Oriental School during the period of racial segregation in the San Francisco school district. A school board appointee, Frank Chong, noted at the renaming that "as a Chinese American member of the Board of Education, this resolution is very special to me, because Gordon Lau was a role model for me" (Lavilla 1998, 12). Lau's daughter Dianne Lau Yee, a teacher herself, remarked that the decision was "a fitting tribute to Dad." She added, "we are proud to know Dad's legacy will live on in educating the youth of San Francisco. I think a lot of things in this city remind us of Dad, even the little things like schools . . . and this was truly representative of him."

Lau is survived by his mother Elizabeth, brother Clifford, wife Mary, and daughters Stephanie, Dianne, and Carolyn.

## Sources

Eljera, Bert. "A Lawmaker's Legacy: S.F. Mourns the Death of its First Elected Asian American Supervisor." *Asian Week.* 29 April 1998, p. 9.

Heredia, Christopher. "S.F.'s First Elected Asian American Supervisor Dies: Gordon Lau Called Trailblazer." *San Francisco Chronicle.* 20 April 1998, p. A13.

Lavilla, Stacy. "School Renamed for Lau: S.F Board Honors Late Supervisor." *Asian Week.* 4 November 1998, p. 12.

"Passing of Pioneer: Gordon Lau Made S.F. Better for Asian Americans." *Asian Week.* 29 April 1998, p. 4.

# Bill Lann Lee

Acting Assistant Attorney General Bill Lann Lee, right, accompanied by Attorney General Janet Reno, meets reporters at the Justice Department in Washington in 1998 to announce the establishment of a national task force to coordinate the investigation of violence against women's health care clinics nationwide. (Dennis Cook, AP/Wide World Photos)

**Born:** 5 February 1949, New York, New York.

**Education:** B.A., Yale University, 1971; J.D., Columbia University, 1974.

**Awards, Honors:** Named to *A. Magazine*'s 25 Most Influential Asians in America, 1997 and 1998 as well as its 100 Most Influential Asian Americans of the Decade list, 1999.

**Summary:** Bill Lann Lee was Acting Assistant Attorney General for Civil Rights, and the nation's top civil rights enforcer.

### Early Years

Bill Lann Lee was born on 5 February 1949 in New York City at the Women's Hospital on West 110th Street to William and Pui-Jen Lee. Like many Chinese immigrants at the time, his parents, who hailed from the Toishan region in China, faced limited opportunities in the job market despite his father's service in the U.S. military during World War II.

In a speech delivered at the Asian American Journalists Association's annual convention in August 1998, Lee recounted the ironic struggle: "His service in the Army Air Corps was one of my father's proudest accomplishments. He demonstrated his loyalty to this country through sweat and blood. The rest of his unit was white, mostly young men in their late teens and early twenties. Yet my father often told us that he began to feel like an American for the first time during the war, because they treated him just like everyone else. Though he had only a sixth grade education, he wrote letters home for a number of men in his unit. When he returned home to New York City from the war, my father found nothing changed. He was called a 'dumb Chinaman' and worse. Searching for an apartment, in uniform, he was turned away because he was Chinese" (Lee 1998). With no other feasible employment options, Lee's father returned to operating Lee's Hand Laundry, located near Harlem first at 91st and Amsterdam and later at 125th and Broadway.

Growing up as a minority on New York's Upper West Side in the 1950s and 1960s left a lasting impression on young Lee. He observed, for example, the sad realities of the historical immigration restrictions on the Chinese American community during his weekly visits to Chinatown after Sunday church services. "As I remember, Chinatown was a kind of refuge, a forlorn place with many elderly men, uncles, who were sojourners cut off from their families back in China," he recalled (Lee 1998). During the rest of the week, Lee and his brother Ernest helped their parents run their business. "To this day, I can still recall the smell, the stench, and the depth of dirty laundry that my parents took in," he remembered. They would not, however, permit the siblings to perform the skilled work, such as ironing, "for fear that we might enjoy the work, and not strive to achieve the American dream" (Lee 1998).

### Education

Lee accepted this parental challenge, graduating from Bronx High School of Science in 1967 and winning a scholarship to attend Yale University as part of its diversity outreach efforts. Upon his arrival on the New Haven campus—alone aboard a Trailways bus—he immediately noticed stark contrasts between himself and his classmates. "I watched as the families of other freshmen drove them onto campus, unloading their belongings from their family cars. I always wore white shirts then, not because I meant to dress well, but because customers would leave old and unwanted white shirts behind at my parents' laundry," he recalled. "I looked different, I felt different, I was different" (Lee 1998). Still, Lee had a successful college career, graduating Phi Beta Kappa, magna cum laude in 1971. He then went on to Columbia University's Law School where he earned his J.D. in 1974.

### Career Highlights

Bill Lann Lee took his first step in the legal world as an associate counsel in New York with the NAACP Legal Defense and Educational Fund (LDF), the civil rights law firm established by the late Supreme Court Justice Thurgood Marshall, a position which helped to prepare him for his future role as the Acting Assistant Attorney General for Civil Rights. "If you wanted to be a civil rights lawyer, there was no better organization to join than the LDF," he explained (Lee 1998).

It was Lee's concurrent volunteer work with New York's Asian American Legal Defense Fund in the late 1970s, however, that really "opened his eyes" to the significance of civil rights advocacy. One of his main tasks was to write appellate briefs arguing that Asian Americans had historically been subject to racist exclusion and discrimination. For Lee, his most memorable moments with the AALDF were representing Chinese American restaurant workers such as waiters, cooks, and dim sum servers in their quests for just wages. "Getting relief for these people made a difference in their lives. I also remember the work I did in the weekly clinics where poor Asian Americans came for advice and representation. The restaurant workers I represented and those who came to the clinics were individuals very much like members of my own family. Not only was my late father a laundryman, my mother is a retired garment worker and my cousins have been garment workers and cooks," he stated. "I learned from these experiences, in the most forceful and direct way, that our nation's civil rights laws are promises of equal opportunity and fair treatment made to all. That I did that early in my career, I am sure, made sure that I would stay a civil rights lawyer, and that I would understand the transcendent importance of the work" (Lee 1998).

After nine years at the LDF, during which he also taught political science as an adjunct professor at Fordham University, Lee moved across the country to work for the Center for Law in the Public Interest in California. After five years as its supervising attorney for Civil Rights Litigation, he rejoined the LDF staff as Western Regional Counsel in Los Angeles.

In December 1997, President Bill Clinton named Lee the Acting Assistant Attorney General for Civil Rights, the nation's highest civil rights post. In doing so, he bypassed the Senate's conventional role in confirming presidential nominees, adding to the partisan controversy sparked by Lee's pro–affirmative action stance. Nevertheless, Lee had the strong backing of a number of prominent organizations, including the NAACP, the National Asian Pacific American Legal Consortium, the Organization of Chinese Americans, and the Japanese American Citizens League. In March 1999, Clinton renominated Lee, whom the White House described as "a skilled consensus builder" and an "excellent litigator" in an official statement (Galvin 1999).

Regardless of his official title, Lee fervently devoted himself to promoting legal justice in the United States, pushing for the removal of cumbersome jurisdictional barriers, fair housing, and rights for Americans with disabilities, while fighting hate crimes and worker exploitation, among other concerns. During his swearing-in ceremony, he pledged to uphold anti-discrimination legislation "without fear or favor" for all Americans (Ross 1997).

As the highest ranking Asian Pacific American in the federal government at the close of the 20th century, Lee, who is married to Carolyn Yee and is the father of three children, holds a significant place in API history, named, for example, by *A. Magazine*'s 25 Most Influential Asians in America in both 1997 and 1998 as well as its 100 Most Influential Asian Americans of the Decade list in 1999. "During my brief time in Washington, D.C., I have learned how it truly makes a difference to have Asian Pacific Americans in the political process and at the policy table in Washington," he reflected in 1998. "For so many years Asian Pacific Americans were not at the table—our issues and interests were not represented and were not raised. Asian Pacific Americans bring new and different perspectives and backgrounds to the table. No one knows this better than I" (Lee 1998).

## Sources

Broder, John M. "Clinton, Softening Slap at Senate, Names 'Acting' Civil Rights Chief." *The New York Times*. 16 December 1997, p. A1.

Galvin, Kevin. "Clinton Nominates Acting Civil Rights Chief Over GOP Objections." The Associated Press View Related Topics. 5 March 1999.

Kim, Jungwon, "Bill Lann Lee." In "The 1998 A. List." *A. Magazine*. December 1998/January 1999, p. 53.

Lee, Bill Lann. Selected Speeches provided by the Office of the Assistant Attorney General, Civil Rights Division, Washington, DC.

Lee, Denny. "Bill Lann Lee." In "The A. 100: 100 Most Influential Asian Americans of the Decade." *A. Magazine*. October/November 1999, p. 95.

"NAACP Supports Clinton Choice." *Sacramento Observer*. 29 October 1997, p. G1.

Park, Charles. "Bill Lann Lee." In "The A List 1997." *A. Magazine*. December 1997/January 1998, p. 65.

Ross, Sonya. "Clinton Names Lee Civil Rights Chief." The Associated Press View Related Topics. 15 December 1997.

United States Department of Justice Web site: www.usdoj.gov [Accessed 17 July 1999].

# Cheryl Lee

Cheryl Lee. (Courtesy of Cheryl Lee)

**Born:** 24 April 1967, Mason, South Korea.

**Education:** B.S., University of Washington, 1990; M.B.A., University of Washington, 2001.

**Positions Held:** Founding Council member, City of Shoreline, Washington, 1995–present.

**Awards, Honors:** Northwest Asian Weekly Foundation Living Pioneer Award, 1998.

**Summary:** Cheryl Lee, one of the nation's youngest Asian Pacific American elected officials, is a founding member of Shoreline, Washington's city council.

### Early Years

Cheryl Lee was born on 24 April 1967 in Mason, South Korea, to Yushin and Yongcha Lee. The oldest of four children, Lee immigrated to Washington State with her family at the age of nine.

### Education

After graduating as salutatorian from Shoreline High School in 1986, Lee attended the University of Washington, where she earned her Bachelor of Science degree in Mechanical Engineering in 1990. Eleven years later, she earned an MBA from UW as well.

### Career Highlights

Diploma in hand, Lee took a position with the Boeing Commercial Airplane Group. For nine years, Lee managed aircraft lease activities of leading European and Asian capital asset management companies as a customer account manager. In 1995, she also started her own consulting agency, Supra International, which provides communication services to small Korean manufacturing firms attempting to enter the U.S. market. Five years later, she left Boeing and returned to the University of Washington to pursue her M.B.A. degree. Meanwhile, she began working as a Business

Development Director with Vendesic Inc., a Seattle-based internet start-up company and opened two local gift and candy boutiques with her sister. In spite of her busy schedule, Lee noted that "I'm there when I can get away in the evenings. I'm there to mop the floor" (London 1998, 4).

In 1995, Lee had the unique opportunity to become part of the Shoreline's first city council following the city's incorporation the previous year, a move largely resulting from Washington's State Growth Management Act. Cheryl Lee captured the second-highest number of votes among all the candidates in the general election, beating her district competitor for the position one seat by 2000 ballots. Basing her campaign on the theme "Building Together," Lee focused a significant part of her energies on encouraging Shoreline's Korean American population to participate. "Actually, a lot of people think Shoreline is a very upper-middle class, all white city, but it's not," she stated. "According to the figures from the school district, about 16 percent of the residents are Asian, and the minority population is about 20 percent." Lee was the first and only Asian Pacific American elected that year in Shoreline (Ee 1995, 5).

Her reason for entering the political arena, she explained, was to "give back something to the community. There is going to be a lot of work, but a lot of diversity in the community is not represented." Continued Lee, "At a lot of transition committees that I go to which involve participation from the community, we don't see any participation [from the Asian community]" (Ee 1995, 5).

As a newly-elected representative, her initial areas of concern included stabilizing the city's treasury, improving public safety, fostering youth-oriented programs, and encouraging a welcoming atmosphere within the municipal government for all peoples. "There's still a perception out there among the minorities that they don't feel like they can go to city hall and do anything, be responded to," she commented. "I want to change that" (London 1998, 4). She also emphasized, "I had been educated in the wonderful Shoreline School District," and she wanted to ensure that "the excellent system is guaranteed with the new city" (Ee 1995, 5).

During her first term, Lee established a legislative internship for area teenagers. "I think it's important everybody participates," she stated (London 1998, 4). She also helped to broker an arrangement between approximately 50 county police officers and the city to promote public safety in Shoreline. In Lee's assessment, the program has been successful, as effective as "a complete in-house police department" (London 1998, 4).

In 1997, Cheryl Lee successfully ran for re-election to the council, receiving the highest number of votes of all candidates. "I am running because I feel strongly the need to complete some of the tasks that the first city council has begun to work on," she said during her campaign (*Northwest Asian Weekly* 1997, 6).

One of Lee's most significant responsibilities as a Shoreline City Council member is her position as a liaison and role model to the city's burgeoning Korean American populace, whose members comprised 10 percent of Shoreline's business owners. Noted her brother Tom Lee, "A lot of people at [Phillippi Presbyterian, a local Korean American] church look up to her, especially the younger adults, ask her for guidance and advice about business or whatever." He added, "She finds a way to take care of everything and finds time to do what she needs to do" (London 1998, 4).

Aside from her professional and civic duties, Lee, who describes herself in her resume as "tenacious, energetic, want[ing] to have an impact, and thriv[ing] in a dynamic environment," is involved in a myriad of outside commitments. She is a member of the Shoreline Community Council Foundation Board, Rotary International Shoreline Breakfast Club, and the Korean American Professional Society, and the Information, Technology, and Communication Steering Committee of the

National League of Cities, where she develops policy and lobbies Congress on technology issues impacting American cities. She has also been a weekly radio columnist on emerging local issues for KWYZ, served on the National League of Cities's nominating committee in 1999, and has been the past treasurer and secretary of Asian Pacific American Municipal Officials, of which she is currently vice president.

Lee is also active in her church as a Sunday school teacher and director and has volunteered as an ESL instructor. In 1998, the Northwest Asian Weekly Foundation named her the "Youngest Asian American Elected to Office in Washington State" and honored her with a Living Asian American Pioneer Award. Her life goal, simply put, is to "make a difference in the lives of others by giving of myself" (London 1998, 4).

### Sources

Angelos, Constantine and Neil Gonzales. "Shoreline Voters Elect 6 to City's 1st Council—Position 4 Race to be Decided by Absentee Ballots." *Seattle Times*. 26 April 1995, p. A1.

"Cheryl Lee: Veteran Says Fledgling Council Still Needs Her." *Northwest Asian Weekly*. 19 September 1997, p. 6.

Ee, Jasmine. "Lee Sweeps to Easy Victory in Shoreline City Council Elections." *Northwest Asian Weekly*. 5 May 1995, p. 5.

London, Melissa. "Pioneer Profile: Shoreline's Council Member is a Role Model for Young People." *Northwest Asian Weekly*. 3 July 1998, p. 4.

# Harry Lee

**Born:** 27 August 1932, New Orleans, Louisiana.

**Education:** B.S., Louisiana State University; J.D., Loyola University, 1967.

**Positions Held:** U.S. magistrate, Eastern District of Louisiana, 1971–1975; Sheriff, Jefferson Parish, Louisiana, 1980–present.

**Summary:** Harry Lee, long-time sheriff of Jefferson Parish near New Orleans, Louisiana, is a pioneer figure among Asian Pacific Americans in law enforcement.

### Early Years and Education

Louisiana's Southern-drawling "Chinese cowboy," Harry Lee, was born to Chinese immigrants on 27 August 1932 in the back of a downtown New Orleans laundry. Together with his parents and siblings, Lee, the third oldest of six children, spent his formative years in a single-room dwelling with no bathtub or hot running water. The family operated their laundry until World War II, when they switched to the restaurant business. There, Lee helped with the day-to-day operations after school and on weekends.

As a student, the popular Lee demonstrated an early penchant for government as both class and student body president. After high school, he attended Louisiana State University as a geology major and became the first in his family to graduate from college.

Harry Lee. (Courtesy of Harry Lee)

Recognized as an outstanding ROTC cadet at LSU, Lee joined the U.S. Air Force. His distinguished three year service in the strategic air command placed him in the top 2 percent of all junior officers nationwide.

## Career Highlights

Upon his return to civilian life, Lee once again immersed himself in the food service industry. As manager of his family's restaurant, House of Lee, located in the Metarie district, he assumed the presidency of the New Orleans chapter of the Louisiana Restaurant Association in 1964. Notably, he facilitated the integration of the city's establishments during his tenure.

It did not take long for Lee to initiate a new career trajectory, however. After his youngest sibling graduated from college, he decided to return to school, balancing his studies at New Orleans's Loyola University Law School with a 72-hour, six-day work week as the House of Lee's opening and closing manager. "You can do it if you really want to," he once said. "For a long time, I was just talking about it. Finally, I had to quit talking, and just do it" (Lum 1998, 9). In addition, he found time to volunteer for one of Louisiana's Congressional Representatives, the late Democrat Hale Boggs, a former majority leader and supporter of civil rights.

After graduating from Loyola in 1967, Lee's professional life was hardly orthodox. Not finding private practice stimulating, he turned to government in 1971 as Eastern Louisiana's appointed U.S. Magistrate. Two years later, he was once again voted president of an organization—this time, the National Council of U.S. Magistrates. Lee was also a member of the Boggs/Ford Delegation to the People's Republic of China in 1972 and was reputedly the first Chinese American officially invited to the Mainland since 1959. Ironically, Lee, who was almost barred from the group because of his ancestry, had claimed an interpreter's fluency in Chinese in order to be allowed on the trip. On the flight to China, however, he confessed to his colleagues, "I don't speak Chinese!" (Lum 1998, 9).

Harry Lee served for four years as a federal magistrate before filling an appointment as the parish attorney for Jefferson Parish, a New Orleans suburb. After another four year term, he made a bid for the Jefferson Parish sheriff's office in 1979. Lee won the election, beating the popular incumbent who had been involved in a wiretapping scandal.

Since April 1980, Lee has served as Jefferson Parish's top law enforcement official, responsible for a $65 million budget and a staff of 1,500. Regarding his accomplishments, he stated, "As far as I'm concerned, the glass ceiling doesn't exist. It's all bullshit" (Lim 1993, 1). A firm believer in the "bootstrap" theory of success and also an opponent of affirmative action, he told Asian Pacific Island police officers during a visit to Houston, "If you believe certain doors are closed to you, then they are. If I can do it . . . you can do it, you can get off your behind. It's not going to be easy, but it can be done. You can go as far as you want to go" (Lum 1998, 9).

Indeed, the colorful Lee is far from being politically correct. "I'm controversial, I say what I feel," he has stated (Lum 1998, 9). Lee cautioned his Texan audience not to organize on the basis of race, arguing that such labor unions undermine "legitimate" labor advocacy. Lee also received criticism from civil rights activists, following a series of local robberies, for declaring in the mid-1980s that young black men driving "rinky dink cars" in the area late at night would be stopped. A number of organizations, including the American Civil Liberties Union and the National Association for the Advancement of Colored Peoples, protested his remarks. In response, he stated that he was just being "honest," that his comments had been misinterpreted, and that he had no control over the fact that a large number of the suspects were African American. Much of the parish's white electorate, on the other hand, applauded Lee's stance, and he was reelected.

Lee remains supported by his constituents. Aside from a fleeting run for Louisiana's gubernatorial race in 1995, he has held firmly to his position as Jefferson Parish sheriff, reelected time and again since first gaining office in 1979 by substantial margins, despite a local Asian Pacific Islander population of less than one percent. Some believe the job is his for as long as he cares to remain; only his physical condition may affect his office. "I've got bifocals, a hearin' aid, artificial knees, and false teeth," he commented (Lim 1993, 1). But for now, the aging Harry Lee prides himself on his commitment to law enforcement. As he explained during the sixth annual National Asian Peace Officers' Conference in 1993, "I'm living proof that you can be fat and old and still succeed."

He is married to Lai Beet Woo; they have a daughter, Cynthia.

### Sources

Lim, Gerard. "Hail to the Chiefs: Asian Pacific American Top Cops Honored." *Asian Week*. 10 September 1993, p. 1.

Lum, Lydia. "Southern Sheriff: A Good ol' Boy Named Lee." *Asian Week*. 14 January 1998, p. 9.

Moy, Kim. "Harry Lee." In *Notable Asian Americans*, ed. Helen Zia and Susan B. Gall. Detroit, MI: Gale Research, Inc., 1995, pp. 194–195.

# Joaquin Lim

**Born:** 8 October 1950, Fukien, China.

**Education:** B.A., San Francisco State University, 1980; M.A., San Francisco State University, 1982.

**Positions Held:** Council member and Mayor, City of Walnut, California.

**Awards and Honors:** 1999 Chinese Americans United for Self-Empowerment (CAUSE) Citizen of the Year.

**Summary:** Joaquin Lim is the first Asian American to hold public office and serve as mayor of Walnut, California.

Joaquin Lim. (Courtesy of Joaquin Lim)

### Early Years and Education

A Chinese American, Joaquin Lim was born on 8 October 1950 in Fukien, China, to Chilay Lim and Siokching Lim. He earned his high school diploma at the Diocesan Boys' School in 1969, his B.A. in economics from San Francisco State University in 1980, and his M.A. in the same field, also at San Francisco State, in 1982.

### Career Highlights

Lim spent 15 years as a Senior Major Contracts Negotiator for the Defense Department and for various Fortune 500 weapon systems manufacturers. In 1995, he was elected to the Walnut, California city council with the highest number of votes, becoming the first Asian Pacific American to hold public office in the city. Four years later, he also became its first Asian Pacific American mayor. He was reelected in April 2000, again with the highest number of votes, to serve his second four-year term.

As mayor of Walnut, Lim has appeared on CBS, CNN, and NBC news broadcasts to "tell America about the beauty and rich diversity of Walnut." Lim's political achievements and potential have been well-noted in the Asian Pacific American community. In 1998, he was elected the first president of Chinese American Elected Officials (CEO), a non-partisan organization consisting of 28 elected representatives in southern California who, Lim explains, are " dedicated to encourage and to support qualified candidates for various local, state, and national political offices." In April 2000, he was reelected for a second term. Additionally, Lim was selected by the Asian Pacific American Institute for Congressional Studies (APAICS) and the UCLA Asian American Studies Center to attend the first annual Political Leader Training Program for Asian Pacific American elected officials, held in 1999. The same year, Lim was honored by Chinese Americans United for Self-Empowerment as a Citizen of the Year.

Lim is the father of Elaine and Janice Lim.

### Source

Personal communication to Ellen D. Wu, 13 July and 28 September 2000.

## John Lim

**Born:** 1935, Yeoju, South Korea.

**Education:** B.A., Seoul Theological College, 1964; Master of Divinity, Western Evangelical Seminary, 1970; Doctor of Humane Letters, Western Evangelical Seminary, 1996.

**Positions Held:** Member, Oregon State Senate, 1992–present.

**Awards, Honors:** Named to A. *Magazine*'s 1998 "A. List," recognizing the year's most influential Asian Pacific Americans.

**Summary:** Korean-born John Lim, who represents District 11 in the Oregon State Senate, is one of the few Asian Pacific Americans in electoral politics in the Pacific Northwest.

### Early Years and Education

Oregon State Senator John Lim was born in 1935 in Yeoju, South Korea. As a youth, Lim developed a taste for competition by winning a pair of rubber shoes in a wrestling match, one of his most vivid childhood memories. Lim completed his primary and secondary education in his homeland, graduating from Yeoju Agricultural High School in 1954. In Korea, he worked as both the assistant executive director of Yo Kwang Children's Home, an orphanage, as well as a chaplain for the U.S. Missile Base in Yepiu. Lim married his wife, Grace, in 1963 before immigrating to the United States three years later. After a decade of stateside residency, he became a naturalized citizen on 15 July 1976. In America, Lim com-

John Lim. (Courtesy of John Lim)

pleted his formal education at Portland's Western Evangelical Seminary with a Master of Divinity degree in 1970 and a Doctorate of Humane Letters in 1996.

### Career Highlights

John Lim, president of the American Royal Jelly Company and a licensed real estate agent, has actively participated in his adopted homeland's civic affairs for a number of years. He has led a number of Asian American organizations, serving as president of the Korean-American society of Oregon in 1986, Bush-Quayle chair of Oregon Asian Americans in 1988, conference chair and national president of the Korean American Chamber of Commerce and Industry in the USA from 1990 to 1991, and chair of the Asian American Voters' Coalition from 1991 to 1992. He has also made use of his business background as a member of the Gresham Area Chamber of Commerce and the Portland Chamber of Commerce, along with the George Fox University Board of Trustees and the Western Evangelical Seminary Board of Regents.

Lim inaugurated his political career in an unsuccessful bid for the Republican gubernatorial nomination in Oregon in 1990. He spent $240,000—most of it his own—in a race with Dave Frohnmayer, the state attorney general. The defeat did not deter him, however, and two years later he successfully campaigned for a seat in the Oregon Senate, becoming the first Republican in 32 years to do so. He repeated his victory in 1996 with reelection as the representative for the state's District 11.

While in the legislature, Lim served as Assistant Senate Majority Leader in 1995. He has been a member of several committees, including Joint Ways and Means, Transportation, and Trade and Economic Development, which he has chaired since 1995. Considered somewhat of a maverick among the GOP caucus, Lim was one of five Republicans to stand against their party in opposing a state school budget, calling for more funding. He also disapproves of the state lottery and has attempted to narrow the range of games available.

During his unsuccessful run for the U.S. Senate in 1998 against incumbent Democrat Ron Wyden, the moderate Lim voiced his support for what he dubbed the "Three-E Policy": Education, Economy, and Ecology, along with open immigration. He also called for reduction in the size of the federal bureaucracy, which he felt "seems to have forgotten that it's a government of the people, by the people and for the people" (Associated Press 1998).

The father of three children, Peter, Bill, and Gloria, Lim was named on A. *Magazine*'s 1998 A. List," recognizing the year's most influential Asian Pacific Americans. Along with his peers Matt Fong, Cecy Groom, and David Wu, noted the editors, "The willingness of Lim ... to venture into rocky political terrain has added much-needed momentum to Asian American participation in politics" (Kim 1998/1999, 50).

### Sources

"John Lim." *AP Candidate Bios*. The Associated Press Political Service. 1998.

Kim, Jungwon. "Matt Fong, Cecy Groom, John Lim, David Wu." In "The 1998 A. List." A. *Magazine*. December 1998/January 1999, p. 50.

## Carol Liu

**Born:** 1941, Oakland, California.

**Education:** San Jose State College, 1963.

**Positions Held:** Member, La Canada Flintridge, California, City Council, 1992–2000; Member, California State Assembly, 2000–present.

**Awards, Honors:** Spirit of Outstanding Service award from the La Canada Flintridge Educational Foundation, 2000; citation for outstanding public service from the Second Baptist Church of Los Angeles, 2000; California's 21st Senatorial District's Woman of the Year Award, 1998.

**Summary:** Carol Liu is one of the first Asian American women to hold a seat in the California State Assembly.

### Early Years and Education

Carol Liu was born in Oakland, California, to a fourth-generation Californian mother and an immigrant father from Beijing, China, in 1941. She attended area public schools and graduated from San Jose State College in 1963. She also earned a lifetime teaching credential from the University of California, Berkeley, in 1964, and an administrative credential in 1978.

### Career Highlights

A longtime educator, Liu taught in California public schools from 1964 to 1978 and worked as executive director of the Richmond Federation of Teachers from 1975 to 1978. After relocating to southern California in 1984, she continued her dedication to education as a PTA president, member of the Berkeley Foundation Board, and president of the Pasadena City College Foundation Board. Her interest in children's issues in particular led her to chair the Board of Directors of San Gabriel Valley Child Care Information Services from 1993 to 1995 and to a position on the Board of Directors of Five Acres Boys and Girls Aid Society in Los Angeles County from 1997 to 1999.

In 1992, Liu was elected to the first of her two terms on the La Canada Flintridge City Council, for which she twice served as mayor in 1995 and in 1999. As a council member, she advocated "livable communities," alternative modes of transportation, and open space and hillside protection.

Liu announced her bid for the 44th district seat in the California State Assembly in 1999. The following year, she made history as one of the first Asian Pacific American women to hold a seat in the legislature. Recognizing the significance of her accomplishment, she stated, "A lot of women are involved in local government, but some of us are a little slower about taking this next step. The women in the new assembly class are generally women who have already raised their families, served time on local school boards, stuff like that" (Fox 2000, B1).

As the 44th district's representative, key priorities on her agenda included improving public education, protecting children, providing adequate health care and coverage for all Californians, backing worker's rights, reforming the state prison system, and preserving the environment.

Liu has received several honors for her accomplishments: the Spirit of Outstanding Service award from the La Canada Flintridge Educational Foundation in March 2000, a citation for outstanding public service from the Second Baptist Church of Los Angeles in May 2000, and California's 21st Senatorial District's Woman of the Year Award in 1998.

### Sources

Fox, Sue. "Wins Cast 2 Women in New Roles." *Los Angeles Times.* 9 November 2000, p. B1.

MacGregor, Hilary E. "Gender Issues at the Fore in Race for 44th District Seat." *Los Angeles Times.* 13 February 2000, p. B1.

## Gary Locke

**Born:** 21 January 1950, Seattle, Washington.

**Education:** B.A., Yale University, 1972; J.D., Boston University, 1975.

**Positions Held:** Representative, Washington State House of Representatives, 1982–1993; Chief Executive, King County, Washington, 1993–1996; Governor, Washington State, 1996–present.

Gary Locke. (Courtesy of the Office of the Governor of Washington, photograph by S. Vento)

**Awards, Honors:** Named one of A. *Magazine*'s 25 Most Influential Asians in America in both 1996 and 1997; named one of A. *Magazine*'s 100 Most Influential Asian Americans of the Decade, 1999.

**Summary:** Gary Locke is the nation's first Chinese American state governor and the first Asian Pacific American governor outside of Hawaii.

## Early Years

Gary Locke, the nation's first Chinese American governor, typifies in many ways the so-called "American Dream." Locke, the second son of Toisanese immigrants James Locke and his wife Julie, was born on 21 January 1950 and grew up in Yesler Terrace, one of Seattle's housing projects built expressly for the families of returning soldiers from World War II (his father had fought in the Normandy Invasion with the 5th armored division). He spent his early years helping out at his family's grocery and Pike Place restaurant, Sadie's Cafe, and participating in the Eagle Scouts. Locke's elementary school years were sometimes troubling—for example, one of his teachers would frequently ask the students what they had eaten in the morning, and "If you didn't eat a conventional breakfast, she'd slap your hand with a ruler," he recalled. "When she asked me, I would say I ate porridge with dried shrimp and pieces of salted pork, a very Chinese breakfast!" (Gong 1996, 32.

## Education

Locke was unable to speak English until kindergarten, but developed into an honors student at Seattle's Franklin High School nevertheless. After meeting an encouraging recruiter from Yale University, he applied and was accepted to the college, which he attended as "a product of affirmative action," in his own words, financing his tuition with scholarships and part-time jobs (Locke 1997). Following his graduation in 1972 with a bachelor of arts degree in political science, he went on to Boston University's law school, where he earned his juris doctorate in 1975.

## Career Highlights

Locke then returned to Seattle to begin work in the local government as a deputy prosecutor for King County. This marked the beginning of Locke's distinguished political career—one inspired by such forces as President John Fitzgerald Kennedy and a meeting with Wing Luke, one of the country's pioneer Asian American city council members, at age 14. "I just happened to meet him in a community setting, and I was completely mesmerized," he recalled (Chen et al. 1996/1997, 55). After serving as a door-to-door campaigner for area hopefuls and a member of the State Senate's higher education committee, he successfully won a seat in Washington's House of Representatives in 1982. As the chair of the House Appropriations Committee for five years, he guided the crafting of bipartisan budgets, which led to higher enrollments in the state's colleges and universities, improved quality of education, especially for poor and minority students, better health care services for children, and heightened environmental protection.

Over the course of his 11-year tenure in the State House, Locke's persona gradually evolved from that of the "angry agitator" to a more diplomatic figure, often facilitating disagreements between differing factions. His negotiating abilities coupled with his skill for budget writing placed him in the state's political spotlight.

1993 marked another major milestone in Locke's career with his election as King County executive, granting him jurisdiction over 12,800 employees, an annual budget of $2 billion, and the 1.6 million area residents comprising the nation's thirteenth-largest county. As he did during his term in the State House, Locke focused his efforts as King County executive on budget management, implementing a reward program to entice county departments to economize, and spearheading a major compromise between pro-growth and environmental groups in the area. Additionally, Locke examined ways to involve the county council more actively with remote, local pockets of the district. In a reference to the Seattle-based department store known for its service, he aimed to provide a "Nordstrom-style," customer-oriented leadership, accessible and accountable to the public (Gupta 1995, 215).

When Washington's incumbent Governor Mike Lowry declined to run for a second term in 1995, Locke seized upon the chance to run for the position. Capturing 58 percent of the vote, Locke triumphed over religious conservative Ellen Craswell to become the United States' first Chinese American governor. Ironically, his quarters in state capital Olympia are located about a mile away from where his grandfather, Suey Gim Locke, once worked as a houseboy.

As Washington's chief executive, Locke's goal has largely been a continuation of his previous efforts. Viewing education as "the great equalizer," he has made it his top priority, proposing college scholarships for promising high school students, standardized teacher certification testing, the hiring of more instructors for Washington's classrooms, and strong measures against school violence (Chen et al. 1996/1997, 55). He also helped to establish the Washington Reading Corps in 1998 to encourage literacy and literary proficiency. "A highly educated work force is the key to our economic future," he declared (Chen et al. 1996/1997, 55). Additionally, Locke, as a self-acknowledged "beneficiary of affirmative action," supports efforts to "act affirmatively to bring women and people of color into the mainstream network," as he told the National Asian Pacific Bar Association in a November 1997 address (Locke 1997).

Among other issues on Locke's agenda are welfare reform—he signed a bill in 1997 that resulted in the reduction of families on government assistance by one-third—lowering of taxes for businesses, rural economic development, transportation, and offender accountability. He has continued to strive for compromise on these divisive issues because "stalemate is not an option" (Associated Press 1998).

Locke's dedication to his work and meticulous attention to detail have earned him a reputation in government circles as an "unabashed nerd" and non-drinking, non-smoking, or swearing "policy wonk." "There's a joke in Seattle," remarked one longtime friend, "if he goes to a dinner party and there's a dripping faucet, Gary's under the sink fixing that leak" (Donahue 1997, 169). However, after his marriage in October 1994 to Mona Lee, a former University of California cheerleader and television reporter for Seattle's KING 5, he has become less of a workaholic. Following the birth of his daughter, Emily, in 1997 (the Lockes also have a son, Dylan, born in 1999), he promised Mona to scale back his gubernatorial duties to devote more time to his family. "I'm a typical doting father," said Locke. Among his parental aspirations are "learning all those [English language] nursery rhymes" he never heard as a young child.

In many ways, Locke is also a father figure for Asian Pacific Islanders in electoral politics, dubbed a rising star by the ethnic press. Daphne Kwok, director of the national Organization of Chinese Americans, Inca, stated, "He is our hope. Asian Americans will be turning to Gary Locke for leadership" (Liu 1997, W18). Eric Liu, contributor to the *Washington Post*, agreed: "Locke has not only benefited from an emerging sense of Asian American identity, he also is actually helping to shape it" (Liu 1997, W18). Among other distinctions, Locke has been named one of *A. Magazine*'s 25 Most Influential Asians in America in both 1996 and 1997 as well as one of its 100 Most Influential Asian Americans of the Decade. Opined *A. Magazine* contributor Denny Lee, "His victory injected new excitement into Asian American politics and inspired a generation of Democrats who view Locke as their new poster boy" (Lee 1999, 92).

Locke's presence extends to the other side of the Pacific as well. In October 1997, Locke visited his grandfather's native village of Jilong, China, for the first time, as part of an envoy to secure the sale of 50 jets from the Seattle-based Boeing company to Beijing.

Locke himself recognizes that he and his wife Mona are "the focal point for a lot of Asian American pride," and that his victory may serve as a "catalyst" for other Asian Pacific Islanders to get involved in politics and run for office. But, like many ethnic government leaders, he faces the challenge of relating API interests to his broader political platform while making certain to give voice and representation for his community. "The best thing I can do for Asian Americans," he declares positively, "is to be the best possible governor of Washington state" (Liu 1997, W18).

### Sources

Access Washington Web site: www.wa.gov/governor.
Chen, Liliana, et al. "Power Brokers 1996: The 25 Most Influential Asian Americans." A. *Magazine*. December 1996/January 1997, p. 55.
Donahue, Bill, Don Campbell and Tina Kelley. "American Tale: Washington Governor Gary Locke Explores His Roots In Jilong, China." *People*. 24 November 1997, p. 169.
"Gary Locke." *AP Candidate Bios*. The Associated Press Political Service. 1998.
Gong, Eric, Jr. "The Man Who Would Be Govenor." A. *Magazine*. August/September 1996, pp. 30–33, 66.
Gupta, Himanee. "Gary Locke." in *Notable Asian Americans*, ed. Helen Zia and Susan B. Gall. Detroit, MI: Gale Research Inc., 1995, pp. 214–215.
Lee, Denny. "Gary Locke: Governor of Washington." In "The A. 100: 100 Most Influential Asian Americans of the Decade." A. *Magazine*. October/November 1999, p. 92.
Liu, Eric. "Locke Step: Is Washington Governor Gary Locke the Breakthrough Politician that Asian Americans are Waiting For?" *Washington Post*. 24 August 1997, p. W18.
Locke, Gary. Remarks to National Asian-Pacific Bar Association, 23 November 1997. www.wa.gov [Accessed 20 April 1999].

# Wing Luke

**Born:** 25 February 1925, Canton, China.

**Died:** 17 May 1965, Snohomish County, Washington.

**Education:** B.A., University of Washington, 1950; M.A., J.D., University of Washington, 1954.

**Positions Held:** Member, Seattle City Council, 1962-1965.

**Awards, Honors:** World War II Army Citations: Bronze Medal, Six Combat Stars; Namesake of Seattle's Wing Luke Asian Museum.

**Summary:** Wing Chong Luke, the first Asian Pacific American elected to public office in the Pacific Northwest, served for three years on Seattle's city council beginning in 1962 before meeting an untimely death in 1965.

## Early Years

Wing Chong Luke was born on 25 February 1925 in Canton, China to Lung Sing Luke and Lew Fung Hai. At the age of five, he immigrated to Seattle, Washington. His father, who had residency, operated a laundry in the city's university district. "The first words I learned were 'yes,' 'no,' and 'he hit me first,'" recalled Luke of his childhood in America. "Not being able to speak English, there were lots of misunderstandings and boyhood fights" (Chin 1976, 4).

In spite of the language barrier, young Luke successfully acclimated himself to his adopted home, drawing cartoons for his classmates, standing at attention to the Star Spangled Banner, crooning Irish ballads on St. Patrick's Day, and even learning to play the Scottish bagpipes and to speak some Spanish, Norwegian, and Swedish. He readily accepted leadership positions—foreshadowing his career in politics—at an early age. As a student at John Marshall Junior High School, he won his run for the presidency of the Boys' Club. Then, while attending Roosevelt High School, he was elected student body president as well as head of the Inter-School Student Council, an organization comprised of representatives from all the city's secondary schools. The experiences undoubtedly shaped his outlook in life. "Roosevelt ... was made up of the 'better' class of kids," remembered Luke in a July, 1963 interview. "I ran for class president and made it. It was a source of satisfaction, even then, to see what others had, compare it with what I had, and succeed with what I had to work with" (Watson 1976, 1).

During his senior year at Roosevelt, Luke was drafted into the army for service in World War II. Ironically, while he fought valiantly for the United States in the Philippines and Korea, earning a bronze medal and six combat stars for his performance, his parents and five U.S.-born siblings experienced racism and discrimination such as bottle-throwing and name calling. After their landlady tripled their rent, reasoning, "We are at war with those people— you can't tell them apart," the Luke family was forced to leave their university district home—something which later shaped his decision to become a specialist in real estate, housing, and land as an attorney (Rochester).

## Education

Upon returning home to Seattle, Wing Luke became a naturalized citizen on his 21st birthday. He also matriculated at the University of Washington. As in high school, he flexed his political muscles on the college campus, presiding over the sophomore class and the UW Young Democrats. He was involved in a number of student organizations, including the local YMCA and Baptist-Disciple Student Center and served as a cartoonist for the *UW Daily and Columns*, receiving several honors in recognition of his activism.

After earning his B.A. in political science in 1950, he spent time at Washington, D.C.'s American University taking graduate courses in the same discipline before returning to UW for law school. Again, as before, Luke demonstrated his political prowess to his peers, serving as president of the King County Young Democrats and the state's national committeeman while completing his studies.

## Career Highlights

Fresh out of the UW law school in 1954, Luke first undertook two years of private practice before joining the office of Washington's attorney general John O'Connell. During his five years on the staff, he served as part of the Civil Rights Division as well as chief legal counsel for the Board Against Discrimination and Real Estate Division in 1957.

In 1961, at the age of 36, he took a leave of absence to bid for Seattle's city council position number five, vacated by outgoing council member Bob Jones, against a field of nine other candidates. As the first person of Chinese [and Asian] ancestry to run for public office in Washington State, Luke's road to victory was far from smooth. "The novelty of being Oriental does not help," he explained after the election. "Being an Oriental does single me out, and one therefore has to work harder. The political Oriental image is not here as yet like in Hawaii, although it is getting that way" (Chin 1976, 4).

In addition to having to work harder, Luke faced blatant opposition and smear tactics during his campaign. Members of one UW fraternity, for example, walked door to door to voice their opposition to him and to accuse him of pro-Communist sympathies. An anonymous adversary also initiated a second smear campaign against Luke, printing and distributing literature which alleged that his candidacy was backed by Communists. Finally, the contenders whom Luke defeated in the primaries all threw their support to Dr. J. G. (Joe) Aiken, the West Seattle physician whom he faced in the general election.

Despite these difficulties, Luke successfully emerged as the victor, largely due to his diverse, bipartisan pool of supporters, such as laborers, educators, and ethnic minority groups. "I had the written endorsement of prominent Seattle citizens who represented an extremely broad cross-section of the community," he stated (Chin 1976, 4). He also drew from the help of between 800-1000 campaign volunteers as well as his own personal dedication, investing approximately $10,000 of his own money and countless hours talking with area constituents, and using such creative tactics as placing "Vote for Wing Luke" messages inside fortune cookies, political posters, and coffee klatches.

In November 1961, he defeated Aiken by over 30,000 votes—the largest margin in that year's election—to make American history. As he was sworn into the city council on 13 March 1962, he stated, "As the first person of Chinese ancestry ever to run for office in Washington State, I have a great obligation to serve well. I accept the challenge of the job, in the spirit of my family, of which I am very proud" (Chin 1976, 4).

Luke's liberal presence on the generally conservative Seattle city council left a lasting impact. He was a staunch advocate of civil rights and was the main force behind the council's 1963 decision to establish a Municipal Human Rights Commission whose chief responsibility was to "carry punitive provisions against racial discrimination in the selling or renting of real estate," as described by journalist Emmett Watson in *Argus* magazine. The meeting, as reported by Watson, was "tense" and "packed," but Luke "adroitly. . . maneuver[ed]" his colleagues into creating the commission and agreeing to pass an open-housing ordinance (Watson 1963, 1).

Described by Watson as "an anomaly in local politics"—being Chinese, a practicing Baptist, an "intellectual," ambitious, and among the "new breed of young conservative-liberals"—Luke envisioned a pluralistic city of harmony fostered through community development projects. Aside from the Municipal Human Rights Commission, he favored the preservation of Pike Place Market to facilitate interaction between urban and rural peoples as well as the planning of a waterfront park for visitors to savor the beauty of the city. He also pushed for bilingual street signs, pea patches (community gardens), abolishing parking meters, historic preservation, fishing programs for city residents, and communal living schemes. Tangible results of his visionary thinking include the use of the downtown area for both businesses and residences, the blooming of Pike Place Market, and regulations requiring large-scale redevelopment projects to replace destroyed low-income housing.

Outside of the civic government, Wing Luke was a member of the Board of Directors of the Urban League, Chinese Community Service Organization, and the Jackson Street Community Council, Save our Ships, and the Gourmet Club, among other groups. He also enjoyed fishing, reading, and spending time with his family, Connie, Ruby, Robert, Marguerite, and Bettie, his sisters and brother, and friends.

In a tragic turn of events, Luke's promising career was cut short on 17 May 1965. As he was flying home from a fishing trip in Okanogan County's Lake Wannacutt, Luke and two other passengers were killed when their plane crashed near Index in Snohomish County. Their remains were not located until three years later.

Although he passed away prematurely, Luke left behind an impressive track record in the Pacific Northwest. Voted "best known" and the "most good," "active," "powerful," "brave," and "wise" city council member in a poll of Seattleites shortly before his accident, he inspired a special concert by the Seattle Youth Symphony and the King County Youth Commission to create a Wing Luke Award in his honor. Monies from his memorial foundation were appropriated for the building of the Wing Luke Memorial Museum (now known as the Wing Luke Asian Museum)—a "long cherished hope" of his, as noted by his close friend Warren Chan—which opened in May 1967 in Seattle's international district (Detera).

Luke's optimism is part of his legacy, honored by the Wing Luke elementary school and Wing Luke Scholarships. "If a man has no more ambition to stay where he is, then he'll soon burn himself out," he said in 1963. "I feel I'm capable of filling any elective job in the state. I have no set design on any office, but I'm young enough to think that opportunities will manifest themselves" (Watson 1963, 1).

## Sources

Chin, Doug. "The Intellectual Politics of Wing Luke." *The International Examiner*. October 1976, p. 4.

Detera, Eydie Calderon. "Wing Luke—a Shared Vision: Celebrating 30 Years of Community." Unpublished essay provided by Wing Luke Asian Museum, Seattle, Washington.

Evans, Walter. "Bicentennial Biographies: Wing Luke." *Seattle Post-Intelligencer*. 12 September 1975.

Rochester, Junius. "Wing Luke: 'Flowers Bloom Fragrantly Among the Riches and Honor,'" Unpublished essay provided by Wing Luke Asian Museum, Seattle, Washington.

Watson, Emmett. "Wing Luke: Anomaly in Seattle Politics." *Argus*. 19 July 1963, 33ff.

# M

## Rene Mansho

**Born:** 28 May 1949, Honolulu, Hawaii.

**Education:** B.Ed. Elementary Education; M.Ed., Educational Administration, University of Hawaii–Manoa.

**Positions Held:** Honolulu City Council member, 1988–2002.

**Awards, Honors:** Small Business of Hawaii Legislator of the Year, *Honolulu Star Bulletin Newspaper* Ten Who Made a Difference, American Transportation Association Transportation Person of the Year, U.S. Representative at 50th Anniversary Hiroshima Memorial.

**Summary:** Rene Mansho has been a member of the Honolulu City Council since 1988.

### Early Years

Rene Mansho was born on 28 May 1949 in Honolulu, Hawaii to Sado and Ethel Nishimoto. "I lived a humble life in Manoa Housing, Kapahulu, and grew up most of my life in Wahaiwa, a rural community on Oahu," recalls Mansho of her childhood. "My parents struggled to make sure that my brother and I had the best that life had to offer."

### Education and Career Highlights

After graduating from Leilehua High School, Mansho attended the University of Hawaii–Manoa, where she earned a bachelor's degree in elementary education and a masters' degree in educational administration. "Being a teacher was the conventional profession for a Japanese [American] female, and I enjoyed every minute of it," she remembers. Mansho spent 17 years as a public elementary school teacher and high school vice principal. Additionally, she was a member of the Hawaii State Teachers Association Board of Directors. "My career path in education led to being a union activist and Democratic Party leader, and eventually elected to office for 14 years," she explained.

Since her election to the Honolulu City Council in 1988, Rene Mansho has been involved in a number of projects, including chairing the Budget and Economic Development Committee, presiding over the Hawaii State Association of Counties, and participating on the National Federation of Women Legislators' Board of Directors. She lists among her proudest accomplishments her work in fostering the fiscal accountability of the council, supporting local businesses, expanding city services, and shoreline preservation. Women's rights, family and child care issues, economic development, environmental and cultural priorities, and "open government for the people" also rank among her interests.

"As a city council member, I take pride in making a difference in my community in passing legislation and funding for neighborhood projects and activities. I learned that I wanted to get the job done with the least amount of politics, which is the greatest challenge," she states. "However, I know deep down inside that I will always want to do whatever I can to help my community."

Although her seat on the Honolulu City Council will conclude in 2002 due to term limitations, she plans to "keep [her] options open." She emphasizes that she "love[s] working with people and solving problems" and will continue to seek employment either in elective office or other government agencies. As for the future, she notes, "I've been blessed as an Asian American to succeed in political life, and want to help my successors to experience the opportunity to serve."

Outside of her official duties, Mansho maintains an active profile both within the community and at home. She chairs both the Leilehua High School Education Foundation and the Carole Kai Charities, Inc.–Great Aloha Run. She also works with the Wahiawa-Waialua Hiroshima Kenjin Kai, the United Japanese Society of Hawaii, and the Honolulu Japanese Chamber of Commerce. Mansho is married to Rodney Mansho, is the mother of Brandon and Selena, and cites "being an active and doting grandmother!" as one of her personal goals.

## Sources

City and County of Honolulu Web site: www.co.honolulu.hi.us/council/d1/ [Accessed 5 October 2001].

Personal communication with Ellen D. Wu, 21 September 2000.

# Robert Matsui

**Born:** 17 September 1941, Sacramento, California.

**Education:** B.S., University of California, Berkeley, 1963; J.D., University of California Hastings College of Law, 1969.

**Positions Held:** Member, Sacramento City Council, 1971–1978; Member, United States House of Representatives, 1978–present.

**Awards, Honors:** Congressional Advocate of the Year, 1992 and 1994; the American Academy of Pediatrics Excellence in Public Service Award, 1992; one of Claremont College's Outstanding California Legislators, 1990 and 1992; Ronald H. Brown Export Enhancement Award from the Small Business Export Association, 1998; the National Health Leadership Award from the National Organization for Rare Disorders, 1998.

**Summary:** Japanese American Robert Matsui has served the United States House of Representatives for over 20 years. He was instrumental in the successful passage of the 1988 Civil Liberties Act granting redress and reparations for the former prisoners of Japanese American concentration camps in World War II.

## Early Years

Born in Sacramento on 17 September 1941, Sansei Robert Takeo Matsui met adversity at an early age. Together with his parents, the infant Matsui was sent to a War Relocation Concentration Camp in April 1942 following President Franklin Delano Roosevelt's signing of Executive Order 9066, the proclamation which called for the imprisonment of 120,000 Japanese Americans during World War II. "For the next three and a half years, my parents, myself, were wanderers, nomads," he stated, capturing the injustice of the situation. "All through that, we didn't know what charges were placed against us, we didn't have a trial." Though Matsui had only fragmented recollections of camp life, he was later to be a key player in the redress and reparations movement.

After the war, the Matsuis returned to Sacramento to resume their interrupted lives. Foreshadowing his future career, one of Matsui's childhood heroes was Clarence Darrow, whose autobiography he had read. He explained that his enthusiasm for the famed trial lawyer bolstered his conviction to "protect the underdog." Later, President John Fitzgerald Kennedy's call to public service would also prove to be one of the signs steering Matsui into government.

## Education

Matsui graduated from Sacramento's C.K. McClatchy High School in 1959 and went on to the University of California, Berkeley, where he earned his B.S. in 1963. Three years later, he obtained his J.D. from the University of California's Hastings College of Law.

## Career Highlights

As a new attorney, Matsui first established his own private practice in Sacramento in 1967. Gradually, he became involved in a number of civic organizations including the Japanese American Citizens League, the Active 20–30 Club, Sacramento Safety Council, United Crusade and Sacramento Rotary Club, and the Sacramento Metropolitan Chamber of Commerce.

Matsui's entrée into the political world first came in 1971 when area districts were reapportioned, freeing the possibility for him to win a spot on the Sacramento City Council. His campaign was, in his own words, "a shoestring operation," relying on friends and a mere $8600 for victory. Matsui also won a second term representing the city's District 8, and served for seven total years, including one as vice mayor and turns as chairman of the budget-finance and law and legislative committees. Meanwhile, Matsui was also active on the California Democrat Central Committee.

From the Sacramento City Council, Matsui moved to the U.S. Congress. In 1978, he decided to run for the state's fifth district seat in the House of Representatives soon to be vacated by retiring Democrat John E. Moss. As with his prior campaigns, his victory was largely due to his widespread network of supporters, including many Asian Pacific Islanders, rather than simply a substantial war chest.

On Capitol Hill, Matsui has been active in children's concerns, such as health insurance and welfare reforms that encourage adult responsibility and initiative without depriving their dependents of adequate care. He also helped to push successfully for the allocation of $1 billion in funding in the federal budget for family preservation programs over a five-year span.

Matsui's work has been widely recognized by a number of organizations nationwide. The Child Welfare League of America honored him as the "Congressional Advocate of the Year" in 1992 and 1994, the American Academy of Pediatrics awarded him its Excellence in Public Service Award in 1992, and Claremont College named him one of California's outstanding legislators in 1990 and 1992. In 1998 he was awarded the Ronald H. Brown Export Enhancement Award by the Small Business Export Association and the National Health Leadership Award by the National Organization for Rare Disorders for his work to promote orphan drug research.

As a member of the weighty House Ways and Means Committee, Matsui has also been closely tied to issues of commerce. Since 1994, he has been acting chair of the Trade Subcommittee, which deals with international projects like the General Agreement on Tariffs and Trade, Most Favored Nation status for China, and U.S.-Japan trade negotiations. Most significantly, Matsui, a loyal Clinton ally, was the congressional leader in the administration's battle to implement the North American Free Trade Agreement (NAFTA) in 1993. As chair of the 30-member bipartisan House NAFTA Liaison Group, he lobbied his colleagues to approve the program, predicting that lowered trade barriers between Canada, Mexico, and the United States would improve overall standards of living in all three countries. Regarding the controversial proposal, large corporations like IBM and General Electric backed Matsui's stance, while many labor, environmental, and consumer groups criticized it. "Matsui sounds more and more like a Republican, and he's carrying water for the corporations that are pushing the same deregulation agenda that the Republicans are," said Craig A. Merrilees, director of the California Fair Trade Campaign (Bradsher 1993, 34).

One of the staunchest supporters of NAFTA was none other than Matsui's wife, Doris K. Okada Matsui, but not sheerly out of marital loyalty—Mrs. Matsui was the White House deputy director of public liaison assigned to garner grassroots support for the program. Their visibility in the campaign made them "the season's hot couple," as they were described in the *New York Times* in 1993. Doris Matsui is now director of government relations at a Washington, DC, law firm. The Matsuis are parents of one son, Brian.

Matsui has also been conscious of discrimination during his time in the House. In response to the opposition to trade with Mexico, but not with Canada, in the NAFTA accord, because "Canadian people's values are similar to ours," Matsui declared, "As an Asian American, all the time I hear the same arguments . . . . I resent those arguments. . . . I hear very credible liberal politicians use the arguments in a way that is offensive." Also, during his first term in Congress, some of Matsui's colleagues assumed that he would most prefer to serve on the Immigration Committee rather than his top choice, the House Judiciary Committee. "I was immediately stereotyped as an Asian," Matsui stated (Yang 1993, 74).

As with other Nikkei members of Congress, Matsui backed the Japanese American Redress Movement. Although initially hesitant to lend his vocal support as a young politician with few Asian Pacific Islander constituents—he would be at risk politically—he attended and testified at every committee meeting on redress bills in the House. Ultimately, however, his well-respected reputation helped to sway his colleagues' votes in favor of reparations for former World War II internees. As he eloquently expressed to his Congressional peers, "we have a responsibility to die for our country, but I tell you one thing that in a democracy, this democracy, with our Constitution, a citizen does not have a responsibility to do: every one of us does not have a responsibility to be incarcerated by our own government without charges, without trial, merely because of our race. That is what our constitutional fathers meant 200 years ago when they wrote the Bill of Rights. That is not a responsibility and an inconvenience of a democracy." When President George H.W. Bush finally signed appropriations legislation in November 1989, Matsui concluded, "This regrettable chapter in American history . . . ends constructively with a reaffirmation of the values this country was built on. This is the end of a long ordeal—an arduous national march toward redemption" (Hatamiya 1993).

## Sources

Bradsher, Keith. "Washington at Work: Campaign for Free-Trade Agreement Creates Capital's New Power Couple." *The New York Times*. 5 September 1993, p. 34.

Congressman Robert T. Matsui [official Web site]: www.house.gov/matsui [Accessed 17 October 2001].

Hatamiya, Leslie T. *Righting a Wrong: Japanese Americans and the Passage of the Civil Liberties Act of 1988*. Stanford: Stanford University Press, 1993.

Henry, Jim. "Robert Matsui." In *Notable Asian Americans*, ed. Helen Zia and Susan B. Gall. Detroit: Gale Research, Inc., 1995, pp. 238–240.

"Robert Takeo Matsui." *AP Candidate Bios*. The Associated Press Political Service. 1998.

Yang, Jeff. "The Power of Two." *A. Magazine*. Fall 1993, pp. 36–37, 73–75.

# "Spark" Masayuki Matsunaga

**Born:** 8 October 1916, Kukuiula, Hawaii.

**Died:** 15 April 1990, Toronto, Ontario, Canada.

**Education:** B.Ed., University of Hawaii, 1941; J.D., Harvard University, 1951.

**Positions Held:** Member, Hawaii Territorial House of Representatives, 1954–1959; Member, United States House of Representatives 1962–1976; Hawaii State Senator, United States Senate, 1976–1990.

**Awards, Honors:** World War II Army Citations: Bronze Star Medal with Valor, Purple Heart with Oak Leaf Cluster, Army Commendation Medal, Five Battle Stars.

**Summary:** "Spark" Masayuki Matsunaga was one of only three U.S. senators of Japanese ancestry to date. He was a crucial figure in the Japanese American redress and reparations movement of the 1980s.

## Early Years and Education

"Spark" Masayuki Matsunaga, the son of Issei Kingoro and Chiyono Fukushima Matsunaga, was born on 8 October 1916 in Kukuiula, Kauai, Hawaii. One of six children—four sons and two daughters—Matsunaga worked a number of jobs during high school, including warehouseman, stevedore, sales clerk, and bookkeeper. He applied himself just as diligently at the University of Hawaii, graduating in 1941 as a Phi Beta Kappa with a bachelor's degree in education.

History, however, interrupted the young Nisei's post-college plans. Matsunaga taught only briefly before joining the army as a second lieutenant later that year. After the December 1941 Pearl Harbor bombing and the February 1942 passage of President Franklin Delano Roosevelt's Executive Order 9066, Matsunaga was shipped to Camp McCoy in Wisconsin. Soon afterwards, the military grouped him and 1400 of his fellow Hawaiian Japanese into the 100th Infantry Battalion.

In the 100th, also known as the "Purple Heart Battalion," Matsunaga fought on the European front in World War II and was wounded twice in Italy. Eventually promoted to Captain, Matsunaga received the Bronze Star Medal with Valor, the Purple Heart with the Oak Leaf Cluster, an Army Commendation Medal, and Five Battle Stars. He continued to serve in the military after the war as a veterans' counselor in the Interior Department from 1945 to 1947 and the chief of the priority division of the War Assets Administration from 1947 to 1948. Thereafter, Matsunaga quickly reestablished himself in civilian life, marrying Helene Hatsumi Tokunaga in 1948 and enrolling in Harvard Law School under the GI Benefits Bill, where he earned his J.D. in 1951.

## Career Highlights

As a fledgling attorney, Matsunaga immersed himself in government. He was an assistant public prosecutor for the city and county of Honolulu from 1952 to 1954, attended the state and county Democratic Convention and served as an executive board member of Hawaii's Democratic Party. He then joined the territorial House of Representatives in 1954, where he was the majority leader in his fifth and final year. After Hawaii attained statehood, Matsunaga became one of the islands' first representatives in Congress, winning the first of seven consecutive elections to the House in 1962.

In the House, Matsunaga sat on the Rule, Aging, Steering and Policy Committees and was the deputy majority whip.

When Hawaii's first senator and incumbent Hiram L. Fong retired in 1976, Matsunaga put his name into the Senate race. Defeating his opponents with 53.7 percent of the vote, he secured the first of his three terms in the upper chamber.

As a liberal Democrat, Matsunaga fought for a number of issues. In regards to

"Reaganomics," a "supply side philosophy which pushed for tax reductions and generous benefits to corporations and wealthy individuals to encourage new investments and stimulate the overall economy, during the early 1980s, for example, he stated that American voters felt that President Ronald Reagan "should not remain on [his] course." A member of the Energy/Natural Resources Committee, he was an advocate of the environment. His last vote, in fact, in the Senate backed the extension of the Clean Air Act in 1990. Additionally, he investigated the possibility of using hydrogen fuel for airplanes and wind-powered commercial ships. He also espoused joint Soviet-American efforts in space exploration.

A firm believer in peace studies, Matsunaga lobbied his colleagues for 22 years to establish a U.S. Peace Institute, which finally came into fruition in 1984. "Peacemaking is as much an art to be learned as war," he once stated (Folkart 1990, A1). The Board of Regents of the University of Hawaii followed suit in 1986 with its creation of the Spark M. Matsunaga Institute for Peace. The mission of the academic organization is "to explore, develop and share knowledge of peace through teaching, research, publication, and public service. In doing so, it seeks to promote peace personally, locally, nationally, and globally through compassionate and nonviolent means. By addressing the major issues of conflict management, community building, and the reduction of violence, the Matsunaga Institute for Peace draws closer to its goal: a world at peace" (www.2.hawaii.edu/mip/mission/html).

As an advocate of social understanding, Matsunaga was a key player in the Japanese redress and reparations movement. Quick to defend his community in the face of racist assaults—he once criticized future Vice President Spiro T. Agnew for calling a reporter a "fat Jap" (Agnew later apologized but lamented what he perceived to be a diminishing sense of humor among Americans)—Matsunaga led the fight in the Senate. In a highly unusual move, he personally lobbied each of the other 99 senators in the 100th Congress at least once, and some even multiple times. The combination of his tireless efforts—the *Washington Post* described him as "the Senator who never sleeps"—his personable demeanor, "Sparkie" was voted one of the two "most popular" members of Congress by his peers in 1981—and his heartfelt testimonies were largely responsible for the willingness of 75 senators to co-sponsor S. 1009, the Japanese American redress bill. Of Matsunaga's invaluable contribution, said the late Mike Masaoka, a Washington lobbyist, "No doubt many who personally did not favor this corrective and remedial measure joined in the co-sponsorship and final endorsement of this extraordinary congressional language because of their personal friendship and affection for the Hawaiian lawmaker" (Hatamiya 1993).

Matsunaga died at age 73 on 15 April 1990 in Toronto, Canada, after a fight with a series of health problems, including prostate and bone cancer, the flu, ulcers, back problems, and a heart attack. He was survived by his wife Helene, his three daughters, Karen, Diane, and Merle, his two sons Keene and Matthew, three grandsons, and five siblings. Praising his "humanitarian" efforts, then Hawaii Governor John D. Waihee declared, "He will be remembered most for his vision of peace and his faith in the human heart. In his memory we will carry on his quest. In his spirit we will strive for the highest of principles and the brightest of worlds" (Folkart 1990, A1).

## Sources

Flint, Peter B. "Spark M. Matsunaga Dies at 73: Senator Led Fight for Reparations." *New York Times*. 16 April 1990, p. 10.

Folkart, Burt A. "Hawaii Sen. S. Matsunaga: Led Fight for Reparations." *Los Angeles Times*. 16 April 1990, p. A24.

Hatamiya, Leslie T. *Righting a Wrong: Japanese Americans and the Passage of the Civil Liberties Act of 1988*. Stanford: Stanford University Press, 1993.

"Spark Masayuki Matsunaga." *AP Candidate Bios*. The Associated Press Political Service. 1988.

"Spark Masayuki Matsunaga." *The Complete Marquis Who's Who Biographies*. Reed Elsevier, Inc., 1992. Last updated 9 July 1992.

# Stanley T. Matsunaka

Stan Matsunaka. (Courtesy of Stan Matsunaka)

**Born:** 12 November 1953, Akron, Colorado.

**Education:** B.S., Colorado State University, 1975; J.D., University of San Diego, 1979.

**Positions Held:** Colorado State Senator, 1994–present.

**Awards, Honors:** Lairmer County, Colorado Outstanding Young Lawyer, 1985; Legislator of the Year awards from the Colorado Association of School Boards, Colorado Bankers Association, and Colorado Association of Commerce and Industry.

**Summary:** Stanley T. Matsunaka is a member of Colorado's State Senate.

## Early Years

Stanley T. Matsunaka, a second-generation Colorado native, was born to Harry and Mary Matsunaka on 12 November 1953 in the town of Akron, Colorado. Matsunaka demonstrated his interest in politics and government at an early age, becoming the student body president of Fort Morgan High School before graduating in 1971.

## Education

From Fort Morgan, Matsunaka went on to Colorado State University, where he earned a bachelor of science degree in biological sciences in 1975. He continued his studies at his alma mater before transferring to the University of San Diego, where he received his juris doctor degree in 1979.

## Career Highlights

Returning to his home state with diploma in hand, Matsunaka established a private legal practice, which he still maintains, in the city of Loveland. Among his specialties are advice and litigation regarding real estate, construction and business contracts, estate planning, representation in personal injury, workers' compensation and employment claims, and other general civil practice matters. For his distinguished work during the early years of his career, Matsunaka was named Larimer County's Oustanding Young Lawyer in 1985. He has participated in a number of professional organizations as a member of the American, Colorado, and Larimer County Bar Associations and as past secretary of both the Young Lawyers Section of Colorado Bar Association and the Larimer County Bar Association.

In 1994, Stanley T. Matsunaka, a Democrat, was elected to the Colorado State Senate representing the heavily-Republican District 15 for the first of his two terms. He defeated incumbent GOP Senator Jim Roberts and became the Rocky Mountain state's first Japanese American elected official. He campaigned on a number of issues, including setting minimum standards in education, contending that schools would strive to surpass these levels. "They'll never settle for just the standards," he opined (Lipsher 1994, B1). Matsunaka also supported the rights of gun owners, pro-choice, and a statewide crime-prevention grant program. "One of the things I don't believe we need is more prisons," he stated. "I think we need tougher sentences for more serious offenders and alternative sentences for minor offenses. Let's see them working on public-work projects wearing bright orange bibs" (Lipsher 1994, B1).

Since assuming office, Matsunaka has served on the Senate's Business Affairs and Labor, Education (where he is presently Chair), Local Government, Joint Legal Services, and Computer Management Committees and has successfully promoted legislation protecting insurance consumers, reducing the size of government, making government more accountable and efficient, and various school-related issues. Matsunaka received Legislator of the Year awards from the Colorado Association of School Boards, Colorado Bankers Association, and Colorado Association of Commerce and Industry. He is currently President of the Colorado State Senate.

Outside of his official duties, Matsunaka has maintained an active community profile. He coaches local youth athletic teams, is a Cub Scout Master and Den Leader, Board Member and Past President of the Loveland Sertoma Club, Deacon and Elder of Mountain View Presbyterian Church, and is committed to pro-bono legal work.

Matsunaka is married to Kathleen Matsunaka, a registered nurse. They are the parents of Melissa, Brian, and Kristi.

## Sources

Lipsher, Steve. "Senate Incumbent, Rival Miles Apart. Race One of Most Divisive in State." *Denver Post.* 6 September 1994, p. B1.

Sanko, John. "Loveland Attorney Finds Out He's A State Senator at 2 A.M." *Denver Rocky Mountain News.* 5 November 1998, p. 51A.

# Dale Minami

Dale Minami. (Courtesy of Dale Minami)

**Born:** 13 October 1946, Los Angeles, California.

**Education:** B.A., University of Southern California, 1968; J.D., University of California, Berkeley, 1972.

**Positions Held:** Co-founder, Asian Law Caucus; co-founder, Asian American Bar Association of the Greater Bay Area; co-founder, Asian Pacific Bar of California; co-founder, Coalition of Asian Pacific Americans.

**Awards, Honors:** State Bar of California's President's Pro Bono Service Award, 1984; Coro Foundation Achievement Award, 1986; the Harry Dow Memorial Fellowship "Justice in Action" Award, 1988; Organization of Chinese Americans Leadership Award, 1989.

**Summary:** Dale Minami is one of the leading Asian Pacific American advocate lawyers today, co-founding a number of Asian Pacific American advocacy organizations and helping to win such significant legal victories as the World War II Japanese American coram nobis cases.

### Early Years

Dale Minami, a third-generation Japanese American, was born in Los Angeles, California, on 13 October 1946 to Nisei parents recently released from the Rohwer, Arkansas, World War II concentration camp. His father was a gardener and proprietor of a small sporting-goods business that also employed his mother.

### Education

After graduating from a public high school in Los Angeles in 1964, Minami attended the University of Southern California. An outstanding student, he was initiated into Phi Beta Kappa and graduated magna cum laude in 1968. He then attended the University of California, Berkeley's Boalt Law School where he earned his J.D. in 1971. Immersed in one of the political hotspots of Asian Americans during that period, Minami later carried its influence into his legal work.

### Career Highlights

As an attorney, Minami divided his time between private practice and teaching. In addition to representing clients in personal injury, entertainment law, and civil litigation cases, he worked as lecturer for Oakland's Mills College Department of Ethnic Studies and the University of California, Berkeley's Asian American studies courses.

It did not take long for Minami to become involved in Asian American legal advocacy. Beginning in 1972, he co-founded a series of organizations dedicated to representing Asian American concerns both within the profession and in larger society. These included: the Asian Law Caucus (Minami served as its first lawyer and director) established in 1972 to address civil rights, employment and housing discrimination, and immigration issues for Asian Pacific Americans; the Asian American Bar Association of the Greater Bay Area in 1976, the premier Asian American Bar organization in the country; the Asian Pacific Bar of California in 1988; and the Coalition of Asian Pacific Americans in 1989, the nation's first APA political action committee.

Throughout his career, Minami has been involved in a number of high-profile cases concerning Asian American civil rights. Among these are *Chan v. City and County of California*, which represented UC Berkeley student Barry Chan who had been assaulted and arrested by area police for photographing random instances of their harassment against Asian men; *Wong v. Younger*, a situation protesting the printing and distribution of pamphlets stereotyping Chinese Americans as gamblers and opium smokers; the Korematsu, Hirabayashi, and Yasui coram nobis cases involving the protests of Japanese Americans against incarceration during World War II; and the Don Nakanishi Tenure battle, in which UCLA Asian American Studies Center director and professor Don Nakanishi sued the school for discriminatory tenure procedures. Of the Nakanishi tenure struggle, Minami remarked, "We achieved victory because we were able to develop a sound legal argument as well as a larger political strategy, capable of mobilizing thousands of allies nationwide.... Don's case became a test of whether our aspirations would be considered seriously or cast aside as inconsequential." He continued, "It was also a test of whether we could effectively coalesce different groups and coordinate a coherent strategy to achieve justice. Finally, it was also a test for the University—not of its strength to withstand our concerted offensive, but of its commitment to its own rhetoric of diversity." Concluded Minami, "I believe we did not gain just another Asian Pacific American professor out of this battle. Nor did we achieve a "victory" over an invincible institution. What we gained was more intangible and also more significant. We gained a sense of empowerment, a sense of confidence that we can fight and we can win, even against great odds" (Minami 1990, 81, 106–107).

Currently a partner in the firm Minami, Lew, Takami, and Lee, which he founded in 1989, Minami has received a number of honors recognizing his contributions to the cause of civil rights. These include the State Bar of California's President's Pro Bono Service Award in 1984, the Coro Foundation Achievement Award in 1986, the Harry Dow Memorial Fellowship "Justice in Action" Award in 1988, and the Organization of Chinese Americans Leadership Award in 1989.

### Sources

Hatamiya, Leslie T. *Righting a Wrong: Japanese Americans and the Passage of the Civil Liberties Act of 1988.* Stanford: Stanford University Press, 1993.

Henry, Jim. "Dale Minami." In *Notable Asian Americans*, ed. Helen Zia and Susan B. Gall. Detroit, MI: Gale Research Inc., 1995, pp. 257–259.

Minami, Dale. "Guerrilla War at UCLA: Political and Legal Dimensions of the Tenure Battle." *Amerasia Journal.* 16:1 1990, pp. 81–107.

## Norman Y. Mineta

**Born:** 12 November 1931, San Jose, California.

**Education:** B.S., University of California, Berkeley, 1953.

**Positions Held:** Mayor, San Jose, California, 1971–1974; Member, U.S. House of Representatives, 1975–1995; U.S. Secretary of Commerce, 2000; U.S. Secretary of Transportation, 2001–present.

**Awards, Honors:** 1995, George Washington University, Martin Luther King, Jr. Commemorative Medal.

Norman Y. Mineta. (Courtesy of the Office of the Secretary of Transportation)

**Summary:** Norman Y. Mineta is the first Japanese American to serve as mayor of a mainland city in the United States. He is also one of the first Asian Pacific Americans elected to the United States House of Representatives and the first Asian Pacific American to hold a Secretary position in a Presidential cabinet.

### Early Years

Born in San Jose, California, on 12 November 1931, Norman Yoshio Mineta had a typical Nisei upbringing. Kay Kunisaki, Mineta's father, traveled by steamship to the United States from Kunmaiden, Japan, to learn new farming techniques. Originally a sojourner, he had intended to return home but instead settled and sent for his bride, Kane Watanabe, the sister of a village friend, in 1912. As with other Japanese immigrants at the time, the Minetas faced a number of discriminatory statutes including California's Alien Land Act of 1913, which prohibited "aliens ineligible to citizenship"—including all Asians—from land ownership. Fortunately, they were able to circumvent this restriction by asking a local attorney, J.B. Peckham, to hold the title to their house, described by Mineta as a "comfortable," three bedroom, "Spanish style stucco with a red tile roof." His father, "making a good living" with the Mineta Insurance Agency, provided a stable lifestyle for his wife and five children (Mineta 1987, 173).

Everything changed for the Minetas following the Pearl Harbor attack on 7 December 1941. With President Franklin Delano Roosevelt's signing of Executive Order 9066 on 19 February 1942, they and all other persons of Japanese ancestry on the West Coast were marked for removal out of "military necessity." The government closed the Mineta Insurance Agency, suspended Kay's license "for the duration of the war," and seized the family's accounts at the Yokohoma Species Bank. The Minetas hurriedly packed a few basic necessities which, for the ten-year-old Mineta meant his Cub Scout uniform, a baseball mitt, and bat (the latter was confiscated as a "weapon"), and were forced to dispense the rest, including their wire-haired terrier Skippy. The family rushed to lease their home before leaving for the Santa Anita racetrack, a detention center in Southern California, where they were assigned to an uncertain future at the Heart Mountain concentration camp in Wyoming. Mineta later recalled, "I only saw my dad cry three times: on December 7, when he couldn't understand why Pearl Harbor was attacked; when we were evacuated, and when my mother died" (Molotsky 1988, A22).

While life in camp was hardly normal, Mineta was able to participate in some of his regular activities, including school and Cub Scouts. As a scout, he had the opportunity to interact with boys from the nearby town of Cody, including the future Senator Alan Simpson. "Somehow we got paired and sort of hit it off," Mineta remembered. Simpson's impressions of the young internee were favorable, describing him as "active, spirited, kind of enthusiastic about things. He seemed to be in everything. I do not remember Norm Mineta being depressed." The two exchanged stories and played games like knot-tying contests. Keeping in touch after the war, Mineta and Simpson would later cross paths on Capitol Hill (Molotsky 1988, A22).

## Education

After being released from Heart Mountain in 1943, Norman Y. Mineta returned to San Jose, where he graduated from high school in 1949. He went on to earn his bachelor's degree in business from the University of California, Berkeley in 1953. Soon afterwards, he began a three year service in the army, working in military intelligence in Japan and Korea.

## Career Highlights

Mineta returned home in 1956 to work for his father's resurrected insurance business. In addition to his job, he was active in the local community, joining a number of organizations such as the Japanese American Citizens League, the Greater San Jose Chamber of Commerce, and the North San Jose Optimist Club. He also took the first steps of his political career with positions on the Santa Clara County Council finance committee, the San Jose Housing Authority, and the San Jose City Council, of which he was the first non-white councilman. In 1971, Mineta made history again as the first Japanese American mayor of a major U.S. mainland city.

Mineta served for three terms as San Jose's mayor before his election to the first of ten consecutive terms in the U.S. House of Representatives. Backed by a supportive Japanese American contingent, he defeated his Republican opponent with 53 percent of the vote in California's 13th Congressional District to claim the seat vacated by retiring Representative Charles S. Gubser.

In his two decades on Capitol Hill, Mineta gradually rose through the ranks of his party, filling such positions as the deputy Democratic whip and serving on the Budget, Policy and Steering Committee, Post Office, and Science,

Space, and Technology Committees. His highest post came in 1993 with his promotion to chair of the Transportation and Infrastructure Committee or Public Works and Transportation Committee. Recognizing Mineta's expertise in transportation, President Bill Clinton considered him for the Secretary of Transportation opening in his cabinet in 1992. Mineta declined in order to remain in the House to chair the Public Works and Transportation Committee, becoming the first Asian American to lead a congressional committee. But two years later with the Democrats' loss of their majority in the House, Mineta lost the chairmanship.

Despite his refusal, however, colleagues still viewed Mineta as a staunch Clintonite. For example, in 1993, he was one of twenty-two House Democrats to vote affirmatively on all nine of the President's budget proposals. Representative Gerald Solomon even suggested that Mineta threw his support behind the North American Free Trade Agreement in exchange for funding for Northern California's Bay Area Rapid Transit system. Mineta described Solomon's accusations as "bull" (Associated Press 1996).

Aside from his authority on public transportation, Mineta is perhaps best known for his crucial role in the passage of the 1988 Civil Liberties Act, granting redress and reparations to the Japanese American prisoners of America's World War II concentration camps. The Japanese American Citizens League first approached him in 1979 to strategize for their campaign. Like Hawaii's Senator Daniel Inouye, Representative Mineta felt that assembling a study commission was the first step toward the public education necessary for a successful effort.

Thereafter, Mineta continued to back the redress movement at considerable political risk—Asian Pacific Islanders comprised only 6 percent of his district, so his support could be construed as self-interest. Regardless, he devoted himself wholeheartedly, offering his office, for example, as the Congressional headquarters for the campaign. His staff was active in the legislative process, serving as liaisons between different committees and Japanese American organizations. Mineta also worked to persuade his fellow Congress members to support redress. His longtime friendship with Senator Alan Simpson, for example, proved to be fruitful—Simpson was one of the redress bill's 73 co-sponsors in the Senate. In addition, as a regent at the Smithsonian Institution, Mineta was also instrumental in the creation of its exhibit, "A More Perfect Union," showcasing the World War II evacuation and internment of Japanese Americans to commemorate the bicentennial of the Constitution in 1987. The timing of this high profile museum event also facilitated the passage of the Civil Liberties Act.

Mineta attended every hearing on redress in the House, sharing his wartime experiences with his colleagues. Following its passage on 10 August 1988, he remarked, "I must confess that this is a moment of great emotion for me," and that the date was one "that I will remember for the rest of my life." He also stated, "We now hope, and pray, that the tragedies of the internment never again occur" (Hatamiya).

The fight, however, did not end there; problems with the subsequent appropriations process prompted Mineta to declare, "In 1988, the president said we made a mistake, that we admit a wrong and will provide a restitution payment. But today, in his fiscal year 1990 budget, the president asks for a $20 million appropriation to provide that payment for no more than 1,000 of the 60,000 individuals eligible" (Hatamiya).

"As president in 1988 and as a veteran of World War II in 1945, Ronald Reagan said that his idea of liberty and justice for all is 'the American way.' Why has the president's vision narrowed now? Why did he not fight for the full $500 million to honor his commitment and our nation's ideals?" (Hatamiya).

After the conclusion of the redress movement, Mineta continued to be a voice for civil rights, working on issues such as the Americans with Disabilities Act, which called for improved access to public buildings, and potential discrimination against Americans of Middle Eastern ancestry during the Persian Gulf War. In 1995, he founded the Congressional Asian Pacific American Caucus Institute, now known as the Asian Pacific Institute for Congressional Studies, which is, according to Mineta, "the only national organization dedicated to increasing the participation of Asian Americans in politics."

Mineta resigned from the House in 1995 before completing his 11th term to become a senior vice president and managing director at Lockheed Martin Corporation, the nation's largest defense contractor. Due to his expertise, he was hired to head a transportation-related division of the company. He made it clear, however, that he left the House on a positive note. "This is not a decision I take lightly," he said. "But for me, I see this as a great new opportunity to build a better society. Part of the challenge and responsibility of public service is to know when to turn back the mandate of the people to the people—even though it may not be at the time we normally set aside for elections. For me, this is that time" (*Aerospace Daily* 1995, 387).

Norman Y. Mineta did not leave public service for long. He chaired the 21-member National Civil Aviation Review Commission, which Congress established to examine the growing crisis in air transport. In its December 1997 report, the commission was one of the first official sources to use the word "gridlock" to describe the state of air traffic. Many of the commission's recommendations were adopted by the Clinton administration, including Federal Aviation Administration reform.

Eight years after declining an invitation to join the Clinton cabinet, President Clinton named Mineta on June 30, 2000, to replace outgoing Commerce Secretary William M. Daley. The Senate unanimously confirmed him as the first Asian American secretary on July 21, 2000.

Although Mineta's tenure as a Cabinet secretary looked short when the Democrat nominee, Vice President Al Gore, lost the 2000 presidential election, Republican President George W. Bush nominated Mineta to become Secretary of Transportation, making him the first Cabinet member to move directly from a Democratic administration into a Republican one. Noting the bipartisan gesture, Mineta declared at his nomination, although he continued to remain a Democrat, "[t]here are no Democratic or Republican highways, no such thing as a Republican or Democratic traffic congestion. . . . Our national transportation policy must have one overriding, bipartisan goal. And that is to give our economy the tools and the infrastructure it needs in order to create and sustain growth and prosperity." On January 25, 2001, the Senate once again unanimously confirmed Mineta as a Cabinet secretary (Eggins and Pianin 2001, A6). Mineta is married to Danealia (Deni) Mineta. He has two sons, David and Stuart Mineta, and two stepsons, Robert and Mark Brantner.

## Sources

Eggen, Dan and Eric Pianin. "Approval for Norton, Battle for Ashcroft; Senate Confirms Mineta, Thompson." *Washington Post.* 25 January 2001, p. A6.

Gupta, Himanee. "Norman Y. Mineta." In *Notable Asian Americans*, ed. Helen Zia and Susan B. Gall. Detroit, MI: Gale Research, Inc., 1995, pp. 259–260.

Hatamiya, Leslie T. *Righting a Wrong: Japanese Americans and the Passage of the Civil Liberties Act of 1988.* Stanford: Stanford University Press, 1993.

Lee, Denny. "Norman Y. Mineta." In "The A. 100: 100 Most Influential Asian Americans of the Decade." *A. Magazine.* October/November 1993, p. 93.

Mineta, Norman, as told to Susan Schindehette. "The Wounds of War: A California Congressman Recalls the Trauma of World War II Internment." *People.* 14 December 1987, p. 173.

Molotsky, Irvin. "Friendships: The Heat of War Welds a Bond that Endures Across Aisles and Years." *The New York Times.* 26 April 1988, p. A22.

"Norman Yoshio Mineta." *AP Candidate Bios.* The Associated Press Political Service. 1996.

"Norman Yoshio Mineta." *The Complete Marquis Who's Who Biographies.* Reed Elsevier, Inc. Last updated 4 June 1997.

"Rep. Mineta Resigns to Take Lockheed Martin Post." *Aerospace Daily*. 12 September 1995.

Wald, Matthew L. "Man in the News: Norman Yoshio Mineta." *New York Times*. 3 January 2001.

## Patsy T. Mink

Patsy T. Mink. (Courtesy of the Office of the Honorable Patsy T. Mink)

**Born:** 6 December 1927, Paia, Hawaii.

**Education:** B.S., University of Hawaii, 1948; J.D., University of Chicago, 1951.

**Positions Held:** Member, Hawaii Territorial/State Legislature, 1956–1959; 1963–1964; Member, U.S. House of Representatives, 1965–1977, 1990–present.

**Awards, Honors:** Americans for Democratic Action 1988 Winn Newman Lifetime Achievement Award, 1992 Hawaii Lawyers Lifetime Achievement Award, 1991 Feminist of the Year Award, named to A. *Magazine*'s top 25 Most Influential Asian Americans of 1996.

**Summary:** Representative Patsy T. Mink is the first Asian Pacific American woman to be elected to the U.S. Congress.

### Early Years

Patsy Takemoto Mink was born in Paia, Hawaii, on 6 December 1927 to Mitama Takeyama and Suematsu Takemoto. Her father's occupation as a civil engineer allowed the family an affluent lifestyle. Mink began her education at the young age of four. A bright pupil, she was one of the few students of color to attend the Kaunoa English Standard School. She later transferred to Maui High School where she was both student body president and the class of 1944 valedictorian.

### Education

The ambitious young Mink next enrolled at the University of Hawaii. A zoology and chemistry major, she intended to become a physician, a dream she had harbored since undergoing an appendectomy as a young girl. Patsy Mink's extracurricular activities in college revealed her original career goals as well as her future in politics—she was the president of the pre-medical students club and a member of the varsity debate team.

Mink attended three different schools during her college career due in part to her dedication to her aspiration of becoming a doctor. Her first transfer out of the University of Hawaii was to Wilson College in Chambersburg, Pennsylvania before switching to the University of Nebraska, an institution that she felt could offer her solid training in the sciences. After she fell ill, however, she returned to the islands to complete her coursework.

Mink's life changed direction once again following her graduation from the University of Hawaii in 1948. Unable to gain entrance into medical school, she worked as an office clerk for awhile before deciding to apply to law school. In 1951, she earned her J.D. from the University of Chicago, becoming the first Hawaiian Nisei woman to earn a law degree. It was there that she also met her husband, a geophysics student named John Francis Mink. The two married that same year and had their only daughter, Gwendolyn (Wendy) Rachel

Mink, now a political science professor at the University of California, Santa Cruz, in 1952.

## Career Highlights

The interracial union proved to be difficult for Mink, not only in terms of her family (her parents were against the marriage), but also in relation to her career. More conservative firms in the islands were reluctant to hire an Asian American woman involved in such a relationship, despite the fact that she had passed the Hawaii Bar Exam. As a result, she spearheaded her own practice, which she operated from 1953 to 1964, specializing in "marginal" issues such as divorce, adoption, and criminal defense. She also lectured in business law at her alma mater.

As part of Hawaii's Democratic Movement largely comprised of Nisei, Mink helped to gain a foothold for her party in the territorial government by establishing Everyman's Organization, which advocated Democratic Party participation among younger adults and by serving as charter president of the Hawaii Young Democrats, an offshoot organization. She was also the national vice president of the Young Democrats of America from 1957 to 1959. Mink's successful bids for election to the territorial House in 1956, the territorial Senate in 1959, and state Senate demonstrated the shift in power from the Republicans to the Democrats in her home state at the time.

In January of 1965, Mink made history as the first Asian Pacific Islander woman to be sworn into Congress, filling the second seat opened by a growing Hawaiian population. Known as an articulate, liberal "political maverick," Mink's beliefs positioned her away from the Democratic mainstream throughout her years in the House. She advocated women's rights in the Hawaii state legislature on campaigns such as "Equal Pay, Equal Work," and in the private sector with a lawsuit against the University of Chicago for distribution of the drug DES (diethylstilbestrol, a synthetic hormone originally believed to prevent miscarriage but in actuality engendered reproductive problems in the children of pregnant women)—Mink herself was prescribed DES while in Chicago. She supported the Women's Educational Equity Act, child care, and abortion. During the Vietnam War, she voiced her opposition to the United States' involvement by traveling to Paris with Representative Bella Abzug (D-NY) to engage in peace talk dialogues. She also set a legal precedent for the handling of the Watergate scandal when she and 23 other members of Congress took the U.S. government to court for issues relating to the Freedom of Information Act.

After her first six terms in the House, Mink switched to the executive branch to serve as President Carter's Assistant Secretary of State for Ocean and International, Environmental, and Scientific Affairs. Beforehand, however, she had lost a Senate race in the 1976 Hawaii Democratic primary and a run for president in 1972. Undaunted, she followed her three year term in the Carter administration with a triple term presidency of the Americans for Democratic Action. "Life is not based on being an elected politician," she once stated. "Politics is a constant involvement in the day-to-day working of society as a whole, one part of which is government" (Saiki 1985, 132).

During the 1980s, Patsy Mink continued to pursue elected offices with mixed success. She was a member of the Honolulu City Council from 1983 to 1987 and chair from 1983 to 1985. While she lost two bids for governor and mayor of Honolulu in 1986 and 1988, respectively, she remained active serving as a delegate to the National Democratic Convention in 1984, managed a private practice from 1987 to 1990, and founded a nonprofit, nonpartisan group to study the proceedings of the state legislature.

Mink stepped back into the national arena in 1990 when she filled the vacancy left in the House by Daniel Akaka, who in turn assumed the late Senator Stanley T. Matsunaga's seat. Later that year, she was elected to a full term, and has since followed her victory with four more terms in 1992, 1994, 1996, and 1998.

In her second run in Congress, Mink has remained a liberal Democrat, earning, for example, a perfect 100 points from the Americans for Democratic Action for her voting record in 1997. In 1991, she worked to expand the numbers of college students eligible for financial aid with legislation. As a member of the Education and Workforce and Budget and Steering Committees, she has facilitated the passage of various bills pertaining to improving the nation's child care and educational system. When asked in 1996 by A. *Magazine* what she believed to be the foremost area of concern in domestic policy, Mink replied, "I think right now, it's all of this anti–Asian Pacific legislation that's going through the Congress. I think all Asian Pacific people, citizen and non citizen, have to be very concerned with what's going on" (A. *Magazine* 1996, 28).

Her performance both in and out of the House has garnered her countless honors, including the Americans for Democratic Action 1988 Winn Newman Lifetime Achievement Award, the 1992 Hawaii Lawyers Lifetime Achievement Award, and the 1991 Feminist of the Year Award. A. *Magazine* ranked Mink as one of the top 25 Most Influential Asian Americans of 1996. Among her achievements highlighted in the publication's "Power Brokers" article was her appointment as chair of the Congressional Asian Pacific American Caucus Institute and her leadership in halting the U.S. Defense Department's violations of the "Don't Ask, Don't Tell Policy" at Hawaii's Hickam Air Force Base. Stated the authors, "Mink's leadership of the Caucus gives her a bully pulpit from which to stare off the threats of legislative attack on immigrants, welfare recipients, and other vulnerable Americans. A true fighter, who's fighting on the right side, at the right time" (Chen et al. 1996/1997, 59).

Patsy Mink died on September 20, 2002 in Honolulu, Hawaii, as this book was going to press.

### Sources

Chan, Sucheng. *Asian Americans: An Interpretive History*. Boston: Twayne Publishers, 1991.

Chen, Liliana et al. "Power Brokers 1996: The 25 Most Influential Asian Americans." A. *Magazine*. December 1996/January 1997, p. 59.

C, Samuel R. "Patsy Takemoto Mink." in *Notable Asian Americans*, ed. Helen Zia and Susan B. Gall. Detroit, MI: Gale Research, Inc., 1995, pp. 261–262.

"The Magnificent 7." A. *Magazine*. 30 November 1996, p. 28.

"Patsy Takemoto Mink," *AP Candidate Bios*. The Associated Press Political Service, 1998.

U.S. House of Representatives Web site: www.house.gov/mink [Accessed 20 April 1999].

## Kenneth Daniel Miyagishima

Ken Miyagishima. (Courtesy of Ken Miyagishima)

**Born:** 15 May 1963, Keesler AFB, Biloxi, Mississippi.

**Education:** B.B.A., New Mexico State University, May 1985.

**Positions Held:** Commissioner, Dona Ana County Government, Las Cruces, New Mexico, 1993–present.

**Awards, Honors:** Farmers Insurance Championship Award, 1997; eight different Topper Club citations.

**Summary:** Kenneth D. Miyagishima is the first American of Japanese ancestry elected to public office in the state of New Mexico.

### Early Years and Education

Kenneth Daniel Miyagishima was born on 15 May 1963 at Keesler AFB, Biloxi, Mississippi to Kazuji Miyagishima and the former Catalina Porras. His father, a Terminal Island, California native, was a member of the Air Force at that time. Miyagishima spent his early childhood in Lompoc, California, before moving with his parents to Alamogordo, New Mexico in 1968. After three years, they relocated to Las Cruces, a town about 45 miles northwest of El Paso, Texas, where he has resided ever since. He attended local public schools, graduating from Las Cruces High School in 1981. He then completed the requirements for two undergraduate degrees, one in Finance and the other in Real Estate, at New Mexico State University in 1985.

### Career Highlights

While in college, the enterprising Miyagishima founded his own company, Ken Miyagishima Insurance Agency Inc. "This business would allow me to sustain an interest in politics and helping people, two things I enjoy very much," he explained (personal communication to Ellen D. Wu, 1999). In 1989, he also began teaching management and finance at Dona Ana Branch Community College. A year later, he waged his first campaign for public office, losing the New Mexico State Representative, District 37 seat by a mere 320 votes out of a total of 6,350 ballots cast.

The defeat, however, did not deter Miyagishima from his goal of public service.

In 1992, at the age of 29, he ran for Commissioner of Dona Ana County—the second most populous in New Mexico—securing 60 percent of the votes in the primary. Though he faced two opponents in the primary, he won the seat uncontested in the general election. With his victory, he became the first elected public official of Japanese ancestry in a state where there are approximately 1,500 Japanese Americans out of a total population of 1.5 million.

One of five commissioners, Miyagishima was elected County Chairman of the Board in 1995, a feat he repeated two years later after winning reelection in 1996.

Aside from his public duties, Miyagishima continues to run his insurance business. A successful real estate broker and licensed insurance agent, he has won a number of awards throughout his career, including the Farmers Insurance Championship Award in 1997 and eight different Topper Club citations. In addition, he is an active member of the Las Cruces Rotary Club and the local chapter of Toastmasters International. Miyagishima is married to the former Kathryn Pacheco of Hatch, New Mexico, with whom he has a daughter, Danielle.

### Sources

"Miyagishima Elected to County Post in New Mexico." *Rafu Shimpo.* 13 February 1995, p. 1.

Personal communication to Ellen D. Wu, 27 September 1999.

## Susan Oki Mollway

**Born:** 6 November 1950, Honolulu, Hawaii.

**Education:** B.A., University of Hawaii, 1971; M.A., University of Hawaii, 1973; J.D., Harvard University, 1981.

**Positions Held:** U.S. District Judge, District of Hawaii, 1998–present.

Susan Oki Mollway. (© 1999 Ed. Gross/Images Photography)

**Awards, Honors:** Outstanding Woman Lawyer of the Year, Hawaii Women Lawyers Association, 1987; named to A. *Magazine*'s 25 Most Influential Asian Americans, 1998.

**Summary:** Susan Oki Mollway is the first Asian Pacific American woman to be appointed as a federal judge. She currently presides over the United States District Court for the District of Hawaii.

## Early Years and Education

Susan Oki Mollway was born to Eichi and Nobuko Oki in Honolulu, Hawaii, on 6 November 1950. Both her family's history and her ancestry shaped her career trajectory from an early age. Her father was one of the most significant influences, having fought in World War II as part of the all-Nisei 442nd infantry in Europe. Upon returning home after the conflict, he made use of the GI-Bill to attend law school. "I benefited from his experiences," she stated. "Not many of us, as Japanese Americans, have been unaffected somehow by the experience of World War II." It was this imprint of history on the Japanese American community that led Mollway to become politically active. "That was part of the reason why I joined the ACLU—to protect the rights of all American citizens" (Panesar 1998, 9).

Before she made civil rights advocacy her life's work, however, Mollway completed her education. She attended the University of Hawaii as a major in English literature, graduating Phi Beta Kappa in 1971. She then continued in the field, earning a masters in 1973 from the same institution. For the following two years, she worked as a writing and literature instructor in the Department of English at the University of Hawaii, Manoa before working in Japan as a lecturer in English at Takushoku University in Tokyo for a year. From 1976 to 1978, she served as an English-language editor for the book publisher Charles E. Tuttle Co. in Tokyo. When her husband Daniel applied to Boston Law College in the late 1970s, she applied to Harvard University's law school. Her decision turned out to be a fruitful one, and Mollway returned to the States to begin coursework. While in Cambridge, she served as Editor-in-Chief of the Harvard Civil Rights–Civil Liberties Law Review, foreshadowing her future career. She graduated second in her class, cum laude, in 1981.

## Career Highlights

As a neophyte J.D., Susan Oki Mollway quickly made her mark on the legal profession. An associate and later partner of Cades, Schutte, Fleming, and Wright in Honolulu, she concentrated in civil litigation. After just six years in the firm, she was named the Outstanding Woman Lawyer of the Year in 1987 by the Hawaii Women Lawyers Association. In 1994, she successfully argued a case before the United States Supreme Court.

Her work both in and out of the courtroom drew the attention of political heavyweights including Senators Daniel Akaka and Daniel Inouye, resulting in her first nomination for federal judgeship in 1995. The deliberation process, however, took several years. "I waited a long time for this to come through and nearly withdrew my application several times because it took so long. At every step, I would ask myself what I was doing," she explained. "I . . . received major opposition from senators on the mainland who were concerned about my services in the past as a director on the board of the Hawaiian branch of the American Civil Liberties Union, because some of my politics might be more liberal than theirs." She continued, "I was asked to spell out my position on issues such as drug testing and same-sex marriages, things that the ACLU had passed resolutions on in Hawaii before I became a director" (Panesar 1998, 9). In the end, Mollway triumphed and assumed her responsibilities on the federal bench in Hawaii in June 1998. Over 700 cases had been left unheard since the 1995 death of her predecessor, District Judge Harold Fong.

Mollway, named one of A. Magazine's 25 Most Influential Asian Americans in 1998, remains down-to-earth about her powerful position. "For any litigator it is a dream job," she commented. "To be honest, I never thought that I would live the dream. I am not that arrogant of my capabilities. I am lucky." Her professional goals are uncomplicated: "I want to be a good judge—giving everyone who comes before me a fair hearing, applying the governing law, writing opinions that give guidance to lawyers" (Panesar 1998, 9).

### Sources

Kim, Jungwon. "Susan Oki Mollway." In "The 1998 A. List." A. Magazine. December 1998/January 1999, p. 59.

Panesar, Randip K. "Setting a Precedent in the Aloha State: Susan Oki Mollway Becomes First APA Female Federal Judge." Asian Week. 9 July 1998, p. 9.

# Hermina M. Morita

Hermina Morita. (Courtesy of Hermina Morita)

**Born:** 2 September 1954, Lanai, Hawaii.

**Education:** George Washington University, University of Hawaii at Manoa.

**Positions Held:** Representative, Hawaii State Assembly, 1996–present.

**Awards, Honors:** Arthur S. Fleming Fellowship, 1997.

**Summary:** Hermina M. Morita is a member of the Hawaii State House of Representatives.

### Early Years and Education

Hermina M. Morita was born on 2 September 1954 in Lanai, Hawaii. She attended the island's Kamehameha Schools, Kauai Community College, George Washington University, and the University of Hawaii at Manoa.

## Career Highlights

Morita was elected in 1996 to the Hawaii State House of Representatives to serve District 12, which includes the north and east portions of the island of Kauai (Kapaa to Haena) and the east portion of Maui (Haiku to Kaupo). Previously, Morita had been involved with the Democratic Party of Hawaii, serving as precinct chair from 1990 to 1996 and was commissioner of the Kauai County Police Commission from 1993 to 1996 and Commissioner of the Kauai County Planning Commission from 1990 to 1993.

In the House, Morita chairs the Energy and Environmental Protection Committee and is a member of the Water and Land Use, Ocean Recreation and Marine Resources, Consumer Protection and Commerce, and Judiciary and Hawaiian Affairs Committees. She also cochairs the Women's Legislative Caucus, participates in the House Policy Committee and Hawaiian Caucus, and is the Assistant Majority Floor Leader of the House. For her efforts, she received the Arthur S. Flemming Fellowship in 1997, a nationwide award recognizing emerging political leaders, becoming the second legislator from Hawaii to do so.

Aside from her official duties, Morita has worked for and managed a variety of businesses and institutions, including the office of U.S. Senator Hiram L. Fong, the Hanalei Bay Resort, Hotel Lanai; the University of Hawaii's Center for Oral History, and the Kilauea Point Natural History Association. She also researched, interviewed, edited, and photographed for the University of Hawaii–Manoa's Center for Oral History's 1989 publication, Lanai Ranch: The People of Koele and Keomuku. Additionally, Morita has been involved with the Democratic Party of Hawaii, serving as precinct chair from 1990 to 1996, and was commissioner of the Kauai County Police Commission from 1993 to 1996 and Commissioner of the Kauai County Planning Commission from 1990 to 1993.

Morita maintains an active profile in her local community, volunteering for a myriad of organizations, including Big Brothers and Big Sisters of Hawaii, the Kauai Children's Discovery Museum, the Kauai Taro Festival, and the Kilauea Point National Wildlife Refuge. She is married to Lance "Kit" Laney, a drywall and plaster contractor, and is mother of two daughters, Misha and Mindy. The Laney-Morita family resides in Hanalei Valley on the island of Kauai.

## Source

Personal communication to Ellen D. Wu, 14 July 2000.

# N

## George Nakano

George Nakano. (Courtesy of George Nakano)

**Born:** 24 November 1935, Los Angeles, California.

**Education:** B.S., California State University, Los Angeles; M.Ed. California State University, Los Angeles, 1977.

**Positions Held:** Member, Torrance City Council; Member, California State Assembly.

**Summary:** George Nakano represents California's 53rd District in the State Assembly.

### Early Years and Education

George Nakano was born in Los Angeles and raised in a lower-income neighborhood on the city's eastside. As a child, Nakano, the oldest of four children, spent four years during World War II with his family in a Japanese American concentration camp. After the war, they returned to Los Angeles where Nakano attended and graduated from John H. Francis Polytechnic High School in June 1954. He next enlisted in the California Air National Guard, serving six years until he was honorably discharged as a staff sergeant in 1960. Back in civilian life, Nakano worked to pay his expenses while studying at El Camino College and California State University, Los Angeles.

## Career Highlights

After graduating with a bachelor's degree in mathematics, George Nakano accepted a position at Jordan High School in the Watts area. He later returned to school, earning his masters in education from his alma mater in 1977. Nakano closed out his career in education as an administrator for the Inglewood Unified School District, retiring in 1991.

In 1984, Nakano successfully bid for a seat on Torrance, California's city council. In this capacity, Nakano represented the South Bay area in several governance-related organizations, including the regional council of the Southern California Association of Governments, the League of California Cities Transportation and Public Works Committees, and the South Bay Cities Association, of which he was elected president.

While on the Torrance City Council, Nakano supported a number of issues, including a Graffiti Abatement Program, which opened a means for Torrance residents to report instances of vandalism. In addition, he advocated continued funding for local libraries and expanded job opportunities and after-school programs for area youth. Nakano also pushed for the creation of a citywide Economic Development Office to foster the establishment and growth of well-paying, high tech jobs in Torrance and adjacent areas. Perhaps one of his proudest moments, however, directly related to Asian Pacific American concerns. "From a personal standpoint, one of my greatest satisfactions was when I was able to get the city council to unanimously support a resolution in support of redress and reparations in 1988," he noted. "The city council supported the resolution. In fact, the mayor at that time sent a letter to President Reagan urging him to sign the bill" (Lim 1996, 9).

After 14 years in municipal government, Nakano entered politics at the state level as the representative for the 53rd District, encompassing the southern coastal region of Los Angeles County stretching from Venice, Westchester, Marina del Rey, Playa del Rey, and the Beach Cities, into Torrance, Lomita and the northern tip of Palos Verdes Estates, in the California State Assembly. In his freshman term in the Assembly, Nakano was named Chair of both the Subcommittee on State Administration and the Select Committee on Aerospace and appointed a member of the Education, Transportation, Veterans Affairs, and International Development committees.

Outside of office, George Nakano maintains an active profile, devoting his time to a number of community organizations throughout the South Bay area, including the California Retired Teachers' Association, Torrance Education Foundation, the Torrance YWCA and the United Way Harbor/Southeast Region advisory boards, and the Salvation Army Advisory Board, which he chaired, and the past presidency of Torrance's branch of the American Association of Retired Persons. Nakano also founded the Torrance chapter of the Japanese American Citizens League in 1983 and is a charter member of the Go For Broke National Veterans Association.

George Nakano has also displayed a special flair for kendo, a Japanese martial art, holding a 5th-degree black belt. Involved in the sport since 1959, Nakano was named to the U.S. Kendo Team in 1966 and established a kendo dojo in Torrance, where he served as head instructor for a decade. Nakano is married to Helen Nakano; the couple are the parents of Laurie, an elementary school teacher, and Kevin, an electrical engineer.

## Sources

Correspondence from George Nakano.
www.democrats/assembly.ca.gov/members/a53 [Accessed 5 October 2001].
Lim, Sam Chu. "Final-Term Mandate in Early Election: City Councilman Top Vote Getter in SoCal Election." *Asian Week*. 15 March 1996, p. 9.
"Nakano Named to Assembly Committees." *Asian Week*. 13 January 1999, p. 8.

# Karen Narasaki

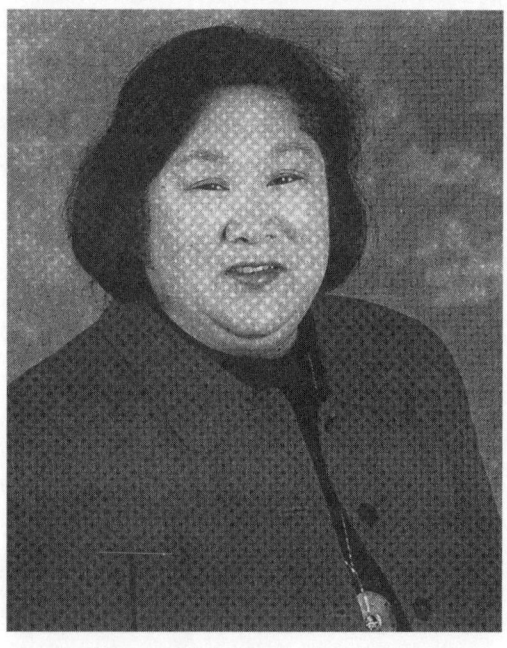

Karen Narasaki. (Courtesy of National Asian Pacific American Legal Consortium)

**Born:** April 1958, Seattle, Washington.

**Education:** B.A., Yale University, 1980; J.D., University of California at Los Angeles, 1985.

**Positions Held:** Washington Representative, Japanese American Citizens League; Member, Executive Committee of the Leadership Conference on Civil Rights; Chair, National Network Against Anti-Asian Violence; Executive Director, National Asian Pacific American Legal Consortium.

**Awards, Honors:** 1997 Wichita Vietnamese Senior Center for Service to the Vietnamese American Community; 1999 Asian Pacific American Labor Alliance Community Award; 1999 A. *Magazine* Award for 100 Most Influential Asian Americans of the Decade; 2000 U.S. Department of Justice Citizen Volunteer Service Award.

**Summary:** Karen Narasaki is the executive director of the National Asian Pacific American Legal Consortium.

## Early Years and Education

Karen Narasaki was born in Seattle, Washington in April 1958 to Richard and Dorothy (Noguchi) Narasaki. A yonsei daughter of World War II prisoners, she recalls, "The fact that my parents and their families were interned during World War II was significant in my choosing a career in civil rights. My father fought as a member of the 442nd Regimental Combat Team and taught us that while we should appreciate the freedom and opportunities that America has to offer, that America was a work in progress and that we had a duty, as Americans, to make it live up to its principles. He and my mother also taught us to have a healthy disregard for authority—to know that people in power were not always right and that we should make up our own minds and stand up for what is right" (personal communication to Ellen D. Wu, 14 January 2001).

She attended Renton High School from 1972 to 1976 before enrolling at Yale University, from which she graduated magna cum laude with a bachelor of arts diploma in political science and economics in 1980. She then earned her juris doctor degree from UCLA's School of Law in 1985, where she was also a member of the Order of the Coif.

## Career Highlights

Narasaki has held a myriad of professional positions related to legal and civil rights issues. As a fledgling lawyer, she clerked for Judge Harry Pregerson on the U.S. Court of Appeals for the Ninth Circuit in Los Angeles from 1986 to 1992 before joining Seattle's Perkins Coie firm, where she worked as a corporate attorney from 1992 to 1994. Currently, she serves on the Board of the Lawyers Committee for Civil Rights Under Law and the Independent Sector.

Asian Pacific American concerns have consistently been top priorities for Narasaki. "When I first came to Washington, Asian Americans were fairly invisible and were not known or well understood by the media or by other civil rights leaders," she stated. "Getting national policy makers and others to take the community seriously and to invest in understanding our issues was a major challenge" (personal communication to Ellen D. Wu, 14 January 2001). Narasaki rose to meet this challenge. In addition to directing the national advocacy program and acting as the Washington, D.C., representative for the Japanese American Citizens League (JACL), the nation's largest membership-based Asian American civil rights organization, she has served on the boards of the National Immigration Law Center, the National Asian Pacific American Bar Association, the Asian Bar Association of Washington, the Asian Pacific American Legal Center of Southern California, and the Organization of Pan Asian American Women. Narasaki is presently the executive director of the National Asian Pacific American Legal Consortium.

As a nationally recognized Asian Pacific American political leader, Narasaki has appeared on ABC and CBS News, Fox News Channel, the Jim Lehrer *Newshour*, *America with Dennis Wholey* and several National Public Radio shows, including *Talk of the Nation* and *Powerpoint*. She has also been quoted by *The New York Times*, *The Washington Post*, *The Wall Street Journal*, and *USA Today*, as well as numerous regional newspapers, including *The Chicago Tribune*, *The Houston Chronicle*, *The Seattle Post-Intelligencer*, and *The Los Angeles Times*. Narasaki has also penned a number of significant columns and op-ed articles addressing a range of civil rights–related topics, including pieces in *Essence*, *The San Francisco Chronicle*, *A. Magazine*, and *Asian Week*.

Karen Narasaki lists among her proudest accomplishments her work on the passage of the reauthorization of Section 203 of the Voting Rights Act, which requires bilingual voting assistance; the Civil Liberties Act amendments of 1992, which guarantees sufficient resources for payment and the redress education fund, blocking passage of legislation that would have eliminated family-based immigration in 1995; the passage of legislation that provided partial restoration of supplemental security income and food stamps to legal permanent residents in 1997 and 1998; the nomination and recess appointment of Bill Lann Lee as assistant attorney general for civil rights; and blocking passage of legislation that would have barred legal permanent residents from being able to provide support to political candidates. Additionally, while at JACL, she helped the organization defend its support of same-sex marriage.

For her many contributions, Narasaki has received a number of honors, including the 1997 Wichita Vietnamese Senior Center for Service to the Vietnamese American Community, the 1999 Asian Pacific American Labor Alliance Community Award, A. *Magazine*'s Award for 100 Most Influential Asian Americans of the Decade, and a 2000 U.S. Department of Justice Citizen Volunteer Service Award.

Regarding her accomplishments, Narasaki states, "I don't really view myself as a 'political' leader since I am not involved in partisan politics. I view myself more as an advocate who seeks to ensure that the Asian American community has the ability to understand and to shape government policies that significantly impact on their lives." (personal communication to Don Nakanishi, 14 January 2001).

## Sources

"The A. 100: 100 Most Influential Asian Americans of the Decade." *A. Magazine*. October/November 1999, p. 85.

www.napalc.org [Accessed 14 January 2001].

Narasaki, Karen. "Affirming the California Experience with Affirmative Action." NEXUS, Chapman University School of Law. Vol. 1, No. 2, Fall 1996.

———. "Discrimination Against Asian Pacific Americans and the Need for Affirmative Action Legislation." *NCJW Journal*. Fall 1996, Vol. 19, No. 3.

———. "Double Talk," A. *Magazine*. February/March 1996.

———. "Fueling Hatred for Immigrants." *San Francisco Chronicle*. 13 August 1996.

———. "I, Too, Am an Affirmative-Action Baby." *Essence.* October 1997.
———. "Welfare and Wedge Politics." *Asian Week.* 24 November 1995.
Personal communication with Don T. Nakanishi, 14 January 2001.
Personal communication with Ellen D. Wu, 14 January 2001.

# Irene Natividad

Irene Natividad. (Courtesy of Natividad & Associates)

**Born:** 14 September 1948, Manila, Philippines.

**Education:** B.A., Long Island University, 1971; M.A., Columbia University, 1973; M.Phil., Columbia University 1976.

**Positions Held:** Chair, National Women's Political Caucus, 1985-1989; Director, Global Forum of Women, 1991-1992; Chair, National Committee on Working Women, 1991–present.

**Awards, Honors:** Women's Congressional Caucus's Women Making History Award in 1985, Americans by Choice's Honored American Award, 1986, Innovator for Women$hare Award from the Women's Funding Coalition, 1987, named to *Ladies Home Journal*'s 100 Most Powerful Women in America, 1988, 25 Most Influential Asian Women, 1989, honorary doctorate, Long Island University, Women of Distinction Award, National Conference for College Women Student Leaders, 1989; Named to 74 Women Who Are Changing American Politics, by *Campaigns and Elections Magazine,* 1993; honorary doctorate, Marymount College, 1994; named to *A. Magazine*'s 25 Most Influential Asians in America, 1993 and 1994.

**Summary:** Irene Natividad is one of the most visible Asian Pacific American women in politics today. She is the first Asian Pacific American woman to head a nationwide women's bipartisan organization as chair of the National Women's Political Caucus from 1985 to 1989.

### Early Years

Pioneer feminist Irene Natividad, once described as a "firebrand" by *A. Magazine*, was born on 14 September 1948 in Manila, Philippines. Young Natividad, one of four children, led a globetrotting lifestyle, spending her first five years on the archipelago before relocating to Okinawa, Iran, Greece, and India as dictated by her father's career as a chemical engineer. As a result of her cosmopolitan childhood, she acquired fluency in an array of languages, including Spanish, French, Italian, and Tagalog as well as a smattering of Greek and Farsi. She also became fluent in English and American culture by attending a succession of American-run international schools before moving to the United States in 1966.

### Education

Natividad proved to be adept in the classroom (although she has admitted a weakness in math), graduating from her high school in Greece as valedictorian. She also took top honors at Long Island University in 1971, due in part to her mother's resolve to attend the commencement ceremony only if she was class valedictorian. Natividad once noted that her family's expectations of her were set quite high—when she informed her mother of her plans to marry Andrea Cortese, now her husband—she promptly replied, "But you can't do that—you don't have your Ph.D. yet" (Brozan 1985, 44). Natividad followed her B.A. with two additional degrees—master of arts in American literature in 1973 and an M.Phil. in 1976 from Columbia University. Her dissertation topic—narratives of slave women—foreshadowed her later accomplishments. She recalled, "I had trouble getting that topic approved. The narratives were not considered to be literature, and to choose only women compounded it" (Brozan 1985, 44).

## Career Highlights

Irene Natividad inaugurated her professional life with several positions in higher education, beginning as an adjunct instructor in English at the City University of New York's Lehman College in 1974 and teaching composition and literature at her alma mater, Columbia, from 1974 to 1976. Between 1976 and 1985, she served as the director of continuing education at both Long Island University and Wayne, New Jersey's William Patterson College, where she built the curriculum up from a few courses to a significant center with over 3,000 students. As with other aspects of her life, Natividad viewed continuing education through a feminist lens. "It is still the stepchild of academia. Colleges are still geared to 18-to-24-year-old males, but the overwhelming majority of continuing education students are women," she stated in a 1985 *New York Times* article (Brozan 1985, 44).

During the presidency of Ronald Reagan, Natividad's career ventured into political advocacy. Her history in grassroots organizing—she had once rallied her fellow wait staff to bargain for better wages from their employer—proved to be valuable training when she became the founding president of Asian American Professional Women and the founding director of the National Network of Asian-Pacific American Women and the Child Care Action Campaign, all in 1980. Two years later, she accepted a two-year position as chair of the New York State Asian Pacific Caucus along with the deputy vice-chairwomanship of the Democratic National Committee's Asian Pacific Caucus. Regarding the latter, Natividad said, "a major project in which I was involved was to create Asian caucuses in every state. We did it in 22 states with no specific goals other than becoming enmeshed in the political process" (Brozan 1985, 44).

Natividad's first major foray into national women's concerns occurred in 1984 with her selection by the Democratic Party as the Asian American liaison for vice-presidential nominee Geraldine Ferraro. Despite Ferraro's defeat at the polls, Natividad reflected positively on the landmark event, noting that Ferraro's nomination and candidacy had been trailblazing for all women, and that it was truly a "win" rather than a "loss" (Gall 1995, 282).

In 1985, Irene became the first API woman to head a nationwide women's bipartisan organization with her election to the presidency of the National Women's Political Caucus. Her campaign slogan was "A national leadership for a national movement." The decision to run came about, she said, "because it became obvious to me that political power is the road to equality. Every aspect of our lives—from the rights of equal access to the preservatives in our food—is impacted on by legislation that is initiated, discussed, and voted on by white males in Washington or Albany" (Brozan 1985, 44). Her proposed agenda included diversifying the membership of the Caucus and supporting abortion rights, pay equity, the equal rights amendment, and affirmative action.

During Natividad's four-year term as president from 1985 to 1989, she successfully guided the 77,000 member NWPC in its efforts to expand the visibility, active role, and status of women in electoral politics. "The prize of citizenship is political involvement. To be silent is to not be counted and we can't afford not to be counted," she once told the *International Examiner* in 1993 (del Rosario 1993, 1). Examples of her work toward this goal included conducting pilot studies on women in congressional races, educating female candidates in campaigning techniques and strategies, publishing an annual survey of Governors' Appointments of Women to State Cabinets, creating the minority women candidates training program, and acknowledging male advocates of women's issues with the association's Good Guy Award. She also advised President George H. W. Bush on the appointment of women to positions in his administration.

Natividad's activism during this period earned her a number of accolades, including the Women's Congressional Caucus's Women Making History Award in 1985, Americans by Choice's Honored American Award in 1986, the 1987 Innovator for Women$hare Award from the Women's Funding Coalition, places on *Ladies Home Journal*'s 1988 100 Most Powerful Women in America and 1989 25 Most Influential Asian Women lists, an honorary doctorate from Long Island University and a Women of Distinction Award in 1989 from the National Conference for College Women Student Leaders.

After leaving office in 1989, Irene Natividad continued her outspoken advocacy on behalf of women. She formed the Women of Color Committee for Clinton/Gore in 1992 to raise money as well as deconstruct the public image of women as "supplicants, rather than donors" (Chi'en 1994). Among her other commitments have been the directorship of the Philippine America Foundation, an agency that promotes anti-poverty actions and other humanitarian efforts in the Philippines (such as raising $50,000 in relief funds for victims of the 1991 Mount Pinatubo eruption) and the chairwomanship of the National Commission on Working Women, which focuses on American women's employment and economic concerns.

In 1992, Natividad assumed the directorship of the Global Forum of Women, an International Caucus of 400 representatives from 58 countries who gathered in Dublin, Ireland to discuss women's issues and outline and implement solutions. She also attended the following conference two years later in Taiwan where she coordinated a political empowerment workshop not unlike those she facilitated in cities around the world. Among her other numerous organizational and institutional memberships are Leadership Washington, Wider Opportunities for Women, Center for Women's Policy Studies, Project Vote Smart, Women's Research and Educational Institutional Advancement Committee, the National Commission on Working Women, and the National Museum for Women in Arts. Currently, she is the head of her own political consulting firm, Natividad and Associates.

Of her many commitments over the years, she once remarked, "Somehow I just kept getting involved. I didn't want to just watch and observe. I wanted to be in the middle of it. The tendency to organize was there. The one constant in my life is that . . . I could get people together to fight a cause" (del Rosario 1993, 1). Natividad has also continued to garner positive attention for her work—in 1993, she was recognized as one of the 74 Women Who Are Changing American Politics, by *Campaigns and Elections Magazine* and in 1994, she received a second honorary doctorate from Marymount College.

A significant dimension of Irene Natividad's activism has been her work within and for the Asian American and Filipino-American communities. She has been "doing her part" through such groups as the Leadership Education for Asian Pacifics, Inc, and through publications including an article on Asian Americans in Politics for Harvard University's *Asian American Review* and the *Asian American Almanac*, which she edited in 1995. One of *A. Magazine*'s 25 Most Influential Asians in America in 1993 and 1994, she stated that year that "[her] goal is to make Asians and women more visible. . . . [Asian Americans] are nowhere near parity, no matter what anyone says. Furthermore, despite the achievements of a number of women that you and I can rattle off, [Asian American women] don't register on the map. There are very few people who break through. But in the end we're Americans too; we happen to be of Asian heritage, but we're Americans, and we want to break through and make a difference. We're not there yet" (Chi'en 1994, 18).

## Sources

"Asian American Elected Chief of Women's Political Caucus." *The Washington Post.* 1 July 1985, p. A6.

Brozan, Nadine. "From Minority Activist to Feminist Leader." *The New York Times.* 6 July 1985, p. 44.

Chi'en, Evelyn. "Sidewalk Talk/Irene Natividad." *A. Magazine.* 30 June 1994, p. 18.

Gall, Susan. "Irene Natividad." In *Notable Asian Americans*, ed. Helen Zia and Susan B. Gall. Detroit, MI: Gale Research, Inc., 1995, pp. 280-282.

Gamarekian, Barbara. "Washington Talk: National Women's Political Caucus; Carrying Word of a Women's Agenda." *New York Times.* 18 November 1997, p. A26.

"Irene Natividad." *Who's Who in American Politics.* Reed Elsevier, Inc., October 1997.

# O

## Angela Eunjin Oh

**Born:** 8 September 1955, Los Angeles, California.

**Education:** B.S., University of California, Los Angeles, 1977; M.PH., University of California, 1981; J.D., University of California, Davis, 1986.

**Positions Held:** Special Counsel, Assembly Special Committee on the Los Angeles Crisis, 1992; Advisory Board Member, President's Initiative on Race, 1997–1998; Commissioner, Los Angeles City Human Relations Commission, 1996–present.

**Awards, Honors:** 1997 UC Davis School of Law Distinguished Alumni Award, 1997 Distinguished Service Award, Ministry of Justice, Republic of South Korea, 1998 Community Service Award, Pat Brown Institute for Policy Studies, 1998 Leadership Award, University of California, Los Angeles Asian American Studies Center, 1998 A. *Magazine* Bridge Builders Award, named as one of A. *Magazine*'s 100 Most Influential Asian Americans of the Decade.

**Summary:** Angela Eunjin Oh has been one of the nation's most recognizable Asian Pacific American figures since her appearance on ABC's *Nightline* representing the Korean American community in the wake of the 1992 Los Angeles riots. The sole Asian Pacific American representative on President Clinton's Initiative on Race Advisory Board in 1997-1998, she continues to engage in advocacy work on behalf of all Asian Americans.

### Early Years

Angela Eunjin Oh, a second-generation Korean American, was born in Los Angeles on 8 September 1955 to Sam Yul and Young Sook Oh, a medical technician and school teacher, respectively. The oldest of four children, Oh developed a strong self-esteem at an early age, due in large part to the influence of her grandmother who cared for her while her father and mother worked or took classes. Oh was active throughout her youth, participating in Girl Scouts and music lessons and holding a job while attending L.A.-area Granada Hills High School.

### Education

In 1973, Oh matriculated at the University of California, Los Angeles with the intention to follow her parents' wishes for her to pursue a career in dentistry. Eventually, however, she abandoned their plans and switched her major to psychology. At this time, she also explored questions of equality and justice and became involved with the Chicano Youth East Barrio Project, foreshadowing her community-oriented career.

After graduating from UCLA in 1977, Oh's interests turned to women's concerns, with a particular focus on public health, leading her to enroll in UCLA's Ph.D. program in public health. In school, she learned of workers' safety and health concerns, spurring her to found the Los Angeles Committee of Occupation Safety and Health (LACOSH). She then left UCLA in 1981 with her masters degree to work full time with LACOSH, and was named the health and safety director of the Federated Firefighters of California.

## Career Highlights

Following her work in public health, Oh returned to school, hoping that a law degree would better equip her to advocate human rights issues. She earned her J.D. from the University of California, Davis, King Hall in 1986, where she engaged in an opposition movement against the school's dealing with South African companies and began working as a political consultant for the "No on Proposition 63" project, an initiative designed to amend California's constitution to designate English the state's "official language." As an organizer in Los Angeles and San Diego counties, she coordinated a public education campaign directed at defeating Proposition 63. Though it passed, Oh gained valuable skills in media relations, campaign finance, and strategic planning that would aid her in subsequent endeavors.

After the election, Angela Oh practiced law at two smaller firms in Los Angeles before becoming a partner at Beck, De Corso, Daly, Barrera and Oh in June 1987, where she specialized in criminal defense. Her work as a trial attorney led to an appearance on ABC's *Nightline*, voicing the concerns of the Korean American community after the devastation of the 1992 Los Angeles uprising. During the broadcast, she critiqued dominant views of inner-city Korean American merchants' economic motivations—"We choose to be there? No. It is out of economic necessity that we are there. It so happens that the overhead is affordable in those areas." Of then-President George Bush's emergency arrival in the city she commented, "I think it's very good that he's here in Los Angeles, for him to be able to survey the damage that his policies and his leadership have yielded. This is the harvest."— "We are seeing around the globe that the American Dream may be the real myth" (Zoroya 1998, 10).

Her remarks catapulted her into the national spotlight, where she continued to illuminate the plight of her community. "Koreans have been blamed out of frustration with the system. It's not us. We're not the problem," she stated (Henry 1995, 295). As special counsel to the California's Assembly Special Committee on the Los Angeles Crisis, Oh assisted members of the State Assembly with a fact-finding mission to examine the root causes of the eruption. She authored a number of articles for national publications including *The New York Times*, *The Los Angeles Times*, and *Ms. Magazine*, and debated issues on radio and television programs.

From June 1997 to September 1998, Angela Oh served as the sole Asian American appointee on President William Jefferson Clinton's Initiative on Race. Oh and the other six members facilitated over 300 forums with Americans nationwide. During the 15 months of the project, Oh advocated a break from the traditional paradigms of race/racism in the American consciousness. As she explained, "On a very fundamental level, I think moving the conversation to be more inclusive of those who are neither black nor white is a more forward, visionary approach . . . to think in terms of including the experiences and insights of people who don't come from that frame of reference." Her remarks, which some perceived to be a blatant dismissal of the centuries-old conflict between blacks and whites in America, elicited criticism from many, including the chair of the Initiative, John Hope Franklin. In response, Oh expressed concern that some believed "that I represent a sector of the population that has not yet paid sufficient dues to sit at the table," despite such Asian American suffering as builders of the transcontinental railroad, prisoners in U.S. concentration camps during World War II, and virtual slaves in the present-day garment industry (Huynh). Oh also highlighted the need to approach the concept of race more deeply by including such issues as educational levels, socioeconomic status, generational differences, and intra-racial diversity.

Since the conclusion of her appointment, Oh, who believes that education is "the only vehicle for combating racism... the only process that we have to share information and raise our consciousness together," has continued to participate in numerous speaking engagements nationwide as a lecturer for the American Program Bureau, Inc. Titles of her talks include "Women and the Third Millennium," "The Multiracial Reality of the 21st Century," and "The Future of Bilingual Education: Race Relations and Language." In January 1999, Oh joined UCLA as a lecturer, visiting scholar, and lawyer in residence, teaching her course, "Race in America," through the school's Asian American Studies Center. She has also continued, if not heightened, her involvement in civic and professional organizations, serving on the Los Angeles City Human Relations Commission, the Board of Directors of Lawyers Mutual Insurance Company, the Asian Pacific American Women's Leadership Institute, and the Korean American Service Center, among others.

A number of groups have recognized Oh's contributions and accomplishments, including the Chicago Area Bar Association 1998 Visions Award, the Pat Brown Institute for Policy Studies 1998 Community Service Award, the Asian American Education Fund of the Asian Bar Association of Washington D.C. 1998 Community Advocate Award, Big Sisters of Los Angeles 1998 Heart of the Community Award, and the Republic of South Korea's Ministry of Justice's 1997 Distinguished Service Award.

### Sources

Henry, Jim. "Angela Eunjin Oh." In *Notable Asian Americans*, ed. Helen Zia and Susan B. Gall. Detroit, MI: Gale Research, Inc., 1995, pp. 294-296.

Huynh, Luan,.."Q & Oh: Angela Oh Answers Questions on Race Relations, the Criminal Justice System, and More." *Pacific Ties.* No. 22, issue 2, Winter 1999, pp. 11, 16, 31.

Resume of Angela E.Oh.

Shepard, Scott. "Race Panel"s Sole Asian-American Rebuts Reputation as a Radical." *The Atlanta Journal and Constitution.* 10 August 1997, p. 8A.

Zoroya, Gregg. "Beautiful Dreamer: Bill Clinton and the Rest of the World Discovered America After the L.A. Riots. But She's Been Carrying the Human Rights Banner for Years." *Los Angeles Times Magazine* 1 February 1998, p.10.

## Wing F. Ong

**Born:** 4 February 1904, Hoiping, China.

**Died:** 19 December 1977.

**Education:** Phoenix College, 1939; J.D., University of Arizona, 1943.

**Positions Held:** Member, Arizona State Legislature, 1946–1950; Member, Arizona State Senate, 1966–1968.

**Summary:** Wing F. Ong was the first Asian Pacific American elected to public office in the United States. He served in the Arizona State Legislature in the 1940s and the Arizona State Senate in the 1960s.

### Early Years

Wing F. Ong was born on 4 February 1904 in Wing On Li Village, Hoiping District, Hoiping, China. As with many Cantonese families of the era, Ong's grandparents had immigrated to America after the gold rush in search of work. Their son, Dao Lung Ong, Wing F. Ong's father, was among the earliest American-born Chinese. Ong himself was conceived and born during one of Dao Lung Ong's periodic trips to his ancestral homeland.

In December 1918, Ong made the arduous journey across the Pacific to join his father in California. Unlike many of his contemporaries, he was able to circumvent the immigration restrictions placed against the Chinese, having inherited American citizenship from his U.S.-born father. Nevertheless, he was still forced to endure three months of isolation on Angel Island, the West Coast's detention station operated by the U.S. government to screen potential immigrants, most of whom were from Asia. In April 1919, Ong finally gained clearance and went to meet his relatives in San Francisco. His father, who lived in nearby Oakland, was unable to support him financially, so one of Ong's uncles became his guardian.

In the early 20th century, employment prospects for Chinese Americans were extremely slim, and Ong was no exception. His uncle had provided him with a job at an herb shop and planned for the young Ong eventually to operate a laundry like so many of their co-ethnics. Ong, however, had conflicting ambitions, and requested instead to be sent to school. Legally, however, as an "Oriental," he was banned from the San Francisco public school system. Instead, Ong attended the Chinese Baptist Mission School located in San Francisco's Chinatown. Although he was not learning English at the Mission School, Ong continued to insist on an education. When his uncle offered him work at a laundry for 50 cents a day, for example, Ong adamantly refused, stating, "I want to go to American schools. I want to become a man of learning and accomplishment, and in America, this can be done if one has the will to do so."

Ultimately, Wing F. Ong was able to pursue his dream when Henry Ong, Sr., an uncle visiting San Francisco from Phoenix, offered to take him to Arizona where Ong would be able to matriculate in the public schools. At the age of 15, he began his formal American education.

An eager student, Ong progressed rapidly through the primary grades at Grant and Monroe Elementary schools in only four years while working concurrently at his uncle's local grocery. He then enrolled at Phoenix Union High School, from which he graduated in 1925, after just two years of study. His diploma notwithstanding, one of Ong's most remarkable accomplishments as a student was his first place award in Arizona's sector of the National Firestone Essay Contest in 1924 for his entry, "The Relation of Improved Highways to Home Life."

During this time, he also worked as a waiter, dishwasher, and cook at different restaurants in the area. In addition, he served as a houseboy for Arizona Governor Thomas E. Campbell and his wife Gayle, an arrangement that proved to be fortuitous for his later career in politics.

## Education

Following high school, Ong spent one year at the University of Arizona in Tucson before dropping out due to financial concerns. He sold insurance for a short time prior to purchasing a Phoenix market in response to family pressure, which he renamed Golden Gate Grocery. On 6 December 1928, he married Rose Wing, a union orchestrated by his uncle, Henry Ong, Sr.

Together, Ong and his wife Rose managed two markets and a delivery service through the difficult years of the Depression. Meanwhile, Rose gave birth to their six children, Catherine, Jack, Patricia, Madeline, Rosalind, and Marvin over a period of 15 years between 1929 and 1944.

Ong's dreams of education were far from dead, however, even with the dual responsibility of work and family. In 1937, he enrolled at the two-year Phoenix College, taking business classes and graduating in 1939. The next year, he made his inaugural attempt at politics with his run for a seat in the Arizona House of Representatives, losing by an incredibly slim margin of 17 votes. His near-victory was due in part to his personal voter registration drive, during which Ong and his brother-in-law trucked his district's residents—most of whom were people of color—to register to vote and later to cast their ballots on election day.

Wing F. Ong's loss was a main factor in his decision to enter the University of Arizona College of Law in September 1941, because, in his view, "What right have I to make laws if I know nothing about the law?" His interaction with his role model, Gov. Campbell, was another source of inspiration. For two years he commuted between Tucson and Phoenix, staying with the Campbells on the weekdays, while completing his coursework. In 1943, he graduated as top student, and upon passing the state bar exam, became one of only eight Chinese American attorneys in the entire country. He then opened his practice next door to his grocery store in Phoenix.

## Career Highlights

In 1946, Ong, armed with his degree, ran again for state office as a Democrat on the slogans, "Let a lawyer help make your laws," and the ironic, "Give me, a Chinaman, a chance." With his defeat of Republican challenger Harry Woodley, Ong became not only a representative in the 18th Arizona Legislature, but also the first Chinese and Asian Pacific American elected to public office in the United States. In 1948, Ong, known as "an Eastern sage in a Far West Assembly," was re-elected to a second term.

During his service in Arizona's House, the enthusiastic Ong, who did not miss a single session during his first two years, fought for such issues as teachers' tenure and minimum salaries, an anti-communist oath for government workers, social security and welfare measures, and federal education grants, while voting against collective bargaining, regulation of insurance companies, and disposal of real property.

After four years as a state representative, Ong was not as fortunate with his next two bids for a seat in the House. He lost in the 1950 primaries and the 1958 general election. In 1964, he defeated other Democratic candidates in a primary race for the State Senate, but Republican B.C. (Bill) Rhodes won the general election. Nevertheless, Ong returned in 1966 to vie successfully for a Senate seat. As a state senator, he advocated government aid for the blind, air pollution controls, legalizing therapeutic abortions, and ending the Vietnam War, among other issues. During his aggregate years in the Senate and State House, he served on the committees of constitutional amendments and referendum, judiciary, ways and means, fact-finding, commerce and industry, labor and management, and county affairs, which he chaired. Ong made one final attempt for the State Senate in 1968 but lost in the primaries.

During and in between his years as a legislator, Ong continued to operate his law practice. In the early 1950s, he moved his family to San Francisco so that he could work more efficiently on immigration cases concerning his fellow Chinese. After failing the California State Bar in the mid-1950s, Ong returned to Phoenix where he opened an office atop the Ong's newest eatery, Wing's Restaurant. To relax from the demands of his profession, he would occasionally perform traditional pieces on the Chinese harp, flute, or fiddle for the restaurant's patrons.

In addition to his presence in government and the legal world, Ong was active in the politics of Arizona's Chinese American community. He was a founder of Phoenix's Chinese Chamber of Commerce, the Chinese Baptist Church, and the city's chapter of the Chinese American Citizens Alliance. From 1965 to 1966, he was the president of the Phoenix branch of the Overseas Chinese Anti-Communist League. In 1965, he was appointed to the city License and Appeals Board and was also appointed by Governor Samuel P. Goddard as the state's Goodwill Ambassador to the Republic of China (Taiwan).

Always an innovator, Ong initiated a number of notable actions among the Phoenix Chinese. For example, in response to accusations in the 1930s by the city's denizens that Chinese grocers were unpatriotic for keeping their stores open on the Fourth of July, Ong suggested that they close their stores and celebrate the holiday with a community picnic. Since then, Chinese American Fourth of July gatherings have been an annual event, complete with food, entertainment, and a beauty contest to select the Phoenix representative for the Miss Chinatown pageant in San Francisco. In another instance, when the state legislature passed a discriminatory sanitation bill aimed at closing Chinese businesses, Ong used his political connections to table the proposal in the State House. And decades later, when Ong founded the Phoenix chapter of the Chinese American Citizens Alliance in 1975, it was he who pushed for the inclusion of women among the membership and the executive board.

Wing F. Ong's political work was not confined to domestic boundaries. A staunch critic of isolationism, neutrality, Japanese aggression in China, and Communism, he engaged in a number of activities in support of his views. As president and executive secretary of the Phoenix chapter of the Chinese War Relief Association, for example, he coordinated relief efforts for Chinese refugees displaced by the Sino-Japanese War. When Chinese pilots arrived in the American Southwest for training during World War II, he organized weekly dinners at the homes of local Chinese American families for the soldiers. In 1961, he embarked on a personal "fact finding tour" of Taiwan and Hong Kong to investigate the uses of American foreign aid in the region and to meet with Taiwan President Chiang Kai-shek to strengthen relations between the ROC and the United States, since he believed that "Formosa [Taiwan] was the strongest defense against the Communist-planned aggression in the Pacific area." In fact, he felt so strongly about U.S. support of the Chinese Nationalists that he pursued an official ambassadorship to the ROC, although to no avail, due to his dearth of formal experience in diplomacy.

Ong's eventful life drew to a close on 19 December 1977 at the age of 73 following two bouts of cancer in the pharynx and bone. His simple epitaph captured the essence of his powerful life story: "Nothing is Impossible."

## Source

Nagasawa, Richard. *Summer Wind: The Story of an Immigrant Chinese Politician.* Tucson: Westernlore Press, 1986.

# P

## Michael Park

Michael Park. (Courtesy of the Clerk's Office, City of Federal Way, WA)

**Born:** 28 July 1946, Wonju, Korea.

**Education:** B.A., National University (Korea), 1971.

**Positions Held:** Federal Way, Washington, City Council, 1995–present; Mayor, Federal Way.

**Awards, Honors:** Living Pioneer Award, Northwest Asian Foundation, Seattle.

**Summary:** Michael Park is the mayor of Federal Way, Washington.

### Early Years and Education

Michael Park was born on 28 July 1946 in Wonju, Korea, to Tae Hee Park and Oak Sun Park. He graduated from Whimoon High School and Korea's National University, where he earned his bachelor's degree in business administration in 1971. Park immigrated to the United States in 1977 and has resided in Federal Way ever since.

### Career Highlights

Park was appointed to the Federal Way City Council on 6 June 1995 to fill a vacated position. He then ran for reelection that fall, successfully securing his seat for an additional four-year term. Currently, Park serves as Federal Way's mayor.

Among Park's many commitments are the Governor's Small Business Improvement Council, the Federal Way School District Superintendent Advisory Committee, Highline Community College's Board of Directors, and co-chairing the Federal Way Community Safety Task Force. For his achievements, Park has received a Living Pioneer Award from Seattle's Northwest Asian Foundation.

Park owns and operates Midway Cleaners in Kent, Washington. He is married to Jin Park; they are the parents of two daughters, Sue and Bo.

## Source

Correspondence from Michael Park.

# Q

## Gordon Quan

**Born:** 16 April 1948, China.

**Education:** B.A., University of Texas, Austin; M.Ed, University of Houston; J.D., South Texas College of Law.

**Positions Held:** Member (At-Large Position 2), Houston City Council 2000–present.

**Awards, Honors:** 1999 Asian American Entrepreneur of the Year, 1999 YMCA International Services Volunteer of the Year.

**Summary:** Gordon Quan is the At-Large Position 2 member of the Houston City Council.

### Early Years and Education

Gordon Quan was born in China in 1948 and raised in Houston's East End. Quan's parents owned and operated a corner grocery store where he and his siblings spent many of their after-school hours. After attending Houston's Franklin Elementary, Edison Junior High, and Mibly High Schools, Quan went on to the University of Texas at Austin, where he earned his bachelor of arts degrees in history and government.

### Career Highlights

Following graduation, he accepted a teaching position in the Houston Independent School District (HISD). Meanwhile, he continued his own education, eventually completing the requirements for a Masters in Education from the University of Houston.

As a teacher and Scout leader, Quan devoted significant attention to underprivileged and troubled students. These concerns pushed him to pursue legal studies at the South Texas College of Law, from where he graduated as a Juris Doctor in 1977.

As an attorney, Quan co-founded the professional legal corporation of Quan, Burdette, and Perez, which specializes in Immigration Law and is the largest firm in this area in the state of Texas. Quan has long been active in the Houston community, serving in a number of capacities, including that of Mayoral Appointee as well as memberships on the boards of the city's Holocaust Museum, Kid Care, Aspiring Youth, Asia Society, Asian Pacific Heritage Association, and Associated Catholic Charities. He is also the vice president of the city of Houston Board of Trust.

In 1999, Gordon Quan was elected to a citywide council member seat out of an initial field of 11 candidates, the first Asian Pacific

American to accomplish this feat in Houston. Notably, his victory was made possible in part by the significant financial support of APA contributors and political backing from Houston's first APA city council member Martha Wong. When asked about the city's APA constituents, which comprised 4 percent of the total population at the time, Quan commented, "I believe we do have an emerging role. One of the things in the campaign was to empower the community to begin to realize how well-respected they are in Houston, and how people want them to participate." However, he also noted, "my big concern is that we are foolish if we think we can do it alone; we have to coalesce with other communities." Emphasized Quan, "Anyone running in Houston as an Asian has to show their pedigree to other communities" (Mason 1999, A37).

Following his inauguration to the city council in January 2000, Organization of Chinese Americans (OCA) National President George M. Ong stated, "OCA congratulates Gordon Quan for taking this gigantic step forward in electoral politics. Quan's path of career achievements, community commitment and 'in the trenches' political participation will be an example for the next generation of Chinese Americans and Asian Pacific Americans to follow. Gordon Quan has been an extremely active and committed member of the APA community both at the local and national level. The citizens of Houston have made an excellent choice in Gordon Quan" (www.ocanatl.org).

Quan lives near downtown Houston with his wife Sylvia. They are the parents of Caroline, Kristen, and Katherine.

## Sources

City of Houston Government Center: www.ci.houston.tx.us [Accessed 17 January 2001].

Mason, Julie. "Asians Coming of Age Politically; Community Emerging as a Significant Force in Houston Area." *The Houston Chronicle.* 12 December 1999, p. A37.

Organization of Chinese-Americans Web site: www.ocanatl.org [Accessed 17 January 2001].

# S

## Patricia Saiki

**Born:** 28 May 1930, Hilo, Hawaii.

**Education:** B.A., University of Hawaii, 1952.

**Positions Held:** Member, Hawaii State House of Representatives, 1968–1974; Member, Hawaii State Senate, 1974–1982; Member, U.S. House of Representatives, 1987–1991; Administrator, Small Business Administration, 1991–1993.

**Awards, Honors:** Most Promising Legislator, Eagleton Institute, 1970; Mainstream America Asian American of the Year Award, Asian Pacific Council, 1992.

**Summary:** Patricia Saiki is the second woman of Asian Pacific ancestry elected to the United States Congress. She served as Hawaii's representative from 1987 to 1991.

### Early Years

Patricia Fukuda Saiki, the eldest child of Kazuo and Shizue Inoue Fukada, was born on 28 May 1930 in Hilo, Hawaii. Although the family lived modestly—her father was a clerk and a Hilo High School tennis coach, while her mother was a seamstress—her parents committed themselves to educating their three daughters. Saiki, who once described her father as "the first feminist," attended college, graduating in 1952 as a history and education major from the University of Hawaii, and both she and her two younger sisters went on to become teachers (Simon 1995, 332).

Reverence for education ran deep within her family. "There were certain commandments I'll remember all my life," she recalled. "One is that we never sit on books. When I was a child, my grandparents would never allow me to use a set of books on the chair so that I could reach the table." Such profound respect was a constant presence in the household, "Which is why, I suppose, they encouraged me to become a teacher" (Saiki 1985, 127).

After marrying her husband, Dr. Stanley Mitsuo Saiki, in 1954 and giving birth to their first three children, Stanley Jr., Sandra, and Margaret, Saiki worked to supplement the family income "grading papers between three loads of laundry . . . nightly" (Simon 1995, 331). When the family, which had been living in Toledo, Ohio, while her husband completed his residency, moved back to Hawaii in 1959,

Saiki became active in local politics. Despite having her hands full with two more babies, Stuart and Laura, she became a precinct officer in the St. Louis Heights area. Meanwhile, she taught American history at area schools, including Punahou, Kaimuki Intermediate, and Kalani High, for a total of twelve years.

## Career Highlights

Education has been a constant theme in Saiki's life. It was through her teaching career that Saiki again pursued politics. As an instructor, she experienced first hand the strengths and weaknesses of Hawaii's education system, and during the 1960s, she was instrumental in the formation of the Teacher's Chapter of the Hawaii Government Employees Association, serving as its first president. Her concerns at the time included teachers' pay, work load, student tracking, and curriculum. She was also appointed as a commissioner of the Western Interstate Commission on Higher Education (WICHE), where she spent two years as chairperson. Her visibility in these circles led her to delegate positions at the 1968 Hawaii State Constitutional Convention and the 1968 Republican National Convention. From 1964 to 1968, she also served on the executive board of the state's Republican Party.

Inheriting feminist values from her parents, Patricia Saiki joined Richard Nixon's Presidential Advisory Council on the Status of Women. An active member until 1976, she monitored the monies disbursed to the Hawaii State Commission on the Status of Women. During her years in the islands' House of Representatives (1968–1974) and Senate (1974–1982), she was a vocal advocate of women's rights, considering herself the author of the Equal Rights Amendment in Hawaii. Saiki pushed the state government to accept the ERA almost immediately after Congress's ratification in 1972. During her 14 years in the state government, she authored 25 bills relating to women. Finally, as head of the Small Business Administration from 1991 to 1993, Saiki emphasized concerns of women in business.

"It is vital that small and medium-sized businesses, the employers of 54.3 million Americans, make the full use of their human resources by being able to recognize glass ceiling barriers and by knowing how to best eliminate them," she argued in 1992. "Many ambitious women and minorities will determine the form and structure of leadership in companies of the future. It is the U.S. economy that will reap the benefits" (*New Pittsburgh Courier* 1992, C1).

In 1983, Saiki re-concentrated her energies on the GOP in Hawaii with her election as the Republican Party chair. Her reasons for this decision were clear. "Having served in the Legislature for 14 years, it became even more apparent to me that balance in government, competition at the polls, and challenges to power are necessary if government is to be responsible to the needs of people," she stated. "All of us get apathetic every so often, and it is only human to get lazy and even arrogant, but not if one is a public servant. So long as our government is based on the two-party system, then it is the responsibility of the two parties to be strong enough to be a check on the other" (Saiki 1985, 128).

Saiki soon refocused on running for office. In 1986, and again in 1988, Saiki won her bids for Hawaii's seat in the U.S. House of Representatives. Other electoral efforts, however, were not as successful. Previously, she had lost her bid for Hawaii's lieutenant governorship in 1982. Saiki was also defeated in her quest to be Hawaii's senator in 1990 and the state's governor in 1994.

As a gubernatorial contender, Saiki highlighted educational reform. "[Hawaiian] SAT scores fall below the national median," she noted during her campaign (Lam 1994, 1). Other issues on her platform included government integrity, economy, and buoying Hawaii's Pacific Rim commerce. "If elected, I want to bring new vision and vitality to our plans for the future. I want the people of Hawaii to enjoy the finest quality of life and provide our children a secure future," she declared (Simon 1995, 332).

While Saiki has clearly been devoted to public service, she remains an educator at heart, as evidenced by her acceptance of a lectureship at Harvard University's Kennedy School of Government in spring 1993. "Anytime anyone invites me to take over a class, I'm more than happy to do so. Getting up in front of a class full of young people whose minds can be affected by learning, I think, is the greatest challenge there is," she remarked (Associated Press, 1994).

Patricia Saiki's commitments have also included the Kapiolano Hospital Auxiliary, the board of governors for the Boys and Girls Clubs Hawaii, the board of directors for the National Fund for Improvement of Post-Secondary Education, and a trusteeship of the University of Hawaii Foundation. She was deemed Most Promising Legislator in 1970 by the Eagleton Institute of Rutgers University and received the Asian Pacific Council's Mainstream American Asian American of the Year award in recognition of her work in the Small Business Association and her career as a whole in 1992.

### Sources

"Effort Made to Shatter 'Glass Ceiling.'" *New Pittsburgh Courier*. 16 September 1992, p. C1.
Lam, May. "Saiki Bidding to be Hawaii's 1st Republican Governor in 32 Years." *Asian Week*. 14 October 1996, p. 1.
"Patricia Saiki." *AP Candidate Bios*. The Associated Press Political Service, 1994.
"Patricia Saiki." *Who's Who in American Politics*. Reed Elsevier, Inc., 1997.
Saiki, Patsy Sumie. *Japanese Women in Hawaii: The First 100 Years*. Honolulu: Kisaku, Inc., 1985.
"Saiki to Receive Asian American of Year Award." *Asian Week*. 11 September 1992, p.1
Simon, Margaret. "Patricia Saiki." In *Notable Asian Americans*, ed. Helen Zia and Susan B. Gall. Detroit, MI: Gale Resesarch, Inc., 1995, pp. 331–332.

# Amy Mah Sangiolo

Amy Mah Sangiolo. (Courtesy of Marcy Stuart Photography, Auburndale, MA)

**Born:** 15 October 1964, Weehawken, New Jersey.

**Education:** A.B., Barnard College, 1986; J.D., Rutgers University, 1991.

**Positions Held:** Alderman-at-Large, Newton, Massachusetts.

**Summary:** Amy Mah Sangiolo is an alderman-at-large in Newton, Massachusetts.

## Early Years and Education

Amy Mah Sangiolo was born on 15 October 1964 in Weehawken, New Jersey, to George and Yuriko Mah. She attended Weehawken High School and Barnard College, where she earned a bachelor's degree in political science in 1986. She studied at Rutgers University College of Law, where she graduated with a J.D. in 1991. Additionally, she attended George Washington University's Masters of Law program in 1993–1994.

## Career Highlights

Sangiolo is involved in a number of professional and civic organizations, including the

New York and District of Columbia State Bars, the New York Bar Association, the DC Bar Association, and the American Bar Association. She is also the vice president of the board of the Asian Pacific American Agenda Coalition (APAAC) and member of NOW, Massachusetts Women's Political Caucus, and the Newton Democratic City Committee. She currently serves as the alderman-at-large for Newton, Massachusetts's Ward 4, and is vice chair of the Programs and Services Committee, chair of the Recodification Committee, and a member of the Zoning and Planning and Post Audit and Oversight Committees.

Sangiolo is married to John Sangiolo; they are the parents of George, Midori, and Joseph. Sangiolo notes that she is the first woman on the Newton Board of Aldermen to give birth to two children while in office as well as the "first to nurse in the Aldermanic Chambers."

As for her political goals, Sangiolo states that she wishes "to improve the process by which an average citizen can access information, obtain any needed assistance, and have concerns addressed." Additionally, she is concerned about the local land use process and would like to make some substantial changes not only in the local Zoning Code but also in the land use process more broadly.

### Source

Personal communication with Ellen D. Wu, 14 July 2000.

# Sharon Tomiko Santos

**Born:** 5 July 1961, San Francisco, California.

**Education:** B.A., Evergreen State College, 1985; M.A., Northeastern University, 1988.

**Positions Held:** Representative, Washington State House of Representatives, 1999–present.

**Awards, Honors:** 1996 Honoree, Washington State Women's Political Caucus; 1996;

Sharon Tomiko Santos. (Courtesy of Washington State House of Representatives)

Honoree, *Northwest Asian Weekly*'s Top 10 Contributors to the Asian American Community; 1993; Recipient, Martin Luther King Jr. Keeping the Dream Alive Award, 1993.

**Summary:** A community activist for more than 20 years, Sharon Tomiko Santos was elected to the Washington State House of Representatives in 1998.

### Early Years and Education

A Japanese American, Sharon Tomiko Santos was born in San Francisco, California in 1961 to Joyce Kyoko Miyake and the Reverend Kenneth T. Miyake. She attended Franklin High School in Washington State from 1976 to 1979 before enrolling at the Evergreen State College, where she studied from 1979 to 1980 and again from 1983 to 1985. After earning her bachelor's degree in history from Evergreen, she continued working toward a master's degree in the same field, which she successfully obtained in 1988 from Boston's Northeastern University.

## Career Highlights

Tomiko Santos's involvement in the political arena began in 1989 when she secured a position as an executive assistant to former U.S. Congressman (later elected Washington state governor) Mike Lowry. In 1992, she began a year-long term as the executive director for the Institute for Global Security Studies, a Seattle-based nonprofit research and educational organization. Among her many projects as the institute's director was the convening of an international conference of women, Women of the Pacific: Confronting the Challenges, in September 1992. Starting in June 1992, Tomiko Santos was a key member of the Gary Locke for King County Executive Campaign. As the campaign's office manager, she developed and implemented a legislative district field plan for endorsements and voter contact. From 1994 to 1995, Tomiko Santos made use of her capabilities as the executive policy assistant for Community Relations and Metropolitan Affairs for the King County Executive Office. As such, she placed a special emphasis on issues related to community and economic development, women and minority programs, and civil rights.

Sharon Tomiko Santos's employment and civic service records reflect her longtime interest in Asian Pacific Affairs. From 1995 to 1997, she served as the Gifts Manager for the International District Village Square, located in Seattle's pan-Asian international district. As a key member of the $19.6 million, community-based, mixed-use development project's management team to revitalize the area as part of the Chinatown–International District Preservation and Development Authority, Tomiko Santos developed individual donors strategies for a $3.5 million campaign. Additionally, she worked with management and governing bodies of community-based social service agencies to develop and implement fund-raising initiatives tailored to unique constituencies. Within the community, she has been involved in such organizations as the Wing Luke Asian Museum, where she has served as a trustee since 1995, the National Asian Pacific American Women's Forum, the Council for Pacific Asian Theology, the Asian Pacific Women's Caucus, the Asian Pacific Islander Women and Family Safety Center, the Asian Pacific American Coalition for Equality, the Asian-Jewish Coalition, the Asian Counseling and Referral Service, and the Asia Pacific Task Force of the Church Council of Greater Seattle. Tomiko Santos lectures on topics concerning Asian Pacific Americans, women, and politics at various conferences and colleges.

Sharon Tomiko Santos first braved the electoral winds in 1997 with her bid for the King County, Washington Council. Although defeated in the three-way primary race, she managed to secure a significant 32 percent of the ballots cast for the district seat representing portions of five municipalities and three unincorporated areas in King County with an aggregate population exceeding 120,000. Undaunted, Tomiko Santos followed this first showing with a successful run for $37^{th}$ Legislative District (Seattle)'s seat in the Washington State House of Representatives in 1998, defeating five other hopefuls in the primaries and Republican Kwame Garrett in the general election.

As a state legislator, Tomiko Santos is a member of the Education, Financial Institutions and Insurance, and Finance Committees and serves as the Assistant Whip in the Democratic Caucus. Her key policy interests include civil rights, women's rights, economic and environmental justice, affordable housing, and quality public education. Some of her goals include reducing class sizes and increasing teacher salaries in public schools and encouraging the legislature to increase resources for students outside of the classroom. "We must recognize that the issues facing students are very different from when I was in high school 20 years ago. We've seen an increase in poverty, violence and single-parent households, and that has increased the challenges facing teachers," she declared "In addition to their regular role, we've asked teachers to be social workers, public health nurses, disciplinarians, and surrogate parents. It's something our schools are not equipped to handle" (Sanders 1998, 5).

In her eyes, one of the greatest challenges is her constituents' racial and economic diversity—the broadest of all areas in Washington.

"I have a responsibility to represent all of the 37th," she stated. Therefore, she looks to addressing "the issues that impact us as human beings and the quality of our lives," regardless of color and class (Sanders 1998, 5).

Sharon Tomiko Santos, who resides with her husband in the Rainier Beach neighborhood of Seattle, maintains a straightforward political philosophy: "I care about what happens here and what happens to us because this is my home" (*Northwest Asian Weekly* 1998, 4).

### Sources

"Election Profile: Santos Aims to Put Experience to Use." *Northwest Asian Weekly.* 18 September 1998, p. 4.

Sanders, Al. "Tomiko-Santos: Diversity is District Strength." *The Skanner.* 7 October 1998, p. 3.

## Dalip Singh Saund

**Born:** 20 September 1889, Punjab, India

**Died:** 23 April 1973.

**Education:** B.A., University of Punjab, 1919; M.S., University of California, Berkeley, 1922; Ph.D., University of California, Berkeley, 1924.

**Positions Held:** California State Representative, U.S. House of Representatives, 1957–1959.

**Awards, Honors:** 1957 Urban League Award, 1958 Lord and Taylor Award.

Dalip Singh Saund. (Reproduced from the Collections of the Library of Congress)

**Summary:** Dalip Singh Saund was the first Asian Pacific American Congressman. He represented California in the House of Representatives from 1957 to 1959. Saund was elected only ten years after the U.S. government granted Asian Indians the rights to naturalization and, consequently, to public office.

### Early Years

Dalip Singh Saund, born on 20 September 1889, spent his childhood in rural Punjab, India. The son of two illiterate but wealthy Sikh parents, Natha Singh Saund and Jeoni Kaur Saund, he had the rare opportunity to attend a one-room schoolhouse in his home village of Chhajalwadi. As a student at Prince of Wales College in Jammu during World War I, Saund first learned of American history and politics, and fast became an ardent admirer of President Woodrow Wilson's 14 points. "I read his speeches over and over again, until I could literally repeat them from memory. His inspiring ideas and ideals—'make the world safe for democracy,' 'the war to end war,' and 'self-determination for all peoples'—appealed to my heart," recalled Saund in his 1960 autobiography, *Congressman from India*.

## Education

The principles of Wilson and other prominent American figures such as Abraham Lincoln and Theodore Roosevelt, which Saund, a follower of Mahatma Gandhi's nationalist movement, believed were applicable to India's struggle for independence from Britain, pulled him to the United States after graduating from the University of Punjab with a B.A. in mathematics in 1919. Originally intending to stay in the United States only long enough to learn food canning in hopes of implementing a canning industry in India, Saund's plans changed like many other Asian "sojourners," as a result of his many experiences in America.

As a graduate student at the University of California, Berkeley, Saund served as the national president of the Hindustan Association of America, often delivering speeches or taking part in debates on Indian independence. At the same time, he continued to gain exposure to the canning industry through his coursework and working in several factories throughout California. Despite his studies in the school's Department of Agriculture, Saund's love for mathematics never diminished, leading him to complete both his masters and doctoral degrees in the discipline in 1922 and 1924, respectively.

## Career Highlights

Upon graduation in 1924, Saund did not leave immediately for India but instead considered several options in the United States, including writing a book on the history of his homeland, pursuing a fellowship, or learning more about the canning industry. He was firm in his love for American democracy and his conviction to stay but was also aware of the limitations that Asians faced in the United States. "The only way Indians in California could make a living at that time was to join with others who had settled in various parts of the state as farmers," he stated (Saund 1960). Consequently, he headed for the Imperial Valley in Southern California where he made a living, first as a foreman on a cotton ranch and later as a produce farmer/grower and fertilizer manufacturer.

During his years in agriculture, Dalip Singh Saund continued to cultivate his interests in Indian independence and American politics through a number of avenues. A frequent visitor to the Los Angeles public library, he researched and wrote his first book, *My Mother India*, sponsored by the Sikh temple of Stockton, California, to be a rebuttal to Katherine Mayo's *Mother India*, a Western account of the subcontinent. Saund was also an avid orator and activist, participating in debates throughout the region as well as the activities of the Toastmasters' Club, the India Association of America, and the Imperial County Democratic Central Committee.

However, Saund was still ineligible for citizenship at this time, much to his dismay. As he recounted, "I had become a close part of the American life. I had married an American girl, and was the father of three American children. I was making America my home. Thus it was only natural that I felt pretty uncomfortable not being able to become a citizen of the United States. My social life may have been full and rewarding, but the political desire in me was sorely frustrated" (Saund 1960). Saund thus helped to lead a lobbying campaign that facilitated the passage of the Luce-Celler bill, granting Asian Indians naturalization rights, in 1946.

After receiving his citizenship in 1949, Saund launched his career in electoral politics. He successfully bid for a local judgeship in 1950, but lost his seat due to a legal technicality. Two years later, he won the election for the same position and served on the bench until 1956, when he ran for the House of Representatives for California's 29th Congressional District. Beating five opponents in the primaries, he had formidable competition—Mrs. Jacqueline Cochran Odlum, a wealthy and famous aviatrix, whose campaign platform *Time* magazine described as "I'm for Americanism." Nevertheless, Saund successfully defeated Odlum, combating nativist sentiments with the aid of his family, volunteers, and "American" elements such as a pro-farm stance, a 1956 blue Buick sedan, "innumerable housecalls," and "barbecue[s] each Sunday" (*Time* 1956, 27).

In 1957, Saund fulfilled his campaign promise of boosting East-West relations "as a living example of American democracy in practice," touring a number of Pacific Rim countries as a one-man subcommittee of the House's Foreign Affairs Committee. With stops in Hawaii, Japan, Okinawa, Taiwan, Hong Kong, Vietnam, Indonesia, Singapore, the Philippines, and India, Saund surveyed the American foreign aid program in Asia while fielding local questions and concerns about issues such as communism, U.S. intervention, and American racism. Saund later commented that "the people of India and the Asiatic world knew the story of my election to the U.S. Congress in 1956 and were proud of the fact that a man born in India had been elected to high office" (Saund 1960).

Saund supported a number of bills while in office, including bills that emphasized better communication between Asia and America, civil rights, and social benefits for citizens. He received a number of honors including the Urban League Award for improving race relations and the Lord and Taylor award for making "perhaps the most effective tour of India by an American on record" (Tilak 1995, 340).

Like his work, Saund's personal life was also affected by American politics. In 1928, he married Marian Kosa, a white woman, who thereupon lost her citizenship due to a discriminatory statute. They stayed together in spite of this restriction and had three children, Dalip Singh Saund Jr., a Korean War veteran, Julie, and Eleanor. Saund died on 23 April 1973.

## Sources

curriculum.calstatela.edu/faculty/jhart2/root/pioneer/ htm [Accessed 14 April 1999].

"The Primaries," *Time*. 18 June 1956, p. 27.

Saund, Dalip Singh. *Congressman from India*. New York: Dutton, 1960.

Tilak, Visi R. "D.S. Saund." In *Notable Asian Americans*, ed. Helen Zia and Susan B. Gall. Detroit, MI: Gale Research, Inc., 1995, pp. 338–340.

# Paull Hobom Shin

**Born:** 27 September 1935, Kyong Ki-Do, Korea.

**Education:** B.A., Brigham Young University, BA, 1962; MPIA, University of Pittsburgh, 1964, MPA, 1970; Ph.D., University of Washington, 1980.

**Positions Held:** Washington State House of Representatives, 1993–1994; Washington State Senate, 1999–present.

**Awards, Honors:** Brigham Young Distinguished Alumni Award, 1997, YMCA Outstanding Service Award, 1998, the Vocational Educational Development Award, and the President of South Korea's Distinguished Service Award.

**Summary:** Paull Shin is a Washington state senator.

## Early Years

Paull Shin was born on 27 September 1935 in Kyong Ki-Do, Korea, under Japanese occupation. His childhood was marked by unusual adversity; at the age of four, his mother died and his father disappeared. At the age of six, he left his grandmother's house for Seoul. "I was hungry. I had no place to go. Therefore my life consisted of standing on street corners begging for food to stay alive," he recalled. "I didn't mind it in summer time, because it was warm, but in the winter time it was awfully difficult." The young Shin lived on the streets of Seoul for nearly a decade—"I had never gone to school, never had a home cooked meal" (Shin 1999).

Shin's life took a fortuitous turn at the age of 15, the year the Korean War broke out. He was able to secure a position as a houseboy with the United States army, polishing shoes, washing clothes, and looking after military personnel. There, he made the acquaintance of Dr. Ray Paull, an American dentist. Dr. Paull adopted Shin, who appropriated Paull's surname as his first, and brought his new son to Salt Lake City, Utah, to join the Paull family, which included three other boys.

The top priority for the 18-year-old Shin was acquiring a formal education, of which he had none. After being turned down by a number of area schools due to his age, Paull hired a special tutor to teach his son English, Social Studies, and History while he himself instructed Shin in chemistry, math, and physics. After 14 months of intensive study, Shin passed the GED.

He followed this feat first with a two-year service in the U.S. Army, stationed in Germany, and second by attending Brigham Young University—his first exposure to formal, institutional schooling—where he earned his bachelor of arts degree in 1962. Eventually, Shin went on to complete requirements for a masters of public and international affairs degree at the University of Pittsburgh (1964), and master's degree and doctorate in public administration (1970) from the University of Washington (1980). For Shin, his Ph.D. graduation ceremony was particularly memorable—"When I was walking down with the degree in my hand, this time my father started to bawl. He bawled like a little kid," recalled Shin. "And this is what he said: 'Thank you, my son, for your accomplishments.' I said, 'Dad, it is I who shall thank you. You brought me out of nowhere, provided a home, love, and education, and above all, my right to be me. How can you thank me for that?' The two of us embraced together and cried" (Shin 1999).

Education has been a dominant theme in Shin's life. After earning his MPIA in 1964, Shin accepted an assistant professorship on the faculty of Brigham Young's Hawaii campus, where he stayed for three years. Meanwhile, he also worked part-time at the University of Maryland's Hawaii Campus. In 1969, he relocated to Seattle's Shoreline Community College, where he taught history for over twenty years.

Shin has also maintained an active business outside the classroom, including work as a legislative advisor on international trade issues and chairman of the board for TTI, a long-distance telecommunications company. Politics, however, captured his interests. As he explained, "I thought about what I can do to minimize some of the obstacles and problems we as immigrants and adoptees have in the mainstream of the country. I want to help some way to minimize that problem. Actually, what came to my mind was yes, I taught 31 years. Yes, I have had 27,000 students that I have experienced the honor of teaching, but I still was not making an immediate and direct impact. And I thought about politics, but it seemed beyond me" (Shin 1999). Initially, he noted, he hesitated to enter the political arena because of his Asian ancestry, which he felt would be a hindrance. However, he was able to "overcome that fear" and ran successfully for Washington State's House of Representatives in 1992 (Shin 1999). During his two-year term, Shin served as vice chair of the Committee on Trade, Economic Development and Housing and as an appointed member on the committees on Transportation and Higher Education. Before landing his position in the Washington State Senate in 1999, Shin competed unsuccessfully for Congress twice, in the 1996 state Democratic primary for the lieutenant governorship, and for the U.S. ambassadorship to South Korea.

Currently, as the representative of the 21st Legislative District in Washington State, Shin is vice-chair of the Commerce, Trade, Housing and Financial Institutions and Education committees and is a member of the Transportation Committee. He also sits on the Governor's Council on Higher Education, the Governor's Council on International Trade, and the Blue Ribbon Study on Washington Trade.

Shin's civic commitments are numerous as well, particularly with regard to the Asian Pacific American community. In addition to participating on the Governor's Commission on Asian American Affairs, he is a board member of Asian American Political Action Civic Affairs, president of the Northwest Region of Korean Americans, and co-founder of Korean Identity Development Society (KIDS), a Seattle-based organization which promotes cultural identity in American adopted children of Korean ancestry. As a native of Korea and a naturalized American citizen, Shin expressed his worldview as such: "America provided an education for me to think, therefore I know who I am. Therefore America is my fatherland. Korea, on the other hand, is my motherland. Korea gave me my life, my blood, and my heritage. . . . As a son, [I want] my mom and dad to get along most beautifully" (Shin 1999).

Within the broader community, Shin is involved with such groups as the YMCA, United Way, United Nations Dolman Society, Snohomish County Boy Scouts, and the World Association of Children and Parents. In recognition of his accomplishments, he has earned such honors as the Brigham Young Distinguished Alumni Award (1997), the YMCA Outstanding Service Award (1998), the Vocational Educational Development Award, and the President of South Korea's Distinguished Service Award.

Shin and his wife Donna have two children and three grandsons.

## Sources

De Leon, Ferdinand M. "Question of Identity—American Adoptees Born in Korea Search for their Cultural Roots in Second Homeland." *The Seattle Times*. 12 March 1992, p. D1.

Kang, Jennifer. "Paull Hobom Shin." In *Distinguished Asian Americans: A Biographical Dictionary*, ed. Hyung-chan Kim. Westport, CT: Greenwood Press, 1999, pp. 318–319.

Korean American AdopteeAdoptive Family Network Web site: www.kaanet.com/keynote.htm. [Accessed 10 July 2000].

Shin, Paull. Keynote speech from 1999 Korean American Adoptee, Adoptive Family Network Conference.

"Shin, Paull H." In *Who's Who Among Asian Americans 1994–1995*. Detroit: Gale Research, 1994, p. 541.

Washington State Legislature Web site: www.leg.wa.gov/senate/members/senmem21.htm [Accessed 10 July 2000].

# Dolores Sibonga

**Education:** B.A., University of Washington, 1952; J.D., University of Washington.

**Positions Held:** Member, Seattle City Council, 1978, 1979–1992.

**Summary:** A woman of many "firsts," Dolores Sibonga was the first Filipino-American to pass the Washington State bar exam and the first minority woman to serve on Seattle's City Council.

## Early Years and Education

Dolores Sibonga spent her childhood in Seattle's International District, living in different hotels with her parents, proprietors of the Estigoy Cafe, a restaurant and pool hall. Sibonga fondly reflected on her colorful youth in 1979: "I was an only child and was terribly spoiled by attention from the customers. If only my children had had the advantages of that kind of upbringing. If only they'd been thrown into close contact with all sorts of different people from all walks of life" (Godden 1979, 4).

The young Sibonga also enjoyed substantial support from her family in her scholastic endeavors. After attending Bailey Gatzert,

Washington Junior High, and Garfield High School, she enrolled at the University of Washington. Her mother's influence, she explained, impacted her educational decisions. "Mother graduated from Wenatchee High at 16 and attended the university for about a year. But it was tough in those days. Women of color had to work their way through doing domestic work. When my time came, I was torn between majoring in music—I admired my violin teacher greatly—and going into journalism. Mother favored journalism," she recalled. "One of the most respected members of our community, Victor Velasco, owned the *Filipino Forum*, a monthly newspaper. So I went into journalism—one of three minority students in the school at the time" (Godden 1979, 4). Sibonga succeeded in her chosen field, earning her B.A. in 1952, becoming the first Filipino American alumnus of UW's journalism school.

## Career Highlights

Dolores Sibonga accepted her first job at Spokane's KHZ, which was making the transition into television at the time. Her principal task at KHZ was as traffic manager, the individual responsible for scheduling programs. As she explained, "[during that period], women got communication jobs by going into the clerical end of the business. They got to do very little writing. The men, however, got to go into writing right away" (Godden 1979, 4).

Her next positions were with various radio and television stations in Seattle. Around 1968, after *Filipino Forum* owner Victor Velasco suffered a fatal accident, Sibonga and her husband, Martin Sibonga, purchased the paper. "We published it for about a year and a half. Through the paper, we'd hoped to get various local ethnic groups to form a bloc. But we were lousy businessmen. We lost a wad of money," she said.

The failure of the *Filipino Forum*, however, indirectly led to Sibonga's career in local politics. By fortuitous circumstances, her husband Martin spotted a newspaper article on the Council on Legal Education Opportunities'

six-week program to assist people of color with the law school admissions process. She took the course, and was subsequently accepted into the University of Washington law school.

Returning to school after 18 years was not an easy task for Sibonga. "At first it was very hard. Partly because I'd been away from my studies for so long, and partly because law's like a foreign language," she remembered. "I had been engaged in a period of community activism and I had to divorce myself from all that to make time to study. Yet that first year was great. Martin was still out of a job, and we were as close to poor as we've ever been. But I'd come home to study and we had a chance to be together. Housekeeping turned out to be a good break from the books, and, as far as the children [Martin, Jr., Randi Maya, and Theresa Escobar Cook] were concerned, I was home when they were home. I was visible" (Godden 1979, 5).

After another two years, Dolores Sibonga successfully completed her coursework and became the first Filipino-American ever to pass the Washington State bar exam. Job prospects were not promising, but she managed to secure a permanent position at the Public Defender's office where she had been an intern. Like school, she found her work to be extremely demanding. "At first . . . [it] was exciting. I went from municipal court to juvenile court and then into the felony program. That's pretty heavy, helping determine people's future lives. I literally burned out after three years" (Godden 1979, 5).

Sibonga then switched jobs, becoming a legislative aide to the King County Council. After six months, she changed hats again, this time as deputy director of the state's Human Rights Commission. In August 1978, she took a leave of absence to fill a vacated seat on Seattle's City Council left open by Phyllis Lamphere, who resigned to accept a federal position. In doing so, she became the first minority woman to serve on the council. Due to technicalities, however, she was ineligible to run for the position the following November.

Nevertheless, the pull toward politics remained strong for Sibonga, and in March 1979, she resigned from the Human Rights Commission to concentrate her efforts on campaigning for a seat on the city council. She found the entire process culturally challenging. "During the campaign, the hardest part for me as a Filipina was to say, 'Vote for me. I've done this and I've done that.' All through school, I'd never vote for myself even when I wanted the position badly. In order to be in politics, you have to speak about your accomplishments and feel good enough about them to have people recognize you" (Chu 1989, 412).

Her electorate took notice of her qualifications, and she won her bid that year, defeating Seattle police officer Bob Moffett by almost 13,000 votes. She was the first minority woman to be elected to Seattle's governing body. When asked about her landmark feat at the time, she replied that she was pleased, "but I wonder why it hasn't happened before. Here I am at 48. There should have been others before" (Chew 1979). During her years on the Seattle City Council, Sibonga served as chair of the Finance Committee. She retired from the council in 1992.

## Sources

Chew, Ron. "Sibonga and Hara Win City Positions." *International Examiner*. November 1979.

Chu, Judy, "Asian Pacific American Women in Mainstream Politics." In *Making Waves: An Anthology of Writings by and about Asian American Women*, ed. Asian Women United of California. Boston: Beacon Press, 1989, pp. 405–421.

Godden, Jean. "Dolores Sibonga." *Northwest*. 18 February 1979, pp. 4, 5.

Nelson, Robert T. "Sibonga Confirms She Will Step Down." *The Seattle Times*. 15 March 1991, p. A1.

# Shamina Singh

**Born:** Chesapeake, Virginia.

**Education:** B.A., Old Dominion University, 1991; M.P.A., University of Texas, Austin.

**Positions Held:** Special Assistant to Secretary of Labor, Senior Lobbyist for the Service Employees International Union, Executive Director, White House Initiative on Asian Americans and Pacific Islanders, 1999–2001.

**Awards, Honors:** Creating a Voice Award, Project-Impact; *A. Magazine*, Twenty Asian Americans to Watch in the 21$^{st}$ Century, Henry Crown Fellowship, Aspen Institute, 2001 Gay Asian Pacific Service Network Pacific Bridge Award.

**Summary:** Shamina Singh is the first executive director of the White House Initiative on Asian Americans and Pacific Islanders.

### Early Years

Shamina Singh was born and raised in Chesapeake, Virginia. As the daughter of Punjabi immigrants, Singh's multicultural upbringing profoundly shaped her future career. "I grew up not seeing many Asians, much less Indians. My parents were one of the first families in that area, so unlike children in California or New York, I did not grow up seeing people who looked like me or talked like me," recalled Singh. "I went to Sikh youth camps and that's where I was first exposed to people my age and I saw the struggles my parents went through to survive in this country" (Melwani).

Continued Singh, "Regardless of income levels, the way mainstream America looks at minorities makes it difficult for them in this country. We were the only Asian family in a large community and although there were pluses there were many issues raised which I saw my family endured." Singh also explained that her parents emphasized "very Indian values" such as "the idea of service and giving back to the community," adding that "My parents were very mindful that we were grounded in this country as Americans and participate fully but always stay grounded in the terms of the cultural identity that we bring to this country" (Melwani).

## Education

Singh attended Old Dominion University in her home state, graduating in 1991. Two years later, she headed for Texas, where she worked for Governor Ann Richards before enrolling at the University of Texas, Austin, where she earned her master's degree in public affairs at the Lyndon B. Johnson School for Public Affairs.

## Career Highlights

En route to the White House, Singh served as special assistant to Secretary of Labor Alexis Herman, specializing in congressional affairs and health care, as well as the senior lobbyist for the Service Employees International Union, the largest union of health care workers in North America. In 1999, President Bill Clinton appointed Singh to head the first White House Initiative on Asian Americans and Pacific Islanders, which, in Singh's view, "is not a paper exercise or a symbolic gesture from the administration but a concrete tool for the community to use.... The Executive order is a tool which empowers people to make a change in their lives."

The commission was institutionalized by Clinton's signing of Executive Order 13125, the first such mandate to target Asian Pacific Americans since Franklin D. Roosevelt's Executive Order 9066 calling for the incarceration of over 100,000 Japanese Americans on the West Coast. Clinton's Executive Order 13125 called for a coordinated federal government effort to improve the quality of life of Asian Pacific Americans in areas where they are underserved, including health, education, housing, labor, economy, and community development. The initiative was part of a broader project of the Administration to eliminate racial and ethnic health disparities for Asian Pacific Americans and other minority groups.

"I'm thrilled to be part of the project that will fulfill the administration's goals of having all groups participate equally in the formation of the vision for American life in the 21st century," stated Singh (U.S. Newswire 1999). Noted Health and Human Services Deputy Secretary Kevin Thurm, "We are pleased that HHS will play a leadership role in this important initiative and that Ms. Singh will head our effort. We are confident that she will work to ensure that the President's goals are met and the needs of Asian American and Pacific Islanders throughout this country are addressed thoroughly and with result" (U.S. Newswire 1999).

Shamina Singh's tasks as executive director included overseeing a federal interagency, closely collaborating with the Department of Health and Human Services, and a presidential advisory commission consulting on the implementation and coordination of federal programs in relation to APAs. More specifically, the initiative was geared toward advising the administration on how the federal government can better serve the APA community, pinpointing strategies for increasing public and private sector involvement in improving the health and well-being of APAs, and developing better ways to foster research and data collection on APAs and public health. While the initiative's findings during its 18-month pilot run were of no surprise to the Asian Pacific American community, they still served an important service in Singh's view. "It wasn't that the federal government representatives were opposed to looking at the issues and looking into how to make government more open and accessible to APIs; it just seemed they had never thought of how they could do it," she explained.

Singh has stressed the importance of dismantling stereotypes about Asian Pacific Americans in order to service effectively the needs of the community. "There is the myth of the model minority that is prevalent for all Asians, but we are finding there's a lot of work that needs to be done within the community," she stated. "For example, heart disease is very prevalent among the South Asian population, and there are issues of cultural adjustment and dealing with the elderly. The fact that we have such a large immigrant population is a very positive thing but it's time for the community in the States to really organize and become involved in the mainstream because that does really affect their daily life." Added Singh, "So no matter what they are doing, whether they are a computer company mogul or a clerk at the 7-Eleven, everybody in this country has access to the government and should definitely be participating both politically and socially, and within the community."

Singh is one of Asian Pacific America's rising stars. In addition to being honored by A. Magazine as one of the Twenty Asian Americans to Watch in the 21st Century, she has received a Project-Impact Creating A Voice Award and a Henry Crown Fellowship from the Aspen Institute.

The one distinction nearest to her heart, however, is the 2001 Pacific Bridge Award presented to her by the Gay Asian Pacific Service Network (GAPSN) on 13 January 2001 in Los Angeles, California. During the evening's ceremonies, Singh publicly acknowledged her homosexuality for the first time. "I am here to proclaim myself as a proud gay woman," she declared. "I felt it was time to come out, and I thought that GAPSN Awards was the best opportunity. I felt very supported here. Out of all the awards I've ever received, this means the most to me" (www.gapsn.org 2001).

### Sources

Gay Asian Pacific Service Network Web site: www.gapsn.org [Accessed 17 January 2001].
Hong, Joseph. "Underscoring Our Needs." *Asian Week online.* 26 January-1 February 2001: www.asianweek.com [Accessed 17 January 2001].
Melwani, Lavina. "Woman in the Middle." Little India online. www.littleindia.com [Accessed 17 January 2001].
"New Executive Director for White House Initiative on Asian Americans and Pacific Islanders Begins New Duties." *U.S. Newswire.* 27 September 1999.
White House Initiative on Asian Americans and Pacific Islanders Web site: www.aapi.gov [Accessed 17 January 2001].

## Sichan Aun Siv

Sichan Aun Siv. (Courtesy of Sichan Aun Siv)

**Born:** March 1948, Phnom Penh, Cambodia.

**Education:** Diplome du Professorat 1972, Bachelier en Droit 1974, and Licence es Lettres in 1975, University of Phnom Penh; M.A., Columbia University, 1981.

**Positions Held:** Deputy Assistant to President for Public Liaison and Deputy Assistant Secretary for South Asian Affairs, 1989–1993; Senior Advisor, International Republican Institute, 1993–present.

**Awards, Honors:** Asian Pacific American Heritage Council's Asian American Award, CARE distinction for "selflessness and courage in pursuit of his lifelong commitment to human freedom, opportunity, and dignity, Reserve Officer's "Twice the Citizen Award."

**Summary:** Sichan Siv, who served as Deputy Assistant to the Secretary of State from 1989 to 1993, is the highest ranking Cambodian American in public office to date.

## Early Years

Sichan ("Beautiful Moon") Aun Siv was born in March 1948 to Chham and Aun (Chea) Siv in Phnom Penh, Cambodia. The middle-class Siv family, supported by Chham's income as a policeman, struggled after he passed away when young Siv was only nine years of age. In his *Notable Asian Americans* biography, Siv recalled his mother's words of advice during the difficult times: "Remember Sichan. Whatever happens, never give up hope" (Rafi 1995, 349). Her comment would prove to be a source of strength to Siv as he faced further adversities.

## Education

Following his graduation from a prestigious Phnom Penh high school in 1968, Siv joined the Royal Air Cambodge as a flight attendant. Cambodia's travel industry was on the decline due to military conflicts, however, and in 1970 he returned to school. At the University of Phnom Penh, he earned his Diplome du Professorat in 1972, Bachelier en Droit in 1974, and Licence es Lettres in 1975. Applying the linguistic skills he had acquired as an employee with Royal Air Cambodge, Siv taught high school English from 1972 to 1974. Next, he worked as a program associate for CARE-Cambodia, an American humanitarian organization, in Phnom Penh from 1974 to 1975.

1975 marked a turning point in the Southeast Asian wars. As the Communist Khmer Rouge prepared to enter Phnom Penh, the city's residents fled to the countryside. Through a connection at the American embassy, Siv learned of an opportunity to evacuate the capital on April 12, five days before the city's capture. Before boarding the helicopter, however, Siv spent his last moments working with local authorities to ship rice and supplies to refugees in a nearby town. "I thought by going to the meeting first I would be able to save many starving families and then leave with a clear conscience," he explained (McAllister 1989, A23). As a result, he missed the final transport by a mere 30 minutes.

Stranded in war-torn Cambodia, Siv did his best to survive the nightmare unfolding around him. He discarded his eyeglasses, which he believed would reveal his educated background and make him a target of the anti-Western, anti-intellectual Khmer Rouge.

After working briefly in the countryside, Siv, carrying false papers, made his solo escape to Thailand on bicycle. Just miles outside the border, Khmer Rouge officials caught him and forced him into hard labor for the Angkar, the "organization," constructing dams, ditches, roads, and canals 18 hours a day. Barely subsisting on rancid broth and minimal sleep, Siv worked fearfully in near silence, worried that the French words and phrases in his daily lexicon would expose his learned past.

A second opportunity for escape presented itself to Siv in January 1976 when he was chosen to fill an opening for a crane operator near the Thai border. On February 12, after learning that his crew was to be moved inland the next day, he broke away and ran into the jungle. "I said, 'Now or never,'" he recalled in 1989. He spent three days and nights without food or water (Weinraub and Shenon 1989, 20).

After a loudspeaker blared announcements for a Buddhist festival on his third day, Siv stumbled into a booby-trapped hole. To his relief, upon emerging from the pit, he realized he was no longer in Cambodia. Siv noticed Thai fruit can labels and footprints from sneakers—footwear forbidden by the Khmer Rouge—a man and woman clad in multicolored dress, and a group of motorcyclers. "Mixed couples were not allowed to ride together in the 'new Cambodia' nor did anyone there wear any thing but black pajamas issued by Angkar," he told the *Washington Post* in 1989 (McAllister 1989, A23).

When Siv finally reached Thailand, police arrested him on charges of illegal entry. Fortunately, June Magnaldi, Siv's co-worker at CARE in Phnom Penh, had notified the U.S. Embassy in Bangkok of his potential escape. They located him at a refugee camp where he was running English classes for his fellow residents. The embassy processed the necessary papers for his leave, and on 4 June 1976, he arrived on American soil.

Notably, Siv's final act before leaving Southeast Asia was becoming a Buddhist monk. His decision came out of gratitude for his mother's strong faith and her merits that he believed saved his life. Although he relinquished his priesthood after settling in the United States, Siv continued to draw strength and peace from his religion. This was especially crucial, when, in the aftermath of his traumatic flight from his homeland, he learned that 15 of his family members, including his mother, older brother, and sister, perished in the Cambodian Holocaust. "I just simply want to separate emotion from reality," he stated in 1989. "If you let your emotions run your life, you'll never get anything done" (McAllister 1989, A23).

In the United States, Siv was initially sponsored by a Peace Corps worker and resettled in Wallingford, Connecticut. To establish himself, he went through a series of jobs, including flipping hamburgers at Friendly's Ice Cream parlor and picking apples in Connecticut, driving a taxi in Manhattan, calculating statistics at the Lower Eastside Service Center in New York City, and counseling other refugees as a staff assistant at the Lutheran Immigration and Refugee Service, also in New York, from 1978 to 1980.

Wanting to return to school, Sichan Siv sent earnest letters to a number of graduate programs detailing his life experiences and ambitions. Dr. Harvey Picker, then dean of Columbia University's School of International and Public Affairs, agreed to admit Siv on a Maguire Scholarship. "I did spot him as quite an unusual student," said Picker. "He had the advantage of having lived through a lot, but he did not come through it with a distorted or radicalized view. He comes through as a winner" (McAllister 1989, A23). Siv, also named an International Fellow, matriculated and earned a masters degree in international affairs in 1981.

Over the next few years, Siv continued to build on his successes. He became a U.S. citizen on 21 December 1982, and married Texan Martha Pattillo almost exactly one year later on 24 December 1983.

## Career Highlights

Sichan Siv secured positions as a management associate at New York City's Marine Midland Bank from 1981 to 1982, an administrator and financial officer for the Episcopal Church from 1982 to 1983, a United Nations representative to the Cambodian Non-Communist Resistance from 1983 to 1987, and the Asia-Pacific manager for the Institute of International Education in New York from 1987 to 1989.

Siv's foray into politics took root in 1987 when he volunteered for George Bush's presidential campaign. "I was very interested in Republican politics," recalled Siv. "I've been a Republican since I became a U.S. citizen ... and I've supported everything George Bush stands for" (Weinraub and Shenon 1989, A20). His performance caught the attention of the Bush administration's communications director David F. Demarest—"It's amazing. There are a couple of things that are amazing about Siv's story; that he lived through it and that he still has a positive attitude," remarked Demarest—and led to his selection as the first Asian Pacific American ranking presidential aide in U.S. history (McAllister 1989, A23). "When I got the call to ask me to work here, I didn't know whether it was true or not," said Siv. "But then I said, 'Yes, it must be true; it is America.' It was the completion of a long journey" (Weinraub and Shenon 1989, A20). Siv began work as one of President Bush's two deputy assistants for public liaison on 13 February 1989, the 13-year anniversary of his escape from Cambodia.

In this position, Siv dealt with both domestic and foreign issues. He coordinated public relations and education on Bush's policies, headed the White House Communications Task Force on national security issues, attended the Geneva conference on refugees, and advised the American delegates to the Paris conference on Cambodia. In March 1992, he participated in the first official U.S. delegation to Cambodia since the Southeast Asian wars. "My relatives in Cambodia called me 'The Man with Golden Bones,'" he said of his trip. "I came to the U.S. with $2 in my pocket. March 13, 1992, exactly 16 years and one month from the time of my arrival in this country, I set foot again in Cambodia and was visiting the village in which my mother was killed. Two weeks later, I was back in Washington, D.C. sitting with the president in the Oval Office, telling him about my trip. I thought to myself, 'Only in the United States could something like this be possible' " (Rian 1992, 4).

From 1992 to 1993, Sichan Siv was named deputy assistant secretary of state for southeast Asian affairs, where he aided Secretary of State James Baker with area policy. After Bush's term ended, New York brokerage Commonwealth Associates courted Siv for its newly-created Asia-Pacific managing directorship as part of the company's emphasis on developing Pacific Rim commerce. Since then, he has served as a financial advisor at Prudential Securities, a managing director of ICG Consulting, and a senior adviser to the International Republican Institute.

Siv has received several honors in recognition of his pioneering work, such as the Asian Pacific American Heritage Council's Asian American Award, and the CARE distinction for "selflessness and courage in pursuit of his lifelong commitment to human freedom, opportunity, and dignity." On 25 June 1992, he was only the third person ever to receive the Reserve Officer's Association's Twice the Citizen Award for "leadership to the nation above and beyond the call of duty"

during the Persian Gulf War. As leader of the White House Office of Public Liaison, he facilitated communications between service men and women and their families and friends back home in the United States. During the emotional ceremony in St. Paul, Minnesota, he stated, "I accept this award on behalf of all refugees in the United States and abroad as well as the entire White House staff" (Rian 1992, 4).

Siv has maintained an active public life beyond the White House as a lieutenant colonel of the U.S. Air Force Auxiliary Civil Air Patrol, and as a board member of the U.S. Committee for Immigration and Refugee Services of America, the Center for Migration Studies, the Smithsonian Institution's Arthur M. Sackler Gallery, and the National Council for Christians and Jews.

Reflecting on his successes in the face of many obstacles, he remarked, "The secret is, I think, strong determination. I was blessed by many things. I was lucky to survive the Khmer Rouge. I was lucky to survive three days in the jungle without having anything to eat. I was lucky to be allowed to resettle in the United States. I was lucky to survive the Manhattan traffic when I was a taxi driver. And . . . I think, more than anything, it was a combination of luck and fate, I'm sure. There are so many qualified people out there, but I'm simply the lucky one" (McAllister 1989, A23).

## Sources

McAllister, Bill. "A Cambodian Emigre's Route from Killing Fields to White House." *Washington Post.* 31 March 1989, p. A23.
Rafi, Natashi. "Sichan Siv." In *Notable Asian Americans*, ed. Helen Zia and Susan B. Gall. Detroit, MI: Gale Research, Inc., 1995, pp. 349–351.
Rian, Joe. "Cambodian Refugee Sichan Siv Accepts Award." *Asian Pages.* 31 July 1992, p.4.
Resume provided by Sichan Siv.
"Sichan Siv." *Securities Week.* 9 January 1995, p. 8.
"Siv, Sichan Aun." *The Complete Marquis Who's Who Biographies.* Updated 22 July 1992.
Weinraub, Bernard and Philip Shenon. "Cambodian Dream." *New York Times.* 21 February 1989, p. A20.

# T

## Shirin R. Tahir-Kheli

Bush appointee Shirin Tahir-Kheli, head of the U.S delegation, addresses the 57th session of the Human Rights Commission prior to the vote on China's human rights record in Geneva, Switzerland, on April 18, 2001.( Donald Stampfli, AP/Wide World Photos)

**Born:** 1944, Hyderabad, India.

**Education:** B.A., Ohio Wesleyan University, 1961; M.A., Ph.D., University of Pennsylvania, 1972.

**Positions Held:** U.S. Ambassador to United Nations, 1990–1993.

**Summary:** Shirin Raziuddin Tahir-Kheli is the first Asian Pacific American delegate to the United Nations for the United States and is also the first Muslim senior government official to be appointed by an American president.

### Early Years

Shirin Raziuddin Tahir-Kheli was born in Hyderabad, India, in 1944 to a family involved in academics and politics. Her grandfather was the premier minister to the nizam of Hyderabad, while her father, a physics professor, became a vice chancellor of Peshawar University in Pakistan and a leading bureaucrat. His high profile positions exposed the young Tahir-Kheli to many world-renowned figures such as China's Chou En-Lai. Following the partition of India in the early 1950s, Tahir-Kheli and her family moved to Pakistan.

### Education

She had an American education, however, attending Ohio Wesleyan University, where she earned a bachelor's degree in textile design at age 17. She then returned to Pakistan where she met and married Dr. Reza Tahir-Kheli, a nuclear physicist and professor at the University of Pennsylvania, before the couple settled in the United States. At Penn, Tahir-Kheli changed her field of study, choosing to concentrate on global affairs. She wrote her dissertation, "Pakistani Elites and Foreign Policy towards the Soviet Union, Iran, and Afghanistan," and earned her doctorate in 1972.

### Career Highlights

Shirin Tahir-Kheli entered academia with a professorship at Temple University from 1973 to 1985. Though granted tenure in 1979, Tahir-Kheli elected to pursue government in her areas of specialty. She began under the secretary of state as part of the State Department's Policy Planning Bureau, considered by many to be the country's diplomatic think tank, in 1982. After two years, she assumed the directorship of political-military affairs coordinating National Security Council staff before being named the director of Near East and South Asian affairs, where she remained from 1986 to 1989.

The following year, President George H.W. Bush appointed her to the position of U.S. ambassador and alternative representative for special political affairs to the United Nations. In this capacity responsibilities for human rights issues formed part of her portfolio, and she participated in two sessions of the U.N. Commission on Human Rights.

Tahir-Kheli received unanimous backing from the Senate Foreign Relations Committee but generated controversy among pro-India interests who raised the issue of Tahir-Kheli's objectivity and possible anti-India biases due to her background and close relationships with certain Pakistani officials, including Pakistan President Mohammed Zia-ul Haq. Despite these claims, she successfully stepped into this high profile role for the duration of the first Bush adminstration, thus becoming the first Asian Pacific American delegate to the United Nations and the first Muslim senior government official to be appointed by an American president. In a 1994 interview, Tahir-Kheli acknowledged the challenges of her position, noting "My goal with regard to United States policy in South Asia was to show that it did not need to be a zero-sum game between India and Pakistan; it was possible to improve U.S. relations with both." She also emphasized, "We [as Asian Pacific Americans] must decide where our loyalties are. . . . My own preference is to be part of the U.S. political system" (Rafi 1995, 364).

Since 1993, Tahir-Kheli has continued to be active in both political and academic circles, contributing to public debates through newspaper editorial writing and affiliating with institutions such as Princeton University's Center for International Studies. She is currently the director of the South Asia Program at the School of Advanced International Studies, Johns Hopkins University and is also a Senior Fellow at the Foreign Policy Research Institute in Philadelphia. In September 2001, President George W. Bush appointed her to serve as a member of the United States Commission on International Religious Freedom for a term of two years.

### Sources

Aziz, Haniffa, "Senators Back Controversial Aide." *India Abroad*. 13 April 1990, p. 9.

———. "Tahir-Kheli Named to U.N. Post." *India Abroad*. 23 March 1990, p. 15.

Rafi, Shazia Z. "Shirin R. Tahir-Kheli." In *Notable Asian Americans*, ed. Helen Zia and Susan B. Gall. Detroit: Gale Research Inc., 1995, pp. 363–364.

Tahir-Kheli, Shirin. "India vs. Pakistan." *Boston Globe*. 12 July 1999, p. A9.

White House News Release Site: www.whitehouse.gov/news/releases/2001/09/20010917-4.html [Accessed 18 October, 2001].

## Paul K. Tanaka

**Born:** 28 July 1958, Los Angeles, California.

**Education:** B.A., Loyola Marymount University, 1980.

Paul Tanaka. (Courtesy of Paul Tanaka)

**Positions Held:** Los Angeles County Sheriff's Department—Deputy, Sergeant, Lieutenant, Captain; Councilmember, Mayor Pro Tem, City of Gardena, California, March 1999–present.

**Awards, Honors:** Sheriff's Department Exemplary Service Award (2), November 1987 and June 1999.

**Summary:** Paul K. Tanaka, a seasoned law enforcement officer, is the mayor pro tem of Gardena, California, one of the largest concentrations of persons of Japanese descent outside of Japan and Hawaii.

## Early Years and Education

Paul K. Tanaka, a fourth-generation Japanese American, was born to Harry and Elaine Tanaka on 28 July 1958 in Los Angeles, California, at the Queen of Angels Hospital. He spent what he describes as a "pretty typical" Japanese American childhood in the city of Gardena, actively participating in sansei athletic leagues for such sports as baseball and basketball. Tanaka attended Gardena High School, where he was involved in a number of service clubs. This experience, he explained, was a "great help" in providing him with a "foundation for going into public service." After graduating from Gardena High School in 1976, Tanaka went on to study at Loyola Marymount University in Los Angeles, receiving his B.A. degree in Accounting in 1980.

## Career Highlights

Tanaka "found out that law enforcement was kind of interesting," and initially decided to "try it for a couple of years, get it out of my system, but it hasn't gotten out of my system yet." He began his career as a patrol officer for the El Segundo, California, Police Department, where he stayed for nearly two years before moving to the Recruitment Unit of the Carson Station of the California Men's Central Jail. After five years as a deputy in Carson, he was promoted to Sergeant of the Field Operations West/Lynwood Station, where he served until 1991.

In July of that year, Tanaka was named a lieutenant of the Los Angeles County Sheriff's Department. For eight years, he served in various capacities at different locations, including managing shift personnel and resources as watch commander for the Mira Loma Facility, Inmate Reception Center, Lennox Station, and West Hollywood Station. He also worked as the Regional Administrator for the Department's Community Oriented Policing Services (COPS) program, as supervision personnel of various stations, operations lieutenant, and as an administrative aide to the sheriff. In August 1999, Tanaka rose to his current standing as captain and accepted the position of bureau commander of the COPS Bureau, supervising 400+ personnel in the following units: COPS, Asian Crime Task Force, Community Law Enforcement Partnership Program, Regional COPS Training Institute, Vital Intervention and Directional Alternatives (VIDA) Juvenile Delinquency Prevention Program.

In addition to his full agenda as a law enforcement officer with the Los Angeles County Sheriff's Department, Tanaka serves on the Gardena City Council. Among others, former Gardena public official Mas Fukai strongly encouraged Tanaka to run for office. At his retirement dinner, remembered Tanaka, Fukai told the young officer, "Now you cannot say no," since there would no longer be any Japanese American representation at the city level. Tanaka also noted that he felt "internal pressure to look out for the aging Issei and Nisei population," since "no one at the Sansei, Yonsei level" seemed to be "remotely interested" in doing so from a formal elected position. As a result, Tanaka successfully bid for a seat on the council, capturing more votes than any other candidate during the March 1999 election.

While Paul Tanaka places Japanese American concerns high on his list of priorities, he also responds to the needs of his other constituents. The diversity of the city—approximately 23–27 percent each Asian Pacific American, African American, Latino, and White—and the need to "bring everyone together for a common cause," presents him with his greatest challenge as a city council member and mayor pro tem. "There is one Gardena," he declared. "No matter what color, what culture, it has to be that way."

While on the council, Tanaka has worked to balance the city's budget, allowing him the opportunity to make use of his accounting skills. When he first started, Gardena was $5.5 million in debt; slowly, Tanaka and his colleagues have worked to reverse the situation. The controversial opening of Larry Flynt's Hustler Casino in Gardena in June 2000 may be one of the most effective remedies. "There are people who are morally opposed to the name, and to gambling, or to Mr. Flynt himself, but I think we're doing what's in the best interests of the majority of the people in Gardena," opined Tanaka (Garrison 2000, B1). Drawing on his experiences with the Sheriff's Department, the mayor pro tem has also co-sponsored the Emergency Preparedness Workshop open to all residents of the Gardena community, and was also instrumental in bringing a special COPS Task Force into the city to assist the local Police Department in locating and eliminating potential and problem drug areas.

Among Tanaka's various council responsibilities are the city's Finance Committee, the Southern California Association of Governments, the South Bay Regional Public Communications Authority, the Southwest Area Planning Council, and the West Basin Water Association.

Aside from his municipal duties, Tanaka remains active in a number of civic organizations, serving on the board of directors for Los Angeles' Harriet Buhai Center for Family Law, the Hollenbeck Youth Center, the Los Angeles Chinese American Sheriff's Advisory, and Keiro Nursing Home Services. He twice received the Los Angeles Sheriff's Department's Service Award—once in November 1987, and again in June 1999. As for his future plans, Tanaka simply stated, "I'm keeping my options open."

### Sources

Garrison, Jessica. "A Helping Hand Some Would Rather Not Grasp." *Los Angeles Times*. 23 June 2000, p. B1.

Telephone interview with Ellen D. Wu, 17 July 2000.

## Mabel Teng

**Born:** Hong Kong.

**Education:** B.S., University of Massachusetts, 1975.

**Positions Held:** Member, San Francisco Board of Supervisors, 1994–present; Chair, Finance Committee, San Francisco County Transportation Authority; Member, Board of Directors, Golden Gate Bridge District.

**Awards, Honors:** Pacific American Women Bay Area Coalition's 1985 Woman Warrior

Mabel Teng. (Courtesy of Mabel Teng)

Award for Outstanding Contributions in Politics and Community Advocacy, 1992 Outstanding Asian Women Award from the Asian Women's Resource Center, 1996 Political Woman of the Year Award, San Francisco chapter of the National Organization for Women.

**Summary:** Mabel Teng is the first Asian Pacific American to be elected to San Francisco's Board of Supervisors. She is also the first non-incumbent Asian Pacific American elected to the board in a city-wide election.

## Early Years and Education

Mabel Teng immigrated to the United States from Hong Kong in 1970. In 1975, she graduated from the University of Massachusetts with a bachelor's degree in biology. She furthered her original career trajectory with genetics research at the Harvard School of Medicine before shifting gears into the realm of community activism and public service.

## Career Highlights

Teng's political career took off with her cross-country move to the Bay Area in 1978. A faculty member of the San Francisco Community College District beginning in 1979, she nonetheless found time to participate in such campaigns as the Justice for Vincent Chin movement in 1983 and the Northern California Chairwoman of the California Democratic Party Asian Pacific Caucus, for which she served as chairwoman in 1986.

In 1990, Teng left her tenured position at the City College of San Francisco to assume responsibilities as a member of the San Francisco Community College Governing Board. The following year, she was elected president. Meanwhile, she served as the Executive Director for two Bay Area nonprofit organizations, the Career Resources Development Center (1991–1995) and the Asian American Donor Program (1995–1996).

Teng made history on 8 November 1994 as the first Asian Pacific American ever to be elected to the powerful San Francisco Board of Supervisors. Furthermore, she was the first non-incumbent Asian Pacific American to be voted onto the board in a citywide election. She followed up her win with another victorious campaign in November 1998.

As a member of the Board of Supervisors, Teng has served in a number of capacities. Her attention has been focused on child care, economic development, and neighborhood concerns. She was the chief author of Universal Child Care Policy for all San Franciscans, a program which included the creation of the High Quality Child Care Fund, the expansion of the Facility Child Care Fund and Affordable Child Care Program, and, most recently, the establishment of C.A.R.E.S. (Compensation and Retention Encourage Stability), which provides scholarships in order to retain child care workers.

Mabel Teng has fought actively against graffiti with her "Partners in Grime" legislation, which she initiated in 1997 in response to a wave of graffiti and hate crimes in the city's Sunset District. "Partners in Grime" marked the first citywide graffiti abatement program.

Additionally, Teng has devoted her energies to economic development and civil rights. Among her projects are the "San Francisco First" policy promoting locally made products, the establishment of the Neighborhood Economic Development Fund and the "Made-by-the-Bay" crusade to save San Francisco's apparel industry, and facilitating the passage of the municipality's welfare-to-work legislation. She also serves as the chair of the Board's Housing and Social Policy Committee and vice-chair of the Rules Committee. As chair of the Finance Committee, Teng has a number of goals. "I also want to work closely with the business community to expand economic growth, especially by expanding small businesses," she said. "I also want to expand our business ties with Pacific Rim countries" (Epstein 1998, A14).

Outside of city hall, Teng divides her time among the San Francisco County Transportation Authority, the Golden Gate Bridge District Board of Directors, the faculty of San Francisco State University, and her husband, Richard Joseph Yuen, assistant dean of students at Stanford University, and daughters Tania and Leticia Yuen.

In recognition of her activism, Mabel Teng has received numerous honors, including the Pacific American Women Bay Area Coalition's 1985 Woman Warrior Award for Outstanding Contributions in Politics and Community Advocacy, the Outstanding Asian Women Award from the Asian Women's Resource Center in 1992, and the Political Woman of the Year Award in 1996, given by the San Francisco chapter of the National Organization for Women.

### Sources

Epstein, Edward. "Teng Will Lead S.F. Finance Panel." *San Francisco Chronicle.* 26 January 1998, p. A14.
"Mabel Teng." *Who's Who in American Politics.* Reed Elsevier, Inc., October 1997.

# Kip Tokuda

Kip Tokuda. (Courtesy of Kip Tokuda)

**Born:** 8 October 1946, Seattle, Washington.

**Education:** B.A., University of Washington, 1969; M.S.W., University of Washington 1973.

**Positions Held:** Member, Washington State House of Representatives, 1995–present.

**Awards, Honors:** Samuel E. Kelley Civil Rights Award, Children's Alliance Children's Advocate of the Year Award, Governor's Child Abuse and Neglect Annual Award.

**Summary:** Kip Tokuda is one of only two Asian Pacific Americans currently serving in the Washington state legislature.

### Early Years and Education

Kip Tokuda was born on 8 October 1946 to George and Tama Tokuda in Seattle, Washington. He attended the University of Washington, where he earned his B.A. in 1969 and M.S.W. in 1973.

## Career Highlights

Before venturing into electoral politics, Tokuda served as the program director of McGraw Center, a residential treatment facility for psychiatrically impaired adolescents. He also worked as the governor-appointed executive director of the Washington Council for Prevention of Child Abuse and Neglect. He also accepted a consultant position for the city of Seattle on children's issues, which he continues to hold.

A Democrat, Kip Tokuda waged a hugely successful campaign for the 37th District's seat in the Washington State legislature in 1995, defeating his contender Republican Daniel Ellis with 85 percent of the popular vote. His platform supported state healthcare reform, increased violence protection efforts, and bilingual education. He noted, however, that his goals would be extremely challenging given the GOP majority in the House. "I think I'm going to have to be less ambitious with what I wanted to accomplish." said Tokuda following the election. "I've always been an advocate for kids, but at a time when there will be limited resources . . . and a philosophical shift, things like funding for violence prevention programs will be a tougher sell. That doesn't mean I'm going to stop being an advocate. I'll continue to push for prevention programs and job training" (Del Rosario 1994, 1).

As a three-term state representative, the liberal Tokuda co-chaired the House Children and Family Services Committee and has been a member of the Appropriations Committee, Transportation Committee, and Corrections Committee. He has sponsored a number of bills, including the Homeless Children's Lawsuit Bill, the Racial Disproportionality Bill, the Special Needs Adoption Bill, and the Early Childhood Education Bill. He was also lead supporter of the Alternative to I-200 Bill (an anti–affirmative action measure) which did not pass, but gave impetus to the NO I-200 movement.

Tokuda has received several honors for his accomplishments, including the Samuel E. Kelly Civil Rights Award, the Children's Alliance Children's Advocate of the Year Award, and the Governor's Child Abuse and Neglect Annual Award.

As one of only two Asian Pacific Americans in the state legislature, Tokuda also emphasized the importance of community participation in politics and government. "It's going to be much more important for communities to get involved with the process," he stated. "They're going to have to put pressure on all levels of legislature" (Del Rosario 1994, 1).

## Sources

Del Rosario, Carina A. "Representatives Veloria, Tokuda Set for Challenging Legislature." *International Examiner*. 6 December 1994, p. 1.

Kuo, Fidelius. "Then There Were Two . . . Velma Veloria and Kip Tokuda, Washington's Only Asian State Representatives." *Northwest Asian Weekly*. 20 January 1995, p. 4.

# U

## Robert Underwood

**Born:** 13 July 1948, Tamuning, Guam.

**Education:** B.A., California State University, Los Angeles, 1969; M.A., California State University, 1971; Ed.D., University of Southern California, 1988.

**Positions Held:** Delegate, Territory of Guam, U.S. House of Representatives, 1993-present.

**Awards, Honors:** Citizen of the Year, National Association for Bilingual Education, 1996; Alumni of the Year, School of Natural and Social Sciences, California State University, Los Angeles, 2000.

**Summary:** Robert Underwood is the sole official of Guamanian ancestry currently serving in the U.S. House of Representatives.

### Early Years and Education

Robert Anacletus Underwood was born on 13 July 1948 in Tamuning, Guam. He spent his childhood on the island in the town of Sinajana and then attended John F. Kennedy High School in Tumon. After graduating in 1965, he journeyed to the American Mainland to pursue a bachelor's degree in history, which he earned in 1969 from California State University, Los Angeles, followed by a master's degree, also in history, from the same institution, in 1971. While in Southern California, Underwood also worked as a loader and sorter for the United Parcel Service for six years.

### Career Highlights

Fresh out of his master's degree program, Underwood returned home to begin his distinguished career in education. Like his parents, Esther Taitano and John Underwood, both schoolteachers, Robert Underwood headed for the classroom, accepting a position at Guam's oldest public secondary school, George Washington, in 1972. After two years of teaching, Underwood was promoted to the position of George Washington's assistant principal for business and student personnel. He then transferred to Inarajan Junior High School in 1976, where he served briefly as the acting principal.

From Inarajan, Underwood made the transition to higher education. Applying his experience as a curriculum writer for the Guam Bilingual Education project from 1973 to 1976, he joined the University of Guam faculty as an instructor in its Bilingual-Bicultural Training Program in 1976, eventually becoming its director. In 1981, Underwood was named an assistant professor at the University of Guam. Two years later, he took the helm of the University's Bilingual Education Assistance for Micronesia Project. His contributions to the field were later recognized when he was honored as "Citizen of the Year" by the National Association of Bilingual Education in 1996.

Underwood's leadership qualifications, including his diverse experience, a certificate in Education Administration from the University of Guam in 1976, and an Ed.D. from the University of Southern California in 1988, next led him to the deanship of the University of Guam's College of Education in 1988. Finally, in 1990, he assumed the school's academic vice presidency. After two years as one of the University of Guam's top administrators, Underwood looked to public office. Resigning from his post, he ran successfully for the territory's Congressional seat in 1992, becoming the third-ever delegate from Guam. Since then, he has won every consecutive election. As Guam's lone representative on Capitol Hill, Underwood has voiced the concerns of the island's indigenous people, the Chamorros, the ethnic group to which he belongs. His interest in Chamorro political issues, language, and culture is deep-rooted. He served on the Territorial Board of Education in 1978 and was named by the U.S. Secretary of Health, Education, and Welfare to the National Advisory Council on Bilingual Education the following year. In addition, he was a 12-year chair of the Chamorro Language Commission until 1991, and a 13-year member of the Guam Historic Preservation Review Board. A staunch supporter of self-determination, Underwood was a founder of PARA'-PADA, a collective of language rights and political activists established in 1975 to counter the passage of a Guam Constitution. He also joined the Guam Commission on Self-Determination's Task Force on Free Association/Independence in 1981 to help investigate the positive and negative repercussions of the two political routes proposed for the territory. Additionally, Underwood was a founder of the Organization of People for Indigenous Rights (OPI-R), a group dedicated to political self-determination for the Chamarros. The island's population voted to back the Guam Commonwealth Act in a 1982 plebiscite, which would allow for internal self-government, and after the Act's Congressional debut in 1987, one of Underwood's initial tasks in the House of Representatives was to reintroduce the legislation to his colleagues. The passage of the Commonwealth Act would be an important victory for Guam's populace, who are barred by law from participating in presidential elections; furthermore, their Congressional delegate cannot vote in House proceedings. Underwood is keenly aware of Guam's predicament. When *A. Magazine* in 1996 posed to the congressman the hypothetical question, "If you were President, what would be first on your executive agenda?" he replied, "My first decision would be to establish a commission to study political status change for the small territories. The small territories are caught in political limbo, and they're never going to get out of it until we get some real high-level national and presidential attention to this issue. How do we implement American ideals in areas that are not states? This continues to be a sore spot for the people of Guam, and a sore spot for the people in the territories in general."

The representative has labored diligently in the House to call attention to Guam's issues, which he believes are often overlooked by those who perceive his home as a tropical paradise. "We have real problems here, too—violence, the economy, and unemployment," he stated. A member of both the Committee on Armed Forces and the Committee on Resources, he has worked to push the passage of Guam-friendly amendments to the Telecommunications Act of 1990, the Magnuson Fisheries Conservation and Management Act, the Defense Department Reauthorization Acts of 1993–1997, and the Omnibus Appropriations Act of 1996. He also facilitated the legislative approval of the return of 3,200 acres of excess federal land to his territory's people and the inclusion of the Chamorro experience in the exhibits of Guam's War in the Pacific National Historic Park. Underwood is also a member of several Caucuses, including the Congressional Asian Pacific American, Hispanic, and Human Rights interest groups. True to his background in education, Underwood also continues to share the history of Guam to advance its self-sufficiency and dignity with the American public.

Aside from his legislative commitments, Underwood spends time with his wife, Lorraine Aguilar, and his five children, Sophia Rosario, Roberto Anacletus, Ricardo Hurao, Ramon John Joseph, and Raphael Vicente. He also often participates in spectator sports and Guamanian community events throughout the country.

### Sources

"The Magnificent 7." *A. Magazine*. 30 November 1996. p. 28.

Official Web Site of Congressional Delegate Robert A. Underwood: www.house.gov/underwood [Accessed 17 October 2001].

"Robert Anacletus Underwood." *The Complete Marquis Who's Who Biographies*. Reed Elsevier, Inc. Last updated 11 March 1997.

# Chanrithy Uong

**Born:** November 1959, Cambodia.

**Education:** B.S., Boston University, 1988; M.Ed., University of Massachusetts–Amherst, 1989.

**Positions Held:** Member, City Council, Lowell, Massachusetts, 1999–present.

**Summary:** Chanrithy "Rithy" Uong is the first Cambodian American elected to city council in Lowell, Massachusetts.

### Early Years and Education

Chanrithy Uong was born in November 1959 in Cambodia and raised in Phnom Penh,

Guidance Counselor Chanrithy Uong, center, is surrounded by some Cambodian students at Lowell High School in Lowell Massachusetts, March 21, 2001. (Elise Amendola, AP/Wide World Photos)

the nation's capital. During the reign of the Khmer Rouge, he labored on a farm in Cambodia's countryside and endured countless other hardships. "My brother was killed [by the Khmer Rouge] because he liked to sing French and English songs," recalled Uong. "The communists loved him, but couldn't help him, because he sang foreign songs"—a forbidden action (Radin 1993, 1). His brother-in-law was also executed for having served in the South Vietnamese outpost of Cambodian embassy.

Following the exodus of the Vietnamese from the country in 1979, Uong's father bicycled around Cambodia—"riding on the rims because there was no rubber"—in order to gather up the family in preparation for fleeing their homeland. Altogether, 20 members of Uong's extended household escaped to refugee camps on the Thai border en route to the United States in 1980 (Radin 1993, 1).

Uong's port of entry was the Dallas–Fort Worth airport, a moment he described as "amazing, unbelievable, very hard to describe" (Radin 1993, 1). In Fort Worth, he found a job assembling antenna cables for Radio Shack for $3.25 an hour. Within months, he was able to produce them so rapidly that he tripled his output as well as his wages, which he set aside in a college fund.

Meanwhile, Uong met his future wife, Diane Leary, a social worker from Massachusetts participating in Jesuit volunteer work. "I told her I really wanted to study," he said. "She was newly graduated from Harvard; she had long hair and looked like a bank robber" (Radin 1993, 1). Recalled Leary, "It was more or less love at first sight. I called my parents . . . and told them I'd fallen in love with a guy who doesn't speak English, who has long hair, who didn't go to school and who is a refugee." Added Uong, "They were shocked. But they gave me a chance" (Cox 1999, 53).

Uong told Leary of his desire to obtain an education, so she first directed him to an area junior college, ultimately a discouraging experience for the young man newly introduced to the English language and American culture. Undaunted, she located sponsors for him—Leonard and Rosemary Peterson of Melrose, Massachusetts—and soon thereafter Uong relocated to New England.

At Boston University, Uong enrolled in an intensive English program followed by coursework leading to an electrical engineering degree in 1988. Science, however, did not seem to be his career of choice, so he accepted a job as a Southeast Asian liaison for the city of Chelsea. He also returned to school at the University of Massachusetts–Amherst, where he earned his masters in education the following year. To fulfill his field requirement, he was placed in Lowell first as teacher and next as a guidance counselor in the public school system. He and Leary, now married, chose Lowell for their new home. There, Uong quickly became involved with the city's sizeable Cambodian community.

## Career Highlights

In an ironic twist, the University of Massachusetts–Amherst's international education center received U.S. Agency for International Development monies earmarked for work in Cambodia. Program officials recruited Uong, and in 1992 he found himself returning with his wife and son, Ravy, to his native country as part of a 70,000-member contingent to assist with free elections and the drafting of a constitution. "I wanted my son to understand where his father came from," said Uong. "I felt it was important. I also wanted to help rebuild Cambodia" (Cox 1999, 53).

Uong, who ran a polling place in the countryside, reflected at the time, "I feel so bad to see the beggars, the street people, the old people sleeping on the ground. Fourteen and fifteen year olds selling themselves on the street, so many bars, so many obscene places. I am very happy to be here doing something" (Radin 1993, 1). Indeed, the project proved successful, with Cambodians turning out in droves to cast their ballots. "The lines stretched down the streets," he marveled. "It was amazing" (Cox 1999, 53).

After four years in Cambodia, the Uongs made their way back to Lowell. Chanrithy Uong not only resumed his position counseling Khmer youth at Lowell High School, but also declared his intention to bid for a seat on the city council. "I'm running, not to win or lose, but to get voices heard in Lowell that have not been heard before," he explained (Cox 1999, 53). Previously, only one other Cambodian, Sambath Chey Fennell, had attempted to win an elective office in Lowell. Both of Fennell's campaigns for school committee in 1995 and 1997, however, ended in defeat.

In a striking parallel to his U.N. assignment on the outskirts of Phnom Penh, one of Uong's main challenges was to encourage members of Lowell's extensive Southeast Asian community to vote. Noting that it was "very, very sad" that only 35 of them had participated in the preceding municipal contest, Uong devoted considerable time to knocking on the doors of the city's Khmer and Laotian residents (Cox 1999, 53). "They don't really understand [the process] and they don't really care that much," he stated. "They think politicians are just politicians. You have to really explain to them they need somebody to listen to them on a city level to make sure their rights and interests are heard." Furthermore, he emphasized, "It's a privilege to have the opportunity to cast the vote" (Cox 1999, 53).

Uong's efforts paid off, and in November 1999, he became the first Cambodian American elected to a city council seat not only in Lowell but in all of New England. His victory was due in large part to his effective coalition building. Among Uong's supporters were not only his co-ethnics but also the Rainbow Coalition, Lowell's Latinos, and affluent liberals including the wife of the late U.S. Senator Paul Tsongas. Uong's students from Lowell High School also campaigned vigorously for their guidance counselor.

Uong's surprising triumph at the polls took over 1,000 votes away from a 30-year veteran of the council. "It was the mainstream voter who voted for Rithy," remarked Samkhann Khoeun, executive director of Lowell's Cambodian Mutual Assistance Association, over which Uong has presided. "That means Lowell is willing to accept a new face." Ratha Yem, executive director of the Cambodian American League, also commented on the significance of Uong's win. "Many have been looking from the outside in, always thinking, 'this is not my city, and we don't belong here.' With the election of Rithy, it changed that" (Lazar 1999, 22).

## Sources

Cox, Christopher. "A Running Start—Cambodian Council Candidate Aims to Change Lowell's Political Landscape." *The Boston Herald*. 13 May 1999, p. O53.

Lazar, Kay. "Lowell Elects N.E.'s 1st Cambodian Councilor." *The Boston Herald*. 7 November 1999, p. O22.

Radin, Charles A. "From Lowell Back to Cambodia, With Hope." *The Boston Globe*. 28 May 1993, p. 1.

# V

## David M. Valderrama

**Born:** 1933, Manila, Philippines.

**Education:** B.Law, Far Eastern University, Manila, Philippines; M.L.L., George Washington University.

**Positions Held:** Probate Judge, Orphans' Court, 1985–1990; Delegate, Legislative District 26, Maryland General Assembly, 1990–present.

**Awards, Honors:** Most Outstanding Filipino Award, Honored American Award, U.S. Delegate to Philippine Centennial Celebration, 1998.

**Summary:** David M. Valderrama, delegate to the Maryland General Assembly, is the first and only probate judge of Filipino ancestry in the United States.

### Early Years

David Valderrama was born in Manila, Philippines, in 1933. As a child, Valderrama displayed unusual gifts in the performing arts, beginning to tap-dance when he was five years old. Following in the footsteps of his older brother, Nick, he took up the violin at the age of seven. Valderrama's talented musicianship led to a spot in a renowned Philippine symphony orchestra at the age of 13. Years later, he joked that he had since faded into a "[musical] has-been" (Lim 1994, 1).

David Valderrama's youth was also marred by extreme tragedy. During World War II, his father, a lawyer, declined a position with the Japanese government that occupied the archipelago. Consequently, Japanese forces cut off the elder Valderrama's hands and legs before murdering him. Reflecting on this violent incident, Valderrama stated, "The lesson I learned from my father's execution was that you stick to your beliefs no matter what" (Tilak 1995, 394).

The young Valderrama continued to be impacted by international politics throughout his 27 years in the Philippines. As a student and fledgling lawyer and judge, he championed the anti-Marcos, "Free Philippine Movement," despite the fact that his brother, Nick, worked for the Philippine establishment. Valderrama, who described the situation as "quite difficult," also fought against apartheid in South Africa and headed the country's Southeast Asian Refugee Task Force (Tilak 1995, 394).

## Education

After immigrating to the United States in 1961, Valderrama continued his legal education. Having earned a bachelor of law degree from Manila's Far Eastern University, he studied for a masters in comparative law from George Washington University in Washington, D.C. Through the years, he authored a number of related works, including *Law and Legal Literature of Peru*, and *Law and Legal Literature of Mexico*, for which he was co-author.

## Career Highlights

During the 1980s, Valderrama resumed his involvement with politics and government with his election into Maryland's Prince George County's Democratic Central Committee, becoming the first Filipino-American elected to office in that district. In 1982, his peers in the organization voted him to the vice-chairmanship, where he was responsible for overseeing the campaigns of Maryland's Democrats vying for seats in the national Congress. As a pioneer Asian Pacific American official, he took his actions very seriously. "The door to equality in this community is politics," he stated in 1988. "We treated it [the DCC race] as if it were the presidency. It was a symbolic act. It proved that we could really work hard" (Hill 1988, M1).

In December 1985, Maryland Governor Harry Hughes appointed Valderrama to fill a vacancy as Judge of the Orphans' Court, becoming the nation's first probate judge of Filipino ancestry. He then ran for, and won, the same position in the next year's election against eleven other opponents. While in office, he represented Maryland at the National College of Probate Judges and served as the Orphans' Court liaison judge from Prince George's County to the Maryland General Assembly.

While not a small accomplishment, Valderrama still felt that his level of social influence as a probate judge was restricted. "Being a judge is nice, [but] what you are doing in that position is limited to interpreting the law. ... The impact for change is greater when you are in the legislature" (Tilak 1995, 393). Thus, on 5 July 1990, he submitted his resignation to the Orphans' Court in order to devote his efforts to campaigning for the Maryland General Assembly.

As a minority candidate, he faced a tough challenge in Maryland's District 26. In 1990, Asian Pacific Americans—half of whom were Filipino American—comprised just 2 percent of the area's registered voters. Still, he waged a successful battle, and in November, he became the first Filipino-American man, and the highest-ranking Filipino-American elected official at the time to be voted into the state legislature.

During his first term, Valderrama often voiced the concerns of Asian Pacific Americans to his colleagues. He attempted to establish an anti-Asian violence task force in response to a series of robberies against Asian-owned and operated businesses in the Washington, D.C. vicinity. Conservative opposition, however, killed his proposal. "There's the belief that Asian Americans don't need any help, because we're the 'model minority,' that we have the money and education, but we need the help," he explained (Lim 1994, 1).

Valderrama also spearheaded efforts to block a number of "English-only" bills in the State Assembly. One of the bills eventually passed, but Valderrama and his supporters effectively persuaded Maryland Governor Donald Schaffer through petitions and a letter-writing campaign to veto the measure. "The Founding Fathers never found any need to make English official, and proponents always fight for it as some unifying force," Valderrama stated (Lim 1994, 1). He argued, however, that designating English as the state's official tongue would alienate and discriminate against non-Anglophone immigrants.

Valderrama's duties include the Constitutional and Administrative Law, Environmental Matters, and Law Enforcement Committees. During Bill Clinton's 1992 presidential campaign, he was a National Surrogate Speaker. The following year, David Valderrama served as the Maryland General Assembly's delegate to the board of directors of the Council of Governments in Washington, D.C.

In 1994 Valderrama won reelection on a platform he dubbed "the DMV equation of the three E's"—enforcement of crime control, excellence in education, and economic revitalization. He credited his Filipino-American and Asian Pacific American constituents for a significant part of his political successes. "Back in 1982, there were only 40 Filipinos registered in my district," he said. "It's a lot more now. The community is certainly vibrant to me" (Lim 1994, 1). Their support held strong through the years, and in 1998, he was reelected to a third term by a landslide.

Valderrama has returned much of his time and energy back to the community, participating in a number of APA organizations. In addition, he has served on the Board of Directors of the Southern Christian Leadership Conference, Prince George's Chapter, and has been a member of the National Association for the Advancement of Colored People, Common Cause, and MD Network Against Domestic Violence. In recognition for his work, he has been named Most Outstanding Filipino and an Honored American. In June 1998, Valderrama was able to bridge relations between his two home countries as a delegate representing President Clinton at the Philippine Centennial Celebration.

Outside of his political work and civic duties, Valderrama keeps busy with his family. He married Nellie, his high school sweetheart from the Philippines, after a chance meeting at her sister's wedding in Canada. The Valderramas have two daughters, Kriselda, born in 1971, and Vida, born in 1973.

Whatever his future endeavors, Valderrama will continue to keep the interests of Asian Pacific Americans at heart. "Many say we're just a minuscule portion of the political machine, but I think we could spell the difference between victory and defeat," he declared (Lim 1994, 1).

### Sources

Andrei, Mercedes Tira. "2 Filipinos Win Maryland Primaries." *Filipina Reporter.* 22 September 1994, 1.

Lim, Gerard. "David Valderrama Bids for Reelection to Maryland's State Legislature." *Asian Week.* 10 June 1994.

Tilak, Visi R. "David Valderrama." In *Notable Asian Americans,* ed. Helen Zia and Susan B. Gall. Detroit, MI: Gale Research, Inc., 1995, pp. 391–394.

## Velma Rosette Veloria

Velma R. Veloria. (Courtesy of Washington State House of Representatives)

**Born:** 22 October 1950, Philippines.

**Education:** B.S., San Francisco State College, 1976.

**Positions Held:** Representative, Washington State Legislature, 1992–present.

**Awards, Honors:** 1994 Leadership Award from the Washington Association of Bilingual Educators, 1996 Pamana Ng Pilipino Award and a citation from Philippines president Fidel V. Ramos, 1996 Pride of the Asian American Community award, 1997 Unsung Heroes Award from the Coalition of Black Trade Unionists, 2000 Paul Robeson Award from Mothers for Police Accountability.

**Summary:** Washington State Representative Velma R. Veloria is the first Filipino-American and first Asian Pacific American woman to be elected to the Washington State legislature.

## Early Years

Velma Rosette Veloria, born 22 October 1950 in the Philippines, first set foot on American soil in 1961 at the age of 11. Her father, Apelino, a veteran of the U.S. Navy, decided to relocate his family to San Francisco's Mission District in search of a better life. However, within a year after their arrival, Veloria's mother succumbed to cancer. As the eldest of four children, Veloria assumed responsibility for the household duties of cooking, cleaning, and child care while her father worked for Happy Boy, a local drive-in restaurant, as a short order cook. Years later, in reflecting on the hardships of her youth, she remarked, "I guess we really were poor. I never really thought about it growing up" (Wilson 1992, F1).

## Education

While a student at San Francisco State College in the early 1970s, Veloria earned her tuition money at an insurance company where she processed medical claims alongside dozens of co-ethnic employees. Because Veloria and her Filipino co-workers were often bypassed for promotions, the company's rank-and-file formed a union to combat the discrimination.

Veloria exercised her activist muscles on campus as well, participating in anti–Vietnam War demonstrations. Her involvement led to a broader understanding of U.S. foreign policy, which she linked to her newly-acquired knowledge of the history of Filipinos in America. "When you're an immigrant into this country, there's a certain situation that happens where you want to be white," she explained. "When you're taught U.S. history, you're not taught about the contributions of people of color.... You begin to dislike being Filipino." With her Asian American Studies classes, she recalled, "I was able to take more pride in my cultural heritage" (Wilson 1992, F1). Upon graduating from San Francisco State in 1976 with a Bachelor of Science degree in Medical Technology, Veloria moved across the country with her husband. In New York, she continued to advocate grassroots concerns by joining an organization that opposed what its members considered to be unfair requirements for foreign medical technicians, such as threats of deportation if citizenship exams were not successfully passed within two years of arrival.

After nearly a decade on the East Coast, Veloria, now divorced, ventured to Seattle in 1984 to join a cannery-workers support campaign in the wake of the murders of labor leaders Gene Viernes and Silme Domingo. Later, she would also work as the staff organizer for the 1199 Northwest National Union of Hospital and Health Care Employees (1989–1990) and the Service Employees International Union (1995–present).

In addition to union organizing, she spearheaded an area movement against Philippine president Ferdinand Marcos, a continuation of her activism in San Francisco and New York. In 1988, Veloria represented the Rainbow Coalition at the Democratic National Convention in San Francisco. In California, Veloria's life took its first turn toward electoral politics upon meeting Dolores Sibonga, a Filipina and member of Seattle's city council. As a result, Veloria agreed to work as field coordinator for Sibonga's mayoral campaign. After Sibonga was defeated, she accepted a spot on Mayor Norm Rice's transition team, followed by a position as administrative assistant to Washington State representative Art Wang from 1990 to 1991. At the time, Veloria did not entertain thoughts of running for office herself. She reconsidered, however, after a number of Asian Pacific American legislators urged her to consider representing Seattle's 11th District, a solid, working-class area covering sections of Seattle, Renton, Tukwila, and SeaTac, with a 19 percent APA population. "They said, 'Well, hey Velma, maybe you should run.' I said, 'Oh yeah, sure, give me a break you guys.' It was the furthest thing from my mind," she recalled. "As days went by, it just started to fall into place" (Wilson 1992, F1). Veloria successfully bid for the seat in the fall of 1992, garnering 54 percent of the primary votes and 71 percent in the general election. With her victory, Veloria became the first Filipino-American as well as the first Asian Pacific American woman in the Washington State legislature.

As a Washington state representative, Velma Rosette Veloria has espoused an "open-door policy" for her constituents, advocating strong linkages between the government body and local communities; during her first term, for example, she passed more legislation than any other freshman member of the house. Her interests span the gamut of living wage jobs, the education system, and tax assistance for small businesses. Veloria's House committee assignments have included co-chair of Economic Development, Housing, and Trade, Finance, and Rules, Education, Trade and Economic Development, State Government, Health Care, Labor and Commerce, and Law and Justice.

The environment is a particularly significant issue to Veloria. District 11, with over 22 toxic waste and three superfund sites, is the most polluted area in Washington State. Veloria has worked to raise consciousness by sitting on the U.S. Environmental Protection Agency's (EPA) National Environmental Justice Advisory Council (NEJAC). As a spokesperson for environmental matters, Veloria aims to connect innovative businesses with countries interested in utilizing unique and safe methods for redevelopment. From 1994 to 1996, she also co-chaired the Jobs Creation Sub Committee of the Duwamish Coalition.

Velma Rosette Veloria has also adopted the expansion of trade relations between Washington State and the Pacific Rim countries of the Philippines, Thailand, Indonesia, Cambodia, and Vietnam as a priority. Beginning in 1993, she organized and headed delegations—which, among others, included Washington Governor Mike Lowry in 1994 and 1995—to these in order to develop direct business links, promote and market various Washington-manufactured products at a mini–trade exhibition, foster cultural and government ties, and support sister-city relationships. The 1995 mission was particularly significant, marking the first U.S. trade envoy to visit Vietnam since the "normalization" of relations between the two nations. As a result of these efforts, a combined total of over $2 million in new revenue flowed to small-, women-, and minority-owned businesses in the Pacific Northwest.

As a native of the Philippines, Veloria paid special attention to links between the archipelago and her adopted home state. When the Republic of the Philippines moved to close its consulate office in Seattle in 1993, she expressed concern to President Fidel V. Ramos for the 70,000 Filipino-Americans living in the region. Due in large part to Veloria's actions, President Ramos agreed to open the Philippine Trade Office in Seattle the following year. In addition to these projects, Veloria pushed for the creation of a sister state arrangement between Washington and Pangasinan, Philippines. In July 1996, over 20 visitors from Pangasinan, including the territory's Governor Oscar Orbos, toured Washington, meeting local dignitaries and businesspersons. During the trip, Governors Lowry and Orbos signed a memorandum of understanding to encourage trade, tourism, and cultural and educational exchange for the broader goals of mutual prosperity, friendship, and understanding between their two constituencies.

After visiting her birthplace for the first time in 12 years in 1992—an "emotional time," since she "felt really out of place there"—Veloria concluded, "It was a breaking point.... It pointed out to me that my home is the U.S." (Wilson 1992, F1). Yet her civic involvement underscores her concern for the Philippines. Veloria has been an active member in Washington Filipino-American and Asian Pacific American organizations and projects. Among her various commitments have been "Alaskeros," an oral history and photo exhibit of the Filipino men who developed the salmon canning industry in Alaska in the 1920s, research for "Shared Dreams: A Pictorial History Exhibit of Asian Pacific American Experience in Washington State," member of the Filipino American Political Action Group of Washington, board member of Seattle's Wing Luke Asian Museum, chair of Asian Elected Officials of Washington, and member of the Asian Pacific Islander Women's Political Caucus. In addition, Veloria has served the greater community as a Washington state advisory committee member to the U.S. Civil Rights Commission, a delegate to the Democratic National Convention, member of the Washington Economic Development Finance Authority (WEDFA), and member of the Community Advisory Board of the University of Washington's Women's Center.

Veloria has received a number of honors for her achievements, including the 1994 Leadership Award from the Washington Association of Bilingual Educators, the 1996 Pamana Ng Pilipino Award and a citation from Philippines president Fidel V. Ramos, 1996 Pride of the Asian American Community award, the 1997 Unsung Heroes Award from the Coalition of Black Trade Unionists, and the 2000 Paul Robeson Award from Mothers for Police Accountability.

### Sources

Biographical materials provided by Velma Veloria.
Wilson, Geordie. "'What You See is What You Get'—Velma Veloria Will be a Working-class Rarity in Legislature." *The Seattle Times*. 31 December 1992, p. F1.

## Philip Villamin Vera Cruz

**Born:** 25 December 1904, Saoang, Philippines.

**Died:** 10 June 1994, Bakersfield, California.

**Education:** Lewis and Clark High School, Spokane, Washington, ca. 1930.

**Positions Held:** Vice President, United Farm Workers, 1960s–1977.

**Awards, Honors:** 1987 Ninoy M. Aquino Award for Lifelong Service to the Filipino Community in the United States, Philippine Government; 1992 Asian Pacific American Labor Alliance Award.

**Summary:** Philip Vera Cruz, a long-time activist, served as the highest-ranking Asian Pacific American official during the United Farm Workers movement.

### Early Years

Philip Villamin Vera Cruz was born on 25 December 1904 in the barrio of Saoang, located in the Ilocos Sur province of Luzon Island in the Philippines. He described his parents, Andriano Sanchez Vera Cruz and Maria Villamin Vera Cruz, as "simple folks." Vera Cruz spent his childhood in Saoang, a small farming and fishing community and other rural towns on the archipelago before immigrating to the United States in 1926.

As part of the predominantly-male first wave manong generation, Vera Cruz's early experiences in America were similar to those of other Filipino immigrants. Inspired in particular by one of his teachers in the Philippines who had told him that "anyone who was willing to work hard could make it in America," he moved to the United States in search of educational opportunities within the public school system. He arrived in the United States planning to stay only long enough to earn a college degree and save money before returning home to support his family. Vera Cruz soon learned, however, "how difficult reality was for us Filipinos living here from the stories we heard back home," finding it hard to maintain even a subsistence-level standard of living through the limited range of menial jobs available to him and other Asians.

## Education

As a migrant worker, Vera Cruz traveled to factories, restaurants, farms, canneries, and private homes in such diverse places as Chicago, Seattle, Minnesota, and North Dakota to earn his wages. He managed to attend classes off and on at different schools, finally graduating from Lewis and Clark High School in Spokane around 1930.

Philip Vera Cruz enrolled in Spokane's Gonzaga University in the fall of 1931, studying for only one year, because he could not afford the tuition while working to support his family in the Philippines. He also attempted night school at the extension of Washington State College in Pullman but quit after one semester. Always on the move, he went to Chicago to find work. He stayed in the city until 1943, when he relocated to California's San Joaquin Valley to pick grapes and perform other tasks for the area's vineyards and farms. Except for a few short, sporadic periods, he remained there in the town of Delano for the rest of his life.

## Career Highlights

Vera Cruz found it difficult to adjust to agriculture's intensive physical labor. "My backache from working in the fields certainly proved wrong a popular saying among racist growers that the Filipinos made good farm workers because they were short and built close to the ground, making it easier for them to bend over," he recounted in his 1992 autobiography, *Philip Vera Cruz: A Personal History of the Filipino Immigrants and the Farmworkers Movement*. He did not readily accept the low wages and poor camp conditions, and in 1948, he participated in the Filipino laborer strike against Stockton's asparagus farmers, and in the late 1950s, he was a member of the National Labor Union (NFLU) of the AFL-CIO, for which he briefly served as the president of the local Stockton chapter.

In the mid-1960s, at the urging of a neighbor, Vera Cruz joined the Agricultural Workers' Organizing Committee (AWOC), marking a turning point in his life. "The $2 I paid for membership was probably the most important and expensive $2 I ever spent in my life. I didn't need anyone to convince me then or now that it was the right decision to make," he recalled.

The all-Filipino membership of AWOC voted to strike against grape growers in the areas surrounding and including Delano on 8 September 1965. The action was partially successful—winning a salary increase, but no contract, for the workers—and ignited the farmworkers' movement of the 1960s. The result was the merging of AWOC with the National Farm Workers' Association (NFWA), forming the United Farm Workers (UFW).

As vice president of UFW, Vera Cruz was one of the few Filipino leaders of the union. In his autobiography, he reflected critically on his experience in the organization, noting "in retrospect, it is true that the Filipino leaders in the UFW have been more showcase than anything else," due largely to the famed union leader, Cesar Chavez and his authoritative control of the UFW agenda. Chavez's power, argued Vera Cruz, "blinded" him at times. However, Vera Cruz was also self-critical, stating, "My biggest shortcoming as a union officer was not fighting like hell for what I knew was right. I took the passive role too often because I had learned from the past struggles in the Filipino community how bad fights at the top can get. I always sacrificed my personal convictions for what I thought or was convinced was the good of the union, and sometimes I think this was a mistake." Despite the growing friction between himself and the other leaders as well as between the Filipino and Mexican members in general, he stayed with the UFW for 12 years "because . . . [for him] the struggle of the workers in this country is the most important struggle."

During his years in the UFW, Philip Vera Cruz oversaw the building of Agbayani village, a retirement community in Delano for aging union members, most of whom were Filipino immigrants. After resigning in 1977, Vera Cruz relocated to Bakersfield, California, in 1979, where he lived until his death on 10 June 1994 from complications following lung surgery. For his lifelong accomplishments, he received the Philippine government's first Ninoy M. Aquino award for lifelong service to the Filipino community in the United States in 1987. He journeyed to his childhood home the following year for the first time since 1926 to receive the prize. Additionally, the Asian Pacific American Labor Alliance honored him at its founding convention in 1992, and the UCLA Asian American Studies Center established an undergraduate scholarship in his name to encourage the study of Asian American labor history.

During his waning years, Vera Cruz recorded his memoirs chronicling his life from the Philippines through his time in the UFW. His story of Filipino-American and labor oral history continues to educate and inspire people. It embodies the communal spirit of Asian American activism. As he stated, "Leadership, I feel, is only incidental to the movement. The movement should be the most important thing. If the leader becomes the most important part of the movement, then you won't have a movement after the leader is gone. The movement must go beyond its leaders. It must be something that is continuous, with goals and ideals that the leadership can then build upon."

## Sources

Henry, Jim, "Phillip [sic] Villamin Vera Cruz." In *Notable Asian Americans*, ed. Helen Zia and Susan B. Gall. Detroit, MI: Gale Research, Inc., 1995, p. 396.

Scharlin, Craig and Lilia V. Villanueva. *Philip Vera Cruz: A Personal History of Filipino Immigrants and the Farmworkers Movement*, ed. by Glenn Omatsu and Augusto Espiritu. Los Angeles: UCLA Labor Center, Institute of Industrial Relations, and UCLA Asian American Studies Center. Memorial Edition, 1994.

# W

## John David Waihee III

**Born:** 19 May 1946, Honokaa, Hawaii.

**Education:** B.A., Andrews University, 1968; J.D., University of Hawaii, 1976.

**Positions Held:** Hawaii House of Representatives, 1980–1982; Hawaii State Lieutenant Governor, 1982–1986; Hawaii State Governor, 1986–1994.

**Awards, Honors:** 1987 Ho'olako (Year of the Hawaiian) Man of the Year Award; 1989 Leadership Education for Asian Pacifics Award for outstanding community leadership; 1989 American Planners Association Award for Affordable Housing Programs; 1990 Earth Trust Award for Protection of Marine Environment.

**Summary:** John David Waihee III served as Hawaii's governor from 1986 to 1994. He is the highest ranking public official of Native Hawaiian ancestry at the state-wide level in the United States to date.

### Early Years

John David Waihee III was born on 19 May 1946 in Honokaa, located on Hawaii's Big Island. His mother, Mary Parker Purdy, was descended from one of King Kamehameha I's advisors and a former Massachusetts sailor, and his father, John D. Waihee II, was employed by a telephone company.

### Education

After graduating from the private Hawaiian Mission Academy in Honolulu, the former Eagle Scout attended Michigan's Andrews University as a major in history and business. He earned his bachelor of arts degree in 1968 and later supplemented his studies with postgraduate urban planning courses at Central Michigan University.

Meanwhile, Waihee worked as a community education administrator for the Benton Harbor, Michigan area schools from 1968 to 1971. He returned to his home state to enroll in the University of Hawaii's William S. Richardson School of Law, and was in its first graduating class in 1976.

### Career Highlights

In Hawaii, John David Waihee continued the career in city planning that he had begun on the Mainland, working for the Honolulu Model Cities Program and the city and county of Honolulu's Office of Human Resources. He then joined the firm of Shim, Sigal, Tan, and Naito in 1975 as an associate before establishing his own practice, Waihee, Manuia, Yap, Pablo, and Hoe, in 1979.

Waihee's entrée into politics came in 1972 with his membership in "Coalition 72," a political collective that aimed to present an alternative to the state's Democratic establishment. The coalition's efforts were unsuccessful, but Waihee stayed involved in local issues, serving as a delegate and majority leader in Hawaii's 1978 Constitutional Convention. Other participants at the event glimpsed Waihee's political prowess as he facilitated the integration of different generations and persuasions of state leaders. In the late 1970s, he was involved with the "Palaka Power" movement, which advocated local, grassroots control of government. He followed this showing with a successful bid for a seat in Hawaii's House of Representatives in 1980, where he served on the powerful Policy Committee.

Two years later, Waihee again sought elected office. He narrowly defeated state senator Dennis O'Connor to secure the lieutenant governor's position. The victory was due in large part to his steady pursuit of support from the denizens of Hawaii's less populous islands.

As lieutenant governor, Waihee arbitrated a number of controversial issues. Governor George Ariyoshi named him the head of a task force that grappled with a United Airlines strike, for example. Waihee also mediated a lawsuit concerning Hawaii's prisons, a disagreement over liquor tax revenues, and facilitated the implementation of tort reform regulations.

In 1986, Waihee joined Hawaii's gubernatorial race. He was able to defeat six opponents in the primary, including former U.S. Representatives Cecil Heftel and Patsy Mink, along with former state senator D. G. "Andy" Anderson, a Republican, in the general election with 52 percent of the vote. On the campaign trail, he shrewdly highlighted his problem-solving capabilities, demonstrated by his years as lieutenant governor, and emphasized his distance from "Old School" Democrats, including Governor Ariyoshi. John David Waihee promoted a "New Hawaii" outlook of encouragement and protection. He was convincing enough that even his mother's relatives, loyal Republicans, backed their more liberal cousin.

Once in office, Waihee expressed his populist leanings. As the state's first governor of Native Hawaiian ancestry, Waihee visibly supported the Native Hawaiian sovereignty movement. In a symbolic gesture during the 100th anniversary of the overthrow of the Hawaiian monarchy, he dictated a five-day removal of the American flag from state office buildings. He also publicly noted the impact of the state's Asian Pacific Islanders in Hawaiin politics. "Asian Americans vote in such large numbers that they can not be ignored," he stated in 1992 (Lee 1992, 30). Additionally, Waihee led educational reforms, which he dubbed "our community voyage," to allow local districts to control their schools (Associated Press, 1994).

Waihee devoted his attention to the state's economy from the start. "I have never treated the finances of state solely as a matter of budget. We always looked at the revenues, how we generate the revenues, how we keep the economy running," he said in 1992 (Associated Press, 1994). He pushed for economic diversification, jobs, and tax reductions that ultimately led the state to salvage $700 million in taxpayer monies. Under his leadership, Hawaii's unemployment rates were among the lowest in the country.

After his reelection in 1990, when he secured 60 percent of the general vote to defeat Republican Fred Hemmings, Waihee continued to back educational and economic improvements. He also voiced his concern for health care and the environment, describing the Hawaiian people as inseparable from nature and calling for more alternative energy sources. In his 1994 state of the state address, Waihee proposed a number of projects for the people of Hawaii, including a mass transit system for the capital, Oahu. "The business of government is never finished," stated the outgoing governor, limited to two terms (Associated Press, 1994).

Waihee's political record, however, was marred by a number of unsavory decisions, including a nepotism case and misuse of state funds to purchase expensive equipment, resulting in a drop in his popularity rates. Nevertheless, Waihee has been widely noted for his contributions, garnering such honors as the 1987 Ho'olako (Year of the Hawaiian) Man of the Year Award, the 1989 Leadership Education for Asian Pacifics Award for outstanding community leadership, the 1989 American Planners Association Award for Affordable Housing Programs, and the 1990 Earth Trust Award for Protection of Marine Environment.

Outside of government, Waihee holds memberships in the Hawaii Bar Association, the National Governor's Association, Kalakaua Lions Club, Honolulu Rotary, and Zonta Club International, among others. He is married to Lynne Kobashigawa with whom he has two children, John David and Jennifer.

### Sources

Gupta, Himanee. "John D. Waihee." In *Notable Asian Americans*, ed. Helen Zia and Susan B. Gall. Detroit, MI: Gale Research, Inc., 1995, pp. 397–398.

"John David Waihee." *AP Candidate Bios*. The Associated Press Political Service. 1994.

Lee, Suzanne. "Reporter's Notebook," *Asian Week*. 18 September 1992, p. 30.

Marable, Manning, "Along the Color Line: Self-Determination for American Minorities," *Metro Reporter*. 28 February 1993, p. 3.

"Waihee III, John David." *The Complete Marquis Who's Who Biographies*. Reed Elsevier, Inc., 1995. Last updated 24 July 1995.

## Barry Wong

**Born:** 29 April 1959, Phoenix, Arizona.

**Education:** B.S., Arizona State University, 1981; J.D., University of Arizona, 1984.

**Positions Held:** Member, Arizona State House of Representatives, 1993–2000.

**Summary:** Barry Wong was a member of the Arizona State House of Representatives from 1993 to 2000.

### Early Years and Education

Chinese American Barry Wong was born on 29 April 1959 in Phoenix, Arizona. A lifelong resident of the state, he attended Phoenix's Alhambra High School, graduating in 1977, before matriculating at Arizona State University as an accounting major. At ASU, Wong earned his Bachelor's degree magna cum laude. He then went on to study law at the University of Arizona, becoming a Juris Doctor in 1984.

### Career Highlights

Within his professional career, Wong has filled a number of different roles, including the manager of a small family business, law clerk, tax accountant, corporate executive, and attorney. On the political side, Wong began his foray into government as a legislative aide for Arizona's House of Representatives in 1981 and bill title/law clerkships with the Arizona State Senate from 1985 to 1986.

In October 1993, Wong was appointed to fill a vacancy in the House for District 18. The following year, he ran in the general election and secured his seat for his first full-length term. In 1996, he again bid successfully to represent his district. As a member of the House, Wong was involved with the Economic Development, Judiciary, Program Authorization Review, Ways and Means, and International Trade, Technology, and Tourism Committees. Among his general policy views were controlling the size and growth of government, restricting tax increases and reducing taxes, encouraging economic expansion, assisting small businesses, crime control and punishment, educational improvement, and welfare reform. In 2000, Barry Wong announced he was retiring from state government to return to his Phoenix law practice.

Outside of his legislative duties, Wong maintains an active profile in community organizations. His myriad commitments include board memberships for the Christown YMCA, Salvation Army, Western International University, the World Affairs Council of Arizona, and the Arizona Asian American Bar Association.

## Sources

azleg.state.az.us/members/bwong.htm [Accessed 12 November 1999].

barrywong.com/pebio.htm [Accessed 12 November 1999].

Personal communication to Ellen Wu, 2000.

# Delbert E. Wong

Delbert E. Wong. (Courtesy of Delbert Wong)

**Born:** California.

**Education:** B.S., University of California, Berkeley, 1942; J.D. Stanford University, 1948.

**Positions Held:** Deputy Legislative Counsel, California State Legislature, 1952–1959; Judge, Los Angeles Municipal Court, 1959–1961; Judge, California Superior Court, 1961–1982.

**Awards, Honors:** World War II, Distinguished Flying Cross, Four Air Medals, Distinguished Army Air Corps Unit Citation; 1994 Organization of Chinese Americans Abacus Award; 1998 Asian Pacific American Legal Center of Southern California Legal Impact Award.

**Summary:** Delbert E. Wong is the first Chinese American judge in the continental United States.

## Education

A native Californian, Delbert E. Wong attended the University of California, Berkeley, where he earned his bachelor of science degree in 1942. Following graduation, he enlisted in the Army Air Corps as an aviation cadet before entering the United States Air Force as a B-17 Flying Fortress navigator, where he attained the rank of first lieutenant. The only Asian Pacific American in his unit, Wong completed 30 bombing missions in the European theatre during World War II and was awarded the Distinguished Flying Cross, an Air Medal on four occasions, and the Distinguished Unit Citation. Upon returning to the United States, Wong continued his service by receiving additional training in statistics at the Harvard University Graduate School of Business in order to work as a statistical control officer of the Air Corps Material Command, a position he held until the end of the war.

After the war, Wong decided to pursue a career in law, despite his parents' wishes for their son to run the family grocery store in Bakersfield, California. The job seemed to be more practical for a young Asian Pacific American man of the era. "My parents said that when most Asians had to go to court, they already have two strikes against them, so why should they hire a Chinese lawyer to represent them," explained Wong. "And to think a non-Chinese would hire you was totally foreign" (Cahill 1998, 15). Nevertheless, Wong decided to take the risk, matriculating at the Stanford University Law School. As with his service in the military, Wong found himself to be the only Asian Pacific American in his cohort, a socially isolating situation, especially considering that APAs were banned from joining the school's law fraternities.

## Career Highlights

Still, Wong managed to succeed in his studies, graduating in 1948 and obtaining a position as a deputy legislative counsel serving the State Legislature in Sacramento for a number of years. "I wanted to do something more than just immigration law, and something more than practice in San Francisco's Chinatown," he recalled. "That was the only avenue for Chinese Americans in private practice at the time. None of them worked in law firms, there were just no opportunities" (Cahill 1998, 15). In 1951, he transferred from the state capital to Los Angeles, becoming only the second Chinese American lawyer south of the San Francisco Bay Area. Initially, however, he was refused a position in the Los Angeles office. "My boss said he didn't think he could send me to Los Angeles, because the Legislature would not feel comfortable having only a Chinese to turn to for advice," stated Wong (Cahill 1998, 15). In spite of the opposition, he received a civil service appointment, becoming the first Asian Pacific American in the Southern California office. For seven years, Wong tried cases in each of the 14 southern counties, from Fresno to the Mexican border, arguing a myriad of cases before the Courts of Appeal and the Supreme Court.

Delbert Wong made history as the first Chinese American judge in the continental United States with his appointment to the Municipal Court in 1959 by California Governor Edmund G. "Pat" Brown. Noting his groundbreaking achievement, the *Los Angeles Examiner* opined in 1959, "Our new judge joins a growing company of scientists, physicians and other savants of Oriental stock who are a credit to California. Their recognition also constitutes a tribute to the democratic process we cherish, because it moves to reward personal merit and thus corrects some ancient discriminations as unworthy of an enlightened society." Two years later, Wong was promoted to the Superior Court where he served for over 20 years, including five years in the three-judge Appellate Department. Upon his retirement from the bench in 1982, he was the senior judge on the 206-member court.

After stepping down from the Superior Court, Wong entered the private judging sector, assisting with arbitrations, mediations, and the settlement and trial of cases outside of the traditional court system. He has maintained an active professional life. In 1986, for example, Wong was appointed by the city of Los Angeles to examine allegations of racial discrimination within the Los Angeles Airport Police Bureau. The following year, he was appointed to the chair of the Asian Pacific American Focus Program of the National Conference of Christians and Jews, where he worked to stem the tide of rising anti-Asian violence. In 1989, L.A. Mayor Tom Bradley selected Wong for the seven-member Commission to Draft an Ethics Code for the Los Angeles City Government, which led to the adoption of the first ethics code by the voters of the city of Los Angeles.

One of Wong's most high-profile assignments came in 1994 with his appointment as special master in the O.J. Simpson murder trial. Wong also served as the judge for a two and a half million dollar settlement in 1997 paid by the County of Los Angeles to a plaintiff for injuries sustained during incarceration in a county jail as well as the appraising of property damage and income loss sustained in the devastating Northridge earthquake.

Outside of the courts, Delbert Wong has maintained steady civic commitments. He is involved with the Asian Pacific American Legal Center, for which he serves as a member of the Trustee Council, the Chinatown Service Center, the National Conference of Community and Justice, the Boy Scouts of

America, and the Chinese American Citizens Alliance.

Wong is married to Dolores Wong, a retired psychiatric social worker and presently a full-time community volunteer. The Wongs have four children: Shelley, a professor of linguistics at Ohio State University, Duane, a country western entertainer, music teacher, and music store owner, Kent, an attorney and director of the UCLA Center for Labor Research, and Marshall, a member of the Los Angeles County Human Relations Commission.

## Sources

Biographical material provided by Delbert E. Wong.
Cahill, Stephanie Francis. "A 'Fair Shot.'" *California Law Business*. 23 February 1998, p. 15.
"Our New Judge." *Los Angeles Examiner*. 24 January 1959.

# Martha J. Wong

Martha J. Wong. (Photo by Alvin Gee)

**Born:** 1939, Houston, Texas.

**Education:** B.A., University of Texas, M.Ed., Ed.D., University of Houston.

**Positions Held:** Member, Houston City Council, 1993–1999.

**Awards, Honors:** Houston Federation of Women's Award for Excellence in Education; the Asian Chamber of Commerce's Commitment to the Community Award; Texas Women's Hall of Fame; Distinguished Alumnus of the University of Houston, 1995; Humanitarian of the Year by the National Conference of Christians and Jews, 1997.

**Summary:** Martha J. Wong is the first Asian Pacific American elected to the Houston City Council.

## Early Years

Martha J. Wong was born to immigrant Chinese parents in 1939. A native Houstonian, Wong spent her formative years as a student in the city's Independent School District before enrolling at the University of Texas. A professional educator, Wong returned to the Houston Independent School District (HISD) as a first grade teacher upon graduation. After taking time off to raise her three children, Wong returned to teaching as a special education instructor. Next, upon accepting the head position at Houston's Kolter Elementary School, where she served for six years, Wong became Texas' first Asian Pacific American school principal. From there, Wong continued to further her career by working as associate superintendent for HISD, a professor at Baylor University, and administrator of the Houston Community College System. In addition, she returned to the classroom, not as a teacher, but as a student, in order to earn her masters' and doctorate degrees in educational administration from the University of Houston.

On 4 December 1993, Martha J. Wong again made history, becoming the first Asian Pacific American elected to the Houston City Council by capturing 62 percent of the votes in a run-off election for the District C council position. Two years later, Wong was reelected with 85 percent of the votes, and in 1997, Wong succeeded in securing her third bid, unopposed, for a seat on the Council. As the city's first Asian Pacific American representative, Wong initially shied away from strongly identifying herself along racial lines. "People are making a lot more out of it than I am," she said in 1993. "We have not identified any Asian issues, or black issues, or Hispanic issues.... The people that represent Asians need to bring that up. My first obligation is to the people of District C," of which Asian Pacific Americans made up only 4.5 percent of the electorate at the time. "I don't necessarily want to play that role," she stated. "It may fall upon my shoulders by virtue of my background and my ethnicity, but I [didn't run] to do that" (Dyer 1993, A34).

On the other hand, acknowledged Wong, a number of Houston's Asian Pacific Americans, including Chinese, Korean, and Pakistani-Americans, offered some of her strongest backing during her campaign. "The Asian community is happy that I am running and I have gotten a lot of support," she admitted. "But I think it's perfectly normal for one person not to get 100 percent support. I don't think every black leader has supported every black candidate, or every Hispanic leader has supported every Hispanic candidate" (Dyer 1993, A34). Wong has publicly advocated a number of APA issues during her time as a Houston city council member. These include the right of the Asian community to erect Asian-language street signs in neighborhoods to reflect the diversity of the city's people. "The Asian community now feels a part of this city of Houston," she argued during a heated debate in 1998. "Having the signs there makes them feel more a part" (Coffee 1998, A31). Wong also declared her support for improved health care information and services for the city's Asian Pacific Americans.

Wong's primary concerns have been neighborhood protection, crime prevention, and economic development. During her first term, she was the only freshman appointed by Mayor Lanier to chair two committees, the Competitive Services Committee and the Education Committee. Since then, she has also been a member of the Redevelopment and Revitalization, Business and Tourism, Ethics, Minority/Women Owned Business Enterprise, Aviation, International Trade, and Fiscal Affairs Committees. Additionally, Wong represented the city of Houston on the National League of Cities Nominating Committee and the Women in Municipal Government Board and served as the treasurer of the National League of Cities Asian Pacific American Municipal Officials, and director of the Texas Municipal League–Region 14.

Outside of office, Wong continues to remain active. Her civic duties span a range of interests, including PTA president, Little League Team Mother, the American Red Cross, the Museum of Fine Arts, the University of Houston Vision Commission, the Greater Houston Women's Foundation, the Houston READ Commission, the Neuhaus Education Center, and the Junior League of Houston. Among her APA activities are the Asian American Coalition, the Organization of Chinese Americans, and the Asian American Heritage Association, of which she was a founding member. For her many achievements, Wong has garnered a number of honors, including the Houston Federation of Women's Award for Excellence in Education, the Asian Chamber of Commerce's Commitment to the Community Award, and a place in the Texas Women's Hall of Fame. In April 1995, Wong was named a Distinguished Alumnus by the University of Houston. Two years later, she was named a Humanitarian of the Year by the National Conference of Christians and Jews.

## Sources

Bernstein, Alan and Jim Simmon. "City Council's New Faces; District C; Martha Wong." *The Houston Chronicle*. 6 December 1993, p. A13.

Coffee, Melanie. "Street Signs Bearing Asian Names Win Support of Emotional Official." *The Houston Chronicle*. 30 July 1998, p. A31.

Dyer, R.A. "Wong wins City Council Seat; 'My first obligation is to the people of District C,' she says." *The Houston Chronicle.* 5 December 1993, p. A34.

Johnson, Stephen. "Asian-American Health Issues Take Spotlight; Must Demand Better Care, Study Group Told." *The Houston Chronicle.* 7 January 1998, p. A16.

"Wong, Martha." In *Who's Who Among Asian Americans 1994/95,* ed. Amy L. Unterburger. Detroit: Gale Research Inc., 1994, p. 650.

# Michael Woo

**Born:** 8 October 1956, Los Angeles, California.

**Education:** B.A., University of California, Santa Cruz; M.S., University of California, Berkeley.

**Positions Held:** Member, Los Angeles City Council, 1985–1993; Western States Director for the Corporation for National Service, Local Initiatives Support Corporation (LISC).

**Summary:** Mike Woo is the first Asian Pacific American to sit on the 15-member Los Angeles City Council. He was also the Democratic candidate for Los Angeles mayor in 1993 but lost to Richard Riordan in the general election.

## Early Years

On 8 October 1956, Wilbur and Beth Woo gave birth to their only son, Michael, at White Memorial Hospital in east Los Angeles. Their new baby boy immediately became the focal point of the Woo household, residents of the city's Wellington Square neighborhood. "You know how Asians are about boys," said Beth Woo years later during her son's campaign for mayor of Los Angeles in 1993. "I was very happy" (Fiore and Scott 1993, A1).

The toddler enjoyed his privileges as the "no. 1 son" of the Woo clan, including promises of rides in the family car with his grandfather, having his laundry done by his grandmother, and being served by his four sisters the choicest cuts of meat from the dinner table. The effects of constant pampering were rather positive on Woo. "I think it helped me build my self-confidence, and my self-confidence is one of my assets.... I grew up with the expectation that I would have major responsibilities," he told the *Los Angeles Times* in 1993 (Clifford and Fiore 1993, A1).

Woo began laying the groundwork for these major responsibilities at an early age. He demonstrated an interest in learning, foregoing conventional toys for magazine reading. A bright student, he actively participated in extracurricular affairs at Alhambra High School, located in the San Gabriel Valley city neighboring Monterey Park, where Woo and his family moved when he was the age of 10. Among his list of activities and accomplishments were managing editor of the school paper, Writers' Guild vice president, speaker of the student body legislature, junior statesmen speaker, Alhambra High School's Boy of the Month in January 1969, and state scholarship semifinalist. He also ran—albeit unsuccessfully—for class president during his senior year.

## Education

After graduating from Alhambra High School, Michael Woo entered the University of California at Santa Cruz. "What could be more different from living in Los Angeles than going to a university in the middle of a redwood forest?" he later asked (Fiore and Scott 1993, A1). At UCSC, Woo delved into the political fervor that seized much of his generation. A third generation Chinese American, Woo proposed and taught a student-run course at UCSC entitled "Children of the Megalopolis," a class that addressed immigrant issues, particularly the struggles of sons and daughters of new Americans. As "Citizen Woo," he authored a column in the campus newspaper, in which he discussed social concerns. During his freshman year, he attended an "exhilarating" San Francisco anti-war protest; he filed for the draft (but was not called to serve) as a conscientious objector. Additionally, he worked on then-Representative George Brown's campaign for the U.S. Senate.

"The political struggles of the 60s definitely influenced my values. I wasn't black, but observing the civil rights movement from afar and getting a sense of the injustice that spawned the movement had a long-lasting effect on me," he explained. "It helped me learn the lesson that there are a lot of people on the outside of this society who are not fairly treated" (Fiore and Scott 1993, A1).

Woo followed his bachelor of arts degree from UCSC with a master's degree in urban planning from the University of California, Berkeley. He then spent eight years as a legislative aide for state senator David A. Roberti (D–Van Nuys) in Sacramento, a position that exposed him first-hand to pressing social dilemmas such as inadequate health care due to closures of hospitals and the difficult experiences of the mentally retarded in jails and prisons.

## Career Highlights

Michael Woo ran for the Los Angeles city council in 1981. He lost, but was not discouraged. In 1985, he again faced his opponent, three-time incumbent Peggy Stevenson, and successfully captured 58 percent of the votes to win the District 13 seat, becoming the first Asian Pacific American to sit on the 15-member board.

Following his victory, which he attributed to a "great coalition effort," Woo noted, "I can't promise any special favors to Asians. I'm not trying to make special claims for myself as an Asian," although he aspired to "go on to develop a good record on the city council that would provide an important role model for young people in the Asian community" (Boyarsky 1985, 1).

During his two terms as the Hollywood area's representative, Woo, a self-described "fighter to change the status quo," drew public attention to a number of issues (Clifford and LaGuire 1993, B1). Conscious of his Latino constituency, he pushed, albeit unsuccessfully, for the designation of Los Angeles as a "city of sanctuary" for political refugees from Latin America. He also backed legislation to suspend police detention of illegal immigrants, although he favored the reporting of undocumented criminals to the INS. Additionally, Woo advocated campaign ethics reform and the restructuring of the Los Angeles Police Department—he was the sole council member to call for resignation of former police chief Darryl F. Gates following the Rodney King beating.

Woo's tenure was not untouched by criticism, however. His critics charged that Woo's pro-environment, pro–slow growth campaign platform wavered over the years. For example, although he was the main force behind legislation aimed at limiting hillside construction, he built a substantial addition to his hillside home in the Silver Lake area just four months before the passage of the ordinance. During his run for Los Angeles' mayorship, he faced accusations of accepting questionable donations to his campaign funds, violating aspects of the very same ethics reform measures that he supported on the city council. In response, he returned the contributions and attributed them to "technical errors" by his campaign managers. Regarding his home expansion project, he stated, "It is unreasonable to expect individuals, whether they are elected officials or not, to comply with laws that are not in effect. I didn't do anything to evade the law, to slow down the ordinance in order to avoid coverage by the law" (Clifford and Fiore 1993, A1).

In spite of the criticism, Woo launched a relatively fruitful bid for mayor of Los Angeles in 1993. He emerged from a field of eleven hopefuls to represent the Democrats in the June general election against Republican Richard Riordan. Supported by a broad coalition of people and interests, including Asian Pacific Americans, homosexuals, laborers, liberals, and African Americans, Woo called for improving relations between communities in the wake of the 1992 Los Angeles uprising. "I want to be the mayor who unites the city," he declared. He emphasized that the elected candidate would need to "enable people to be comfortable with" the orientation of Los Angeles towards an "involuntary diversity," yet still characterized by ethnic, race, and class isolation. One of his primary goals was to tear down "invisible walls...closing the gap between haves and have-nots" (Clifford and Fiore 1993, A1).

Michael Woo proposed economic revitalization, particularly of low income areas, using tactics such as loans to small businesses, boosting the numbers of the Los Angeles police force, establishing an office of immigrant affairs, appointing a gay representative to the city's police commission, and balancing the budget.

To the disappointment of many Asian Pacific Americans, the 46 percent of the votes cast in the general election for Woo were not enough to surpass the 54 percent in favor of Riordan. Woo cited Riordan's hefty campaign war chest—including $6 million out of pocket—and the anti-incumbency sentiments among the public as two of the main factors in his defeat.

After his landmark run, Woo delved into education. In the spring of 1994, he taught a course entitled "Asian Americans in politics: from private identity to public responsibility" at Caltech.

He is currently director of the Los Angeles office of the Local Initiatives Support Corporation (LISC), a program that provides technical and low-interest loan support to locally based neighborhood conservation/community development organizations.

### Sources

Boyarsky, Bill. "Measure to Add 1,000 LAPD Officers Loses; Woo Captures Stevenson's City Council Seat; Tuttle Defeats Shapiro in Controller's Race." *Los Angeles Times*. 5 June 1985, p. 1:1.

Clifford, Frank. "Decision '93/A Look at the Elections in Los Angeles County; Los Angeles Mayor; Separated From the Pack by their Public Service, 11 Candidates are Given a Fighting Chance to Win a Runoff Spot; Michael Woo; Ethnic Coalition in Bradley style." *Los Angeles Times*. 11 April 1993, p. T4.

Clifford, Frank and Faye Fiore. "Woo Tries to Reconcile Pressures of Two Cultures; Campaign: Councilman Born into Affluence Speaks of Downtrodden. Critics Say He Tries to Please Everyone." *Los Angeles Times*. 30 March 1993, p. A1.

Clifford, Frank and Lennie La Guire, "Decision '93/ Los Angeles County Elections; Interviews with the Mayoral Candidates; Michael Woo." *Los Angeles Times*. 30 May 1993, p. B1.

Fiore, Faye and Janny Scott. "L.A. Mayoral Race a Clash of Generations, Visions; Politics: Riordan and Woo Were Shaped by Different Eras. Now, Their Divergent Paths Have Crossed." *Los Angeles Times*. 6 June 1993, p. A1.

Mydans, Seth. "Los Angeles Elects a Conservative as Mayor and Turns to a New Era." *Los Angeles Times*. 10 June 1993, p. A1.

"Where We Work: Los Angeles." Local Initiatives Support Corporation. www.liscnet.org [Accessed 6 October 2001].

"Woo will Teach Course at Caltech." *Los Angeles Times*. 15 April 1994, p. B4.

## S.B. (Shien-Biau) Woo

S.B. (Shien-Biau) Woo. (Courtesy of S.B. Woo)

**Born:** 13 August 1937, Shanghai, China.

**Education:** B.S., Georgetown College; Ph.D., Washington University, 1964.

**Positions Held:** Delaware State Lieutenant Governor, 1985–1989.

**Awards, Honors:** Fellow, Harvard University Kennedy School of Government, 1989.

**Summary:** S.B. Woo served as Delaware's first Asian Pacific American elected public official. He was Delaware's lieutenant governor from 1985 to 1989.

### Early Years

A self-described "American by choice," Shien-Biau (S.B.) Woo was born in Shanghai, China, on 13 August 1937 (Associated Press 1992). Like many other families during the Chinese Civil War, 12-year-old Woo fled the political unrest on the Mainland with his parents, Koo-ing, a homemaker, and C.K., a wool merchant, a brother and two sisters to the island of Taiwan in 1949. They then migrated a second time to Hong Kong. After spending the bulk of his teen years in the British colony, Woo immigrated to the United States, where his parents believed educational and occupational opportunities for their young son would be much greater.

### Education

Woo took the first step toward his promising future by attending Georgetown College in Kentucky. After graduating summa cum laude with a bachelor's degree in math and physics, he went on to earn his doctorate in physics from St. Louis's Washington University in 1964, a year after he married his wife Katy K.N. As a new Ph.D., he completed two years of postdoctoral work at the Joint Institute for Laboratory Astrophysics (JILA) in Boulder, Colorado, before accepting a faculty appointment at the University of Delaware in 1966.

As a Delaware professor Woo began to ponder the connection between government, technology, and education. He reasoned that increased involvement of scientists at administrative levels would improve American technology and scientific education. He first practiced this theory through active involvement on the UDE campus as a member of the college steering committee and as the founder of the faculty bargaining unit. Woo also served as the president of the American Association of University Professors' University of Delaware chapter for two years, and was one of the school's trustees from 1976 to 1982. During this time, he faced opposition to his education policies concerning tuition and enrollment, which some viewed as too radical; nevertheless, he made a name for himself.

### Career Highlights

Declared a naturalized citizen in 1972, S.B. Woo was both willing and eligible to expand his influence to the state level. In 1984, Woo ran for Delaware's lieutenant governor position. A Democrat, Woo won both the primary and the general election after a recount, becoming the nation's highest ranking Chinese American elected state official at the time. While in office, he bridged science and government by investigating ways to foster the state's involvement and investment in high-tech industries. Regarding education, however, Woo felt his capacities were limited by the governor, Republican Michael N. Castle.

In 1988, rather than try for reelection, Woo sought Delaware's seat in the U.S. Senate. He won the party primary but lost the general election to Republican Senator William V. Roth. Four years later, he bid for a place in the U.S. House of Representatives against his former boss, Michael N. Castle.

During the campaign, Woo named the economy and employment as his top priorities. He called for the United States to create high paying manufacturing jobs and to promote the marketing of American products. "We have got to stop exporting jobs to foreign countries," he argued. "America's wealth is gushing out" (Lim 1992, 3). He also advocated a single-payer health insurance system, competitive salaries for teachers, the Family Leave Act, and a national system for background checks on daycare workers. Woo supported women's rights, including equal pay and pro-choice—"It's time for us to be equal," he declared (Lim 1992, 3). He also advocated the establishment of an independent body to administer Social Security so that "the federal government cannot use these payments to cover the deficit," because "retirement should be worry free."

Despite strong support from segments of the electorate, including Delaware's African Americans, Woo lost to Castle in the November count. Thereafter, he returned to teaching at the university.

S.B. Woo's activism has not been stifled by his defeats, however. In 1989, he was an institute fellow at Harvard University's Kennedy School of Government. A leader in the Chinese American community, he was founder of both the Chinese School of St. Louis in 1963 and the Chinese School of Delaware in 1967. He served as president of the National Organization of Chinese Americans in 1990–1991. Woo has contributed opinion pieces to publications like *Asian Week*, and is currently a member of political collectives such as the Committee of 100, which strategizes on ways to boost U.S.-China relations and the visibility and clout of Asian Americans domestically. He has proposed, for example, that Asian Americans vote as an ethnic bloc, as do Jewish Americans and African Americans. As one of the 120 Chinese Americans outlining a "blueprint" for APAs to consider during the 2000 presidential election, Woo stated, "[The] time has come for Asian Americans to practice 'real politics,' the kind practiced by other immigrant groups in their paths to equality. We must reward the political leaders and parties that fight for equal opportunity. We must punish those who don't—through the ballot box" (*Northwest Asian Weekly* 1998, 11).

### Sources

"Asian Partners Eye Vote 2000." *Northwest Asian Weekly*. 3 July 1998, p. 11.

Ketchum, Susan "S.B. Woo." In *Notable Asian-Americans*, ed. Helen Zia and Susan B. Gall. Detroit, MI: Gale Research, Inc., 1995, pp. 419–420.

Lim, Gerard. "Woo Making Late Surge for Congressional Seat." *Asian Week*. 2 October 1992, p. 3.

Lin, Sam Chu and Wong Gerrye. "Committee of 100 Converges Near S.F.: Luminaries Inspire, Excite Convention-Goers." *Asian Week*. 17 June 1998, p. 6.

"S.B. Woo." *AP Candidate Bios*. The Associated Press Political Service. 1992.

# David Wu

**Born:** 8 April 1955, Taiwan.

**Education:** B.S., Stanford University, 1977; J.D., Yale University, 1982.

**Positions Held:** Member, U.S. House of Representatives, 1999–present.

**Awards, Honors:** Named to A. *Magazine*'s 25 Most Influential Asians In America, 1998.

**Summary:** David Wu is the first Asian Pacific American elected from Oregon to the United States House of Representatives.

### Early Years and Education

Born in Taiwan on 8 April 1955 to K.C. and Helen Wu, David Wu spent his first six years on the island before moving with his family to the United States following a change in the nation's stringent immigrant legislation. The Wus first settled in New York before migrating to Orange County, California. Educated in public school, Wu graduated as valedictorian of his class of 700 from Westminster High School. He went on to earn his B.S. at Stanford University in 1977, took courses in medicine at Harvard University for a period, and finally graduated with his J.D. from Yale Law School in 1982.

## Career Highlights

As an attorney, Wu has held a number of civic and professional positions, working with the Portland Planning Commission, the Japan American Society of Oregon, a federal judge in Portland, and West Coast–based International law firms. In addition, he is the founder of both the Portland-Suzhou Sister City Association and his own practice, Cohen and Wu, which specializes in high-tech industries and small businesses. He has focused many of his efforts on developing trade opportunities along the Pacific Rim and Oregon in particular, and has facilitated the growth of businesses and jobs in the "Silicon Forest" of the Northwest.

On 6 January 1999, Wu, the first Chinese American member of the House of Representatives, was sworn into the 106th Congress, with his wife Michelle, mother Helen, and sister Alice cheering him on in the House gallery. Perhaps not unlike many other dutiful Asian Pacific American sons and daughters, an ironic but somewhat humorous thought crossed his mind during the ceremony. "When I was being sworn in to Congress, it was the proudest moment of my life," he said. "But I recall thinking, 'Do my parents still wish I had finished medical school?'" (Ch'ien 1999, 29).

Having defeated Republican nominee Molly Bordonaro, Wu was elected to represent Oregon's First Congressional District, encompassing the region from Portland to the coast, the second-most-populous district in the state. David Wu, who captured 50 percent of the popular vote, advocated public education by restricting class sizes and modernizing schools, maintain the current social security system, and supported environmental protection, economic growth through job training and research, abortion rights, and safe streets (in part by limiting the use of firearms).

Wu adopted an unorthodox campaign method in the region, comprised of 93 percent whites, less than 4 percent Asians, and significantly populated by Republicans. Instead of a slick advertising and media campaign, he canvassed from door to door and phoned voters personally to discuss personally the issues on their minds.

Eager to "maximize" his "chances of getting a good committee assignment," Wu, the first freshman to move to Washington, D.C., after his victory, was named to the House Committee on Education and the Workforce, Committee on Science, and Subcommittees on Aeronautics, Early Childhood, Youth, and Families, and Technology and Space (Lin 1998, 16). His staff members have taken note of his devotion to technology and jokingly describe him as too "wonkish" (Ch'ien 1999, 28).

Coming to office in the wake of the Democrats' campaign finance scandals, Wu understood that his own actions might be questioned. "All Americans are entitled to participate in politics, and shouldn't be intimidated from the process," he stated (Wenger 1998, 9). Consequently, he has acknowledged the importance of API representation in national government. "Just focusing on 1996, the largest campaign fundraising convictions were of non-Asian people, but that got little attention," he observed. "There has been particular attention being given to the Asian factor, if you will, and that can be much more effectively addressed by having a 'voice at the table,' and I fully intend to be that voice" (Lin 1998, 16). Congressman Wu is active within API political circles, serving as vice-chair of the Congressional Asian Pacific Caucus. While some observers have questioned his support from the Portland Chinese community, his Asian Pacific Islander colleagues are pleased with his views and have welcomed him into their fold. Randy Okamura, a board member of California's Cupertino-Sunnyvale Fremont Union High School district, noted that he was "impressed with Wu's commitment," while Barry Chang, one of Wu's campaign fund-raisers, stated, "I would like to see a Chinese American become a U.S. congressman, a U.S. senator, and hopefully one day president of the United States. Electing David to Congress is the answer to the first part of that dream" (Lin 1998, 16).

## Sources

Ch'ien, Evelyn. "The Freshman." *A. Magazine.* June/July 1999, pp. 26–29.

Kim, Jungwon. "The 1998 A. List." *A. Magazine,* December 1998/January 1999, p. 50.

Lin, Sam Chu. "Congressman David Wu Hits Office." *Rafu Shimpo.* 11 January 1999, p. 1.

———. "Oregon's David Wu Victorious." *Rafu Shimpo.* 7 November 1998, pp. 1, 3.

———. "Oregon Win Hits Home in Silicon Valley: Supporters Turn Out to Congratulate David Wu." *Asian Week.* 2 December 1998, p. 16.

London, Melissa. "Wu Wins Congressional Seat: There are Now Seven Asian Pacific Americans in National Office." *Northwest Asian Weekly.* 20 November 1998, p. 1.

U.S. House of Representatives Web site: www.house.gov/wu [Accessed 20 April 1999].

Wenger, Jeff. "Lost in Chinatown: Congressional Hopeful David Wu Says He's Victim of Identity Politics." *International Examiner.* 4 November 1998, p. 9.

# Joe Bee Xiong

**Born:** 10 August 1961, Mong Cha, Laos.

**Education:** B.S., Mount Senario College, 1988.

**Positions Held:** Member-At-Large, Eau Claire, Wisconsin City Council.

**Awards, Honors:** The Defenders of Freedom Citation, United States Congresss, 1995; Commendation and Citation for Vietnam War Service in Laos, 1996; Outstanding Alumnus of the Year, Mount Scenario College, 1996.

**Summary:** Joe Bee Xiong is the first Hmong American to be elected to office in the state of Wisconsin.

## Early Years and Education

Joe Bee Xiong was born in Mong Cha, Laos on 10 August 1961. He spent much of his childhood learning to farm and surviving the jungle environment of Laos. "The two experiences we knew the most were fighting and shooting, and agriculture," he recalled. His father, for example, engaged in anti-communist combat. At the age of 12, the young Xiong, replacing his father, entered a CIA program in his native country whose purpose was to enlist Hmong in the American efforts against communism in Northeast Laos. Soon thereafter, the United States, fighting a losing battle in this "Secret War," eventually withdrew its forces in 1975. Like many of his countrymen, however, he remained to battle North Vietnamese troops. "We just used the ammunition, the guns and hid them in the tunnels. We just fought to protect our villages and for our families," stated Xiong ("Adjustment").

"There were three types of people in Laos," explained Xiong in a 1996 interview. "The first group flees the country. The second group surrenders and accepts the communist system. I am part of the third group, the group that fights back and will not accept their ways. After the Americans left, those of us in the third group fled our villages and lived in the jungle. Like animals. Like the fox. Like the tiger" (Hannah 1996, 2A).

He continued, "We have no choice. There is no future. We fight to save our families, to protect our villages. We kill many. We poison their water. We are very mad" (Hannah 1996, 2A). Recalling one particular confrontation in April 1978, he described, "During the fight that day, I was never scared. I am always the one who calls out to the others to continue fighting. But maybe I call too loud. Ever since I am growing up, I have the behavior of leadership" (Hannah 1996, 2A). Twenty years later, the United States Congress would recognize his bravery with a Defenders of Freedom Citation in 1995 and a Citation for Vietnam War Service in Laos in 1996.

Eventually, Xiong and his family members—his mother, father, five brothers, and one sister—decided to flee their homeland as part of a mass exodus of 1,300 Hmong refugees. They headed first to Thailand before immigrating to Philadelphia in 1979 en route to settling in Eau Claire, Wisconsin. In the new city, he attended Memorial High School and Chippewa Valley Technical College from 1982 to 1985, where he received 334 hours of police training in conjunction with the Eau Claire Police Department, also earning an associate degree in data procession. On 21 May 1987, Xiong became a naturalized citizen of the United States, and the following year he graduated from Ladysmith, Wisconsin's Mount Senario College with a bachelor of science degree in criminal justice. At Mount Senario, he served as the president of the school's Lao/Hmong/American Student Organization. "I'm proud that I've been able to get an education, have a job, and my family," he declared. "I'm the first generation in my family to get a college degree, and we're talking since 5000 years before Christ." Xiong not only earned his diploma but was named Mount Senario's Outstanding Alumnus of the Year in 1996 ("Adjustment").

## Career Highlights

Xiong has actively embraced his adopted community, holding a myriad of professional, civic, and political positions in the area. From 1987 to 1991, as a part of the Eau Claire Police Reserve, Xiong was involved with patrolling, report writing, and educating local residents about police services. Since 1987, he has regularly offered presentations on Hmong history, music, and culture to organizations and schools in the upper Midwest area under the auspices of the University of Wisconsin–Eau Claire. Occasionally, Xiong also performs on the qeej, a Hmong reed instrument, at various community festivals and events. Beginning in 1988, he worked for a decade with the Eau Claire County Department of Human Services as a case manager and financial planner, and from 1998 to 1999 he served as a teacher assistant and interpreter for the Menomonie School District. Currently, Xiong is the KEYS (Keeping Education among Youth for Success Program) Coordinator of the Eau Claire Area Hmong Assistance Association, Inc. As KEYS coordinator and counselor, he assists Hmong youth in overcoming cultural and language barriers that prevent successful participation in school and community life. He devotes significant attention to developing self-esteem and ethnic pride among youth, promoting bicultural skills, and strengthening family relationships in order to help them integrate better into mainstream American life.

Xiong's bicultural approach is also evident from his other volunteer positions within the community. For example, he was a board member of both the Eau Claire United Way from 1994 to 1995 and the city's Housing Authority from 1996 to 1998. He is currently Eau Claire's Water Way and Park commissioner and an active member of the local chapter of the Kiwanis Club. In addition, he has served for one year as the president of the Eau Claire Area Hmong Mutual Assistance Association, Inc., and has been president of Eau Claire's Asian Cross Culture, Inc., since 1992.

One of Xiong's most significant accomplishments is his 1996 election to the city council of Eau Claire as member-at-large, making him the first Hmong to win an elected position in the state of Wisconsin and one of only a handful of Hmong legislators nationwide. Soon after his victory, he stated simply, "I am not scared. I have seen much life and death. The city council is a big job, but, you know, I am not scared" (Hannah 1996, 2A). Most of his constituents were white, but racial differences did not prevent him from securing his seat a second time in 1998. His bid, however, was not uncontested, as demonstrated by an anonymous letter voicing one voter's unwillingness to vote for Xiong, because "he had too many kids" ("Adjustment"). Despite any prejudices, however, the campaign "was a major step for Hmong community when Joe Bee was elected. He's addressed not only issues affecting the Hmong but others that have addressed the entire city," stated Bill Nielsen, the president of Eau Claire's City Council at the time (*Duluth News* 2000). These have included keeping taxes low and improving city services.

Xiong's success in politics has inspired many of his co-ethnics. "It was a really big deal when Joe Bee was elected," explained Ka Ying Yang, executive director of the Southeast Asia Action Resource Center in Washington, D.C. "That event has really encouraged Hmong people across the country to run for public office. It showed them that 'Hey, we really do have a chance.'" She added, "We have to face it. There is a lot of racism in Wisconsin but Joe Bee was able to overcome that. Electing Hmong public officials is a great way to get some of those issues addressed" (*Duluth News* 2000).

Xiong, who is married to Ta Moua and the father of eight, takes his public profile seriously. "There is nothing better in life than to be a leader or a good role model," he stated. "[The youth] can say, if Joe can do it, then we shouldn't have any trouble. . . . I often tell my family how lucky we are. Here we are in the country of opportunity and education, the richest country in the world" ("Adjustment").

## Sources

"Adjustment to U.S. Was Tough." News clipping provided by Joe Bee Xiong, no author, date available.

Hannah, Steve. "Many Years and Miles Later, Joe Bee Finds a New Fight." *Capital Times*. 30 March 1996, p. 2A.

"Hmong Citizens Finding a Place on Wisconsin Ballots. Candidates Getting National Attention." *Duluth News*. 10 January 2000.

# Y

## Michael Yaki

Michael Yaki. (Courtesy of Michael Yaki)

**Born:** 15 February 1961, Los Angeles, California.

**Education:** B.A., University of California, 1983; J.D., Yale University, 1986.

**Positions Held:** Member, San Francisco Board of Supervisors, 1996–present.

**Summary:** As a member of the San Francisco Board of Supervisors, Michael Yaki is one of the pioneering Asian Pacific Americans in elected politics in Northern California.

### Early Years and Education

The son of a United States Foreign Service Career Officer, Michael John Yaki was born in Los Angeles, California on 15 February 1961 to Michael M. Yaki, third-generation Japanese-Hawaiian American, and Madeleine Yaki, a first-generation Chinese American. Yaki spent much of his childhood abroad, living in Manila, Philippines, Hong Kong, Taichung, Taiwan, Jakarta, Indonesia, and Ottawa, Canada.

Yaki attended the University of California, Berkeley, graduating in 1983 with a B.A. in East Asian studies. He then enrolled at the Yale University Law School, where he earned his J.D. in 1986. Afterwards, he spent one year clerking for Justice Harry Low of the California Court of Appeal. Yaki then went into private practice as an attorney for San Francisco's Morrison and Foerster in 1987.

## Career Highlights

Two years later, Michael Yaki moved to the office of Congresswoman Nancy Pelosi, eighth congressional district representative, where he served as district director (chief of staff for the local branch). He remained as the senior advisor to Pelosi until 1996.

Yaki's personal foray into electoral politics began on 5 February 1996, when Mayor Willie L. Brown, Jr. appointed him to fill the unexpired term of newly-elected District Attorney Terence Hallinan on the San Francisco Board of Supervisors. Several months later, he claimed the seat at the polls, securing his position for an additional four years.

As a member of San Francisco's powerful board, Yaki has devoted his energies to a variety of issues. An advocate of strict gun control, he authored legislation banning the sale of Saturday Night Specials in the city. He also crafted the First Source hiring ordinance allowing the city's denizens top priority for new jobs created by new city contracts or permits. Yaki has also been a principal player behind the Juvenile Justice Action plan, base conversion and development at Treasure Island, the design of the new San Francisco Giants ballpark at China Basin, and a historic charter amendment to reform MUNI, one of the city's public transportation lines. Yaki also chaired the first San Francisco Children and Youth Summit and worked with the YMCA to found the Presidio Day Camp for underpriviledged children.

Currently, Yaki chairs the San Francisco County Transportation Authority, which oversees programming local transportation projects funded by federal and state monies. He also sits as vice chair of the board's Transportation and Land Use Committee and as a member of the Committee on Public Health and Environment.

## Source

Resume provided by Michael Yaki.

# Brian Y. Yamane

Brian Y. Yamane. (Courtesy of Brian Yamane)

**Born:** 14 January 1947, Honolulu, Hawaii.

**Education:** B.A., University of Hawaii, 1982.

**Positions Held:** Member, Hawaii State House of Representatives, 1994–present.

**Summary:** Brian Y. Yamane is a member of the Hawaii State House of Representatives.

## Early Years and Education

Brian Y. Yamane was born on 14 January 1947 in Honolulu, Hawaii, to Ernest and Usano Yamane. He attended the University Laboratory High School in Hawaii, graduating in 1964. He continued his education at the University of Hawaii, earning his bachelor's degree in economics in 1982.

## Career Highlights

Professionally, Yamane has been affiliated with several insurance agencies in the Honolulu area. He currently works as an independent agent, specializing in business property insurance.

Politically, Yamane was elected to Hawaii's House of Representatives in November 1994, serving the state's 19th District, which includes Kaimuki, Diamond Head, Kapahulu, and Waikiki. During his time in the legislature, he has served as the vice chair of the Judiciary and Health Committees.

Outside of his official duties, Yamane is involved with a number of organizations, including the Diamond Head Lions Club, the Free and Accepted Masons, the Neighborhood Justice Center, the Kaimuki Neighborhood Board, and Citizens Patrol. He is married to the former Jean Kobayashi; they are the parents of two sons, Ryan and Aaron.

### Source

Resume provided by Brian Yamane.

# Leland Yee

**Born:** 1948, China.

**Education:** B.S., University of California, Berkeley; M.S., San Francisco State University; Ph.D., University of Hawaii.

**Positions Held:** Member, Vice President, President, San Francisco School Board, 1989–1996; Member, San Francisco Board of Supervisors, 1997–present.

**Summary:** Leland Yee is a member of the San Francisco Board of Supervisors.

### Early Years and Education

Leland Yee was born in China in 1948 and immigrated to the United States at the age of three, settling in San Francisco. After graduating from the city's public school system, he attended the University of California, Berkeley, earning his bachelor's degree before going on to graduate from San Francisco State University with a master's in developmental psychology. Yee rounded out his formal education with a doctoral degree, also in developmental psychology, from the University of Hawaii.

### Career Highlights

Putting his training to good use, Yee, a national board certified school psychologist, has served as an education consultant to several California school districts. He has also been an administrator of private and public mental health and social service programs and has worked as a psychologist with school districts and children's mental health services. In addition, he participated in the California Senate Task Force on Child Abuse Laws and the Technical Group–National Assessment of Educational Programs and chaired the Ethnic and Multicultural Concerns Committee of the Council for Exceptional Children.

From 1989 to 1996, Yee was a member of San Francisco's Board of Education. During this time, he served as chair of the Council of Urban Boards of Education and was on the Board of Directors of the California School Boards Association and the National School Boards Association.

In 1996, Yee successfully bid for a seat on San Francisco's powerful Board of Supervisors. As a supervisor, he has held a number of important positions, including chair of Finance and Labor and vice chair of Public Utilities and Deregulation. He worked with the San Francisco Transportation Authority Finance Committee, Transportation and Land Use, and the Retirement Board.

Children, education, and family issues have ranked as some of the top priorities on Yee's agenda. Among his many accomplishments are the crafting of a budget as Finance Chair that Coleman Advocates for Youth called "one of the best ever for children, youth, and families." As a member of the school board, he established a budget committee to monitor the school district's finances and require performance standards and financial disclosures when awarding instructional and facilities contracts. He also developed the pioneering Integrated Services Model, which opened schools in the evenings to provide tutoring, adult education, child care, sports, counseling, and health services for families. In addition, Yee facilitated the development and implementation of a parent help-line to assist parents whose children are struggling with social, emotional, educational, and physical stresses. Other concerns that Yee actively advocates are "Open, Honest Government" and public safety.

Yee and his wife Maxine are the parents of four children, all graduates of San Francisco public schools.

## Sources

Bowman, Catherine and John King. "S.F. Supervisor Incumbents Triumph." *San Francisco Chronicle*. 6 November 1996, p. A1.

Supervisor Leland Y. Yee, Ph.D. Web site: www.lelandyee.com.

# Mae Yih

Mae Yih. (Courtesy of Mae Yih)

**Born:** 24 May 1928, Shanghai, China.

**Education:** B.A., Barnard College.

**Positions Held:** Oregon State Representative, 1976–1982; Oregon State Senator, 1982–present; Oregon Senate President Pro Tempore, 1993–1995.

**Awards, Honors:** Honorary Citizen of Fujian Province, China.

**Summary:** Mae Yih has served for over 25 years in the Oregon State Legislature.

## Early Years

Mae Yih was born on 24 May 1928 in Shanghai, China, to Chun Woo Duan and Fung Wen Feng Duan. Having survived the 1936–1945 Japanese occupation of her hometown as a young child, she states simply that she "appreciate[s] freedom" (personal communication to Ellen D. Wu, 2000).

## Education

Yih graduated from the Shanghai's McTyeire High School for Girls and spent her first year in college at the local St. John's University. After moving to the United States in 1948, she attended New York City's Barnard College, where she earned a bachelor's degree in economics. In addition, she completed coursework in accounting at the neighboring Columbia University's Graduate School of Business.

## Career Highlights

Following her initial public service involvement as a member of local school boards, Yih inaugurated her long-running career in the Oregon State Legislature by challenging a 14-year incumbent for a seat in the State House in 1976. That year, she won the first of three successful bids for state representative, followed by five consecutive terms as Oregon state senator for District 19, encompassing portions of Linn and Benton Counties, a feat she considers to be one of her proudest accomplishments "as a Chinese American" (personal communication to Ellen D. Wu, 2000). In 1993, she was also chosen by her colleagues as the Senate's president pro tempore for a biennium.

As an Oregon State senator, Yih has participated on the Joint Legislative Ways and Means Committee, the Subcommittee on Human Resources, and the Transportation/Trade and Economic Development Committee. She has also served as the vice chair of the Senate Transportation Committee and a member of the Joint Legislative Emergency Board.

Two of Mae Yih's main goals for her political career are to "improve trust and accountability in government" and facilitate trade and friendly relations between her home state and the nation of her birth (personal communication to Ellen D. Wu, 2000). Among her noteworthy projects toward these ends have been the co-sponsorship of legislation to correct the Measure 50 draft oversight to ensure Linn and Deschutes counties' property owners property tax relief, and the spearheading efforts to establish an Oregon Trade Representative office in Shanghai, China, to help promote commerce and increased job opportunities for Oregonians. For her dedication to Pacific Rim ties, Yih has been named an honorary citizen of China's Fujian Province.

Yih and her husband, Stephen, a retired executive of Teledyne Wah Chang Corporation in Albany, New York, have two sons, Donald, a physician, who resides in Philadelphia, and Daniel, an attorney, who lives in Chicago.

### Sources

landru.leg.state.or.us/yih/bio.html [Accessed 28 October 1999].
Personal communication to Ellen Wu, 2000.

# Karl Goso Yoneda

**Born:** 15 July 1906, Glendale, California.

**Died:** 9 May 1999, Mendocino County, California.

**Education:** High School in Hiroshima, Japan.

**Positions Held:** Trade-unionist, longshoreman, writer.

**Awards, Honors:** AFL-CIO Asian Pacific American Labor Alliance Award, 1992.

**Summary:** Karl G. Yoneda was one of Asian America's most radical activists. Over his lifetime, he was involved in a myriad of movements, including the Communist Party, labor organizing, anti-imperialist protests, and the Japanese American redress and reparations campaign.

### Early Years and Education

Karl Goso Yoneda was born in 1906 in Glendale, California, to Hideo and Kazu Yoneda, Japanese immigrant farmers hailing from Hiroshima, Japan. After seven years in the United States, Yoneda ventured with his father and brother across the Pacific to his parents' native country, where he embarked on his "proper Japanese education."

Young Yoneda showed early signs of his passionate personality. An avid reader, Yoneda was profoundly influenced by the works of Vasily Eroshenko, a Russian anarchist and Esperantist who authored a number of fairy tales in Japanese before being expelled from Japan for his political views. Deeply influenced, Yoneda set out in 1922 to find Eroshenko, who had gone to China to teach Esperanto at Peking University. He hitchhiked his way to Beijing, working odd jobs along the way. After four months, he finally located Eroshenko, staying with him for another two months, taking dictations in order to earn travel fare back home. Upon returning to Japan, recalled Yoneda, "I decided I no longer wanted to return to school. Instead, I joined the labor movement," engaging in strikes in Osaka, Tokyo, and Hiroshima and publishing *Tsuchi* (Earth), a progressive monthly for poor farmers.

## Career Highlights

At the age of 20, Yoneda left for the United States to eschew conscription by the Japanese Imperial Army. After a two-month detention at the Angel Island Immigration Center, Yoneda left the Bay Area for Los Angeles to find his brothers and sisters. Spurred by his labor-advocacy activism in Japan and conversations with Einosuke Yamaguchi, an area radical, he joined the Los Angeles–based Japanese Workers Association (JWA) and the American Communist Party. A card-carrying member of the CP, Yoneda took the name "Karl" after Karl Marx. In Los Angeles and around the state, Yoneda devoted his time to organizing farm workers and participating in pro-labor and anti-Japanese imperialism/anti-war actions while supporting himself through part-time work as an agricultural laborer, gardener, dishwasher, or domestic worker.

During this time, noted Yoneda in his 1983 autobiography, *Ganbatte: Sixty-Year Struggle of a Kibei Worker*, "A couple of JWA/CP members criticized me for not devoting enough time to the Japanese community as a whole. I had begun to paint English posters, a time-consuming task, for demonstrations and indoor meetings. I explained that working with non-Japanese groups was essential for our mutual understanding, as they too would become interested in the plight of the Japanese in this country." He continued, "Working together and building unity, keeping faith in the workers and rank-and-filers, and advocating a socialism based on Marxism-Leninism, were, I believed, the main ingredients to build the movement. That was, and still is, my firm conviction."

In 1931, Yoneda's involvement with the National Unemployment Council's National Unemployment Insurance Day demonstrations resulted in an arrest for "disturbing the peace." His future wife, Elaine Black, the New York–born daughter of Russian Jewish revolutionaries and the International Labor Defense Committee office secretary, nicknamed the "Red Angel" and "Tiger Woman" for her militancy, posted bail for him. The pair became close companions, but were legally barred from marriage in California due to an anti-miscegenation statute. As a result, they had to travel to Seattle to wed.

Throughout the Depression Era, Yoneda continued to be involved in a myriad of political causes, including agricultural laborer, longshoremen, and cannery worker advocacy and anti-Japanese imperialism. He also served as the editor of the *Rodo Shimbun*, a San Francisco–based Japanese socialist newspaper.

After President Franklin D. Roosevelt issued Executive Order 9066 mandating the "evacuation" and internment of all people of Japanese ancestry from the west coast, Yoneda, along with his fellow Kibei, Nisei, and Issei Communists and sympathizers decided not to fight or speak out publicly against the violation. "Our rationale was we would lose all rights if the Germany-Italy-Japan fascist Axis powers were victorious," he explained. "The menace of worldwide fascism was knocking at our nation's doorstep. We had to do everything to insure Allied victory. We had no choice but to accept the racist U.S. dictum at that time over Hitler's ovens and Japan's military rapists of Nanking." In accordance, Yoneda "volunteered" to help construct the Manzanar, California concentration camp, where he was subsequently imprisoned. In solidarity, his wife Elaine demanded to be confined with him and their son Tommy. Eventually, she was authorized to relocate with Tommy to San Francisco, but had to remain in monthly contact with government authorities in order to report on his status.

Beginning in late 1942, Yoneda served as a translator for the U.S. Military Intelligence Service in the Pacific Theatre until he was honorably discharged in November 1945. After the war, Yoneda was unsuccessful, due to his political leanings, in finding work as a longshoreman despite being a military veteran. In addition, as an interracial couple, he and his wife were unable to secure housing in San Francisco. Consequently, the Yonedas moved to rural Sonoma County, California, where they purchased and operated a six-acre chicken farm. "I painfully learned that it was unrewarding, endless toil. As the years progressed, big feed companies, hatcheries, and many chicken raisers became mere sharecroppers," he recalled. "We couldn't compete against the big mechanized ranchers. The end of our farming career was inevitable." In 1957, Yoneda resumed his work as a longshoreman in San Francisco.

Despite the constant threats of McCarthyism during the Cold War, the Yonedas managed to persist with their leftist involvement such as helping to establish a branch of the California Labor School in Santa Rosa, supporting CP candidates, and campaigning against attempts to deport International Longshoremen and Warehousemen's Union President Harry Bridges. Additionally, the Yonedas protested against the atomic bomb and the Vietnam War and supported the "Free Angela Davis" campaign. In 1967, Yoneda published his Japanese-language manuscript *The Labor History of U.S. Japanese*, which inaugurated his many years of guest lecturing at various university campuses, high schools, and Marxist studies classes. He was also invited to speak at a number of academic conferences, including the Southwest Labor Studies Conference, the American Sociological Association, and the Organization of American Historians, on Japanese American labor history. Throughout the 1960s-1990s, the Yonedas participated in personal, and later community-wide pilgrimages to Manzanar concentration camp as well as the Japanese American redress and reparations movement. The AFL-CIO Asian Pacific American Labor Alliance honored Yoneda's union contributions in 1992.

In 1982, reflecting on his six decades of struggle, Yoneda remarked: "I find it has been a mixture of bad and good, failures and successes, rueful days and joyous memories. I have been surrounded by family, comrades, and fellow workers of all ages in causes against evil and for human dignity. . . . I have great faith in the multi-racial working people and their allies of this nation."

Yoneda died on 9 May 1999 in Mendocino County, California.

### Sources

"Karl Yoneda; Japanese American Radical, Union Activist." *Los Angeles Times*. 16 May 1999, p. B6.

Yoneda, Karl G., with an introduction by Yuji Ichioka. *Ganbatte: Sixty-Year Struggle of a Kibei Worker*. Los Angeles: Asian American Studies Center. 1983.

# Appendix 1: Distinguished Asian American Political and Governmental Leaders by Birth Date

| | | | |
|---|---|---|---|
| 1889–1973 | Dalip Singh Saund | 1940– | James Y. Arakaki |
| 1904–1977 | Wing F. Ong | 1941– | Mike Honda |
| 1904–1994 | Philip Villamin Vera Cruz | 1941–1998 | Gordon Lau |
| 1906– | Hiram L. Fong | 1941– | Carol Liu |
| 1906–1992 | Samuel Ichiye Hayakawa | 1941– | Robert Matsui |
| 1906–1999 | Karl Goso Yoneda | 1942– | Julia Chang Bloch |
| 1909–1987 | John Fujio Aiso | 1943– | Eni F.H. Faleomavaega |
| 1909–1983 | James Kimo Kealoha | 1944– | Cheryl Ann Lau |
| 1915– | Grace Lee Boggs | 1944– | Shirin R. Tahir-Kheli |
| 1916– | Herbert Young Cho Choy | 1946– | Jose S. Esteves |
| 1916–1990 | "Spark" Masayuki Matsunaga | 1946– | Dale Minami |
| 1920– | Ruby Chow | 1946– | Michael Park |
| 1921– | Yuri Kochiyama | 1946– | Kip Tokuda |
| 1924– | Daniel K. Akaka | 1946– | John David Waihee III |
| 1924– | Daniel K. Inouye | 1947– | Warren Furutani |
| 1925– | Jean Sadako King | 1947– | Mazie Hirono |
| 1925–1965 | Wing Luke | 1947– | Brian Y. Yamane |
| 1926– | George R. Ariyoshi | 1948– | Harry J. Joe |
| 1927– | Patsy T. Mink | 1948– | Stewart Kwok |
| 1928– | Mae Yih | 1948– | Irene Natividad |
| 1929– | March Fong Eu | 1948– | Gordon Quan |
| 1930– | Patricia Saiki | 1948– | Sichan Aun Siv |
| 1931– | Norman Y. Mineta | 1948– | Robert Underwood |
| 1932– | Harry Lee | 1948– | Leland Yee |
| 1933– | David M. Valderrama | 1949– | Bill Lann Lee |
| 1935– | John Lim | 1949– | Rene Mansho |
| 1935– | George Nakano | 1950– | Lance A. Ito |
| 1935– | Paull Hobom Shin | 1950– | Joaquin Lim |
| 1936– | Tony Lam | 1950– | Gary Locke |
| 1937– | Nguyen Minh Chau | 1950– | Susan Oki Mollway |
| 1937– | S.B. (Shien-Biau) Woo | 1950– | Velma Rosette Veloria |
| 1939– | Benjamin Cayetano | 1952– | Dennis W. Hayashi |
| 1939– | Jay C. Kim | 1953– | Elaine L. Chao |
| 1939– | Martha J. Wong | 1953– | Judy Chu |

Appendix 1. Leaders by Birth Date

| | | | |
|---|---|---|---|
| 1953– | Matthew K. Fong | 1962– | Michael P. Guingona |
| 1953– | Stanley T. Matsunaka | 1962– | Daphne Kwok |
| 1954– | Harold Hongju Koh | 1963– | Mike Gin |
| 1954– | Hermina M. Morita | 1963– | Kenneth Daniel Miyagishima |
| 1955– | Angela Eunjin Oh | 1964– | Amy Mah Sangiolo |
| 1955– | David Wu | 1967– | Cheryl Lee |
| 1956– | Michael Woo | 1969– | Satveer Chaudhary |
| 1958– | Kumar Barve | | |
| 1958– | Karen Narasaki | | |
| 1958– | Paul K. Tanaka | | |
| 1959– | Chanrithy Uong | | |
| 1959– | Barry Wong | | |
| 1961– | Sharon Tomiko Santos | | |
| 1961– | Joe Bee Xiong | | |
| 1961– | Michael Yaki | | |

**No Date**

Thelma Buchholdt
Wilma Chan
Dolores Sibonga
Shamina Singh
Mabel Teng
Delbert E. Wong

# Appendix 2: Distinguished Asian American Political and Governmental Leaders by Position

**Activists**
Grace Lee Boggs
Yuri Kochiyama
Stewart Kwoh
Daphne Kwok
Dale Minami
Karen Narasaki
Irene Natividad
Angela Oh
Amy Mah Sangiolo
Philip Villamin Vera Cruz
Michael Woo
Karl Goso Yoneda

**City Government Officials**
Nguyen Minh Chau, Garret Park, Maryland
Judy Chu, Monterey Park, California
Jose S. Esteves, Milpitas, California
Warren Furutani, Los Angeles, California
Mike Gin, Redondo Beach, California
Michael Guingona, Dale City, California
Harry J. Joe, Irving, Texas
Tony Lam, Westminster, California
Gordon Lau, San Francisco, California
Cheryl Lee, Shoreline, Washington
Harry Lee, Jefferson Parish, Louisiana
Wing Luke, Seattle, Washington
Rene Mansho, Honolulu, Hawaii
Angela Eunjin Oh, Los Angeles, California
Gordon Quan, Houston, Texas
Amy Mah Sangiolo, Newton Massachusetts
Dolores Sibonga, Seattle, Washington
Paul K. Tanaka, Gardena, California
Mabel Teng, San Francisco, California
Chanrithy Uong, Lowell, Massachusetts
Martha J. Wong, Houston, Texas
Michael Woo, Los Angeles, California
Joe Bee Xiong, Eau Claire, Wisconsin
Michael Yaki, San Francisco, California
Leland Yee, San Francisco, California

**County Government Officials**
James Y. Arakaki, Hawaii Co., Hawaii
Wilma Chan, Alameda Co., California
Ruby Chow, King Co., Washington
Mike Honda, Santa Clara Co., California
Kenneth Daniel Miyagishima, Dona Ana Co., New Mexico

**Governors**
George R. Ariyoshi, Hawaii
Benjamin Cayetano, Hawaii
Gary Locke, Washington
John David Waihee III, Hawaii

**Justices**
John Fujio Aiso
Herbert Young Cho Choy
Lance A. Ito
Susan Oki Mollway
David M. Valderrama
Delbert E. Wong

**Lieutenant Governors**
George R. Ariyoshi, Hawaii
Benjamin Cayetano, Hawaii
Eni F.H. Faleomavaega, American Samoa
Mazie Hirono, Hawaii
James Kimo Kealoha, Hawaii

Jean Sadako King, Hawaii
John David Waihee III, Hawaii
S.B. (Shien-Biau) Woo, Delaware

**Mayors**
Judy Chu, Monterey Park, California
Michael P. Guingona, Daly City, California
Harry J. Joe, Irving, Texas
Jay C. Kim, Diamond Bar, California
Joaquin Lim, Walnut, California
Norman Y. Mineta, San Jose, California
Michael Park, Federal Way, Washington

**National Government Officials**
Julia Chang Bloch
Elaine L. Chao
Dennis Hayashi
Harold Hongju Koh
Bill Lann Lee
Norman Y. Mineta
Shamina Singh
Sichan Aun Siv

**State Government Officials**
George R. Ariyoshi, Hawaii
Kumar Barve, Maryland
Thelma Buchholdt, Alaska
Benjamin Cayetano, Hawaii
Wilma Chan, California
Satveer Chaudhay, Minnesota
Judy Chu, California
March Fong Eu, California
Matthew K. Fong, California
Jean Sadako King, Hawaii
Cheryl Ann Lau, Nevada
John Lim, Oregon
Carol Liu, California
Gary Locke, Washington
Stanley T. Matsanaka, Colorado
Patsy T. Mink, Hawaii
Hermina M. Morita, Hawaii
George Nakano, California

Wing F. Ong, Arizona
Patricia Saiki, Hawaii
Paull Hobom Shin, Washington
Kip Tokuda, Washington
Sharon Tomiko Santos, Washington
David M. Valderrama, Maryland
Velma Rosette Veloria, Washington
John David Waihee III, Hawaii
Barry Wong, Arizona
Brian Y. Yamane, Hawaii
Mae Yih, Oregon

**U.S. Ambassadors and Diplomats**
Julia Chang Bloch, ambassador, Kingdom of Nepal
March Fong, ambassador, Micronesia
Shirin R. Tahir-Kheli, ambassador, United Nations

**U.S. Cabinet Members**
Elaine L. Chao, U.S. Secretary of Labor
Norman Y. Mineta, U.S. Secretary of Transportation

**U.S. Representatives**
Daniel K. Akaka, Hawaii
Eni F.H. Faleomavaega, American Somoa
Mike Honda, California
Daniel K. Inouye, Hawaii
Jay C. Kim, California
"Spark" Masayuki Matsunaga, Hawaii
Robert Matsui, California
Norman Y. Mineta, California
Patsy T. Mink, Hawaii
Patricia Saiki, Hawaii
Dalip Singh Saund, California
Robert Underwood, Guam
David Wu, Oregon

**U.S. Senators**
Daniel K. Akaka, Hawaii
Hiram L. Fong, Hawaii
Samuel Ichiya Hayakawa, California
Daniel K. Inouye, Hawaii
"Spark" Masayuki Matsunaga, Hawaii

# Selected Bibliography

In compiling the entries for this book, we relied on a number of invaluable reference sources. Previously published collections of Asian Pacific American biographies such as *Notable Asian Americans* (Zia and Gall 1995) and *Distinguished Asian Americans* (Kim 1999) proved to be helpful starting points, as was Judy Chu's seminal article, "Asian Pacific American Women in Mainstream Politics" (Chu 1989). Asian American periodicals such as *A. Magazine*, *Asian Week*, and others included in the Ethnic News Watch electronic database offered important insights and information on contemporary Asian Pacific American politics. Indeed, we cannot emphasize enough the important role which Asian Pacific American journalists in community-based and mainstream media play in documenting issues and events relevant to Asian Pacific American communities. At the same time, in order to incorporate regional, ethnic, and gender diversity in our project, we turned to the *National Asian Pacific American Political Almanac* (Nakanishi and Lai 2001), which is the only annual directory of Asian Pacific Americans in elected and major appointed positions, along with other information about the status of Asian Pacific American political activities. We used the almanac to contact individuals for information that we were unable to uncover from other sources. We would like to thank those who took the time to respond. Finally, we would like to extend our deepest appreciation to Bob Fisher, Collections Associate at Seattle's Wing Luke Asian Museum; Oliver J. Kim, Esq.; and Marjorie Lee of the UCLA Asian American Studies Center Reading Room and Library for their assistance in compiling the information for this book.

*Note:* In addition to the below sources, in many cases the authors directly interviewed the distinguished politicians and government leaders who are included. This information is included in the sources listed at the ends of the individual profiles.

Bai, Su Sun. "Affirmative Pursuit of Political Equality for Asian Pacific Americans: Reclaiming the Voting Rights Act." *University of Pennsylvania Law Review* vol. 139, no. 3, pp. 731–767.

Carmody, Deirdre. "Secrecy and Tenure: An Issue for High Court." *New York Times* December 6 1989, p. B8.

Chu, Judy. "Asian Pacific American Women in Mainstream Politics," in *Asian Women United of California.* Boston: Beacon Press, 1989, pp. 405–421.

Chuman, Frank. *The Bamboo People: Japanese Americans and the Law.* Del Mar, CA: Publisher's, Inc., 1976.

Chun, Ki-Taek. "The Myth of Asian Pacific American Success and Its Educational Ramifications." *IRCD Bulletin* vol. 15, 1980, pp. 1–12.

Daniels, Roger. *The Politics of Prejudice*. New York: Atheneum, 1968.

De Vera, Arleen. "Without Parallel: The Local 7 Deportation Cases, 1949–1955." *Amerasia Journal* 1994, vol. 20, pp. 1–26.

DeWitt, Howard. *Violence in the Fields: California Filipino Farm Labor Organizing During the Great Depression*. Saratoga, CA: Century Twenty-One Publishing, 1980.

Erie, Steven P. and Harold Brackman. *Paths to Political Incorporation for Latinos and Asian Pacifics in California*. Berkeley: The California Policy Seminar, 1993.

Horton, John. *The Politics of Diversity*. Philadelphia: Temple University Press, 1995.

Ichioka, Yuji. "The Early Japanese Quest for Citizenship: The Background of the 1922 Ozawa Case." *Amerasia Journal* vol. 4, 1977, pp. 1–22; republished in *The Issei*, New York: Free Press, 1988.

Irons, Peter. *Justice at War*. New York: Oxford University Press, 1983.

Kim, Hyung-chan, ed. *Distinguished Asian Americans*. Westport, CT: Greenwood Press, 1999.

Kwoh, Stewart and Mindy Hui. "Empowering Our Communities: Political Policy," in *The State of Asian Pacific America: Policy Issues to the Year 2020*. Los Angeles: LEAP Asian Pacific American Public Policy Institute and the UCLA Asian Pacific American Studies Center, 1993, pp. 189–197.

Kwong, Peter. *Chinatown, New York: Labor and Politics, 1930–1950*. New York: Monthly Review Press, 1981.

Louie, Steven and Glenn Omatsu, eds. *Asian Americans: The Movement and the Moment*. Los Angeles: UCLA Asian American Studies Center, 2001.

Nakanishi, Don T. "When Numbers Do Not Add Up: Asian Pacific Americans and California Politics," in *Racial and Ethnic Politics in California*, vol.2, Michael B. Preston, Bruce E. Cain, and Sandra Bass, eds. Berkeley: Institute of Governmental Studies Press, University of California, Berkeley, 1998, pp. 3–44.

Nakanishi, Don and James Lai. *2001–2002 National Asian Pacific American Political Almanac*. Los Angeles: UCLA Asian American Studies Center, 2001.

Ong, Paul and Suzanne Hee. "The Growth of the Asian Pacific American Population: 20 Million in 2020." in *The State of Asian Pacific America: Policy Issues to the Year 2020*. Los Angeles: LEAP Asian Pacific American Public Policy Institute and the UCLA Asian Pacific American Studies Center, 1993, pp. 11–24.

Ong, Paul and Don Nakanishi. "Becoming Citizens, Becoming Voters: The Naturalization and Political Participation of Asian Pacific Immigrants," in *Reframing the Immigration Debate*, ed. Bill Ong Hing and Ronald Lee. Los Angeles: LEAP Asian Pacific American Public Policy Institute and the UCLA Asian American Studies Center, 1996, pp. 275–305.

Saxton, Alexander. *The Indispensable Enemy*. Berkeley: University of California Press, 1971.

Scharlin, Craig and Lilia V. Villanueva. *Philip Vera Cruz: A Personal History of Filipino Immigrants and the Farmworkers Movement*. Los Angeles: UCLA Asian Pacific American Studies Center and UCLA Labor Center, 1992.

Suzuki, Bob H. "Education and the Socialization of Asian Americas: A Revisionist Analysis of the 'Model Minority' Thesis." *Amerasia Journal* 1977, vol. 4, pp. 23–51.

Wang, L. Ling-Chi. "Lau v. Nichols: History of a Struggle for Equal and Quality Education," in *Counterpoint*, ed. Emma Gee et al. Los Angeles: UCLA Asian Pacific American Studies Center, 1976, pp. 240–263.

Yoneda, Karl. *Ganbatte*. Los Angeles: UCLA Asian Pacific American Studies Center, 1983.

Youngberg, Francey Lim. "Census 2000: Asian Pacific Americans Changing the Face of America At A Rapid Pace." In *The National Asian Pacific American Political Almanac*, ed. Don Nakanishi and James Lai. Los Angeles: UCLA Asian American Studies Center, 2001, pp. 42–55.

Zia, Helen and Susan B. Gall, eds. *Notable Asian Americans*. Detroit: Gale Research Inc., 1995.

# Index

Page numbers in **bold-face** type indicate main entries.

abortion rights, 7, 50, 71, 80, 123, 130, 148, 202
Abu-Jamal, Mumia, 83, 85
Abzug, Bella, 130
ACLU (American Civil Liberties Union), 105, 133, 134
adoptee's rights, 162, 163
affirmative action, 22, 30, 35–36, 63, 98, 101, 105, 111
Africa, famine in, 14–15
Agency of International Development (AID), 14–15
Agnew, Spiro T., 121
AIDS, 91
Aiken, J.G. (Joe), Dr., 114
Aiso, John Fujio, **3–5**
Akaka, Daniel K., **5–8**, 130, 133
Alaska, Filipinos in, 22
Alaskeros, 188
Albright, Madeline, 87
Alien Land Act of 1913 (California), 125–26
Alioto, Angela, 98
Alioto, Joseph, 98
All Souls College (Oxford), 86
alternative energy, 121, 192
America, first impressions of, 13, 29, 150, 180
American Civil Liberties Union (ACLU), 105, 133, 134
American Communist Party, 213
American Legion, speech contest, 3–4
American University, 113
Americans with Disabilities Act, 127–28
Anderson, D.G. "Andy," 10, 192

Andrews University, 191
Angel Island Immigration Center, 147, 213
anti-miscegenation laws, 213
Antioch College, 52
ANWAR (Arctic National Wildlife Refuge), 7
APA (Asian Political Alliance), 18–19
Apacible, Galiciano, 57
APALC (Asian Pacific American Legal Center), 89
Arakaki, James Y., **8–9**
Aramony, William, 30
Arctic National Wildlife Refuge (ANWAR), 7
Ariyoshi, George R., 6, **9–11,** 192
Arizona State University, 193
Asian Alaskan Cultural Center, 22
Asian American Studies programs, 52, 60
Asian American women, in politics, 142–43
Asian Americans in politics, 28, 53, 67
Asian Joint Communications, 39
Asian Law Caucus, 62, 63, 124
Asian Pacific American Agenda, 157
Asian Pacific American Institute for Congressional Studies (APAICS), 107, 128
Asian Pacific American Legal Center (APALC), 89
Asian Political Alliance (APA), 18–19

Baker, Bob, 80
Baker, James, 170
Baliles, Gerald, 90–91
Barnard College, 17, 19, 156, 211
Barnes, Ramona, 22

*221*

Barve, Kumar, **12–13**
Bender, Kandace, 99
Beye, Don, 91
Big Brothers, 38
bilingual issues, 40, 43, 114. *See also* education, bilingual
Birendra, King of Nepal, 15
Black, Elaine, 213
Blackmun, Harry A., 87
Bloch, Julia Chang, **13–16**
Bloch, Stuart Marshall, 15
Boggs, Grace Lee, **16–19**
Boggs, Hale, 105
Boggs, Jimmy, 18
Boggs/Ford Delegation to the People's Republic of China (1972), 105
books authored: *Chinese Home Cooking* (Bloch), 16; *Congressman from India* (Saund), 159–60; *Filipinos in Alaska: 1788-1958* (Buchholdt), 22; *Ganbatte: Sixty-Year Struggle of a Kibei Worker* (Yoneda), 213; *The Labor History of U.S. Japanese* (Yoneda), 214; *Language in Action* (Hayakawa), 60; *Law and Legal Literature of Mexico* (Valderrama), 184; *Law and Legal Literature of Peru* (Valderrama), 184; *Linking Our Lives* (Chu), 39; *Living for Change* (Boggs), 16, 19; *Manifest for a Black Revolutionary Party* (Boggs and Boggs), 18; *My Mother India* (Saund), 160; *Philip Vera Cruz: A Personal History of the Filipino Immigrants and the Farmworkers Movement* (Vera Cruz), 189; *Revolution and Evolution in the Twentieth Century* (Boggs), 18
Bordonaro, Molly, 203
Boston University, 110, 181
Boxer, Barbara, 50
Bradley, Tom, 195
Bridges, Harry, 214
Brigham Young University, 45, 162
Brown, Edmund G. "Pat," 195
Brown, George, 199
Brown, Willie L., Jr., 99, 209
Brown University, 4, 5
Bryn Mawr College, 17
Buchholdt, Thelma, **20–23**
Bulos, Alice, 57
Burns, John A., 10, 25, 77
Burton, John, 99
Bush, George H. W., 15, 30, 119, 142, 145, 169–70, 172
Bush, George W., 30, 128, 172
Bush/Quayle campaign (1988), 30, 49

California School of Professional Psychology, 39
California State College-Hayward, 43
California State University, Los Angeles, 79, 136, 178
Cambodia, war in, 168
Cambodian Holocaust, 169
Camp Asan, Agana, Guam, 94
Campbell, Gayle, 147, 148
Campbell, Thomas E., 67, 147, 148
Campbell Estate, 26
capital punishment, 7
Carmichael, Stokely, 52
Carson, Johnny, 61
Carter, Jimmy, 130
Castle, Michael N., 201
Cayetano, Benjamin, **24–27,** 64
Center for International Affairs at Harvard, 15
Central Michigan University, 191
Chamorro issues, 179
Chan, Barry, 124
Chan, Warren, 115
Chan, Wilma, **27–28**
*Chan v. City and County of California,* 124
Chang, Barry, 203
Chao, Elaine L., **29–31**
Chau, Nguyen Minh, **31–32**
Chaudhary, Satveer, **32–33**
Chavez, Cesar, 189
Chavez, Linda, 30
Chiang Kai-shek, 149
child care, 40, 131, 175
Chin, Frank, 35
Chin Lee restaurant, 17
Chinese American Citizens Alliance, 149, 196
Chinese American Elected Officials (CEO), 107
Chinese American Fourth of July (Phoenix), 149
Chinese Civil War, 201
Chinn, George, 98
Chippewa Valley Technical College, 206
Chong Wah Benevolent Association, 35
Chou En-Lai, 171
Chow, Ping, 34, 35
Chow, Ruby, **33–36**
Choy, Herbert Young Cho, **36–38**
Chu, Judy, **38–40**
Chuo University (Japan), 4
citizenship, 160
City University of New York, 87
Civil Liberties Act (1988), 71, 127, 139
civil rights: advocacy, 62, 91, 98, 101, 114, 124, 127, 158; movement, 75, 88, 138–39, 199
Civil Rights Act (1991), 30
Clinton, William Jefferson (Bill), 7, 43, 62, 87, 101, 127, 144, 145, 166, 185
College of San Mateo, 52
Colorado State University, 122

Columbia University, 29, 31, 43, 169, 211
communism, 161, 213
community organization, 18–19, 20, 114, 192
Community Oriented Policing (COPS), 173–74
community service, 34–35
commute, longest, 15
concentration camps, 136; avoided, 60; Camp McCoy, WI, 120; Heart Mountain, WY, 73, 126; Jerome, Arkansas, 84; and the law, 61, 62, 66, 71, 117; Manzanar, CA, 213; and political activism, 83–84, 138, 146; Rohwer, AK, 51, 124; Santa Anita racetrack, 126
Congressional Asian Pacific Caucus, 7, 71, 91, 203
consumer advocacy, 71
consumer protection, 12, 135
Cook, Captain James, 81
COPS (Community Oriented Policing), 173–74
Cortese, Andrea, 142
Craswell, Ellen, 111
crime prevention, 123, 185, 197
Crossley, Randolph, 10
Cunneen, Jim, 68

Daley, William M., 128
D'Amato, Alfonse, 73
Darrow, Clarence, 25, 118
Dartmouth College, 29
Davis, Angela, 214
Davis, Gray, 49
Defense Language Institute, 5
Delta Upsilon, 4
Demarest, David F., 169
Democratic National Committee, campaign finance scandal (1990's), 65, 67, 80–81, 91, 97, 203
Democratic National Convention (1968), 71
Der, Henry, 98
DES (diethylstilbestrol), 130
desegregation, 71
development: community, 158, 200; economic, 12, 175–76, 197; international, 14–15, 43, 93, 161, 181; redevelopment, 187; workforce, 65
disability rights, 101
discrimination: in America, 52, 70–71, 110; employment, 25, 88, 91, 100, 124, 186; racial, 3, 62–63, 101, 113, 119, 147, 195
District of Columbia School of Law, 22
diversity, 40, 46–47, 124, 159, 174
Dole, Bob, 50
Dole, Elizabeth, 29–30
Dooley, Tom, 93
drinking fountains, 13
drunk driving, 91
Dukmejian, George, 73

early jobs, 37, 47, 69–70, 74, 82, 91–92, 104, 147, 186, 189
East Los Angeles College, 39
e-commerce, 12
economy: diversification of, 26; policies on, 49–50, 108, 111, 158, 174, 192; revitalization of, 185, 200
education: advocacy for, 52–53; bilingual, 61, 178–79; funding for, 67–68, 108, 110, 148, 210–11; lasting influence of, 82; policies on, 6, 28, 66–67, 116, 131, 155, 158–59, 175, 201; public, 103, 109, 111, 152, 203
Effective Parenting Information for Children, 27–28
e-government, 56
El Camino College, 136
Ellis, Daniel, 177
English-only movement, 61, 145, 184
environment: justice, 19; policies on, 7, 50, 109, 148, 187; priorities on, 117; protection of, 83, 121, 199
Equal Pay, Equal Work, 130
Eroshenko, Vasily, 212
Esperanto, 212
Estes, Jane, 35
Esteves, Jose S., **41–42**
Eu, Henry, 43
Eu, March Fong, **42–44**, 49
Evergreen State College, 157
Executive Order 13125 (Clinton), 166
Executive Order 9066 (Roosevelt), 117, 120, 126, 166, 213

Faleomavaega, Eni F.H., **45–47**
Family Leave Act, 202
family preservation programs, 118
family values, 50
Fang, James, 99
Far Eastern University, Manila, 184
farmworkers' movement, 189–90
Fasi, Frank, 10, 26
Feinstein, Dianne, 67, 98
FEMA (Federal Emergency Management Agency), 7
feminism, 16, 32, 141, 142, 154. *See also* women's rights
Fennell, Sambath Chey, 181
Ferraro, Geraldine, 141
*Filipino Forum* (magazine), 164
Flynt, Larry, 174
Fong, Harold, 134
Fong, Hiram L., **47–48,** 120, 135
Fong, Matthew K., 44, **48–51**
foreign aid, 161
14 Points (Wilson), 159–60

## Index

442nd Regimental Combat Team, 70, 71, 133, 138
Franklin, John Hope, 146
Frohnmayer, Dave, 108
Fuimaono, A.U., 46
Fujino, Diane C., 85
Fukai, Mas, 174
Furutani, Warren, **51–53**

gambling, 108, 174
Gandhi, Mahatma, 160
gangs, youth, 73
garment industry, present day, 146
Garrett, Kwame, 158
Gates, Darryl F., 199
gay rights, 50
genius grants, 88, 89
George Washington University, 70, 86, 134, 156, 184
Georgetown College, 201
Georgetown University, 12, 64
Gibbons, Jim, 97
Gin, Mike, **54–56**
Gingrich, Newt, 50, 97
Giuliani, Rudolph, 50
Global Forum of Women, 142
"Go For Broke" soldiers, 70
Goddard, Samuel P., 148–49
Gonzaga University, 189
Gordon J. Lau Elementary School, 99
Gore, Al, 128
graffiti, 137, 175–76
Great Society, 48
Grier, Rosie, 49
growth management, 10, 103
Gubser, Charles S., 126
Guingona, Michael P., **56–58**
Guingona, Teofisto, 57
gun control, 71, 209
gun owners' rights, 123

Hague Academy of International Law, 86
Hallinan, Terence, 209
Harvard Law School, 37, 47, 120
Harvard School of Medicine, 175
Harvard University, 3, 4, 13, 14, 29, 86, 133, 202
hate crimes, 65, 101, 175–76
Hawaiian monarchy, overthrow of, 7
Hayakawa, Samuel Ichiye, **59–61**
Hayashi, Dennis W., **61–63**
Health and Human Services (HHS), 166
health care: access to, 28, 197; public, 110–11, 166; reform, 63, 145, 177, 199, 210
health insurance, 12, 21, 118, 202
Heftel, Cecil, 192
Hemmings, Fred, 192
Herman, Alexis, 166

HHS (Health and Human Services), 166
Hirono, Mazie, **64–65**
Hiroshima Maidens, 84
Holmes, Oliver Wendell, 59
homelessness, 161–62
homosexuality, 26–27, 50, 167
Honda, Mike, **65–68**
Hormel, James, 50
House of Lee restaurant, 105
housing, 98, 158, 206
housing rights, 101, 113
Hsieh, Tom, 98
Hughes, Harry, 184
human rights, 83, 84, 87, 172. *See also* civil rights
Humphrey, Hubert H. III, 33
Hurd, Mrs., 82

Illinois Institute of Technology, 60
immigrants in the community, 166–67
immigrants' rights, 62, 131, 139, 148, 152, 162, 186, 199
immigration policy, 64, 108
Indiana University School of Music, 96
Inouye, Daniel K., **69–72,** 127, 133
Institution Saint Paul (Saigon), 31
insurance, 65. *See also* health insurance
integration, 84, 105
international affairs, 35, 48, 67, 85, 105, 170, 172
international trade, 43–44, 49, 118–19, 127
internment camps. *See* concentration camps
Iran-Contra affair, 71
Ito, Lance A., **72–75**

jail sentences, 25
James, CLR, 17–18
Japan, atrocities during wartime, 67
Japanese American Citizens League, 52, 61, 62, 101, 118, 139
Japanese American redress and reparations, 59, 83, 85, 117–18, 119, 121, 127, 137
Jaykim Engineers, 79–80
Jefferson, Julie, 51–52
JILA (Joint Institute for Laboratory Astrophysics), 201
Joe, Harry J., **75–76**
Johnson, Lyndon B., 48, 71
Johnson-Forest Tendency, 17–18
Jones, Bob, 113
Jordan, Frank, 98
journalism, 164
justice, environmental, 19

Kealoha, James Kimo, **77–78**
Keating, Charles, 73
Kemp, Jack, 50
Ken, Miyamoto, 82

Kennedy, Edward M., 33
Kennedy, John F., 66, 71, 110, 118
Khmer Rouge, 168–69, 170, 180
Khoeun, Samkhann, 182
Kido, Mitsuyuki, 77
Kikumara, Yu, 83, 85
Kim, Jay C., **78–81**
King, James A., 83
King, Jean Sadako, 10, **81–83**
King, Rodney, 199
Kissinger, Henry, 80
Knowles, Tony, 22
Kochiyama, Bill, 84
Kochiyama, Yuri, **83–85**
Koh, Harold Hongju, **86–87**
Korean American Political Association, 79
Korean War, 79, 162
Korematsu, Fred, 62
*Korematsu v. United States*, 62, 124
Korzybski, Alfred, 60
Kosa, Marian, 161
Kwoh, Stewart, **88–90**
Kwok, Daphne, **90–91**, 112

Lam, Tony, **92–95**
Lam Brothers Corporation, 93–94
Lamphere, Phyllis, 164
land use, 10, 55, 64, 157
language issues, 4, 105, 113, 179, 197
Laos, Hmong exodus from, 206
Laos, war in, 205
Lau, Cheryl Ann, **96–97**
Lau, Gordon, **97–99**
laundries and laundry workers, 42, 100, 101, 104, 113
law enforcement, 106, 173–74, 206
Leary, Diane, 181
Lee, Bill Lann, **99–102,** 139
Lee, Bruce, 34
Lee, Cheryl, **102–4**
Lee, Denny, 112
Lee, Harry, **104–6**
Lee, Mona, 111
Lee, Tom, 103
Leopold, John, 10
libraries, 137
Lim, Joaquin, **106–7**
Lim, John, **107–8**
Lincoln, Abraham, 160
Lingle, Linda, 26
Little Saigon, Westminster, CA, 95
Liu, Carol, **108–9**
Liu, Eric, 112
living wages, 187
Locke, Gary, 28, **109–12,** 158

Long Island University, 140
Loo, Jim, 62
Los Angeles Harbor College, 25
Lott, Trent, 50
Louisiana State University, 104
Low, Harry, 208
Lowry, Mike, 111, 158, 187
Loyloa University, 25, 105
Loyola Marymount University, 173
Luce-Celler bill, 160
Luke, Wing, 110, **112–15**

MacArthur, Douglas, 4
Macarthur Foundation, 88, 89
MacLaine, Shirley, 49
Magdalen College (Oxford), 86
Magnaldi, June, 169
Malcom X, 84–85
Mansho, Rene, **116–17**
Manzanar Pilgrimage, 52
March on Washington, 18
Marcos, Ferdinand, 186
marriage, interracial, 81–82, 130, 181, 213
marriage, same sex, 26–27, 134, 139
Marshall, Thurgood, 100
Marx, Karl, 213
Masaoka, Mike, 121
Mascone, George, 98
Massachusetts Institute of Technology, 29
Matsui, Doris K. Okada, 119
Matsui, Robert, **117–19**
Matsunaga, "Spark" Masayuki, 6, 78, **120–22,** 130
Matsunaka, Stanley T., **122–23**
Mayo, Katherine, 160
McCarthyism, 214
McConnell, Mitch, 30
McGill University, 59
McKay, Brian, 96
Mead, George, 17
Merrilees, Craig A., 119
Michigan State University, 9–10
Micronesia, 43–44
Military Intelligence Service Language School (MISLS), 3, 4
Mills College, 43
Minami, Dale, **123–25**
Mineta, Norman Y., 61, **125–29**
minimum wage, 61
Mink, Patsy T., 82, **129–31,** 192
minorities in America, 39, 165
Miyagishima, Kenneth Daniel, **131–32**
model minority, 89, 166, 184
Moffett, Bob, 165
Mollway, Susan Oki, **132–34**
Morita, Hermina M., **134–35**

Moss, John E., 118
motor voter registration, 43, 80
Mount Holyoke College, 29, 31
Mount Senario College, 206
Mount St. Mary's College, 20

NAACP (National Association for the Advancement of Colored People), 100–101, 105
NAFTA (North American Free Trade Agreement), 118–19, 127
Nakahara, Seichi, 83
Nakanishi, Don, 124–25
Nakano, George, 67, **136–37**
Narasaki, Karen, **138–40**
narcolepsy, 60
Nash, Phil Tajitsu, 80, 81
National University (Korea), 150
National Women's Political Caucus, 141
Native Americans, 38, 72
Native Hawaiian sovereignty movement, 192
Natividad, Irene, **140–43**
Nepal, 15
nepotism, 193
New Mexico State University, 132
New York University, 82
Nguyen, Jimmy Tong, 95
Nielsen, Bill, 207
Nixon, Richard M., 37, 48, 71, 155
Nkrumah, Kwame, Dr., 18
Normandy Invasion, 110
North American Free Trade Agreement (NAFTA), 118–19, 127
Northeastern University, 158

O'Brian, Leo, 70–71
Occidental College, 62
O'Connell, John, 113
O'Connor, Dennis, 192
Odlum, Jacqueline Cochran, 160–61
Oh, Angela Eunjin, **144–46**
Ohio Wesleyan University, 171
Okamura, Randy, 203
Old Dominion University, 166
100th Infantry Battalion, 120
Ong, Henry Sr., 147
Ong, Wing F., **146–49**
Opportunity System, Inc., 31–32
Orbos, Oscar, 187
Organization of African Unity, 18
Organization of Chinese Americans, Inc., 40, 90, 91, 101
Overseas Chinese Affairs Commission, 35

Palaka Power movement, 192
Panama Canal, 61
Panoringan, Mario, 57

Park, Michael, **150–51**
"Partners in Grime," 175–76
Patel, Marilyn, 62
patients' rights, 67–68
Paull, Ray, Dr., 162
Peace Corps, 14, 30, 66, 169
Peacock, Bill, 67
Pearl Harbor, attack on, 70, 120, 126
Peckham, J.B., 126
Pelosi, Nancy, 209
Pepperdine University, 49
Percy, Charles, 14
Persian Gulf War, 30, 170
Peterson, Leonard and Rosemary, 181
Phi Beta Kappa, 64, 100, 124, 133
Phi Delta Phi, 70
Phoenix College, 147
Piche, Robert and Lloyd, 62
Picker, Harvey, Dr., 169
Pike Place Market, 114
police harassment, 124
political correctness, 105
political prisoners, 83
politics in the family, 44, 49, 192
Pregerson, Harry, 138
Prince of Wales College, India, 159
prison reform, 109, 123
prisons, 192
Proposition 63 (English only), 145
Purple Heart Battalion, 120

Quan, Gordon, **152–53**
Quan, Roland, 98
Quinn, William F., 77–78
quotas. *See* affirmative action

racism, 7, 21, 73–74, 145–46, 161
Rainbow Coalition, 182, 186
*Rainbow Warrior* (ship), 45
Ramos, Fidel V., 27, 57, 187, 188
Randolph, A. Phillip, 18
Rayburn, Sam, 71
Reagan, Ronald, 7, 60, 121, 127, 137, 141
Reaganomics, 120–21
redress and reparations. *See* Japanese American redress and reparations
restaurant workers, 101
restrooms, pay, 43
Rhodes, B.C. (Bill), 148
Rice, Norm, 187
Richards, Ann, 166
Riordan, Richard, 198, 199–200
Roberti, David A., 199
Roberts, Jim, 122
Robinson, Jackie, 99
Roosevelt, Franklin D., 117, 120, 126, 166, 213

Roosevelt, Theodore, 160
Roth, William V., 201
Ruby Chow's Restaurant, 34–35
Rutgers University College, 156

safety, public, 55, 66–67, 103
Saiki, Patricia, 26, **154–56**
Saiki, Stanley Mitsuo, Dr., 154
Salinas Junior College, 43
San Francisco State College (now San Francisco State University), 60, 186
San Francisco State University, 106, 210
San Jose State University, 66
Sangiolo, Amy Mah, **156–57**
Santos, Sharon Tomiko, **157–59**
Saund, Dalip Singh, **159–61**
Schaffer, Donald, 184
Schultz, George, 61
senior citizen issues, 21, 28
sex slaves, 67
Shabada, Victor, 52
Shin, Paull Hobom, **161–63**
Short, Walter, 37
Sibonga, Dolores, **163–65,** 186–87
Sibonga, Martin, 164
Sijo Gakuen (Japan), 4
Simpson, Alan, 126, 127
Simpson, O.J., 72, 73, 195
Sing, Lillian, 98
Singh, Shamina, **165–67**
Siv, Sichan Aun, **167–70**
slave women, narratives of, 141
smear campaigns, 114
Smith, Chuck, 95
Smithsonian Institution, 127
Social Security, 148, 202
Solomon, Eric, 60
Solomon, Gerald, 127
South Africa, boycott against, 145
Southwestern Law School, 49
space exploration, 121
St. John's University, Shanghai, 211
St. Olaf College, 33
Stanford University, 43, 195, 202
Stevenson, Peggy, 199
Stewart, Chris, 80
street gangs, 73
strikes: agricultural, 82, 189; student, 60; sugar (1946), 82
sugar production, 6, 7
superfund sites, 187

Tahir-Kheli, Shirin R., **171–72**
Takasugi, Robert, 62
Takushoku University, 133
Tanaka, Paul K., **172–74**
tax policy, 50, 80, 193, 207, 212
technology and government, 201
Teng, Mabel, 98, **174–76**
Tennant, Forest, Dr., 80
territories, status of, 179
Texas Southern University, 45–46
Third World Student Strike, 60
Thomas, Clarence, 7
Thurm, Kevin, 166
Tokuda, Kip, **176–77**
tourism, 6, 10, 26, 65
Tran, Van, 95
transportation, public, 35, 48, 209
transportation issues, 29–30, 57, 127, 128
Tunney, John V., 60

Underwood, Robert, **178–80**
unions, 82, 116, 186
United States Agency for International Development (USAID), 93
United States Air Force Academy, 49
United Way, 30
University of Arizona, 148
University of California, 62
University of California, Berkeley, 13, 14, 43, 46, 73, 124, 126, 160, 194, 208, 210
University of California, Davis, 145
University of California, Los Angeles, 25, 39, 56, 73, 89, 138, 144
University of California at Santa Cruz, 198
University of Chicago, 129
University of Guam, 179
University of Hawaii, 6, 8, 26, 37, 47, 64, 70, 82, 116, 129, 133, 134, 154, 191, 209
University of Houston, 46, 152, 196
University of Manitoba, 59
University of Massachusetts, 175
University of Massachusetts-Amherst, 181
University of Michigan, 31
University of Minnesota, 33
University of Nebraska, 129
University of North Texas, 75
University of Phnom Penh, 168
University of Pittsburgh, 162
University of Punjab, 160
University of San Diego, 122
University of San Francisco, 56, 96, 97
University of Southern California, 55, 79, 124
University of Texas, 196
University of Texas at Austin, 152, 166
University of the Philippines, 41
University of Toronto, 86
University of Washington, 102, 113, 164, 177
University of Wisconsin at La Crosse, 59

Uong, Chanrithy, **180–82**
U.S. Air Force, 105
U.S. Peace Institute, 121
USAID (United States Agency for International Development), 93
USO for Japanese American soldiers, 84

Valderrama, David M., **183–85**
vandalism, 137
Velasco, Victor, 164
Veloria, Velma Rosette, **185–88**
Vera Cruz, Philip Villamin, **188–90**
victims' rights, 43
Viendong restaurant, 95
Vietnam, war in, 93–94
Vietnam War, opposition to, 39, 71, 89, 130, 148, 186, 214
violence: anti-Asian, 145, 184, 195; domestic, 96; gun, 40
violence protection programs, 177
voter registration, 40, 43, 91, 148
voter turnout, 181–82
voters, multilingual, 139
voting, as an ethnic bloc, 202
voting procedures, 65
Voting Rights Act, 139

Waihee, John David III, 121, **191–93**
Wang, Art, 187
Wang, L. Lingchi, 98
Washington State College, 189
Washington University, 75, 201
Watergate scandal, 71, 130
Watson, Emmett, 114
Weiss, Paul, 17
welfare, 71, 131, 148
welfare reform, 66, 111, 118, 176, 193
Wellesley College, 27
Wenig, Herbert, 4
Wesleyan University (Middletown, CT), 90
Western Evangelical Seminary, 108
White House Initiative on Asian Americans and Pacific Islanders, 166

Wilkey, Malcolm Richard, 87
Wilson, Pete, 30, 49
Wilson, Woodrow, 159
Wilson College, 129
Wing Luke Asian Museum, 115, 158
Wing Luke Elementary School, 115
Wing's Restaurant, 148
women in business, 155
women in politics, 21, 109, 165
women's rights, 43, 64, 96, 117, 130, 155, 157, 158, 202
Wong, Barry, **193–94**
Wong, David, 83, 85
Wong, Delbert E., **194–96**
Wong, Martha J., 153, **196–98**
*Wong v. Younger*, 124
Woo, Michael, **198–200**
Woo, S.B. (Shien-Biau), **200–202**
Woodley, Harry, 148
Wu, David, 28, **202–4**
Wyden, Ron, 108

Xiong, Joe Bee, **205–7**

Yaki, Michael, 98, **208–9**
Yale Law School, 202, 208
Yale University, 100, 110, 138
Yamaguchi, Einosuke, 213
Yamane, Brian Y., **209–10**
Yang, Ka Ying, 207
Yee, Carolyn, 101
Yee, Harold, 98
Yee, Leland, 98, **210–11**
Yem, Ratha, 182
Yih, Mae, **211–12**
Yoneda, Karl Goso, **212–14**
youth: advocacy, 28, 109, 177, 210; justice, 209; programs for, 26, 103, 137, 163, 206; at risk, 24–25

Zia-ul Haq, Mohammed, 172

## About the Authors

**DON T. NAKANISHI** is the director of the Asian American Studies Center at the University of California, Los Angeles, and co-editor of the National Asian Pacific Almanac and Directory.

**ELLEN D. WU** is a Ph.D. candidate at the University of Chicago.

MAR 2004